Identity in Britain

A cradle-to-grave atlas

Bethan Thomas and Daniel Dorling

First published in Great Britain in 2007 by

The Policy Press
University of Bristol
Fourth Floor, Beacon House
Queen's Road
Bristol BS8 1QU
UK

Tel +44 (0)117 331 4054
Fax +44 (0)117 331 4093
e-mail tpp-info@bristol.ac.uk
www.policypress.org.uk

British Library Cataloguing in Publication Data
A catalogue record for this book is available from the British Library

Library of Congress Cataloging-in-Publication Data
A catalog record for this book has been requested

ISBN 978 1 86134 820 3 paperback
ISBN 978 1 86134 821 0 hardcover

Bethan Thomas and **Daniel Dorling** work in the Social and Spatial Inequalities Research Group in the Department of Geography at the University of Sheffield.

Cover design by Blakebrough Design, Bristol.
Printed and bound in Great Britain by Latimer Trend, Plymouth.

All the world's a stage,
And all the men and women merely players;
They have their exits and their entrances,
And one man in his time plays many parts,
His Acts being seven ages. At first the infant,
Mewling and puking in the nurse's arms;
Then, the whining schoolboy, with his satchel
And shining morning face, creeping like snail
Unwillingly to school; and then the lover,
Sighing like furnace, with a woeful ballad
Made to his mistress' eyebrow; then, a soldier,
Full of strange oaths, and bearded like the pard,
Jealous in honour, sudden and quick in quarrel,
Seeking the bubble reputation
Even in the cannon's mouth; and then, the justice,
In fair round belly, with good capon lined,
With eyes severe, and beard of formal cut,
Full of wise saws and modern instances,
And so he plays his part; the sixth age shifts
Into the lean and slippered pantaloon,
With spectacles on nose and pouch on side,
His youthful hose, well saved, a world too wide
For his shrunk shank, and his big manly voice,
Turning again toward childish treble, pipes
And whistles in his sound; last Scene of all,
That ends this strange eventful history,
Is second childishness, and mere oblivion,
Sans teeth, sans eyes, sans taste, sans everything.

William Shakespeare, *As You Like It,* **II.7 (2005, London: Penguin)**

For Michael Quinlan.
For Solomon Dorling,
born 10 August 2006.

Contents

Acknowledgements

Thanks to John Pritchard for the initial work in creating the neighbourhoods used throughout this book and to Bronwen Dorling for commenting on an initial draft of this text. Also to officials in what is now the Department for Communities and Local Government, for funding part of the development of the neighbourhood geography used here, and to the Economic and Social Research Council (ESRC) for their support of the network on the 'development and persistence of human capability and resilience in their social and geographical context', coordinated by Mel Bartley, work on which, initially with Richard Mitchell and Helena Tunstall, helped in our thinking on life stages. Thanks also to Julia Mortimer, Dave Worth, Emily Watt and Jacqueline Lawless at The Policy Press, to Steve Blakeborough, for design and consultation, to Dawn Rushen, for superb copy-editing, and to Mary Shaw, for the photographs. We thank Sainsbury's Plc for permission to include the photographs taken in its stores. Thanks to Helen Durham and Phil Rees at the University of Leeds with whom we worked on an earlier version of the base map. For more information on the base map see the companion volume to this: Danny Dorling and Bethan Thomas (2004) *People and places: A 2001 Census atlas of the UK*, Bristol: The Policy Press

Information derived from the population censuses of Scotland and England and Wales and digital boundaries are Crown Copyright and reproduced with the permission of the Controller of HMSO and the Queen's Printer for Scotland. Census data used in this book were obtained from the Census Dissemination Unit at the University of Manchester and digital boundaries were obtained from the Census Geography Data Unit (UKBORDERS), EDINA (University of Edinburgh).

Much of the data in this book is Census data, with other data obtained from Neighbourhood Statistics and a variety of sources: benefits data from the Department for Work and Pensions Statistical Tabulations tool; school educational data for England from the Department for Education and Skills, for Wales from Statistics Wales, and for Scotland from Scottish Neighbourhood Statistics; higher education participation data from Mark Corver of the Higher Education Funding Council for England; mortality and age of mother at giving birth data were supplied by the Office for National Statistics and the General Register Office for Scotland (as was data on deaths). Election data was obtained from Richard Kimber's Political Science Resources website at the University of Keele (www.psr.keele.ac.uk/) and housing wealth data was derived from data provided by HM Land Registry and Registers of Scotland. Estimates of the numbers of households in Britain living in wealth and poverty were derived from a project that included collaboration with our colleagues at the Universities of Sheffield, Bristol and in London: Jan Rigby, Ben Wheeler, Dimitris Ballas, Eldin Fahmy, Dave Gordon and Ruth Lupton, to whom we are grateful for their collaboration, and to the Joseph Rowntree Foundation who funded the work that led to those estimates being made. National estimates of mortality rates were taken from the most recent British life tables produced by the Government Actuary's Department.

Daniel Dorling acknowledges current funding supporting this work under a British Academy Research Leave Fellowship to study the social and spatial transformation of society.

The maps on the inside covers show the location of some cities and towns on both the cartogram and conventional map as an aid to navigation.

1 Introduction: seven stages

All the world's a stage,
And all the men and women merely players;
They have their exits and their entrances,
And one man in his time plays many parts,
His Acts being seven ages.

Introduction

One hundredth of the world is an island, the island of Britain. One hundredth of the world of people, that is. What does this stage look like if we try to view all the players? Imagine the island were reconfigured so we could easily view it all from the air, just below the clouds. Space out everyone equally. An hexagonal arrangement is best. And give them each 50 coloured placards. The kind of placards you see used in mass games. Then ask the crowd a question to which the correct answer for each is just one of their 50 colours. What would you see? It might be a little confusing. What questions would be relevant to all?

Start again. Take just the children. Just the school-age children. Arrange them as a map of Britain in which each is given roughly equal space and has 50 placards. Now ask them: how are they doing at school? What kind of home do they live in? What do their parent(s) do? That makes a little more sense. Different questions make sense to different age groups. There is little point in asking a teenager about retirement. But too many age groups and the answers will not be that different. For old time's sake let us choose seven stages and play out our acts on them. For an encore we will briefly bring everyone back on at the end.

But what is it that we wish to see on these seven stages? What questions do we want to ask? Well, let us start at the beginning and ask a simple one: are they all merely players? Do all men and women have their part to play, their exits and entrances to make and by and large perform as the playwright directs? Can you see evidence of the stage directions from how they move about the stage? Do they show any signs of autonomy or are they just delivering the lines that have been given them? To what extent are most people merely players? What identities do they each appear to have been allotted?

When the play starts the action is, of course, a little random, the lines somewhat garbled. It is, after all, not easy to orchestrate a perfect performance from several million players, especially when they are all mewling infants to begin with. But pull your camera back so that no individual placard is identifiable, just the colour created by thousands next to one another. Blur the image, squint slightly. Now, now do you see it? But what is it that you are actually seeing? Is it a pattern, a pattern made up of human identities, a human mosaic, human cartography?

1.1 Human identity

We *are constantly informed that to share an identity is to be bonded on the most fundamental levels: national, 'racial', ethnic, regional, and local. Identity is always bounded and particular. It marks out the divisions and subsets in our social lives and helps to define the boundaries between our uneven, local attempts, to make sense of the world. Nobody ever speaks of a human identity.* (Paul Gilroy, 2000 [2004 edn], *Between camps, nations, cultures and the allure of race*, London: Routledge, p 98)

Identify yourself!

Who are you? What are you? Why are you?

It is no coincidence that in British newspaper articles two forms of identity are usually given, one implicit (gender) in our first names or titles, the other explicit (age):

In 2007, with Bethan Thomas, Daniel Dorling (aged 39) wrote a book.

Gender tells you a lot, age tells others much more about you, and so here we use age first to identify different groups of Britons that share common experience of their ages. To avoid being novel, we use seven ages as identified by the long-dead English playwright whose words introduce each of our chapters. The world as a stage is an old metaphor for adding geographical context to understanding life courses. Our age groups cannot be as ambiguous as his and therefore, following this introduction, this atlas is divided into seven chapters relating to the seven ages. Note from the table below that we avoid the modern habit of trying to pretend that we are not deteriorating physically as we age. There is no 'third age' in this book and middle age is centred

From sonnet to statistic: the seven ages of modern British (wo)man

Age limits	Title	Description
0-4	Infancy	Mewling and puking
5-15	Childhood	Whining and shining
16-24	Young adulthood	Sighing and woeful
25-39	Midlife	Jealous and quarrelsome
40-59	Maturity	Wise and severe
60-74	Old age	Lean and shrunk
75+	Truly elderly	Sans teeth, taste and eyes

around half life expectancy, not reserved as a title for later years to try to make our dotage appear less daunting.

Once gender and age are ascribed, other identities quickly follow: 'mother', 'husband', 'sister' in families; 'friend', 'colleague', 'boss' at work; 'acquaintance', 'mate', 'lover' at play; and so on. And, as Paul Gilroy makes clear, many identities have overtly geographical overtones: national (English/British), 'racial' (White/Black) and ethnic (British/Irish); but as Paul (male) Gilroy (early 50s) goes on to say, regional and local also matter in creating human identities where lives are structured across space by so much more than just the simplest of social classifications (class). Pictures drawn of our collective lives depict a human mosaic. The mosaic should be of what our collective human identity looks like.

So what might the view from Olympus be? To mimic it, we need to create a new device, a new technique, and it is always nice to name such a device after people who have described what it is you are trying to look for. Instead of a Hubble telescope, let future inventors create a Gilroy-scope, pointed back to Earth rather than to the heavens and back in time to around the start of the second millennium of the present era. Just as few know who Hubble was now, no one may know who Gilroy was by then. That does not matter. What matters is that instead of registering wavelengths of light, the Gilroy-scope registers social identities and it can do this on many bands. Turn it to remotely sense the human geography of this small island. Pan left a bit, it is the strange-looking blob off the coast of mainland Europe. Focus in on the decades we are currently living through. Turn up the contrast and the colour. Simplify the signals coming in, but show image after image after image and here is what you might see. Oh, a little auto-rectifying is needed to ensure that the projection is stable and everyone can be seen.

In your hands here, then, is a crude attempt at that device, so crude that it was drawn by hand. Its prototype and origins are described in Daniel Dorling and Bethan Thomas (2004) *People and places: A 2001 Census atlas*, Bristol: The Policy Press. There is nothing very revolutionary about this device. Just as the microscope was invented by turning round a telescope (or was it the other way round?), we have just altered a few basic principals of mapping, inverted the image so people are shown rather than land and used up to 50 colours rather than the five that modern-day cartographers appear to believe are the limit. The result is an atlas of people, showing through places how they share identities, many identities that when collected together often appear to form a common set of human identities expressed through a human mosaic.

1.2 A human mosaic

Ever wondered where the lines of fracture lie? How the fragments of society splinter and are stuck together? Ever wondered where the fault lines run, where the wrong and right sides of the tracks divide? At a particular crossroads have you ever thought you had crossed into another place? Just felt that between this street and that road something had changed?

Imagine a map of what matters. Not a map of where pylons run or where land is currently built on, but a map of where people and their lives change. Dream up a map in which the fields are coloured by hopes and fears, chance and circumstance. Imagine a map that shows who plays with whom, where children have brothers and sisters, how they learn, love, toil, rest, recuperate, age, wither, dither and die. See a human mosaic.

Social creatures do not live lives that make sense examined in solitude. A honeycomb of neighbourhoods is not revealed through a focus on one journey. Travel through a few of the cells of community in which we live and you will gain a very partial image of the whole. A day in the life of one individual in a million, or 60 individuals in sixty million, is just a day, is just a couple of months, just touches the edge. Sixty stories are too many to follow. Sixty million is a deceptively simple dozen letters, eight digits, five syllables, two words, one country.

Sixty million people live in Britain. Sixty million breaths are taken every second. Sixty million thoughts are about to be. And be gone. Imagine sixty million. Imagine a map of sixty million. Better, imagine 60 maps of 60 sides to sixty million. Sixty stories are too many to follow but 60 snapshots of time are an album of instance that constitute a story. An album tells a tale, even if each image is just of some 60 people: a wedding, a funeral, the faces, expressions, placings. Pictures tell stories of people through images of places, or groups, of position and juxtaposition. Can you imagine what stories there would be in an album of sixty million?

Zoom out from the face and you see the crowd. Out from the crowd and you see the stadium, out from the stadium and you see the streets. Out from the streets and you see the neighbourhoods. Out from the neighbourhoods and you see the city. Then out from the city and its hinterland to see the country. Sharpen your focus and you see a country made up of cities. Cities made up of neighbourhoods. Look further in and you lose your peripheral image of the country. Sixty cities each averaging a score of neighbourhoods, suburbs, exurbs and innards is enough for most minds. Sixty score, twelve hundred, six squared, squared, places of people, 1,200 faces in each picture in an album of a society.

Each face of a place reflects thousands more faces. Start with the six faces in a large family living in a close of six large family homes, strung along a street of six such closes, a street that with another five comes off a main road, six of those main roads makes a suburb and six of them a quarter of a town. A quarter of a town is usually what each of our faces represents. Thus one of our neighbourhoods is an image of thousands of faces, a face of a place. And placed all together these neighbourhoods are faces, each different yet still faces of places. Each face of a place came to be there with care, people moved in and out within narrow bands of choice and constraint, without much chance to create, maintain or change that face.

Each place is a story of thousands of stories, a composite, collage, collection, a human mosaic.

1.3 Human boundaries

The maps that follow are of parliamentary constituencies, the areas that were used to elect members of the Westminster Parliament at the 2001 General Election, or more frequently, of subdivisions of constituencies. Note that we are unable to include Northern Ireland as some of the datasets we used to subdivide constituencies did not include the province. Each of the 641 constituencies is shown as a hexagon. We have added a little detail by splitting each constituency in two and have tried to make reading of the maps easier by separating the regions and marking out the lower course of the River Thames. We call each half of each constituency a neighbourhood because, with the help of colleagues, we have tried to best split each into the two most distinct halves possible, splitting the more affluent half from the less affluent.

The neighbourhoods shown in this atlas are thus 1,282 distinct areas that have many characteristics in common in terms of the lives of the people who live there. The boundaries of constituencies themselves are also partly supposed to be drawn to ensure this. And why have we chosen to only split these areas and not to split them into smaller places? Because this is as much as we think is humanly possible: it ensures that no smaller units (wards) are split and that all neighbourhoods are of comparable population size; and because by this simple split alone, enough detail is revealed, avoiding highlighting the spurious and unrepresentative. A more complex subdivision is possible by algorithm, but not where each result is checked by hand to see if it results in anomalies that require us to revisit all our previous decisions.

On each map each neighbourhood is represented by a half hexagon. It would have been much easier to split each hexagon vertically, but would have made the ensuing cartogram virtually impossible to navigate visually. Therefore, we have split each hexagon representing a constituency into its two constituent neighbourhoods as they are related to each other in real space. Thus, for example, Aberavon West lies to the left of Aberavon East, and Kirkcaldy South lies below Kirkcaldy North as depicted in the mosaic on the page.

The two following maps show the regions and countries of Great Britain on the hexagonal cartogram used in this atlas and also on a conventional area map. In order to make the cartogram easier to read, the regions are slightly separated out.

The next two maps show the location of some cities and towns on both the cartogram and conventional map as an aid to navigation. Note that the outer boundary of Outer London coincides with the London region boundary. On all of the mosaics mapped, the outlines of these urban areas are shown.

The mosaics are complex to interpret and therefore detailed, labelled cartograms of regions, countries and their constituent constituencies and neighbourhoods, together with a look-up table, can be found on the accompanying website (https://www.policypress.org.uk/page.php?name=9781861348203). Those maps and accompanying text explain how to find a location given a name and a name given a location. Space limits precluded the inclusion of these maps in this atlas.

In this atlas, only the full-page maps are numbered and they take the number of the section in which they fall. The first full-page map is in Section 1.4 and is numbered Figure 1.4; there are no Figures 1.1, 1.2 or 1.3.

Compass directions are in capitals if they refer to a proper place name: Aberavon West, South East region. If they refer to a more general and less specific area they are in lower case: west Wales, southern England.

At the time of writing, each hexagon in England and Wales on the map represents a Westminster Parliamentary constituency. In Scotland, each hexagon represents a Scottish Parliamentary constituency.

1.3 Human boundaries

1.3 Human boundaries

1.3 Human boundaries

Many of the maps in this atlas have keys of a type that are probably unfamiliar to readers and so here we provide an explanation of how the maps should be interpreted. The maps are categorical rather than of simple proportions and require some study to enable them to be understood.

Some of the maps are of conventional proportions always measured as percentages, such as the example key shown below left of the percentage of people aged 16-24 who are female. This type of map (the map itself is shown on page 89) is probably familiar and does not require much further explanation, save to say that the colour indicates the band of proportions within which each neighbourhood so coloured lies.

Example modal and second modal key

Council Tax Band
	Band A/Band B
	Band A/Band C
	Band A/Band D
	Band A/Band E
	Band A/Band G
	Band B/Band A
	Band B/Band C
	Band B/Band D
	Band B/Band E
	Band C/Band A
	Band C/Band B
	Band C/Band D
	Band C/Band E
	Band C/Band G
	Band D/Band C
	Band D/Band E
	Band D/Band F
	Band D/Band G
	Band E/Band B
	Band E/Band C
	Band E/Band D
	Band E/Band F
	Band E/Band G
	Band F/Band D
	Band F/Band E
	Band G/Band C
	Band G/Band D
	Band G/Band E
	Band G/Band F
	Band G/Band H

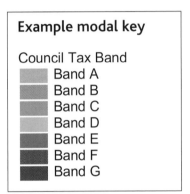

Example percentage key

Females 16–24 (%)
	34.0 – 39.9
	40.0 – 47.4
	47.5 – 52.4
	52.5 – 54.9
	55.0 – 59.9

Example modal key

Council Tax Band
	Band A
	Band B
	Band C
	Band D
	Band E
	Band F
	Band G

Other maps show the most common (modal) category of the topic under consideration in each neighbourhood. An example is given above, centre, of the modal (most commonly found) Council Tax Band for each neighbourhood, taken from the map on page 14. Although these maps are less common in conventional mapping of human geography, they are analogous to, for example, geology maps. However, these maps are simple to interpret: in the example here, anywhere where the most common Council Tax Band is Band A is coloured pink on the map. It is important to remember that the most common category may constitute less than 50%.

Many of the maps are of the most common and second most common occurrences of particular categories. Second most common is often referred to as majority–minority in this atlas. These are the most complex maps and will almost certainly be unfamiliar to readers. Hence, they require a little more study to understand. The example key above right shows the most common and second most common Council Tax Bands. This key is taken from the map on page 15.

Where we have shown two maps of the same topic, one showing the modal, and the other the modal with the second most common category, we have tried to link the colours, as can be seen in the two Council Tax Band keys above. Thus, using either key, everywhere where the most common Council Tax Band is Band A, neighbourhoods are coloured pink/red. In the combination map, the different shades of pink and red enable us to discriminate between those places where the most common category is Band A and where the second most common category is Band B, C, D, E or G. From this we can also see the combinations that do not exist. Here, for example, in the neighbourhoods where the most common Council Tax Band is A, the second most common Band is never F. If a combination does not occur anywhere on the map then it does not appear anywhere on the key.

1.4 Human cartography

Sometimes *peculiar things happened during the lengthy work with analyses, comparisons, drawing, checking. It sometimes seemed as if the red symbols and yellow ground colour of the urban landscape faded away and were replaced by forests, lakes and fields, criss-crossed by roads, which turned out to be filled with streams of sleepy early-morning travellers in cars, buses and trains, on their way to work in the towns. There were times when the coloured areas on the colour ink-jet map were suddenly obscured by white summer clouds which seemed to scud in from nowhere between the map and the author's eyes, and among which he could glimpse the sparkle of the sea by the coast, the rivers which rolled down to meet it, the towns and villages and people. Sometimes old people materialised out of the map of Norrland and observed with melancholy the exodus of the young towards the coast and the south. From the diagrams which display households suddenly appeared a throng of people who with muted voices told of their lives, of their loneliness, of their joy in their children and of their hopes on their behalf.* (Janos Szegö, 1984, *A census atlas of Sweden*, Stockholm: Swedish Council for Building Research, p 20)

Janos Szegö is credited with the invention of the concept of human cartography. In 1994 he published *Mapping hidden dimensions of the urban scene* (Stockholm: Swedish Council for

Building Research); his story began with a view from the sky, from a hot air balloon containing a magical machine. The machine is an early prototype of the Gilroy-scope but less focused on identity and more simply on existence. It is a scanner that allows the locations of people to be viewed, through walls and roofs, as coloured dots. At night most dots are stationary, but a new one suddenly appears when a child is born. Shortly after dawn the dots begin to move frantically, quickly forming lines commuting to work, going to school or milling around when shopping in local neighbourhoods. Showing movement and change is difficult and only makes sense once the structure that is being changed and within which people are moving is appreciated. Let us start with the dot that is the birth of a child, but colour the dot by just one aspect of that child's identity: the mother's age.

Almost every minute of every hour of every day of the year, a baby is born in Britain. An extra thousand people are born between when you brush your teeth in the morning and at night. Of those thousand, just twenty-five are born to mothers aged under 18, fifty to mothers aged 18 or 19 and twenty to mothers aged over 40, with the remaining 900 odd being born to mothers between the ages of 20 and 39. With every year that passes a few additional older women and a few less younger ones have children.

Birth is where we begin our story of the myriad geographies to life in Britain. Babies are differentiated in innumerable ways. The ways in which they differ tell us in turn of how neighbourhoods differ, and those babies themselves contribute to making different neighbourhoods distinct. An aspect of the first instances of their lives that sets infants apart subsequently (and that is recorded for all) is the age of their mother at the point of their birth. If there were no geographical patterning to mother's age, there would be little structure to be seen on the maps on the following pages. The patterning that there is reveals much about the social worlds into which British babies are now born.

The age distribution of 1,000 typical mothers in Britain

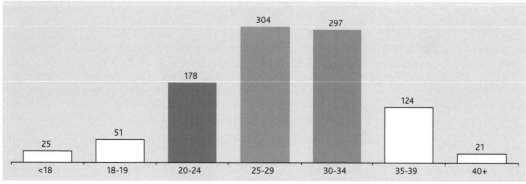

<18	18-19	20-24	25-29	30-34	35-39	40+
25	51	178	304	297	124	21

1.4 Human cartography

To understand what comes next, three concepts need to be understood in ascending order of probable unfamiliarity: modal/ majority group, spatial detail/complexity, and visual equality/ population cartogram. We show the modal group in each area, that is, the most common. Often we call this the majority group. Note that just as politicians do not need over 50% of the vote to win a majority in an election, majority means 'most', and not 'more than half'.

In some instances where there is remarkable uniformity across the country we show the modal group of difference from the national distribution. In every case where we do this we just show 'below average', 'average' and 'above average'. We will show the distribution of these areas over space and how they relate to each other in spatial detail. By spatial detail/complexity we mean that we will use a detailed enough geographical and social resolution that areas similarly shaded can coalesce to visible structure, and many shades can be shown simultaneously. We often show the second most commonly found group in an area simultaneously with the most common. And we show the characteristics of the

people in these areas visually equal, ensuring that each area is drawn in proportion to population. One person, one pixel. This necessitates the use of a population cartogram of these 1,282 neighbourhoods.

Here, we begin by showing a series of simple maps that are easy to interpret, and follow these by maps of more complexity. The first three maps show those neighbourhoods where the modal (that is, the most common) age for mothers to give birth is age 20-24, 25-29 and 30-34 respectively. These are the only age ranges for which most mothers in any neighbourhood fall. Clearly, in most of the country, most mothers are aged between 25 and 29 when they give birth, with older mothers concentrated in the South East. The fourth map is a composite of the first three maps.

Modal mother's age 20-24

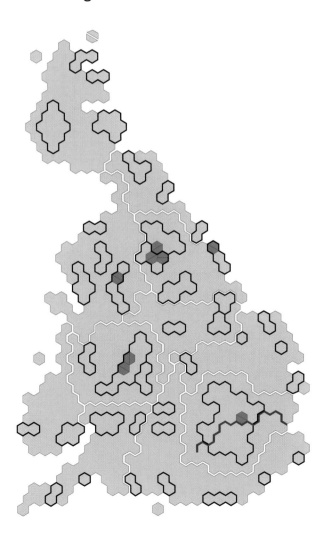

Modal mother's age 25-29

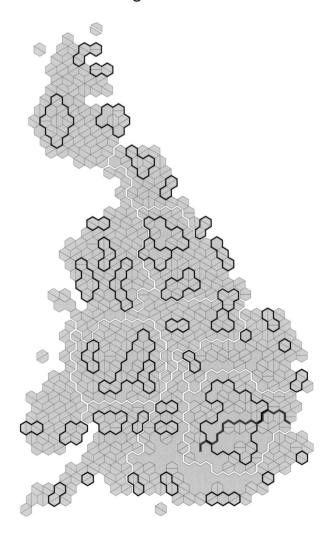

1.4 Human cartography

Modal mother's age 30-34

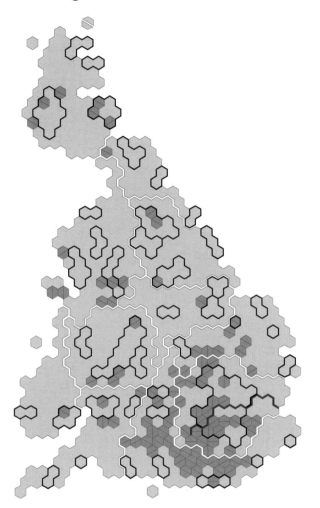

Modal mother's age

Modal mother's age
Age 20-24
Age 25-29
Age 30-34

Figure 1.4 opposite is of the most common and second most common age, by five-year age bands, at which mothers give birth. Of the 1,282 neighbourhoods, in 1,076 the most common age for mothers to give birth is 25-29, shown by the two blue hues. In 190 neighbourhoods the modal mother's age is 30-34 (coloured pink) and only in 16 neighbourhoods are births to mothers aged 20-24 (coloured green) the most common. Nowhere are mothers aged below 20 in the majority. In each case, the second most common mother's age is in an adjacent age band. This increased amount of visual detail means that the 25-29 age band of modal mother's age is now split into two, showing where the second most common age of giving birth is either 20-24 or 30-34. Older mothers are more likely to be found in London and the South East, while young mothers are more common in northern and midlands cities, as well as in Stepney and Bow in east London.

By adding the second most common to the most common age of giving birth, we have added a level of visual complexity to the map. Most of the maps in this atlas are of this type and we often refer to these as 'mosaic' maps. By this means we can start to typify particular neighbourhoods: this is a neighbourhood where the most common age of giving birth is age 25-29, followed by 20-24; this is a neighbourhood where the modal ethnicity is 'White British' followed by 'Black Caribbean', and so on. Note that the key to Figure 1.4 is very simply labelled. The most common group that is implied by a shade is shown before the solidus and the second most common group is shown after the solidus.

1.4 Human cartography

Figure 1.4

Modal mother's age at giving birth
- Age 20-24/Age 25-29
- Age 25-29/Age 20-24
- Age 25-29/Age 30-34
- Age 30-34/Age 25-29

1.5 Human geography

The use of one base map throughout this atlas allows all images to be compared. Take for instance the maps of modal mother's age shown in Section 1.4. Just what kinds of places are the mothers aged under 25 or over 30 clustered into? Compare the maps in the previous section with the one below and it perhaps becomes more obvious. This map is of the modal (most common) Council Tax Band of property in each neighbourhood. It should immediately be clear that older mothers tend to take their infants home to more valuable properties. This we can simply guess, given where such properties are and where the mothers give birth. It is theoretically possible that this is not the case, but in practice ecological associations are not usually fallacious and as Council Tax Bands are not recorded on birth certificates a little supposition may not go amiss.

Although the ecological fallacy is rarely invoked, a more common error is to assume uniformity where there is variance. For the ecological fallacy to be invoked, the opposite has to be the case from that which you might assume. The classic example of the ecological fallacy is that on hearing that literacy levels are low in areas where high numbers of people were labelled 'Black' in 1950s North America, you might assume that literacy among Black people was low. You would be wrong, but more often than not you would be right to assume that spatial coincidence implies individual coincidence. However, there are varying levels of coincidence ranging from 'weakly related to' to 'substitutes for'. Usually, there is greater variance within areas than that which is being shown. For instance, property values as measured by Council Tax banding can only at best be weakly related to some other aspect of life at the individual level, such as the ages at which women choose to try to give birth.

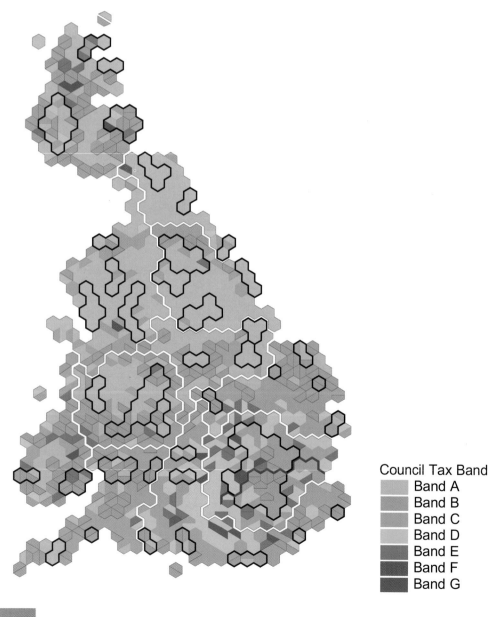

Council Tax Band
- Band A
- Band B
- Band C
- Band D
- Band E
- Band F
- Band G

1.5 Human geography

Figure 1.5

Figure 1.5 shows which Council Tax Band is most common and which is second most common in each area. After a little examination, it can be seen that there is not a great variation within neighbourhoods. To help clarify this, the first table overleaf shows the proportion of dwellings in Britain located in neighbourhoods according to which band is most and second most common there. Some 86.1% of dwellings are found in bands either side of the main diagonal of the table overleaf. A further 12.3% are in the next band, leaving only 1.6% of dwellings in neighbourhoods where there are two bands or more between the most and second most common Council Tax Bands (highlighted in the table). These neighbourhoods are the rarest to be found on the map and this lack of heterogeneous neighbourhoods becomes a theme running through this entire work. For information, we also provide a table overleaf of the property value of each Council Tax Band for England, Scotland and Wales.

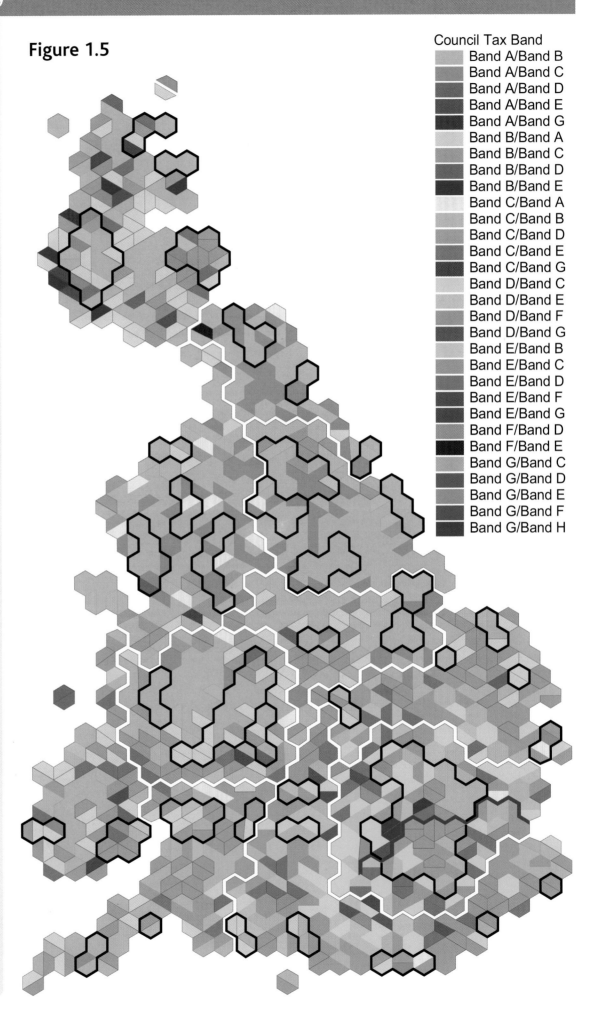

Council Tax Band
Band A/Band B
Band A/Band C
Band A/Band D
Band A/Band E
Band A/Band G
Band B/Band A
Band B/Band C
Band B/Band D
Band B/Band E
Band C/Band A
Band C/Band B
Band C/Band D
Band C/Band E
Band C/Band G
Band D/Band C
Band D/Band E
Band D/Band F
Band D/Band G
Band E/Band B
Band E/Band C
Band E/Band D
Band E/Band F
Band E/Band G
Band F/Band D
Band F/Band E
Band G/Band C
Band G/Band D
Band G/Band E
Band G/Band F
Band G/Band H

1.5 Human geography

Proportion of dwellings in Britain by neighbourhood classified by Council Tax banding

% dwellings	Second most common band								
Most common band	Band A	Band B	Band C	Band D	Band E	Band F	Band G	Band H	Total
A		27.5	8.0	0.3	0.2	–	<0.1	–	36.0
B	8.1		12.2	0.3	0.4	–	–	–	20.9
C	1.3	11.7		12.3	1.6	–	0.1	–	27.0
D	–	–	6.1		4.5	<0.1	0.2	–	10.9
E	–	0.1	0.5	2.8		0.2	0.2	–	3.9
F	–	–	–	0.1	<0.1		–	–	0.1
G	–	–	0.1	0.3	0.2	0.2		0.4	1.2
Grand total	9.4	39.3	26.9	16.1	6.9	0.4	0.5	0.4	100.0

Note: Cells are coloured in the table above by the colours used in Figure 1.5, but only when there are at least two bands between the most and second most common Council Tax Bands.

Council Tax Bands and the valuation of the property associated with them by country

England		Wales		Scotland	
Band A	Up to £40,000	Band A	Up to £30,000	Band A	Up to £27,000
Band B	£40,001-£52,000	Band B	£30,001-£39,000	Band B	£27,001-£35,000
Band C	£52,001-£68,000	Band C	£39,001-£51,000	Band C	£35,001-£45,000
Band D	£68,001-£88,000	Band D	£51,001-£66,000	Band D	£45,001-£58,000
Band E	£88,001-£120,000	Band E	£66,001-£90,000	Band E	£58,001-£80,000
Band F	£120,001-£160,000	Band F	£90,001-£120,000	Band F	£80,001-£106,000
Band G	£160,001-£320,000	Band G	£120,001-£240,000	Band G	£106,001-£212,000
Band H	£320,001+	Band H	£240,001+	Band H	£212,001+

Note: Council Tax valuations are based on the price a property would have fetched if it had been sold on the open market on 1 April 1991. The Council Tax Band of a property is related to its market value at the valuation base date and not the value at March 2003 when the data were collected. Each dwelling is assigned to one of the eight bands shown above (note also that this is before the Welsh revaluation in 2005).

2 At first the infant: ages 0-4

At first the infant,
Mewling and puking in the nurse's arms;

2.1 Introduction

We start this, and each chapter that follows, with a map showing the proportions of people of the relevant age group living in each neighbourhood. This distribution should be borne in mind when studying the maps in the rest of this chapter.

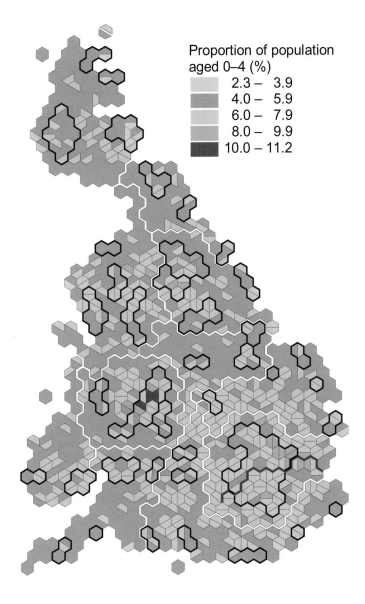

Proportion of population aged 0–4 (%)

	2.3 – 3.9
	4.0 – 5.9
	6.0 – 7.9
	8.0 – 9.9
	10.0 – 11.2

The map on the right is clearly only of the locations of infants that applied when the snapshot used throughout most of this atlas was taken in 2001. Note that at the extreme some neighbourhoods have five times as many infants as others. The patterns of age distribution tend to change slowly over time, but those of the very young change more quickly, influenced by trends in the popularity of having children in particular places at particular times for particular groups of people. However, this map most reflects where women of the ages most common to give birth live in their highest numbers.

Most people are not average and the same is true of infants. To appreciate this and its implications, babies need to be put into a few categories, homes have to be valued, mothers' ages must be ascertained, and a scattering of comparisons has to be made. Just from what has been mapped in the introduction to this atlas we can tell that it is, for instance, true that the most common Council Tax Band in neighbourhoods containing 57% of dwellings is Band A or B, and that the second most common modal age band for giving birth in is 30-34. However, in those neighbourhoods where the majority of mothers are in their early thirties, the most common Council Tax Band for properties is Band D (not A or B). What is perhaps most telling is that there are no neighbourhoods in which most mothers give birth at age 20-24 where the modal Council Tax Band of property is Band D, E, F or G. Furthermore, by Band A and mother's age, almost all infants living in areas where the most or the second most new mothers are in their early twenties are born in Wales, Scotland or the north of England. And almost all of those born where mothers are older and property more valuable are born in the south of England. In 12 out of 15 majority Band G neighbourhoods the modal mother's age is 30-34. All but one of these 12 are in the south. All of the remaining three are in Scotland or Wales (where the band levels differ).

2.1 Introduction

Dwelling by neighbourhood categorised by modal mother's age and Council Tax Band

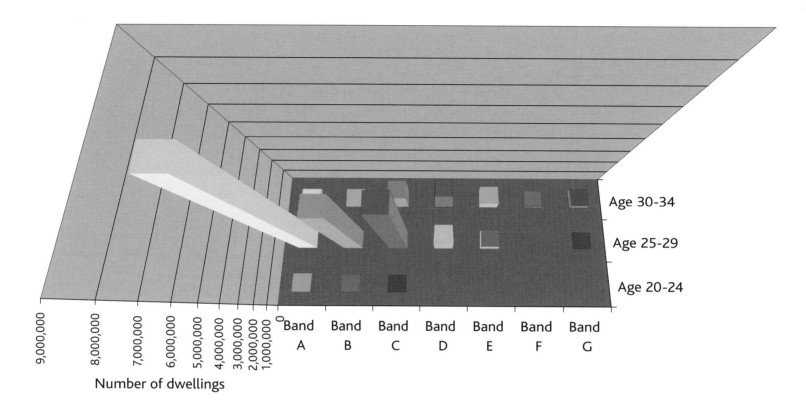

Modal mother's age and Council Tax Band by neighbourhood in Britain

Modal (%)	Band A	Band B	Band C	Band D	Band E	Band F	Band G	Total (%)
Age 20-24	1.2	0.1	0.1	0.0	0.0	0.0	0.0	1.4
Age 25-29	34.0	20.3	21.9	5.2	1.7	0.0	0.1	83.1
Age 30-34	0.8	0.6	5.1	5.7	2.2	0.1	1.1	15.5
Total (%)	36.0	20.9	27.0	10.9	3.9	0.1	1.2	100.0

2.1 Introduction

Look at Figure 2.1 and you begin to see that there are rigid rules governing where infants come to be born, in aggregate, in Britain. If you know a little bit about the rules, you can surmise much else. There are combinations of characteristics that are simply not found anywhere in Britain. There are no areas with most mothers aged under 20, no Band F with most aged under 30. If you know one thing about the area in which a child is born, you can surmise much else about that area. If you know two or three things, there may be less and less you can learn later. And this is simply on the basis of what we mapped above. However, how much you can assume about any particular infant on the basis of where they were born is far less exact. But you can assume a great deal about who else they are growing up with.

Figure 2.1

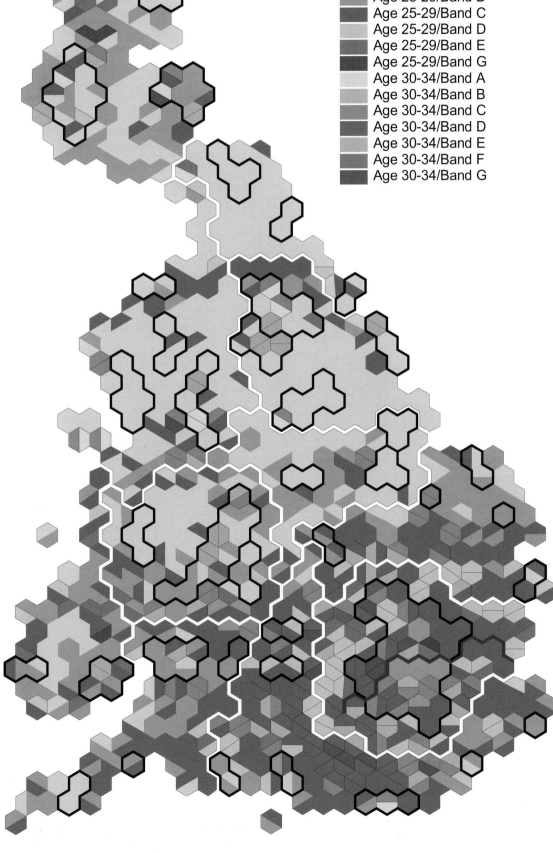

Mother's age & Council Tax Band

- Age 20-24/Band A
- Age 20-24/Band B
- Age 20-24/Band C
- Age 25-29/Band A
- Age 25-29/Band B
- Age 25-29/Band C
- Age 25-29/Band D
- Age 25-29/Band E
- Age 25-29/Band G
- Age 30-34/Band A
- Age 30-34/Band B
- Age 30-34/Band C
- Age 30-34/Band D
- Age 30-34/Band E
- Age 30-34/Band F
- Age 30-34/Band G

2.2 The family of infants

What is the typical family? According to the 1851 Census of Great Britain:

> **The** *English family in its essential type is composed of husband, wife, children and servants, or less perfectly, but more commonly, as husband, wife and children.*
> (British Parliamentary Papers, 1851 Census Great Britain, Volume I, p xxviii)

One hundred years later, the typical family would have consisted of a married couple with two point something children, the father in employment and the mother a housewife. The expectation was that married women, let alone mothers, did not work. Although the civil service raised its marriage bar in 1946, many companies continued with one through the 1950s; Barclays Bank did not raise its bar until 1961. In 1951 most children lived with both of their biological parents; step-parenthood usually resulted from the remarriage of the surviving spouse following the death of one of the birth parents. The few lone parent families that existed were almost entirely the result of widowhood.

Today there is a much wider range of family types. While most small children live in a married couple family, a lower proportion of such families consist of both biological parents. Increasing divorce and remarriage rates mean that more children live with a step-parent. Many couples choose not to marry and therefore more children are living in cohabiting couple families; however, such families are not in a majority in any part of the country.

Although there has been a steady increase in the number of lone parent families, in very few places are they in the majority. Most such families are created through separation or divorce. Women's participation in the workforce has increased for a variety of reasons: equal opportunities and equal pay legislation, rising house prices necessitating higher family income, remarkable recent changes in educational opportunities and achievements, and changing expectations have all had a role to play.

Given the plethora of ways in which families at the start of the current century are given identities, a choice has to be made as to what matters most when classifying infants by their family type. The most simple, pertinent and revealing division of families into three kinds is by the number of adults in each infant's household who are in employment. In all neighbourhoods the modal number is none, one, or two and more.

Figure 2.2 shows where these different neighbourhoods are found. A fifth of infants live in a household where no one works and just under two fifths where one adult works. The majority of infants (43%) live in households where at least two adults work. Most often this is the father full-time and mother part-time. This arrangement is the dominant (largest) group to be found in the vast majority of neighbourhoods: all those shaded blue here.

2.2 The family of infants

Figure 2.2

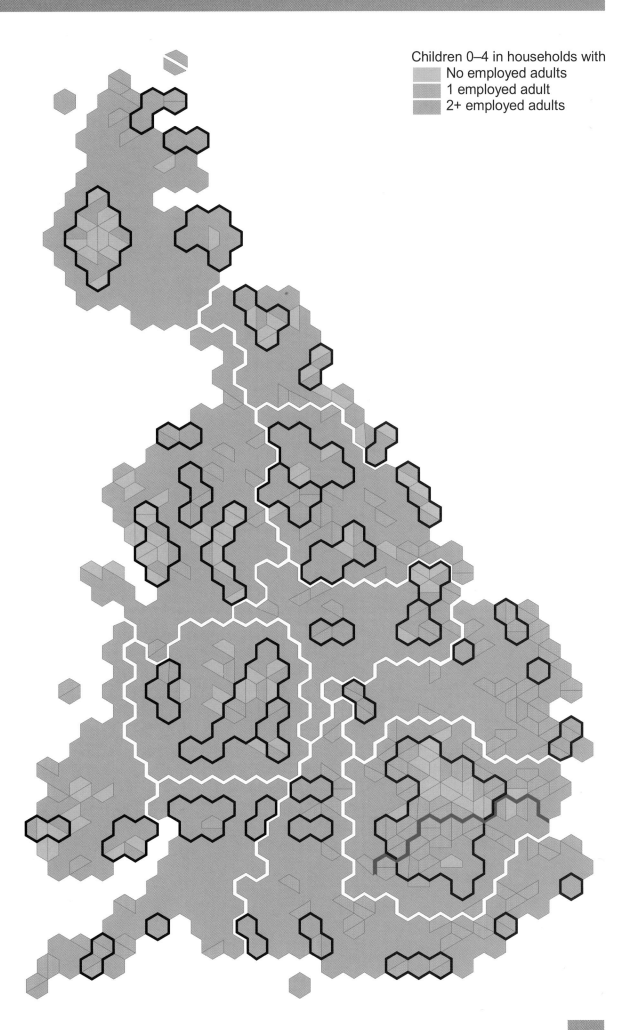

Children 0–4 in households with
- No employed adults
- 1 employed adult
- 2+ employed adults

2.3 Marriage versus lone parenthood of the parents of infants

Taking the three-way division of families by the number of adults in employment and adding a second dimension related to marriage reveals that often, but far from always, where no adults are in employment there is usually only one adult to look after the infant, infants and/or other children. Figure 2.3 opposite shows the mosaic of the modal type of family by marriage/relationship status together with the modal number of adults in employment for each neighbourhood. For most of the country, the most common category is that of children under the age of five living in households consisting of a married couple and where there are two or more adults in employment. Usually, both parents will be in employment, but there will be cases where only one parent works and the second (and any subsequent) working adult might be an older sibling, a grandparent or other, unrelated adult.

The next but far less common category found in Figure 2.3 is that of the traditional 'typical' family: married parents and one adult in employment. Such employment patterns might still be common in a few areas for a number of reasons: traditional customs, one high earner, comparatively low house prices or scarcity of suitable employment for both parents. The high cost of childcare in London is also clearly important there. In some areas there might well be a change from the typical male breadwinner, as women find work in the new service industries that have replaced much of traditional, male-dominated, blue-collar employment.

The least common modal category where married families are in the majority, as shown in Figure 2.3, are where there are also no adults in the household in paid employment, with north east London, the Welsh Valleys, Birmingham and Tyneside as obvious clusters. Clearly, such families are likely to be found in areas with fewer employment prospects as well as where there are high levels of ill health. Less clearly, but also possibly, areas can be assigned to this category where there are both high numbers of children living *with* a single parent who does not work, *and* high numbers of children living with married couples where one or both parents work. This is the case within parts of London and Birmingham. Just because most households in an area contain a married couple and most households contain no adults in work does not mean that most married couples there are without work.

The other category of family that composes the mode in many of the neighbourhoods shown here is the lone parent family. Again, the mosaic shows the mode for pre-school-age children living in families with no, one, or two or more adults in employment. Areas where lone parent families are the norm are concentrated in Glasgow, Liverpool, Manchester and Nottingham, together with parts of Cardiff. The majority consist of lone parent families and no working adults; such families with one working adult are only found in Vauxhall in London and in Blackpool. Finally, lone parent families and households with more than one working adult are only in the majority in Linwood in Scotland.

For those interested in the anomaly of Linwood (which features again in later life), Linwood is the only such area of its type shown on this map of family type. With the opening of a car plant in the 1950s 'on the grounds of social as well as business impact, including the case for building a new community around the plant at Linwood' (page 311 of R. Boyle, 1993, 'Changing the partners: the experience of urban economic policy in West Central Scotland 1980-90', *Urban Studies*, vol 30, no 2, pp 309-23), Linwood expanded from a small village to a substantial town. The creation and closure of the plant created a new community, which, by the 21st century, saw the majority of under-fives living in a neighbourhood where most did not live with their father but where most adults they lived with had to work. Further subdividing families by type and number of children shows that there are more children living in 'married couple with two children' families than in any other family type in Linwood (as we see in the next section when considering siblings).

2.3   Marriage versus lone parenthood of the parents of infants

Figure 2.3

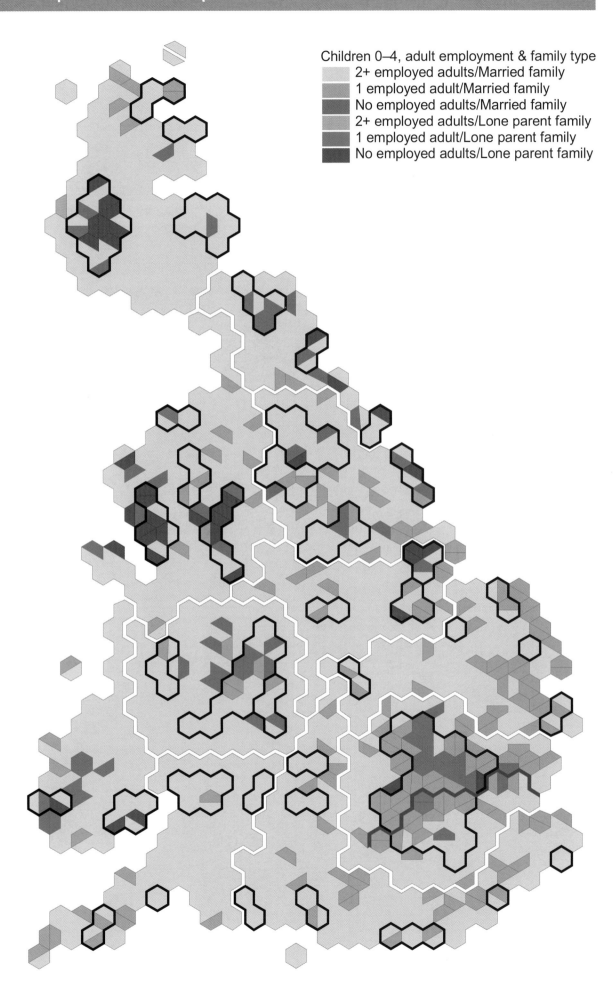

Children 0–4, adult employment & family type
- 2+ employed adults/Married family
- 1 employed adult/Married family
- No employed adults/Married family
- 2+ employed adults/Lone parent family
- 1 employed adult/Lone parent family
- No employed adults/Lone parent family

2.4 Brothers and sisters of infants and children

The early lives of children in Britain vary according to the number of siblings and parents they live with as much as by whether their parents are married. However, the mosaic of family size does not reflect as much variation in the geography of family size. Here we are concerned with all children, not just those aged under five (as there is little point distinguishing by age). Six in every seven children live in neighbourhoods where the modal family is two married parents with two children, and the next most common family consists of two married parents with three or more children. These areas are the light pink expanse of conformity that dominates 1,119 of the 1,282 neighbourhoods shown in Figure 2.4 opposite. Couple these areas with the only slightly more adventurous neighbourhoods where there are slightly more children living with two or more siblings and their married parents than with one, and 95% of neighbourhoods are coloured either light or darker pink.

Families do tend to have slightly more children within the major cities, excluding Bristol and Edinburgh. Lone parent families with one child are the modal group only in neighbourhoods in Scotland, almost all being in Glasgow, where the neighbourhoods are coloured a variety of blue shades in Figure 2.4 opposite, depending on the second most common type of family. Around Glasgow, south east Dundee, the old town of Aberdeen and central Brighton are the few areas like Linwood where single parent families with a single child are the second most typical kind of family to grow up in after two-child married parent families. In contrast, single parent families with two children are the most common type of family, from the point of view of children, only in the North West of England (almost all being in Liverpool in the neighbourhoods that are shades of green).

Nowhere in the country is there a neighbourhood where either the largest or second largest group of children are in families where their parents are cohabiting. Only a third of children in Britain are growing up in families with two or more siblings, less than a quarter are living with just one parent, less than a sixth as the only child in their family, and only a tenth with cohabiting parents. The majority of children live in a family with at least one sibling and both parents who are married. The table below shows the proportions living in each kind of family for all dependent children in Britain.

Children in Britain by family size and marriage

Family type	%
Married with 1 child	13
Married with 2 children	31
Married with 3+ children	22
Cohabiting with 1 child	3
Cohabiting with 2 children	4
Cohabiting with 3+ children	3
Lone parent with 1 child	8
Lone parent with 2 children	9
Lone parent with 3+ children	7
All children	100

2.4 Brothers and sisters of infants and children

Figure 2.4

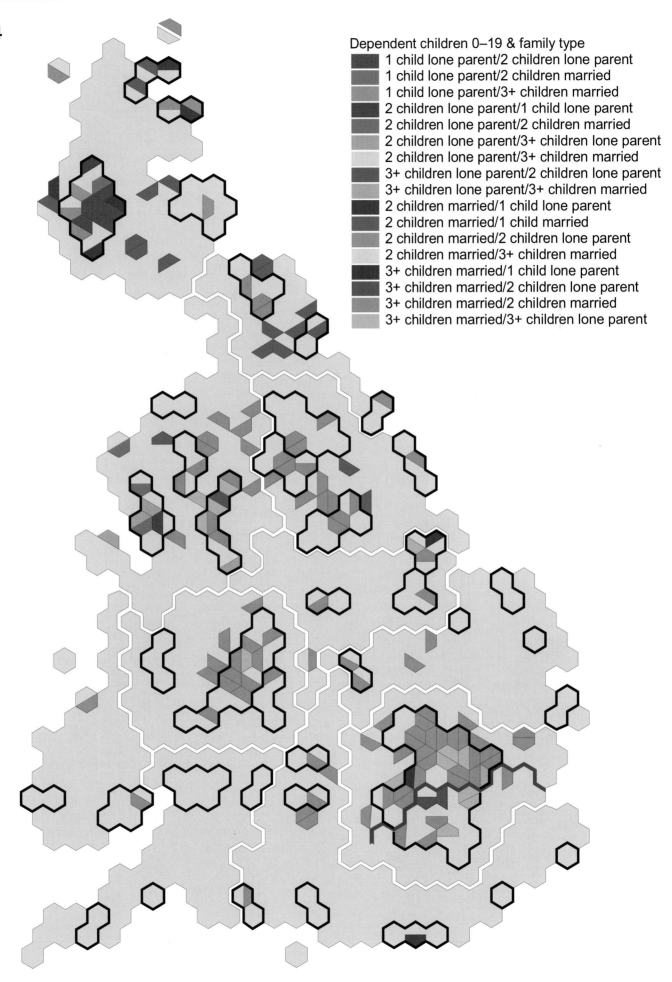

Dependent children 0–19 & family type
- 1 child lone parent/2 children lone parent
- 1 child lone parent/2 children married
- 1 child lone parent/3+ children married
- 2 children lone parent/1 child lone parent
- 2 children lone parent/2 children married
- 2 children lone parent/3+ children lone parent
- 2 children lone parent/3+ children married
- 3+ children lone parent/2 children lone parent
- 3+ children lone parent/3+ children married
- 2 children married/1 child lone parent
- 2 children married/1 child married
- 2 children married/2 children lone parent
- 2 children married/3+ children married
- 3+ children married/1 child lone parent
- 3+ children married/2 children lone parent
- 3+ children married/2 children married
- 3+ children married/3+ children lone parent

2.5 Girls and boys: the balance in infancy

More boys are born than girls in most neighbourhoods (but not all). There is no geographical pattern to where girls are more likely to be born than boys and thus the mosaic below of neighbourhoods coloured light pinks and blues shows little spatial structure between those shades of sex. However, the colours are a little darker towards the coasts and lighter in the cities. More children are born in the latter and move towards the former, net, over time in their first few years of life. This is most striking in the capital where the clustering of the lightest shades of blues highlights areas people are most likely to leave once they have had their first child. And it is at the start of the first year of life that the highest proportion is male.

The more complex mosaic opposite (Figure 2.5) highlights this urban trend. Here the sex of infants is ignored and neighbourhoods are shaded by the year groups that are most numerous. The pinks are where those aged under a year are found in greatest numbers. Other urban areas are evident, but it is London that dominates, while suburban London is where the next age group, those aged one year, are most clustered.

The net outwards migration of young children is confirmed by the rural, highland and coastal concentration of blues and purples in the mosaic interspersed with the odd dark red or green for when

children aged four are the second largest group of all those aged under five. That there is such a pattern to be found, even within our geographies of just the first five years of life, shows how quickly we move (and of course are moved) around to establish these patterns.

Part of the reason for the high numbers of babies in London is recent high fertility there. But the rise also has its origins in migration, especially migration from overseas into the capital, of young people, by definition, of the usual ages to have children.

Lastly, in 1,097 of the 1,282 neighbourhoods shown here, more children aged under five are boys than girls. The frequency distribution of neighbourhoods by percentage female aged under five is shown in the graph below. Less than nine in 20 young children are girls in Aberdare South, Salford West, Inverness West and Liverpool Riverside South (all relatively poor neighbourhoods).

Girls in neighbourhoods

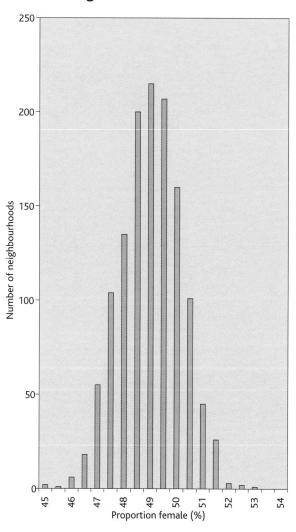

Note: The bars are coloured pink where a majority of under-fives are girls, otherwise they are coloured blue.

Children 0–4
- Girls aged 0
- Girls aged 1
- Girls aged 2
- Girls aged 3
- Girls aged 4
- Boys aged 0
- Boys aged 1
- Boys aged 2
- Boys aged 3
- Boys aged 4

2.5 Girls and boys: the balance in infancy

Figure 2.5

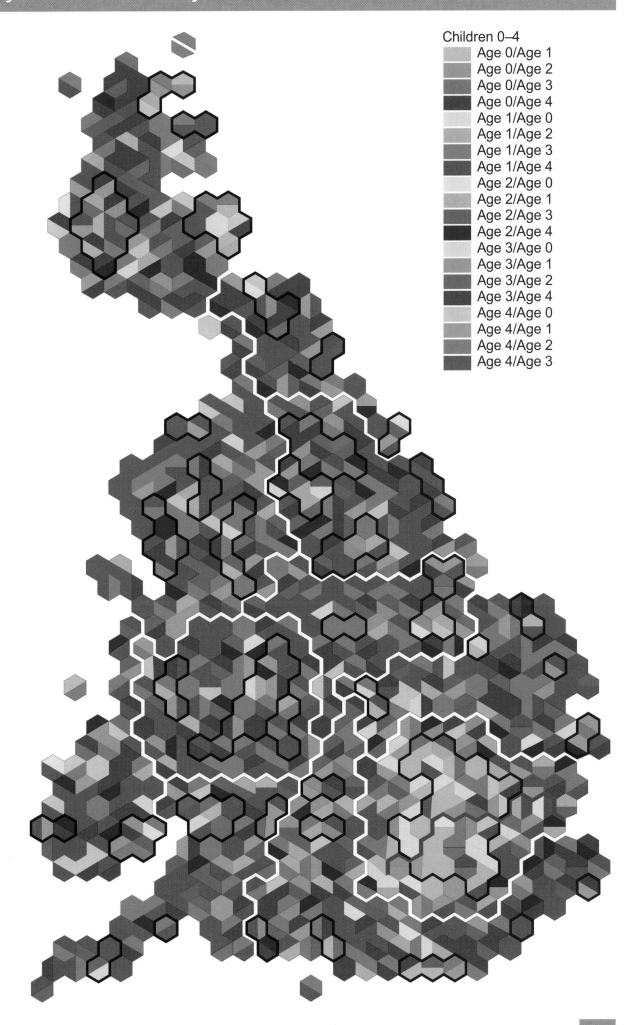

Children 0–4
- Age 0/Age 1
- Age 0/Age 2
- Age 0/Age 3
- Age 0/Age 4
- Age 1/Age 0
- Age 1/Age 2
- Age 1/Age 3
- Age 1/Age 4
- Age 2/Age 0
- Age 2/Age 1
- Age 2/Age 3
- Age 2/Age 4
- Age 3/Age 0
- Age 3/Age 1
- Age 3/Age 2
- Age 3/Age 4
- Age 4/Age 0
- Age 4/Age 1
- Age 4/Age 2
- Age 4/Age 3

2.6 Over-crowding in families with infants

A *house may be large or small; as long as the surrounding houses are equally small it satisfies all social demands for a dwelling. But if a palace arises beside the little house, the little house shrinks to a hovel … [and] the dweller will feel more and more uncomfortable, dissatisfied and cramped within its four walls.*
(K. Marx, 1847, *Wage labour and capital*, p 268)

In three dozen neighbourhoods of London and three in Glasgow most children aged under five are living in housing provided by the state, with too few rooms for their family. In 2001 Census terminology these are neighbourhoods where a majority of children live in homes with an 'occupancy rating' of –1 or less. Elsewhere most under-fives in Britain are growing up in homes, small palaces, with a surfeit of rooms.

Many of our great-grandparents will have shared homes with other families; our grandparents shared beds with siblings; our parents shared rooms with siblings; and we, mostly, grew up sleeping in a room of our own. From the viewpoint of today's under-fives, most live in areas where their families have spare rooms. In a generation's time how many children will expect to have both playrooms and bedrooms?

Here places are classified by tenure and over-crowding measured by occupancy rating. The occupancy rating provides a measure of under-occupancy and over-crowding. For example, a value of –1 implies that there is one room too few and that there is over-crowding in the household. The occupancy rating assumes that every household requires a minimum of two common rooms (excluding bathrooms). Tenure, the ownership categorisation here, has been collapsed into two main types: owner occupied or social rented, as nowhere is private renting the majority tenure for families with children.

Most rare are the places where social renting dominates and the majority of under-fives live in a home with one spare room. All 13 shown in Figure 2.6 opposite are found in England, none in London. Here homes were built for larger families and demand for housing is no longer so high. In twice as many (25) places the majority tenure is owner occupied and households with under-fives have fewer rooms than they need. All but five of these over-crowded places are in or around London. In a further 36 areas where social renting is most common the largest groups of children live in homes with just enough rooms for everyone. This may include the sharing of rooms by same-sex children aged under 10 and is mostly found in the north of England and within Glasgow. In the remaining 38 areas where social renting is most common among under-fives there are too few rooms for their family. All but three of these areas are in London and those three are in Glasgow. These children will mostly live in flats or tenements.

2.6 Over-crowding in families with infants

Figure 2.6

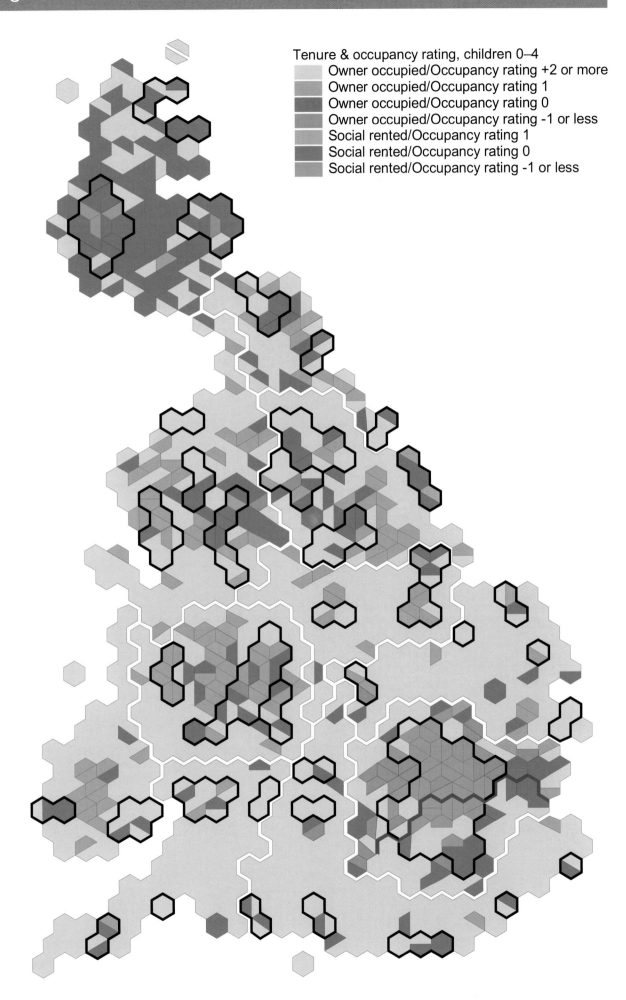

Tenure & occupancy rating, children 0–4
- Owner occupied/Occupancy rating +2 or more
- Owner occupied/Occupancy rating 1
- Owner occupied/Occupancy rating 0
- Owner occupied/Occupancy rating -1 or less
- Social rented/Occupancy rating 1
- Social rented/Occupancy rating 0
- Social rented/Occupancy rating -1 or less

2.7 Home ownership among the families of infants

In most neighbourhoods classified by tenure and over-crowding, owner occupation is the most dominant tenure and the largest group of under-fives is not over-crowded (see Figure 2.6). These areas divide into three groups. The first comprises just over 100 neighbourhoods where the largest group of families with children aged under five live in owner occupied housing and have a single spare room. These are mainly found in Birmingham, the Welsh Valleys and across the Yorkshire–Cheshire conurbation. The second comprises just over 200 neighbourhoods, places where the majority of under-fives live in owner occupied housing and have as many rooms as they are deemed to need. The majority of places within Scotland fall into this group. The third, of substantially more than 800 neighbourhoods, represents most places in Britain where under-fives are most usually found living in owner occupied dwellings with two or more spare rooms. Their parents may not view the rooms as spare, but compared with what significant numbers of children and families still contend with, they are spare. Found where semi-detached and detached houses dominate, in rural areas and especially in the south of England, most under-fives are growing up in homes with enough room for all, and also with a little more spare for when people come to stay. Tenure is key to understanding over-crowding.

What is the typical way we pay to be housed? Sir Joseph Bowley, Dickens' fictional Member of Parliament and 'poor man's friend and father', suggested that the poor a century-and-a-half ago should:

> **Live** *hard and temperately, be respectful, exercise your self-denial, bring up your family on next to nothing, pay your rent as regularly as the clock strikes, be punctual in your dealings.*
> (C. Dickens, 1844, The *chimes*)

A century ago nine out of 10 families rented. Now the typical family still pays for its housing but more usually through a mortgage rather than rent. On average we became richer, and some, more propertied. Many think they own their home, but actually they do not. When tenure is viewed from the eye-line of the under-fives even fewer of their parents actually own the home they are growing up in. In fact there are no neighbourhoods in Britain where most under-fives live in a home that is owned outright by their parents, although there are a few where that is the second most common tenure (tenure meaning the form of holding property).

Across the vast majority of Britain, in 94% of neighbourhoods, mortgaging dominates. For the typical child in the typical street, 'our house' is being paid for by our mum and dad. That monopoly is shown starkly on the simplified map opposite (Figure 2.7). Only three categories of tenure are shown here and only two form the majority tenure in any neighbourhood. The other 6% of areas see more children aged under five growing up in social housing than any other tenure. Social renting is in almost all cases the second most common alternative in any neighbourhood to owner occupation, but in the countryside, and on the coast, private renting is more often the largest minority tenure. In all areas but one owner occupation is most common after social renting (where social renting is in the majority).

2.7 Home ownership among the families of infants

Figure 2.7

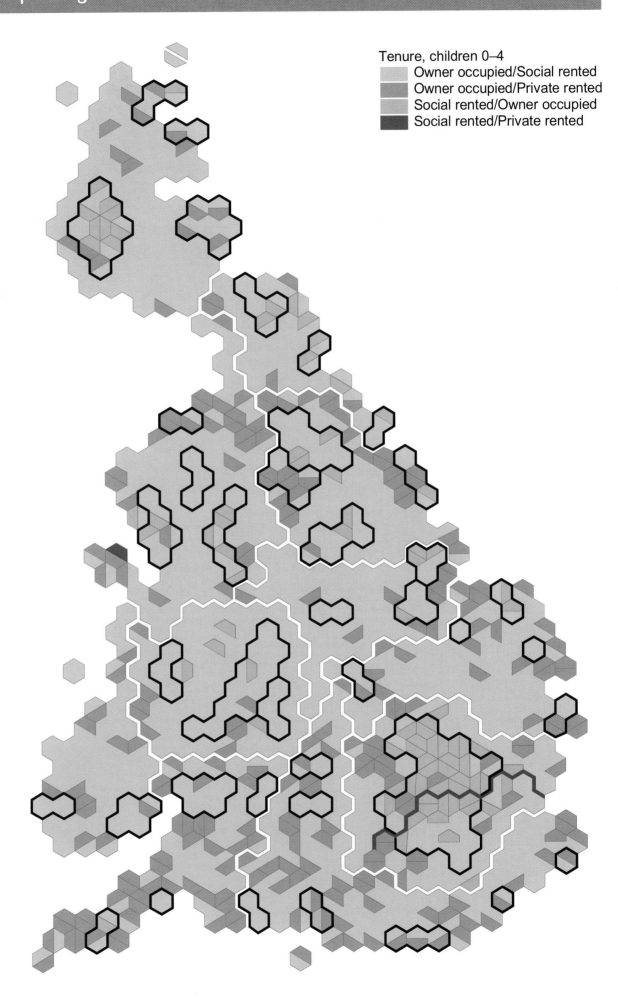

Tenure, children 0–4
- Owner occupied/Social rented
- Owner occupied/Private rented
- Social rented/Owner occupied
- Social rented/Private rented

2.8 Tenure of the homes of infants

When owner occupation is subdivided into owned outright and having a mortgage (buying), and social renting is also subdivided, a more detailed picture emerges (see Figure 2.8 opposite). Mortgaging is the dominant sub-tenure, and typical streets are found in four contrasting types of area depending on which tenure is next most common (counted by infant children) after mortgaging. In half the areas of Britain it is renting from the local authority (LA) that is the largest minority tenure. These typical areas are mostly found in Scotland, Wales and the north of England and in north and suburban London.

Mortgaging dominates with private renting the second most common tenure (when counted by under-fives) in a quarter of Britain's areas, often in more rural and coastal areas. These are places where the remnants of an older pattern of agricultural tenure remain, and where there is almost no social housing. Half as commonly found again are areas where mortgaged is most common and other social rented next most common. These tend to be areas near to more rural places and again concentrated in the south. Lastly, mortgaged dominates with owned outright as the second most common tenure in a similar number of more affluent localities. These are located, in the main, nearer to the cities and sometimes in their more affluent suburbs.

In the remaining 6% of the country places are almost always dominated by LA tenure, most usually where mortgaging is second. These areas are rare outside of Inner London or the urban north. Urban again are a dozen neighbourhoods where 'LA rented/other social rented' is the order of popularity (through the eyes of the under-fives). These places are only found in Inner London and Glasgow, places again connected to poverty: from the south bank of the Thames up through central London to Holborn and across to areas around the East End, and in Glasgow in parts of Govan and Maryhill constituencies. Contrast these to the four addresses where 'private renting' is most common and 'mortgaged' next: Hyde Park, Kensington, Chelsea, parts of Richmond (Yorkshire), places perhaps less common than you might think, synonymous now with luxury apartments or rural idyll (if marred slightly by a military presence). Then in four areas the most common tenure is 'other social rented/LA rented': Harlesden, Hackney, Kensal Town, the northern end of Liverpool Riverside; synonymous with concrete stereotype, such places are also more rare than you might think.

Finally, Birkenhead North-East is the one place where 'LA rented' is the most common tenure followed by 'private rented', the only place in Britain where this combination is found for under-fives. Many of those who own property there choose not to live there but rent out. Next and equally unusual is Hackney North where the dominant tenure pairing is 'other social rented/private rented', a similar story to Birkenhead North-East other than that the LA housing has been transferred to a housing association. And last, Glasgow Parkhead, with 'other social rented/mortgaged', home of Celtic football club, the Parkhead Housing Association, early shared ownership schemes, and one of the few mixed tenure neighbourhoods in all of Britain from the point of view of children.

2.8 Tenure of the homes of infants

Figure 2.8

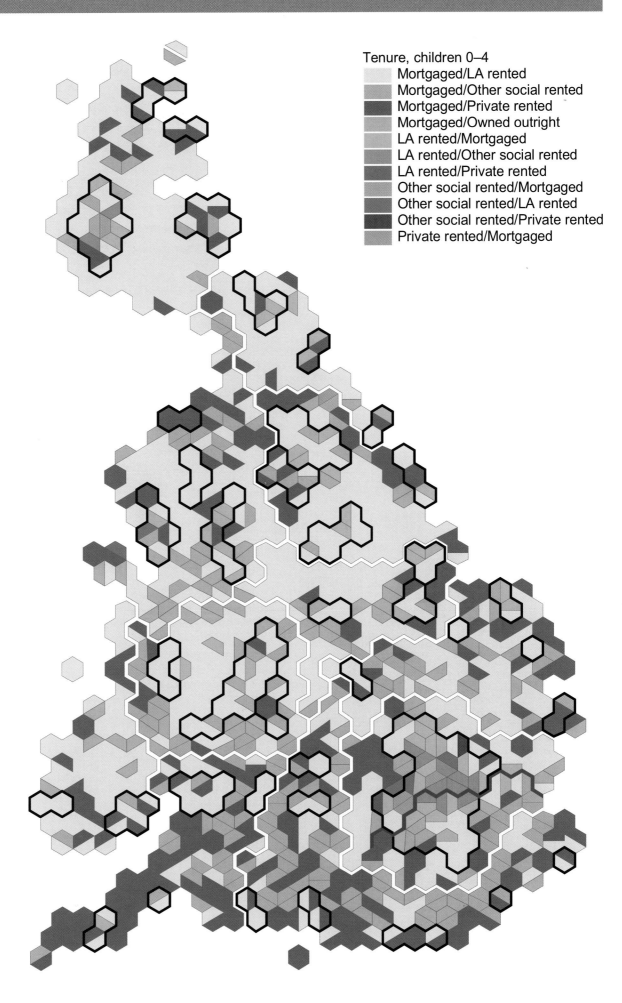

Tenure, children 0–4
- Mortgaged/LA rented
- Mortgaged/Other social rented
- Mortgaged/Private rented
- Mortgaged/Owned outright
- LA rented/Mortgaged
- LA rented/Other social rented
- LA rented/Private rented
- Other social rented/Mortgaged
- Other social rented/LA rented
- Other social rented/Private rented
- Private rented/Mortgaged

2.9 Cars and houses of the families of infants

Infants will have little idea as to whether their parent(s) own the home they are growing up in, whether they are buying or renting it. They will probably not appreciate whether their home is over- or under-crowded, their family large or small, rich or poor. Most infants lead lives similar to the majority around them, thus they are lives organised geographically in Britain. However, there are two material positions that, at least by the age of four, most children will be very aware of: first, to what extent their family has access to cars and second, whether they live in a house or a flat. They might even just be beginning to notice how their family's possessions compare with those of their friends.

We no longer live in those slightly more sexist and size-ist of times when the question was whether your dad's car was bigger or not. The key issue now is whether your family has a car at all, or two, or more. Having access to one car is no longer the norm. In wealthy and rural Britain, and especially in wealthy rural Britain, the norm is that most families of infants have two, and if not two at least one car, as shown in the map below. In urban areas none or one, or one or none, is most common. There is no mixed neighbourhood where most parents either have two or more cars, or none. Such places are the figments of social planners' imaginations.

Add housing type to the mix and even more clearly what is normal depends on where you are, as shown in Figure 2.9 opposite. For every introductory reading book that stars an infant living in a flat in London or one of the four Scottish cities within which flats and occasionally also no cars are the norm, there should also be several dozen books in which the star is a child living in a house in suburbia with two cars in the drive and perhaps a third parked by the kerb. In the north there is still a scattering of neighbourhoods where tightly packed terraces and lack of finance make no access to a car the norm. But nowhere south of Birmingham are such places still found, at least not when seen through the lives (and eyes) of the under-fives.

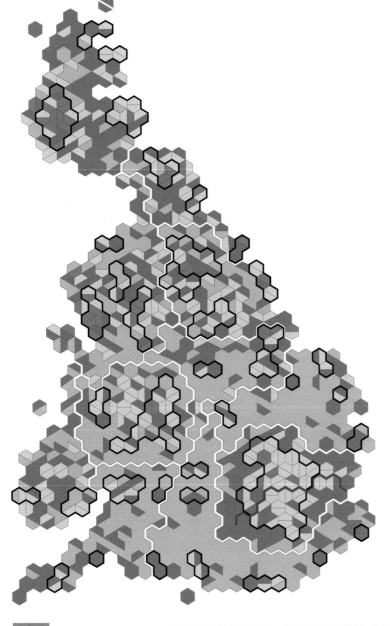

Children 0–4 in households with
- No car/1 car
- 1 car/No car
- 1 car/2+ cars
- 2+ cars/1 car

2.9 Cars and houses of the families of infants

Figure 2.9

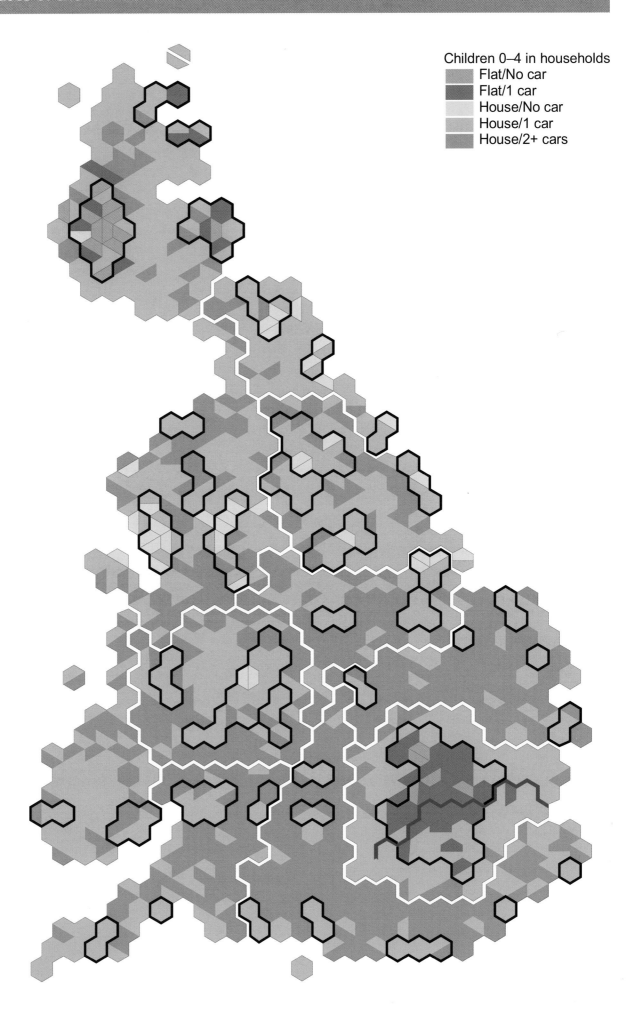

Children 0–4 in households
- Flat/No car
- Flat/1 car
- House/No car
- House/1 car
- House/2+ cars

2.10 Social class of the family of infants

Social class is in the main inherited from parents. Here class is defined by the title of the job a child's head of household (or, more correctly, Household Reference Person) does, but, like family identity, there are many components to class. Wealth is a key aspect of class that parental job title only indirectly captures. Wealthier children are more likely to have parents with more affluently titled occupations, but the link is not direct. For instance, the very rich have no need to work.

Social class also appears to vary by age when measured through occupation more than it actually does. People tend to work in more menial, routine, jobs when young. The best rewarded tend to be older higher managers. Some social classes also contain more people than others. Because of this the map opposite (Figure 2.10) showing modal social class of parents is dominated by the red shade of lower management but with the pink shade of higher management located mainly in the Home Counties, Cheshire, Hallam and around Edinburgh. Higher managers tend to have children (if any) later in life. Young children's parents are most likely to have 'never worked', have 'routine' or 'semi-routine' work in south Wales, the midlands and northern cities of England, and Glasgow. Only in a handful of remoter more agricultural areas is the 'middle' class – 'lower supervisory' – dominant in the lives of young children.

The table below gives the full title of the social classes used in the maps and also shows the proportion of children aged below five in Britain assigned to each social class in 2001. This excludes all children for whom a class could not be assigned. The change column refers to the change in that percentage between children aged 0-2 and 3-4. It is evident that a significant number of parents begin to work on their own account, often from home, following the birth of a child and before school age. It is also possible that fewer people who have never worked had children in 1999-2001 compared with 1997-98.

Social classes: proportion of children in Britain aged 0-4 in each class and % change

Social class	NS-SeC category	Children aged 0-4 (%)	Change (%)
1. Higher managers	Higher managerial and professional occupations	16	−0.4
2. Lower managers	Lower managerial and professional occupations	24	−0.2
3. Intermediate	Intermediate occupations	7	−0.1
4. Small employers	Small employers and own account workers	11	0.9
5. Lower supervisory	Lower supervisory and technical occupations	12	−0.2
6. Semi-routine	Semi-routine occupations	13	0.0
7. Routine	Routine occupations	12	−0.2
8. Never worked	Never worked or long-term unemployed	5	0.3
Total	All 1 to 8	100	0.0

Note: NS-SeC = National Statistics Socioeconomic Classification.

2.10 Social class of the family of infants

Figure 2.10

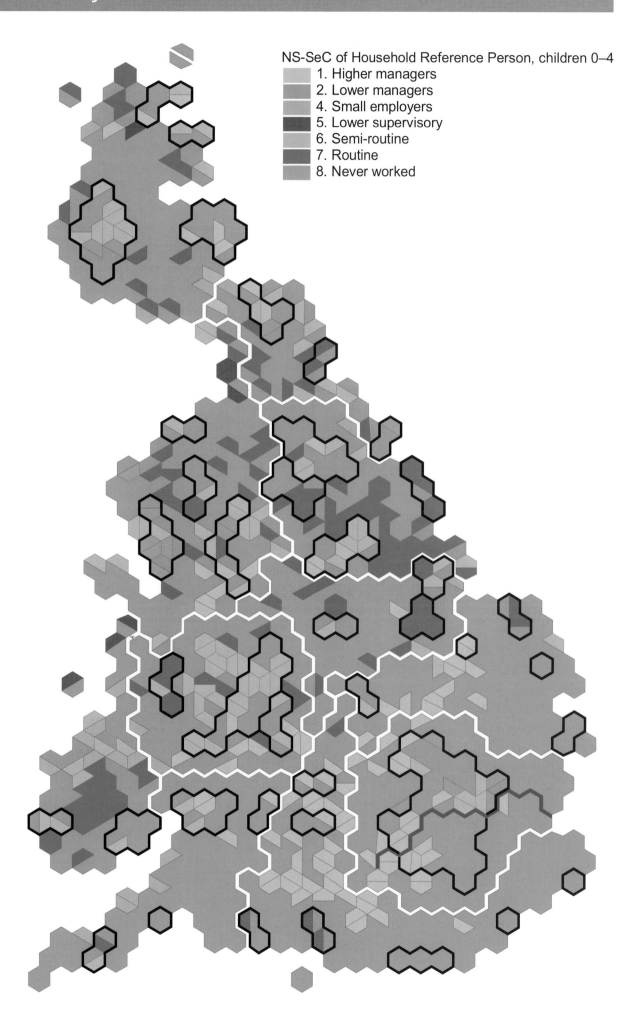

NS-SeC of Household Reference Person, children 0–4
1. Higher managers
2. Lower managers
4. Small employers
5. Lower supervisory
6. Semi-routine
7. Routine
8. Never worked

2.11 Class mixing in infancy

Simply considering which group of children aged 0-4 is the largest when grouped by the class of their 'Household Reference Person' (breadwinner) produces a misleading map. It is misleading because there is some mixing of children by social class within neighbourhoods. To counter this simplification, the detailed mosaic opposite (Figure 2.11) distinguishes between 22 shades of neighbourhood, rather than the eight used in Figure 2.10. These shades reflect which group of children by class is both the largest and second largest in any neighbourhood. Then, in theory, some 56 (8×7) shades of combination are possible but more than half do not occur anywhere. This distinction is telling. In all of the 102 neighbourhoods where the majority of parents are 'higher managers' the next largest group are 'lower managers'. None of the six other possible mixings occurs where the children of 'higher managers' are most numerous. Those who can invariably do, as a group, pay for their children not to mix socially by neighbourhood. They do this mainly through the prices they pay for their homes and usually end up owning their homes outright, hence the partial correspondence between this map and that of tenure earlier. Combine tenure, price and class (as defined by occupation) and you have a fair idea of the bulk of financial resources that will become available to the infants of Britain in the near future.

The bulk of the 102 'higher manager' neighbourhoods are to be found in the Home Counties and west London. They in turn are surrounded by some 470 neighbourhoods where 'higher managers' are the second most common class classification for infants. In every one of those areas the most common classification is 'lower manager'. Nowhere do the infant children of 'higher managers' mix most with any other class. Conversely, 'lower managers' mix with all classes except the children of those in 'intermediate occupations' who are too few and too evenly spread to appear in this map. From then on down the social order the map is a visual metaphor for the old comedy sketch that begins, 'I look up to him because he is upper class, but I look down on him because he is lower class ...'.

Similarly, in the 17 neighbourhoods where the majority of parents have never worked or are long-term unemployed, only seven see the most common group of parents of under-fives nationally in second place locally: three within Manchester and Liverpool and four within London. Nine see parents with 'semi-routine' work as their next most likely neighbours, all areas a fraction further from city centres: parts of East Ham in London, parts of Glasgow, Manchester, Liverpool and Knowsley and Tyne Bridge West (the neighbourhoods made up of Benwell, Elswick and Scotswood in Newcastle). In only one neighbourhood are 'routine' jobs second most common to having no job: Middlesbrough East. The social class of children is determined by their parents, which in turn is defined by their neighbourhood. Nowhere in Britain is socially mixed from the point of view of where and with whom children are growing up. The closest any area comes to this is the Clifton neighbourhood of Nottingham for under-threes, but that is not a success story.

The neighbourhood that we have labelled as Clifton within Nottingham was one of the most difficult to design within the constraints we used. It was quite anomalous, enough so, in fact, for it to be used as an example in a report to a government department of the limits of trying to define neighbourhoods. It stretches from Wollaton in the north, through the University over a lake, the A6005, the railway tracks, industrial and sewage works, the Beeston Canal and the river Trent through to the actual suburb of Clifton in the south. Very few neighbourhoods are bisected by a major road, railway line, canal and river running east to west across them. Furthermore, it is also divided by the multi-lane ring road running from the north and exiting through the south of the neighbourhood. It is telling that the only neighbourhood in Britain that appears to tolerate mixing of children by class — albeit only up to age two — is so well divided. Within this area physical barriers mean that parents cannot mix.

2.11 Class mixing in infancy

Figure 2.11

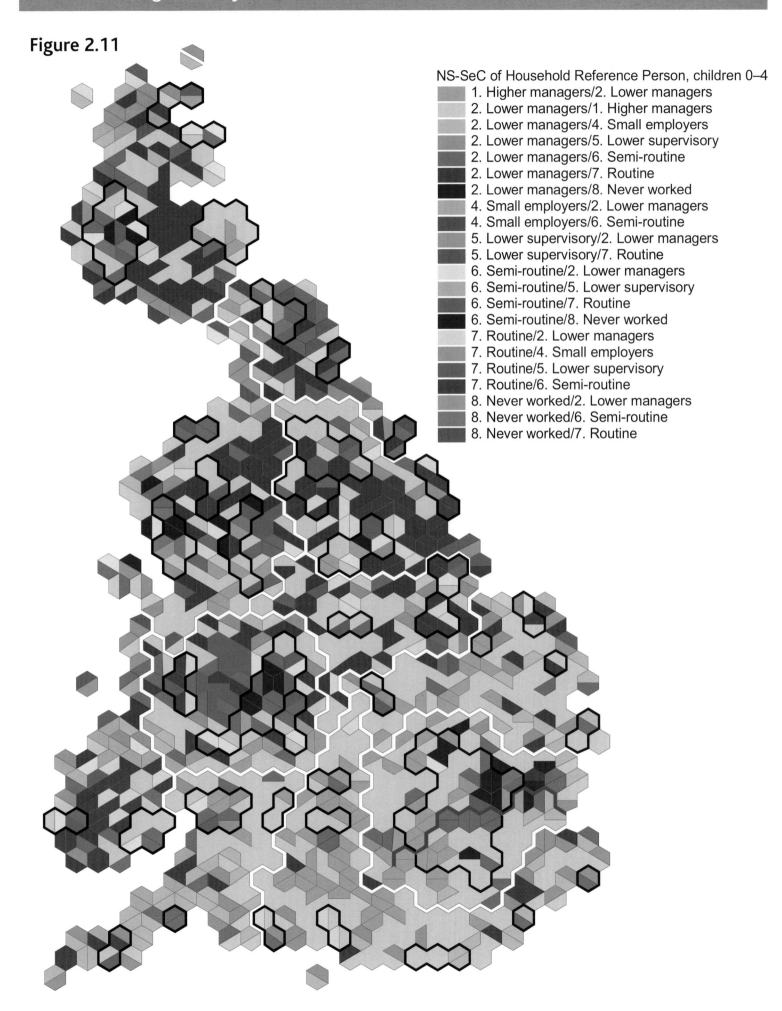

NS-SeC of Household Reference Person, children 0–4
1. Higher managers/2. Lower managers
2. Lower managers/1. Higher managers
2. Lower managers/4. Small employers
2. Lower managers/5. Lower supervisory
2. Lower managers/6. Semi-routine
2. Lower managers/7. Routine
2. Lower managers/8. Never worked
4. Small employers/2. Lower managers
4. Small employers/6. Semi-routine
5. Lower supervisory/2. Lower managers
5. Lower supervisory/7. Routine
6. Semi-routine/2. Lower managers
6. Semi-routine/5. Lower supervisory
6. Semi-routine/7. Routine
6. Semi-routine/8. Never worked
7. Routine/2. Lower managers
7. Routine/4. Small employers
7. Routine/5. Lower supervisory
7. Routine/6. Semi-routine
8. Never worked/2. Lower managers
8. Never worked/6. Semi-routine
8. Never worked/7. Routine

2.12 Disability and health of infants

Thankfully, everywhere in Britain the large majority of young children are growing up in good health and without disability. Children aged under five are most likely to be reported as having a disability (living with a disabling limiting long-term illness [LLTI]) if they live in Middlesbrough East, the area that had the unique class structure just detailed: 7% of children there, followed by 6.7% in Liverpool Riverside North (as also just listed). These rates contrast with a minimum of just over 1% in North East Dorset and Weybridge. Of the roughly 260 children in the east of Middlesbrough with such disabilities, equal numbers are also reported to have good and poor health and just a few more to have fair health. Thus the area is shaded a middling pink in Figure 2.12 opposite, which is of the health of children cross-referenced by the level of disabilities in each neighbourhood.

To create the map, each neighbourhood is shaded red, green or blue depending on whether the rate of disability in young children found there is above average, average or below the national average. Next a shade of that colour from light to dark is chosen depending on whether the majority of children are growing up in good, fair or poor health respectively. Thus only in the neighbourhoods shaded darker red are more children growing up with a disability than on average and a majority of children are suffering poor health. Half of those neighbourhoods are in Scotland. That may partly be due to parents in Scotland being more likely to label their child as having a disability if they think that their health is also poor.

Figure 2.12 shows both the complexity and some of the simplicity of the patterns of how parents across Britain describe their youngest children's health when asked. Light pink signifies places reporting above-average rates of disability but where most children enjoy good health. Note that the light pinks are more prevalent towards the north, in Wales and in urban areas around the south coast and in east London. Only in Scotland is there an obvious clustering of neighbourhoods where above-average numbers of children have a disability and the majority of those also have poor health.

Less than 26,000 children aged 0-4 have both poor health and a disability, a quarter of all those with a disability (LLTI). At the extremes it is some of the poorest parts of the country where children are most likely to be ill and some of the most affluent, where adult health fares best, where children appear also to do best. Between those extremes different groups of adults have different propensities to label what may be similar conditions in different ways. Parents in Scotland may be more reticent to tick the disability box for their children (as we know they are for themselves). Once they do tick that box though, they often also say their child's health is poor. Other groups of parents living elsewhere with, as they report, very healthy children, may treat more minor complaints as disabilities. Finally, and counter to what might be expected by all this and more, where pre-school children are healthier mothers tend to be older.

2.12 Disability and health of infants

Figure 2.12

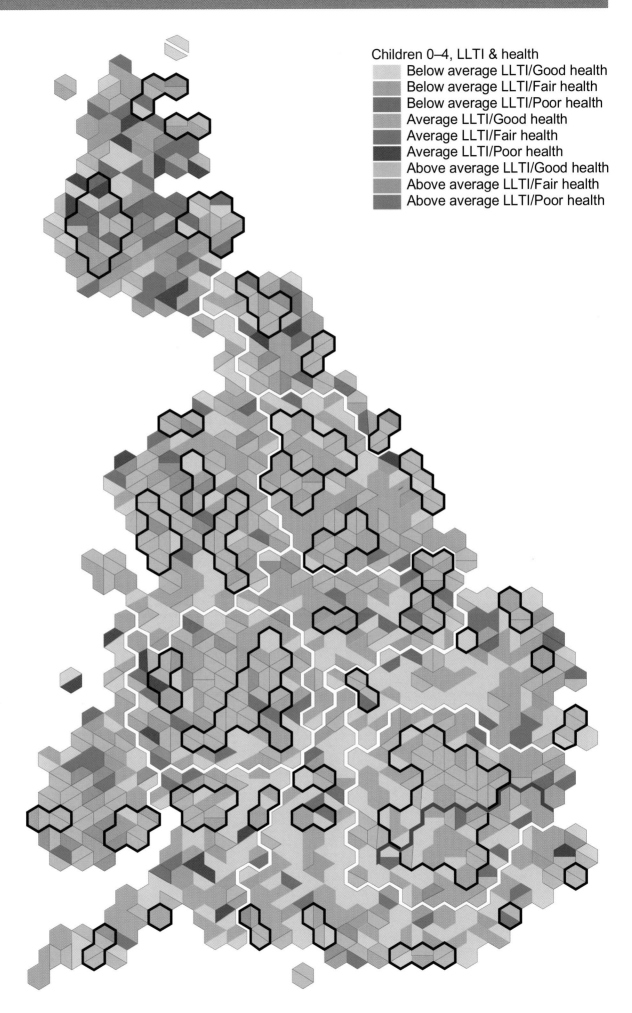

Children 0–4, LLTI & health
- Below average LLTI/Good health
- Below average LLTI/Fair health
- Below average LLTI/Poor health
- Average LLTI/Good health
- Average LLTI/Fair health
- Average LLTI/Poor health
- Above average LLTI/Good health
- Above average LLTI/Fair health
- Above average LLTI/Poor health

2.13 Born abroad for all infants

Many infants in Britain were not born in the UK and so for them there is no record of their mother's age held centrally, nor any other information from any certification of their birth. Between 2% and 3% of infants aged under five were born abroad, but by neighbourhood this ranges downwards from 21.6% in Mildenhall to near zero at the minima. More than one in seven infants were also born abroad in Walton, Hyde Park, Chelsea and Kensington, the areas of Britain with most immigrant children. As far as we can tell, in almost no neighbourhoods were all infants living there born in Britain. However, in some areas the proportion as well as the absolute number is as near to zero as makes no difference, as Figure 2.13 opposite shows.

There were too few infants born abroad to reliably map the diversity of their countries of birth. Instead the table below shows the numbers of children aged 0-15 by the countries and groups of countries in which they were born, as recorded in 2001.

Country of birth of children aged 0-15 living in Britain by number of children

Number	Country	Number	Country
9,555,856	England	4,404	Spain
950,178	Scotland	4,374	Cyprus
549,352	Wales	4,031	Italy
37,546	Germany	3,835	New Zealand
32,742	USA	3,663	China
21,196	Pakistan	3,227	Iran
18,223	South Africa	2,577	Channel Islands and Isle of Man
14,171	India	2,538	Malaysia
14,142	Bangladesh	2,460	UK (part not specified)
11,277	France	2,102	Singapore
11,255	Australia	1,595	Poland
10,243	Northern Ireland	**Number**	**Region**
10,181	Caribbean	24,272	Other South and East Africa
10,098	Ireland	21,640	Other Eastern Europe
9,646	Hong Kong	17,954	Other Middle East
9,623	Nigeria	14,827	Other EU
6,496	North Africa	9,873	Other Far East
6,367	Japan	9,857	Other Central and West Africa
6,219	South America	8,644	Other South Asia
5,978	Canada	6,225	Non-EU Western Europe
5,534	Netherlands	3,464	Any other
5,494	Zimbabwe	1,309	Other North America
4,666	Kenya	510	Other Oceania

2.13 Born abroad for all infants

Figure 2.13

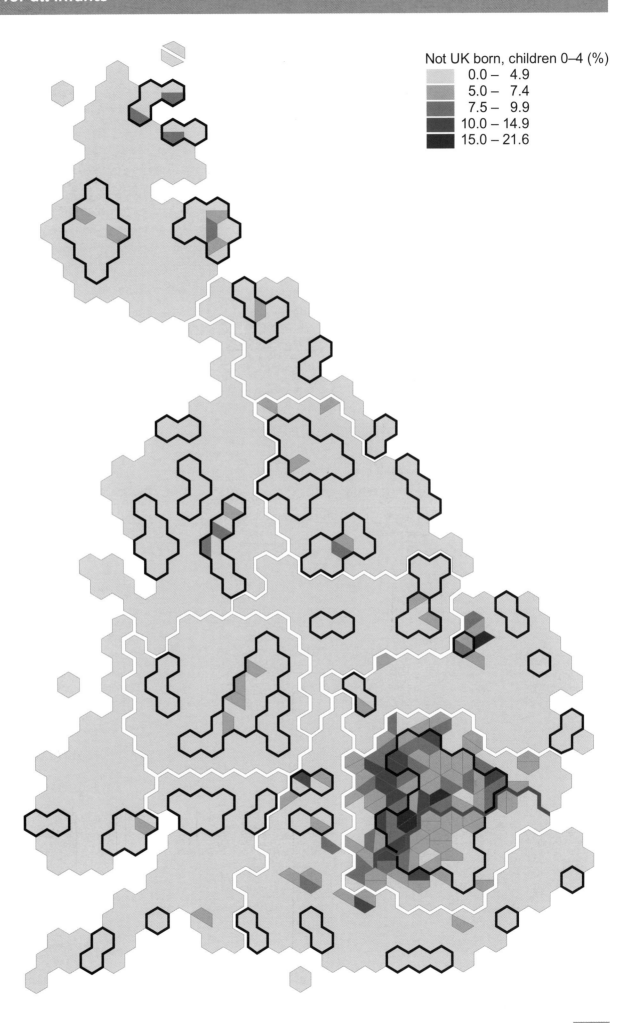

Not UK born, children 0–4 (%)
- 0.0 – 4.9
- 5.0 – 7.4
- 7.5 – 9.9
- 10.0 – 14.9
- 15.0 – 21.6

2.14 Majority–minority birthplace of infants and children

Because there were too few infants born abroad to reliably map the diversity of their countries of birth, here we map in detail the mosaic for all children aged under 16 in Britain. The second most common country of birth is shown opposite (Figure 2.14) as the map of most common country of birth is monotonous. Most children in all neighbourhoods in England, Scotland and Wales are born in those respective countries except for there being slightly more England- than Wales-born children in Buckley, Connah's Quay and rural Montgomeryshire, possibly due to maternity hospitals being located in England.

The story of children born outside of Britain is partly a military story. After the three home countries it is Germany where the next largest numbers of children living in Britain were born, followed by the USA. In all the five areas listed in Section 2.13 where more than a seventh of children were born abroad the largest immigrant group is from the USA. The mosaic map shows clearly how these two groups of children tend to cluster either in areas with military facilities or in areas from which the British armed forces tend to recruit heavily and areas to which military families with their children born in Germany tend to settle when they leave the armed forces. Britain also has very strong commercial ties to North America and has had an extremely long history of immigration from Germany. Those links are also reflected here.

The next most common overseas countries of birth of children in Britain are Pakistan, South Africa, India and Bangladesh, but fewer children born in these four countries combined are living in Britain than were born in the USA and Germany combined. Fewer again, than from the USA and Germany combined, are from the next seven highest contributing countries and provinces: France, Australia, Northern Ireland, Ireland, Hong Kong, Nigeria and Japan. And underlying this, the largest minority groups in most neighbourhoods in Britain are the England-born children living in Scotland and Wales, and the Scotland- and Wales-born living in England. The 21st-century mosaic of children's birthplace reflects the military, colonial and imperial histories of the generations born before them, current internal migration between the home countries, and only then, although to the most colourful extent on the map, the movement of families with young children from abroad with no military, colonial or imperial connection.

2.14 Majority–minority birthplace of infants and children

Figure 2.14

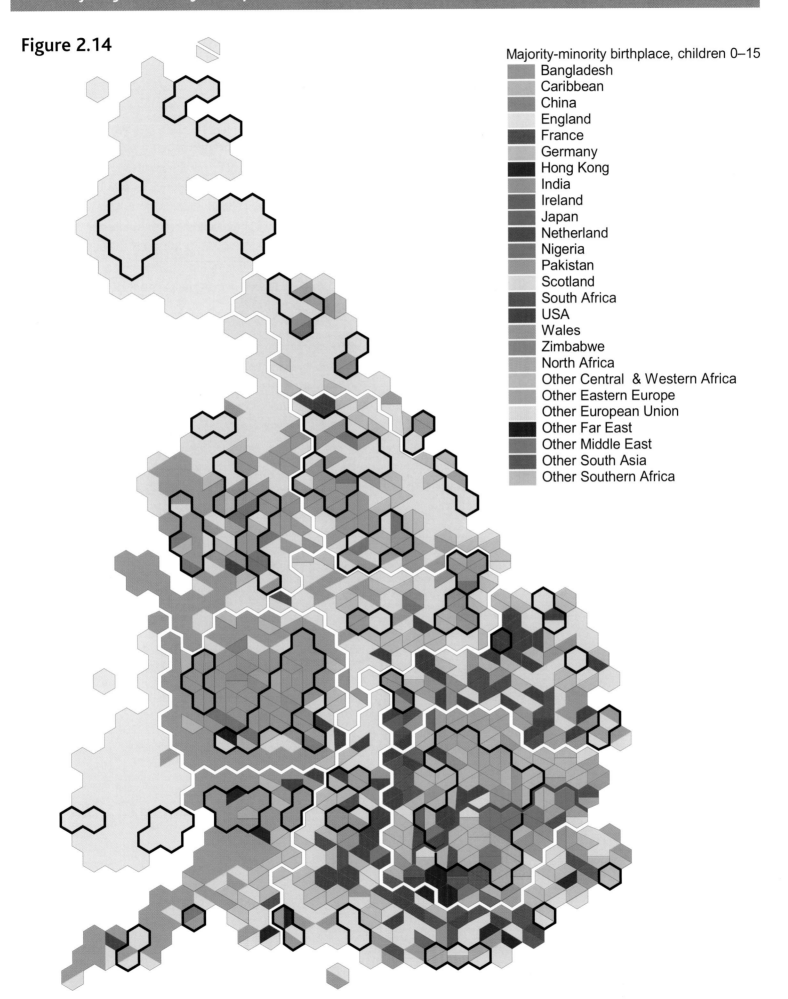

Majority-minority birthplace, children 0–15
- Bangladesh
- Caribbean
- China
- England
- France
- Germany
- Hong Kong
- India
- Ireland
- Japan
- Netherland
- Nigeria
- Pakistan
- Scotland
- South Africa
- USA
- Wales
- Zimbabwe
- North Africa
- Other Central & Western Africa
- Other Eastern Europe
- Other European Union
- Other Far East
- Other Middle East
- Other South Asia
- Other Southern Africa

2.15 Ethnicity of UK born infants and dependent children

One way in which children in Britain are often distinguished is through their ethnicity. All children are given an ethnicity by their parents or by the authorities that do the counting for various forms of 'ethnic monitoring'. We have excluded the few children born abroad from Figure 2.15 opposite so that it is clear that we are not looking at any pattern of immigration. All children mapped here were born in Britain despite their ethnicity label often including the name of a country or continent overseas. Suitable data have not been released for Scotland to allow the neighbourhoods of that country to be included. In England and Wales the majority of dependent children born in Britain have been labelled 'White British' by their parents in all but a handful of neighbourhoods. Dependent children are those under 16 or aged 16-19 living at home and in full-time education.

To be able to show anything of the subtleties of the geography of ascribed ethnic origin, the second most common ethnicity has to be mapped. In almost all of Wales and where there are large numbers of North Americans or people from Europe, 'Other White' is the second most common label we give our children. There are then more neighbourhoods where the second largest ethnicity for children is 'Mixed White and Black Caribbean' than any other minority group: the lighter green shaded areas in Figure 2.15.

Neither 'Other White' nor 'Mixed White and Black Caribbean' are the largest of minority groups but they are those most often found as the second largest in areas where most children are 'White British'. In contrast, 'Black Caribbean' and 'Black African' children are the second largest groups in significant numbers only in London. In no neighbourhood are they the largest group of children born in Britain by ethnicity. In three London neighbourhoods 'Bangladeshi' children born in Britain are the largest group, in 12 neighbourhoods 'Indian' Britain-born children, and in six neighbourhoods children of 'Pakistani' ethnicity born in Britain. Nowhere are 'Other White' or any of the Mixed groups in the majority, as is also the case for children of 'Chinese' ethnicity, constituting the second largest groups mainly in the North West of England.

Six in every seven children born in Britain are labelled as 'White British': 87 in every 100. In contrast, two in every 100 are 'Indian', two 'Pakistani', and to the nearest whole child one in 100 is 'Bangladeshi', one is 'Other White', one is 'Mixed White and Black Caribbean', one is 'Mixed White and Asian', one is 'Other Mixed', one is 'Black African' and one 'Black Caribbean'.

Ethnicity of children in Britain

Ethnicity	%	Ethnicity	%
White British	87.12	Mixed White and Asian	0.79
Indian	2.31	Other Mixed	0.58
Pakistani	2.27	Other Asian	0.42
Mixed White and Black Caribbean	1.28	Other Black	0.34
Black Caribbean	1.06	Chinese	0.34
Bangladeshi	0.92	White Irish	0.30
Other White	0.90	Mixed White and Black African	0.29
Black African	0.89	Other ethnic group	0.21

2.15 Ethnicity of UK born infants and dependent children

Figure 2.15

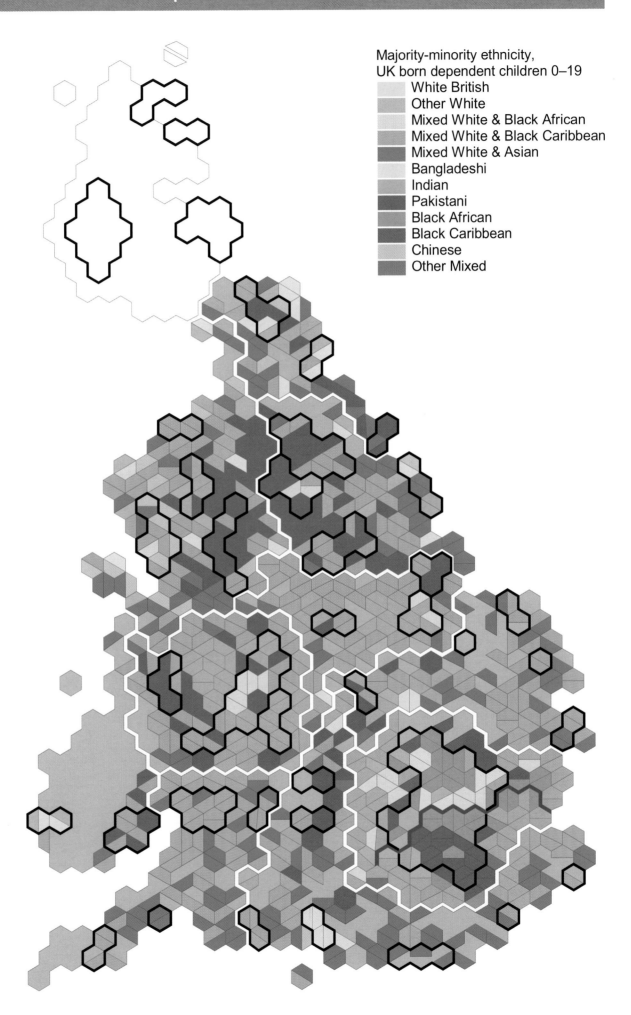

Majority-minority ethnicity,
UK born dependent children 0–19
- White British
- Other White
- Mixed White & Black African
- Mixed White & Black Caribbean
- Mixed White & Asian
- Bangladeshi
- Indian
- Pakistani
- Black African
- Black Caribbean
- Chinese
- Other Mixed

2.16 Religion ascribed to infants

Some parents assign a religion to their pre-school children when completing official forms. The most commonly stated religion for the under-fives is 'Christian', followed by 'None'. Of course, more than half of all children of these ages cannot speak clearly enough to express an opinion. Almost no children of these ages are expected to make a choice over whether they wish to belong to a particular religious group or have any religious beliefs. Figure 2.16 opposite shows for each neighbourhood in Britain which religion was most often used to label pre-school children and which was used second most often.

When mapped to show diversity of children's birthplace Scotland did not show any visible variation across its territory and insufficient information on ethnicity was released for the children of Scotland to allow variation in that form of identity to be shown. Had it been released, it is unlikely to have shown particularly interesting patterns as the variety of ethnicities in England are not found in Scotland. In contrast, the religious geographies of Scotland are far more interesting. On the eastern side of the country the majority of children under five are labelled as being of 'no religion'. Only in a scattering of places south of the border does that occur. Many Scots on that side of Scotland hence either do not ascribe a religion to their youngest children or do not believe that if they do so it is any business of the state to know.

In England, where Christian denomination was not asked, more parents than usual did not state any religion (or stated 'None') for their pre-school children in many parts of the North West, some parts of the North East and a scattering of neighbourhoods in London. Ironically, some may have done this because they did believe their children were of a particular Christian denomination but they did not want that to be confused with another.

After Christian, 'None' and 'Not stated' (3.1 million pre-school children), the next most populous ascribing was to Islam (0.2 million pre-school children). More often in second place (orange on Figure 2.16 opposite) than first (shades of blue), Muslim pre-school children are almost all growing up in densely populated parts of towns and cities. In contrast, the 32,000 Hindu pre-schoolers are mainly growing up in the suburbs. The 23,000 Sikh 0-4-year olds are more urbanly concentrated. Just over a thousand of the 14,000 religious Jewish under-fives live in Golders Green, a very different distribution to the scattering of the 5,000 Buddhists toddlers and babies, found for some reason in highest numbers (but even there only 70 in total and so not featuring on the map) in Woolwich. However, were you thinking of starting a nursery geared towards the needs of the Buddhist toddler, Woolwich would be the place to begin.

2.16 Religion ascribed to infants

Figure 2.16

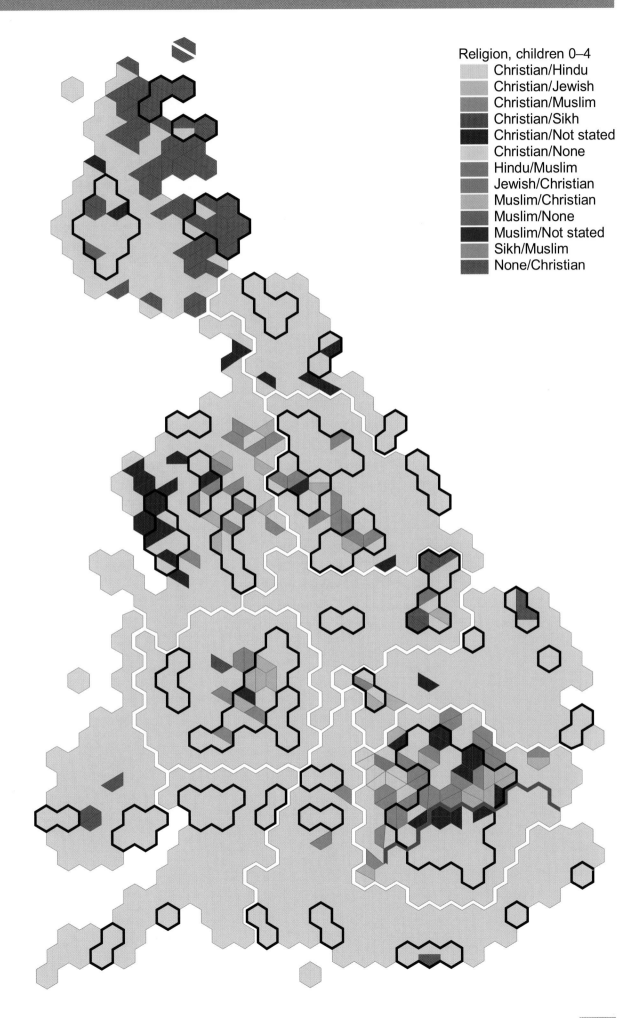

Religion, children 0–4
- Christian/Hindu
- Christian/Jewish
- Christian/Muslim
- Christian/Sikh
- Christian/Not stated
- Christian/None
- Hindu/Muslim
- Jewish/Christian
- Muslim/Christian
- Muslim/None
- Muslim/Not stated
- Sikh/Muslim
- None/Christian

2.17 Conclusion: the lives of the under-fives

Children in Britain are born into neighbourhoods that differ substantially from each other when characterised through the early lives of those children. The differences between what is normal, what is modal, in one neighbourhood as compared to another, are so great that it would be misleading to suggest that there is a particularly British experience of growing up. Instead there are a multitude of experiences of growing up in Britain in a large but finite set of contexts. Each child is different, every family differs, and each neighbourhood is distinct, yet it is possible to summarise the variety and show both the breadth of possibilities and, just as important, what does not appear possible. In this chapter that is perhaps best summed up by the implicit listing of the kinds of neighbourhoods that do not exist in Britain, the ones that have been shown on none of the maps in these pages.

There are no neighbourhoods where the majority of young children have parents who cohabit. There is only one neighbourhood in which most children are growing up with at least two siblings but just one parent, and also where the second largest group is also likely to be living with just one parent (it is in the centre of Manchester). There is nowhere where most children are growing up in social housing with many others in the same area living in homes where they have more rooms than they need. In only one neighbourhood are most children growing up in social housing with the next largest group in privately rented accommodation (Birkenhead North-East). There are both places that do not exist and places that are unique. However, most neighbourhoods are not, and could not be, unique. Many places look like many others from the point of view of the children who live there.

Just a few dominant tenure mixes typify most of the country. Across just over half of Britain the largest group of parents by occupation are in 'lower managerial and professional occupations', neither boss nor labourer. However, it is only with the children of this ubiquitous class that those above them will mix. It is where both of these classes are found that children are likely to enjoy the best health, even though it is again here where they are most likely to have been born to much older mothers than elsewhere (and hence to be growing up in quite different households). And almost everywhere most young children who have been born in Britain are labelled 'White' and given either a Christian, 'None', or 'Not-stated' religious tag.

The minority of children born outside of the country they are living in help make the social map of majority–minority birthplace, at least in England, a far more interesting mosaic. For those born in England the mosaic of majority–minority ethnicity is similarly complex but not as complex as to not be easily understandable. In contrast, the mosaic of majority combined with second largest religious affiliation ascribed to the under-fives presents a remarkably simple map (Figure 2.17 opposite). Excluding 'None' and 'Not-stated' makes the map a little more intricate. But most of Britain's neighbourhoods when classified by their children are 'Christian/None' or 'Christian/Muslim', depending on whether those with no religion are included.

2.17 Conclusion: the lives of the under-fives

Figure 2.17

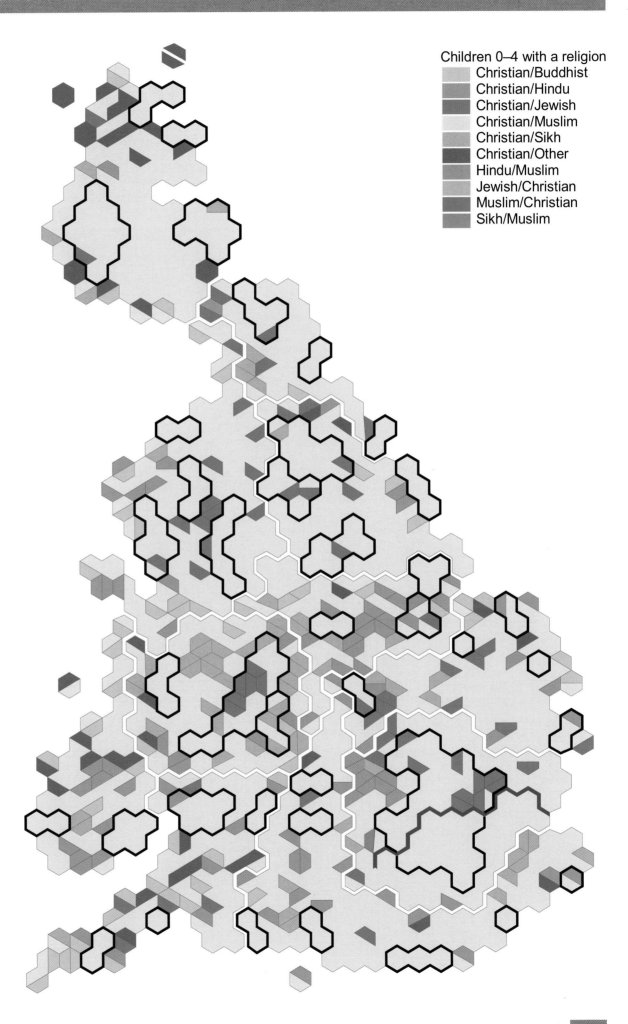

Children 0–4 with a religion
- Christian/Buddhist
- Christian/Hindu
- Christian/Jewish
- Christian/Muslim
- Christian/Sikh
- Christian/Other
- Hindu/Muslim
- Jewish/Christian
- Muslim/Christian
- Sikh/Muslim

3 Then, the whining schoolboy: ages 5-15

Then, the whining schoolboy, with his satchel
And shining morning face, creeping like snail
Unwillingly to school;

3.1 Introduction

The ages of 5-15 are the compulsory years of schooling in Britain. Many children begin schooling a little earlier and most now carry on a little later, but these are the years at which almost all are in school and thus it makes sense to combine them. We know that almost all children spend their days with other children aged 5-15 and mostly live with a parent or parents, but within which social worlds are schoolchildren really growing up in Britain?

Here we look into the homes, lives and neighbourhoods of Britain's older children: where the mode live in neighbourhoods where their parents do not work, and the few in areas where most have one breadwinner. We show how these exceptions are islands in a sea of uniformity where typically both mum and dad are at work, at least for a lot of the time, when the children are at school. 'What does your mum do?' is as sensible a question in most of Britain today as asking father's occupation of a child a couple of generations ago.

We move on to show where you would be wise not to ask about a child's father's occupation, where the odds are high that there is no father at home, and show how that mixes with the patterns of parents' or parent's employment. Then we turn to the main and largely hidden repercussion of lone parenthood: the transformation to step-childhood and how it shows a surprisingly different geography. If daddy was a rolling stone, mummy is more likely than ever to have moved on and out of the cities with a new man. Thus the sea of apparent two-parent uniformity with which this chapter begins is something of an illusion. However, simply by looking at where original parents cohabit against where reconstitution of families occurs, the boundaries of two different kinds of family life can be seen etched across the map of Britain. There are two very different ways for parents to 'live in sin' today and different places for such living to happen. It is not just that as children age their families leave cities; much more is going on than that.

Of course, for a variety of reasons, not all children get to live with a family. Some parents pay a lot of money not to have to live with their children, and we go on to show here where the homes of those children would be if they did live at home. Parents not only have the right to exile their children; they can also tell them what to believe. And so the map of religion is clearly not a map of what children themselves have decided to think.

Adults also get to be the main deciders of where their children live and when they move, although those moves are much influenced by their hopes for their children as expressed through the sudden exodus of many 10- and 11-year-olds each year from our cities to areas where most families have two or more cars and a mortgaged house, and are more wealthy than average. In these areas, few are poor and fewer still rely on benefits, and the children living here are ever so slightly more likely to 'do better' at school.

Clearly, parents (who can) move neighbourhood as much to choose their and their children's friends and future boyfriends and girlfriends as to aid their academic progress. Thus children are at least as segregated by social class by area while at school as they were before they reached the age of five. Lastly, a clearly class-related factor is that some children have to grow up a little earlier than others. We end the chapter by looking at where those children who care for their disabled parents call home. Not all children whine on their way to school.

3.1 Introduction

Figure 3.1 shows the spatial distribution of children aged 5-15 recorded in the 2001 Census. The geography of the most likely locations of childhood tends not to change much over time. The places to which people tend to move in greatest numbers in the years before or the years when they have children remain much the same decade by decade. It is useful to try to memorise this distribution, or at least to have a rough idea of it, for understanding the remainder of this chapter. Note also the differences between the maps of some characteristics shown in this chapter and the equivalent maps in the preceding chapter on infants. For example, where do all the infants growing up in central London (see page 19) move to so that less than an eighth of people there are schoolchildren.

Figure 3.1

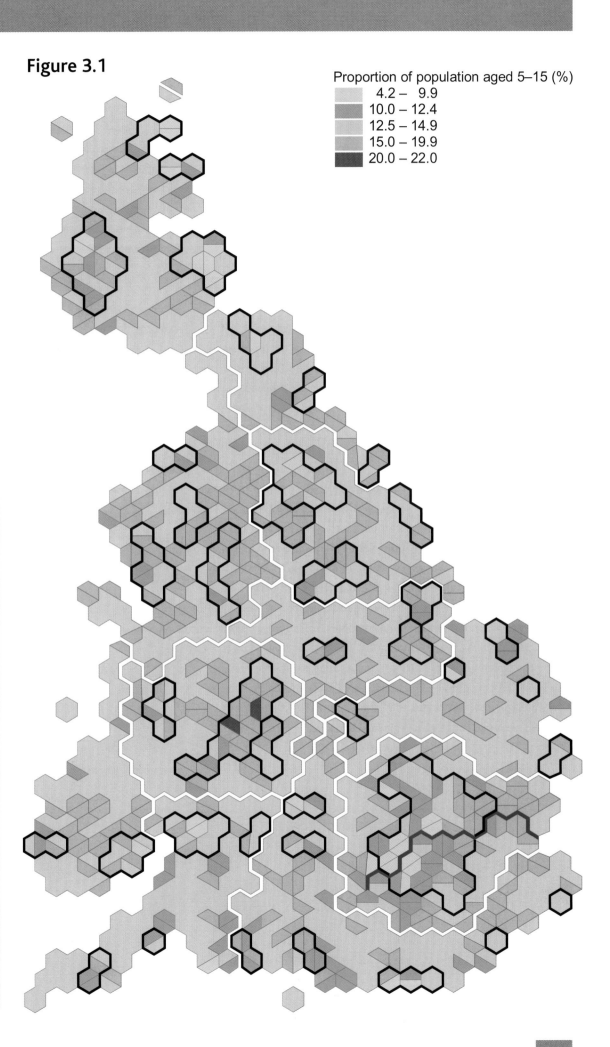

Proportion of population aged 5–15 (%)
- 4.2 – 9.9
- 10.0 – 12.4
- 12.5 – 14.9
- 15.0 – 19.9
- 20.0 – 22.0

3.2 The family you grow up with in childhood

The simplest division of families that also distinguishes between children likely to be having quite different experiences of life is by whether no adults, one adult, or two or more adults are in work in their household. Where there are no earnings coming in, home life is very different from the vast majority of families who rely on the earnings of two and sometimes more adults to bring up children. In between these two extremes are the increasingly rare single earner families.

Families, of course, change. Throughout most children's lives there will be times when either one or both of their parents (or step-parents) are earning. Most children with no earning adult in their household will not be in that situation for many years. Either their parent, or one or even both of their parents, will find or be forced into a job, or another adult who works will join their household. Families are in constant flux, often slow, some more chaotic. However, children in families where there has been no work are more likely to be in that situation again, just as children living with two working parents are likely to return to that state sometime soon after one stops work.

Nothing is certain, but the trends are very strong and, most importantly for Figure 3.2 shown opposite, once those trends are averaged out across hundreds of families in each neighbourhood, they describe not just the chances a family has of being in one of the three groups, but also its chances of remaining in that group if it remains in that area. Children living in a neighbourhood where most of their friends' families also consist of two adults working are very unlikely to find their family incomes fall suddenly due to both parents being made redundant. That rarely happens where they live. If it does happen, those families that are affected tend to leave the area quickly. The same is well known to be the case for families who gain work while living in an area where almost none have work. Those who gain work often leave.

The most striking difference between Figure 3.2 and the map for children aged 0-4 shown on page 23 is how many fewer areas are typified by having no adults working in families with older children. Clearly, once children go to school, in all but a small minority of areas most of their parents work. Even more remarkable, however, is the dramatic reduction in the number of neighbourhoods where on average only one adult is working. This is despite some neighbourhoods where at younger ages most parents were not working reverting to 'one parent working' majority areas for older children.

Clearly, once children are at school, almost all live in places where it is now normal for there to be at least two sets of earnings financing their home. The largest concentration of places where that is not the case are found in south west London, in neighbourhoods where people are so affluent that it would appear that some families can get by without a second salary. The phrase 'ladies that lunch' was imported from the USA to describe what may be happening in some affluent parts of Britain. Just as travelling by train is now more and more for the rich, and those who cannot afford to use the train have to fly, the traditional family may be becoming the preserve of the wealthy.

3.2 The family you grow up with in childhood

Figure 3.2

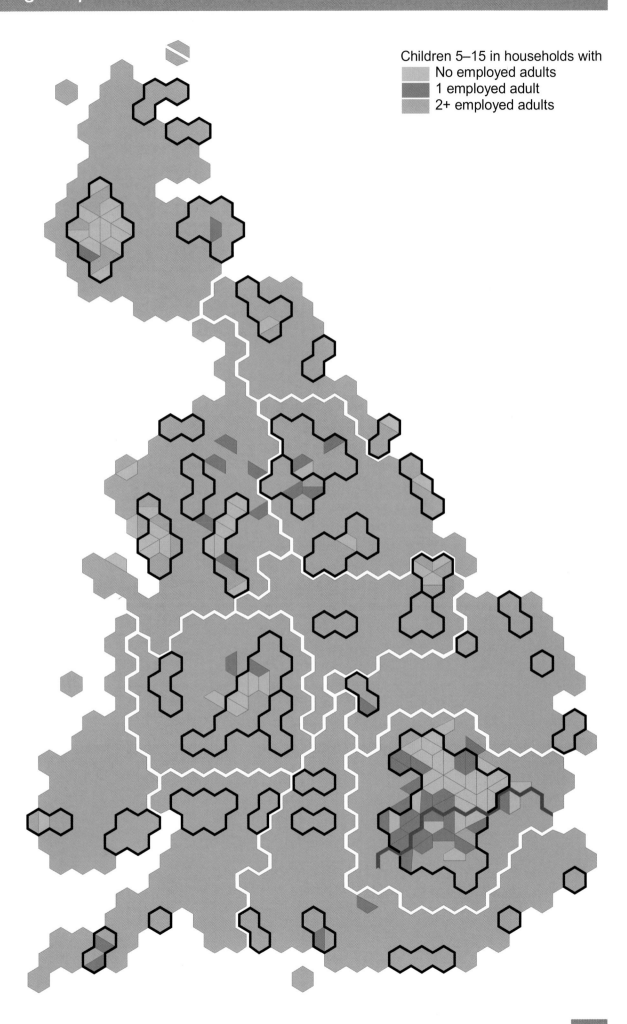

Children 5–15 in households with
- No employed adults
- 1 employed adult
- 2+ employed adults

3.3 The marriages of parents of children

Few weddings are complete today without extraneous former partners still tied into the family, the fun of arranging the order of step-parents and other paramours on the top table, and of course the various children of the bride or groom (or occasionally of both) to take the places formerly reserved for nephews and nieces. New self-help books are being written on how to adjust to your parent's latest remarriage, and just what to wear as the daughter of the bride so as not to upstage your mother. Sadly, at least from the point of view of drawing colourful mosaics, life in Britain is not yet as complex as this. In fact, by area it becomes remarkably neat for the parents of school-age children. To have become so neat many have had to find a new partner to replace a previous one. Many of the few still cohabiting have had to tie the knot and accept the old and ancient people-into-property ceremony (marriage) that we dress up as if it were all about love and had nothing to do with access to children, inheritance, pensions and wealth. Yes, by the time their children go to school, if not before, the adults of Britain conform to turn the varied map of family type by marriage and employment for under-fives shown on page 25 into the more uniform one opposite (Figure 3.3), showing the families in which most school-aged children in most areas are growing up in.

Across the vast majority of Britain most schoolchildren are growing up in homes where their two married parents both work (the mother often part-time). This is the new conformity, just as homogenous as the 1950s breadwinner, but now involving two sets of earnings and a marriage that may have happened a little later or have involved reconstituting previously separate groups. Financial needs and desires still cajole people into behaving in remarkably similar ways, especially those who have children. It is just that they now have a little longer to choose whom they end up with, and have a couple of options to change their mind along the way. Aberrant areas are thus fewer and even further between than was the case for families of the under-fives.

There is now only one neighbourhood *both* where most school-aged children live with only one parent *and* in homes where two adults work: the 'new community' of Linwood (see page 24). The scattering of more interesting areas seen across the country for the under-fives has now been confined to a few cities, and even there conformity is rising. For example, in Wales there is only one neighbourhood where school-age children are not in the majority when living with two earners. There were more than a dozen for such children aged under five. There is also no neighbourhood in that country, nor the whole of the South West, Eastern, West Midlands or North East regions of England, where most school-age children are not living with married parents.

There are a few interesting changes away from conformity as children age. For instance, in the one neighbourhood in Edinburgh where most under-fives live in homes receiving only one set of earnings, most school-age children's parent is working, but lone parenthood is now the majority family type for school-age children. However, over nine in 10 children do not live in places other than those representing the mode.

3.3   The marriages of parents of children

Figure 3.3

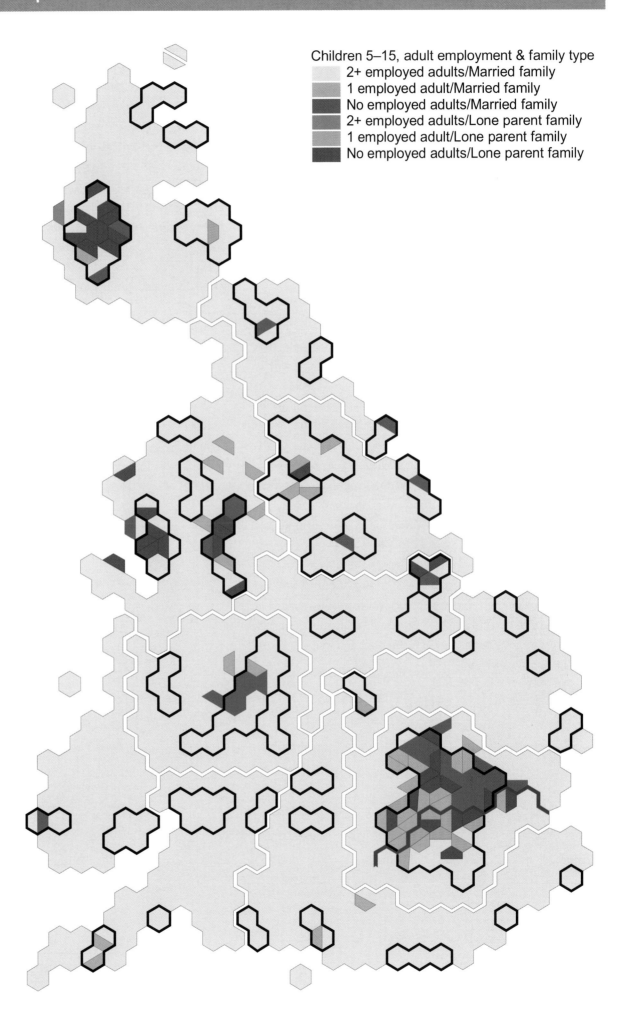

Children 5–15, adult employment & family type
- 2+ employed adults/Married family
- 1 employed adult/Married family
- No employed adults/Married family
- 2+ employed adults/Lone parent family
- 1 employed adult/Lone parent family
- No employed adults/Lone parent family

3.4 Step-children

When considering the apparent uniformity of family life for school-age children in Britain, consider the amount of effort it takes to achieve the picture of rural and suburban tranquillity just painted. Step-children are children in a married or cohabiting couple family who are not the son or daughter of both adults. Their families did not arrange themselves to have two parents without a little mixing and matching. The legacy of the history of family constitution post-birth is captured through Figure 3.4 opposite. This is a map of step-children in Britain, where new families have been formed from previous, often dissolved, family units. These families often start life in quite different places to where they have ended up, or at least those where that part of the family with the school-age children has ended up.

By neighbourhood, the proportion of school-age children in Britain living with at least one parent different to those they began with varies from less than one in 20 to almost one in five. Almost a million children live in such step-families. The geographical pattern of where these families are could not be much clearer. The further from the cities you go and the further into what appears to be the monotonous rural fringes of the country (monotonous in the sense of little variation in family life), the more step-children you find. The countryside and the suburbs, far from being havens of conventional family life where marriage occurs before children and couples stay together and work, are increasingly the places to where new families move once they have formed and old ties have dissolved. And the furthest extremes of the countries, the tips of peninsulas and remote coastlines, see the highest incidences of step-children. It is possible that families resulting from more than one set of such changes tend to be located even further out and that this partly explains the extremes.

What we can be sure of is that the pattern seen is not the result of children being more likely to be step-children the older they are or of older children being found further from cities. Both of those trends occur, but the map of the likelihood of all children aged 12-15 living in step-families is very similar to that shown in Figure 3.4, so this map is not a map of migration. Instead, it is better seen as a map of both conforming and of economic necessity/possibility. Bringing up children with two parents is conformist; there is no need for those two parents to be the original two. Further, pooling the resources of two adults increases the purchasing power of the family. One parent living alone could not afford to live easily in many of the places where most step-families are found.

To put it another way, if the Railway Children saw their father imprisoned today, their mother would either have to move so they could wave at trains passing Clapham Junction, or she would have to quickly become friendly with the affluent but somewhat lonely man currently commuting to Leeds from the idyllic cottage in the Dales, a cottage that a century ago was a home for the poor.

3.4 Step-children

Figure 3.4

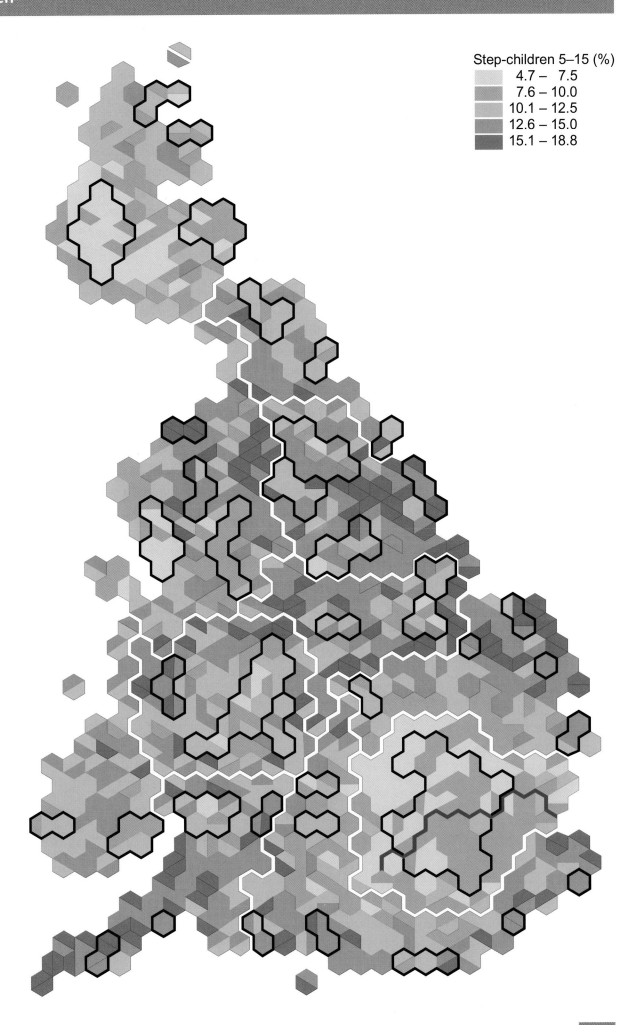

Step-children 5–15 (%)
- 4.7 – 7.5
- 7.6 – 10.0
- 10.1 – 12.5
- 12.6 – 15.0
- 15.1 – 18.8

3.5 Splitting up and coming together of families of children

It is worth remembering that in every neighbourhood in Britain the most common families in which school-age children are growing up are married non-step-families or female-headed lone parent families. And also that in each case, the second most common category is the reverse of this. Step-families are nowhere yet the norm and cohabiting couple families even further from ever becoming the norm anywhere. Nevertheless, the mosaic of cohabiting couple families can give insight into where families split up and come together. That is because many step-families go through a period of trying to live together, with the adults cohabiting and different sets of children trying to get along, before they decide whether or not to continue the arrangement and in many cases marry or remarry.

Cohabiting families with school-age children can be divided into two groups: first, those that are non-step-families that have not changed since the children were born or perhaps where the natural father is now living with a former single mother; second, those that are step-families, where at least one of the parents is not the children's natural or adoptive parent and the adults in the household are not married. Often this latter group, cohabiting step-families, are newly constituted families. There are three quarters of a million school-age children living in cohabiting couple families, with the majority (of just over 400,000) living in cohabiting step-families. Figure 3.5 opposite shows locally where there are more step- and non-step-children in such families.

If you were looking for a single measure that better separates urban Britain from the remainder of the country, it would be difficult to find one as good as this. In general, the two shades of neighbourhood in this mosaic skirt the city boundaries, most clearly around London. There are a few areas where the distinction is not so clear, especially in Yorkshire. But in general, if children of school age are living with unmarried parents, the odds are that they are their original parents if they are living in a city, or that at least one is a step-father or mother if they are living outside of the major conurbations.

Families change as children grow older and move their location as well as sometimes changing their adult membership. What is expected, affordable, tolerated and possible also changes over time and across space. Neighbourhoods change more slowly. Some are places through which different types of family are more likely to pass at different points in their children's lives. The different odds of these events, measured according to who is being considered (in this case, schoolchildren), are mapped as a kind of litmus test of the social soil of places. It is in cities that most variety in ways of growing up is found, but it is only because of family reconstitution (and much other effort to create conformity) that a swathe of what appears on the surface to be uniform lives can be drawn around our cities. That swathe is the result of changes in many disparate lives, mostly in a direction to make them appear more similar.

3.5 Splitting up and coming together of families of children

Figure 3.5

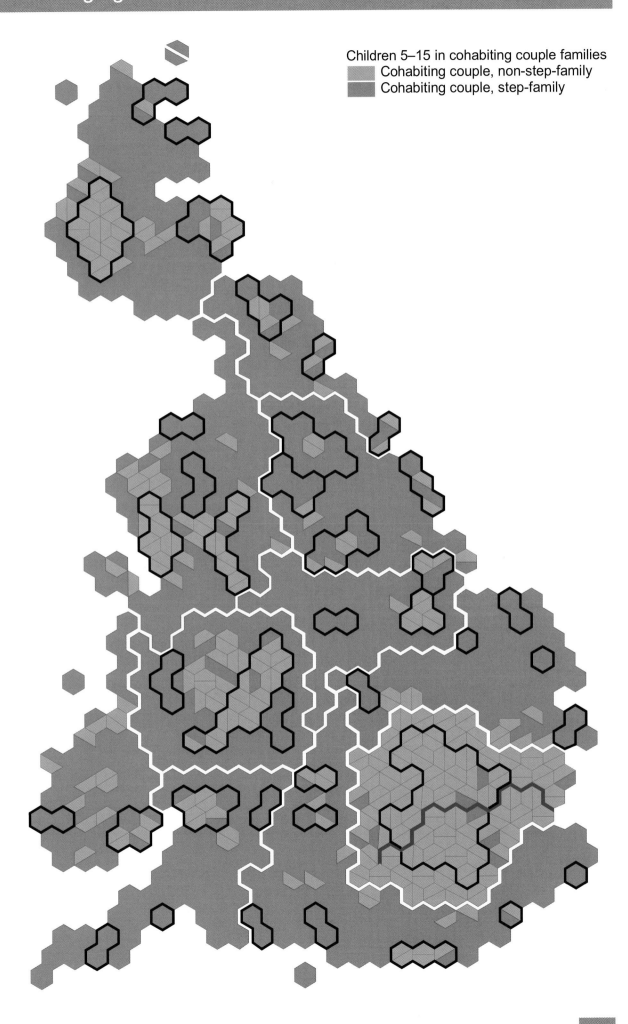

Children 5–15 in cohabiting couple families
- Cohabiting couple, non-step-family
- Cohabiting couple, step-family

3.6 Boarding: living away from home for children

Not all children live in families. A few are growing up in children's homes, ranging from short-stay establishments located near to their natural, adopted or foster parents to a few buildings that are all but child prisons in name. However, the number of children in all such types of state care and punishment has fallen dramatically in recent decades.

In contrast, over 50,000 children from the ages of 4-15 are each year legally placed in private care, sent away from their family home to live, eat and sleep elsewhere. They may see their parents out of term time or they may be sent to holiday camps or mainly cared for by nannies. For most of the time they do not see their parents. These children's lives are so different from those of almost everyone else of their age that they need to be mapped separately. Figure 3.6 opposite shows the estimated proportion of children, by their home address, who are sent away each year to board.

It would make little difference to the lives of many of these children if their parents split up and formed new partnerships; they perhaps would not be affected other than perhaps noticing a new adult or two when on holiday. When considering the range of families in which children grow up it is important not to forget this group: children who neither live with parents nor step-parents but who are cared for outside the home by other adults, almost all in educational establishments called boarding schools. Note also that for these children boarding can begin as early as the age of four.

More than 5% of the school-age children from Chelsea are boarders and do not live in that neighbourhood. Next most likely to be sent away are the children from the Hyde Park, Kensington, and Fulham neighbourhoods: 4%-5% of these children do not live at home. Areas where military families are likely to live are included in those neighbourhoods where between 3% and 4% are sent away to school: Salisbury Rural, Chichester North, Devizes Rural, Tooting West, Cotswold North East and Putney East. Finally, a few more military areas and more very affluent areas are included in all those neighbourhoods where between 2% and 3% of children are not found at home: London Central, Warminster, Battersea East, West Dorset Rural, Henley South, Walton, Wantage West, Newbury Rural, Winchester East, Whitchurch, Witney West, Wimbledon North, Lewes North, Crowborough, Wootton Bassett, Romsey Rural, Swanage, Somerton, Battersea West, Horsham Rural, Salisbury Urban, Lorn, Richmond North, Andover, North West Dorset, Richmond (Yorkshire) West and Tooting East. In total, some 7,000 children are missing from these 37 neighbourhoods alone. Almost 12,000 more are missing from the next 129 neighbourhoods shown in Figure 3.6. The mosaic is, in effect, the route map of the Pied Piper of boarding school education. Only in the far north east of Scotland are schools so remote that this is the only way of teaching older children.

3.6   Boarding: living away from home for children

Figure 3.6

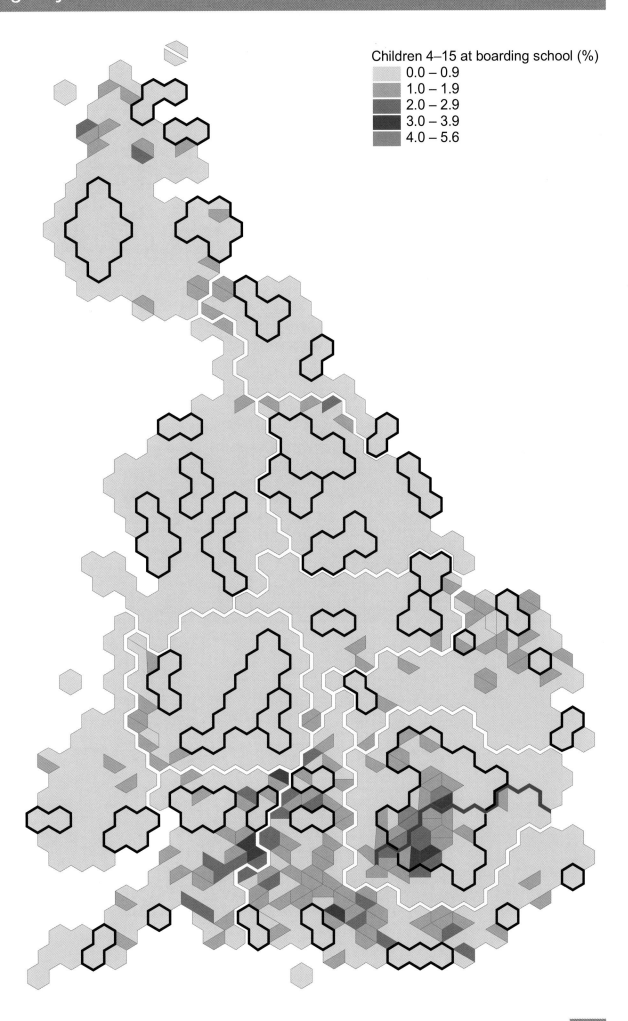

Children 4–15 at boarding school (%)
- 0.0 – 0.9
- 1.0 – 1.9
- 2.0 – 2.9
- 3.0 – 3.9
- 4.0 – 5.6

3.7 Religion: beliefs from home given to children

Just as children have little or no choice over who they are born to, whether their parents are together when they are born, stay together, split up or find new friends, or even whether they are sent away to school, so too do children have little influence over the religious beliefs of their parent(s). Thus Figure 3.7 opposite, which ascribes religious belief to school-age children, is very much a map of what religion parents ascribe to themselves.

Here only those children who have had religion ascribed to them are shown: the religion of the majority and then of the next largest group. Of the eight million school-age children in Britain, almost exactly a quarter have 'no religion' or 'no religion stated' and these are not shown here. In almost all neighbourhoods the majority have been labelled 'Christian' where any labels are given. In 23 neighbourhoods 'Christian' is the second largest religious affiliation of children aged 5-15. In just one neighbourhood 'Christian' does not feature in first or second place.

Looking just at the religious beliefs ascribed to children by their parents on completing a census form, Britain may appear mono-religious. However, in the large majority of cases, neighbourhoods are mixed 'Christian/Muslim', even if 49 times out of 50 there are more 'Christian' than 'Muslim' children living there.

Were children to be asked themselves what, if any, religious or other faith beliefs they hold, very different images may emerge. Respect might be greater for the footballer Wayne Rooney than Jesus Christ in many areas, but as such questions are almost never asked, such maps of actual adherence are never drawn.

Number of neighbourhoods in Britain by most common religion of children aged 5-15

Number of areas	Second most common religion of all children aged 5-15 who are ascribed one							
Most common religion	Buddhist	Christian	Hindu	Jewish	Muslim	Sikh	Other	Total
Christian	36		83	39	934	84	82	1,258
Hindu		3						3
Jewish		1						1
Muslim		19						19
Sikh					1			1
Total	36	23	83	39	935	84	82	1,282

3.7 Religion: beliefs from home given to children

Figure 3.7

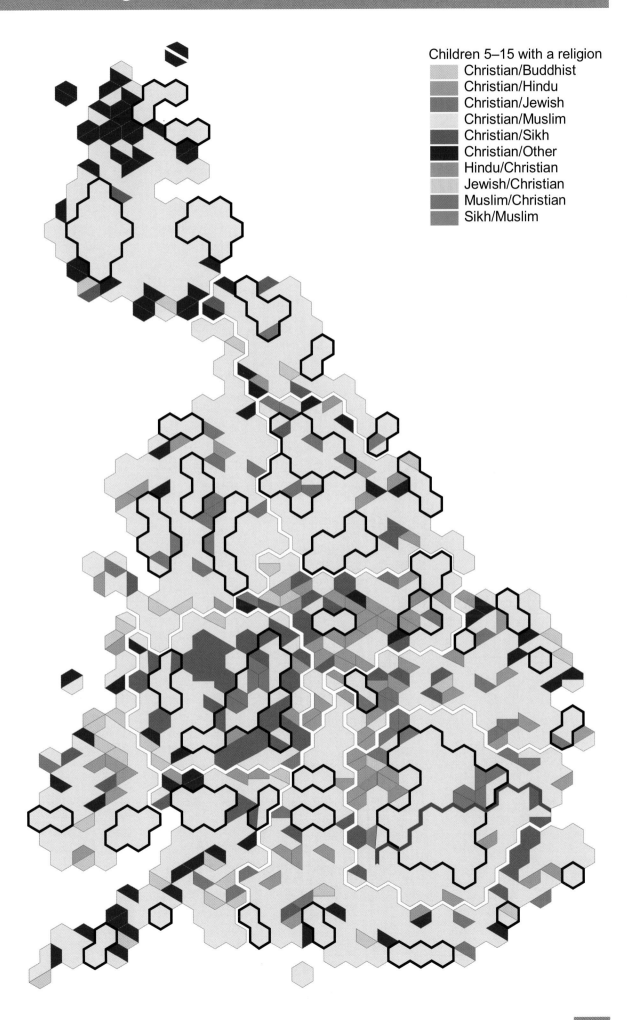

Children 5–15 with a religion
- Christian/Buddhist
- Christian/Hindu
- Christian/Jewish
- Christian/Muslim
- Christian/Sikh
- Christian/Other
- Hindu/Christian
- Jewish/Christian
- Muslim/Christian
- Sikh/Muslim

3.8 Age and moving home for children

The map below of the most common children's age tells us only one fact clearly: that London is different. For it is only in central London that children under the age of five dominate many areas. With a little imagination, it may also be possible to discern visually from this image the effects of out-of-city migration peaking around the time children are aged 10, most probably to secure school places from age 11. However, for a clearer picture of the geography of younger ages, fewer categories and mapping the runner-up as well as winning age group help greatly.

In Figure 3.8 opposite, London still clearly stands out, but so too are the areas of coastal and northern retreat where children are most commonly aged 12+ and then eight or more. Here, perhaps, is to where parents move when their youngest reaches a certain age, or on splitting up a marriage (which often occurs with the same time cue).

In between these extremes is another slice of Britain where those aged between four and 11 dominate in number. Out of the core cities but not yet properly away from it all, the elementary school years form a swathe of similar hues across the country, reflecting fears over children's futures, the desire to buy more space for expanding families, job opportunities, relationship changes, moving aspirations and the securing in many cases of more financial resources as children age; and all this simply to be seen in the residual geography of just a few more children living here or there.

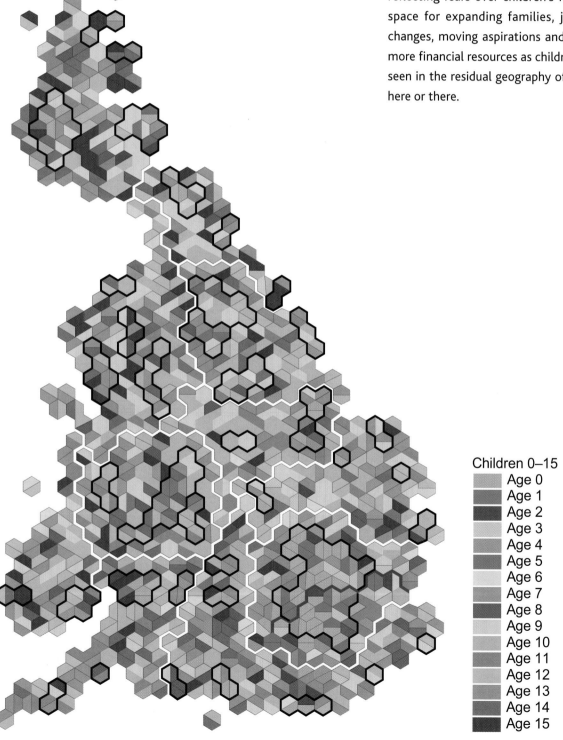

Children 0–15
- Age 0
- Age 1
- Age 2
- Age 3
- Age 4
- Age 5
- Age 6
- Age 7
- Age 8
- Age 9
- Age 10
- Age 11
- Age 12
- Age 13
- Age 14
- Age 15

3.8 Age and moving home for children

Figure 3.8

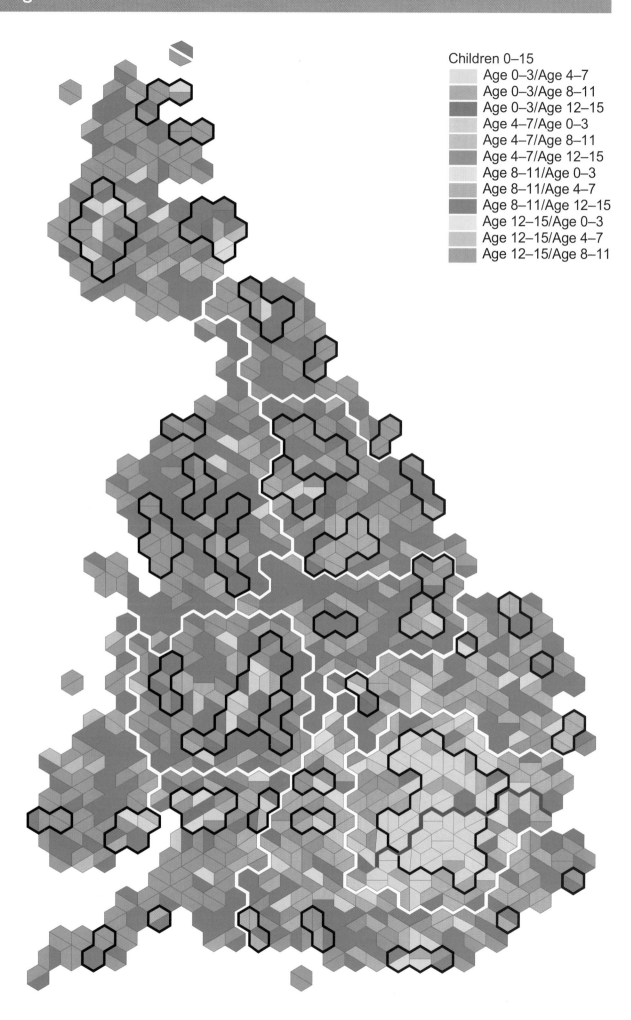

Children 0–15
- Age 0–3/Age 4–7
- Age 0–3/Age 8–11
- Age 0–3/Age 12–15
- Age 4–7/Age 0–3
- Age 4–7/Age 8–11
- Age 4–7/Age 12–15
- Age 8–11/Age 0–3
- Age 8–11/Age 4–7
- Age 8–11/Age 12–15
- Age 12–15/Age 0–3
- Age 12–15/Age 4–7
- Age 12–15/Age 8–11

3.9 Cars and houses: five to 10 years on, for children

The differences in material circumstances are so slight compared to the under-fives, that it is almost not worth showing these images, and yet those differences that there are show how the material lives of older children differ from that of infants, not only through the fact that they and their parents are ageing, but also through their slightly different geographies resulting from the migration just described. The map below of the modal number of cars is remarkably similar to that on page 36. All but 102 neighbourhoods are coloured identically.

Of those that have changed, in two thirds (67) of cases the modal average number of cars has risen by one car and in the remaining third (35) of neighbourhoods it has fallen by one, and then most often downsizing from two cars to one. Nowhere where it is most common for under-fives to have access through their family to two or more cars do most over-fives have access to none, nor is there anywhere where most under-fives live in families with none and over-fives with two or more. Everything changes slowly and changes predictably.

When housing type is also included (Figure 3.9 opposite), again children aged 5-15 live in very similar material circumstances to those aged under five and in all but 116 neighbourhoods what is modal is identical. However, in only half as many neighbourhoods is it normal to be bring up older children in a flat with access to a car as it was for infants. Of those areas changing, half see parents moving to presumably larger houses and that becomes the norm (along with now having a car and in one case two cars). However, half of these neighbourhoods where most infants live in a flat with a family with a car see most older children still living in flats but no longer with the car. It can be assumed from this that in these places the car proves too costly to run as other expenses rise. The differences between these images and those for children half a generation younger are slight, but telling. By ages 5-15 the southern-most neighbourhood where most live in a house with no car is in Nottingham.

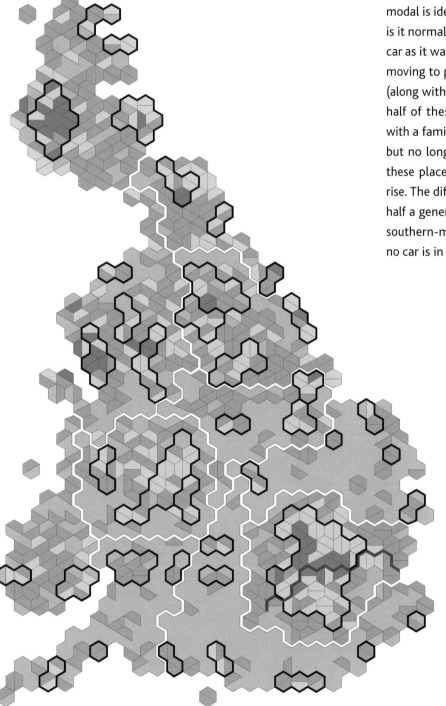

Children 5–15 in households with
- No car/1 car
- 1 car/No car
- 1 car/2+ cars
- 2+ cars/1 car

3.9 Cars and houses: five to 10 years on, for children

Figure 3.9

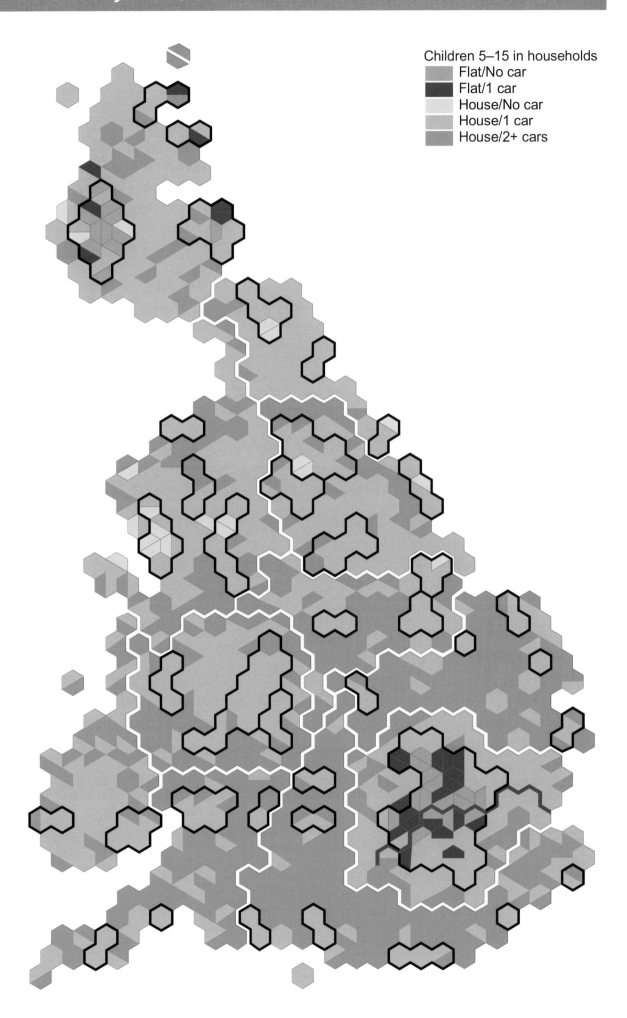

Children 5–15 in households
- Flat/No car
- Flat/1 car
- House/No car
- House/1 car
- House/2+ cars

3.10 No place like home: tenure of families for children

Just as with cars and housing type there is little change in the dominant tenure in each neighbourhood between the ages of 0-4 and 5-15, but perhaps just enough to warrant presenting Figure 3.10 opposite and documenting the changes there are. Four neighbourhoods where most under-fives are housed by the local authority (LA) see most over-fives in a mortgaged property. In all four cases 'mortgaged' was the second most common tenure in the area for infants. Conversely, in the 1,191 neighbourhoods where mortgaging was the norm for infants, in just 13 cases 'LA rented' became the norm for older children and in one case, 'other social rented'. Again, the direction (if not the occurrence) of both switches was predictable from the second most common tenure housing infants. Then, as the remainder of the table below shows, only three other neighbourhoods are recoloured from their dominant tenure to that which was second most common for infants.

Perhaps what is most telling about the similarities in the tenure map for infants and older children are the categories and transitions that do not exist. Renting of any kind never exists alongside 'owned outright' as the two largest tenures of a neighbourhood. The rural idyll where the wealthy own their manor house and the less affluent rent their cottage is a fiction. So too is the affluent urban suburb where those who own live next to those who rent privately. Most clearly, those who own live only in largest numbers alongside those who aspire to own.

In terms of transitions that do not occur, if 'mortgaged' is not even second most common for infants it will not be modal for older children; nowhere does 'private rented' grow in popularity; and the only place where the majority of children live in property that is owned outright by their parents is Kensington, a transition from renting but most probably not of the same families. Families that rent in Kensington tend to have very young children and move out of the borough before these children reach school age.

Neighbourhoods in Britain by tenure mix for infants and modal tenure for children aged 5-15

Number of neighbourhoods	Most common tenure for households with children aged 5-15					
Most and second most common tenure for the homes of infants aged 0-4	LA rented	Mortgaged	Other social rented	Owned outright	Private rented	Total
LA rented/Mortgaged	50	4				54
LA rented/Other social rented	12					12
LA rented/Private rented	1					1
Mortgaged/LA rented	13	647				660
Mortgaged/Other social rented		129	1			130
Mortgaged/Owned outright		129				129
Mortgaged/Private rented		286				286
Other social rented/LA rented			4			4
Other social rented/Mortgaged		1				1
Other social rented/Private rented			1			1
Private rented/Mortgaged		1		1	2	4
Total	76	1,197	6	1	2	1,282

3.10 No place like home: tenure of families for children

Figure 3.10

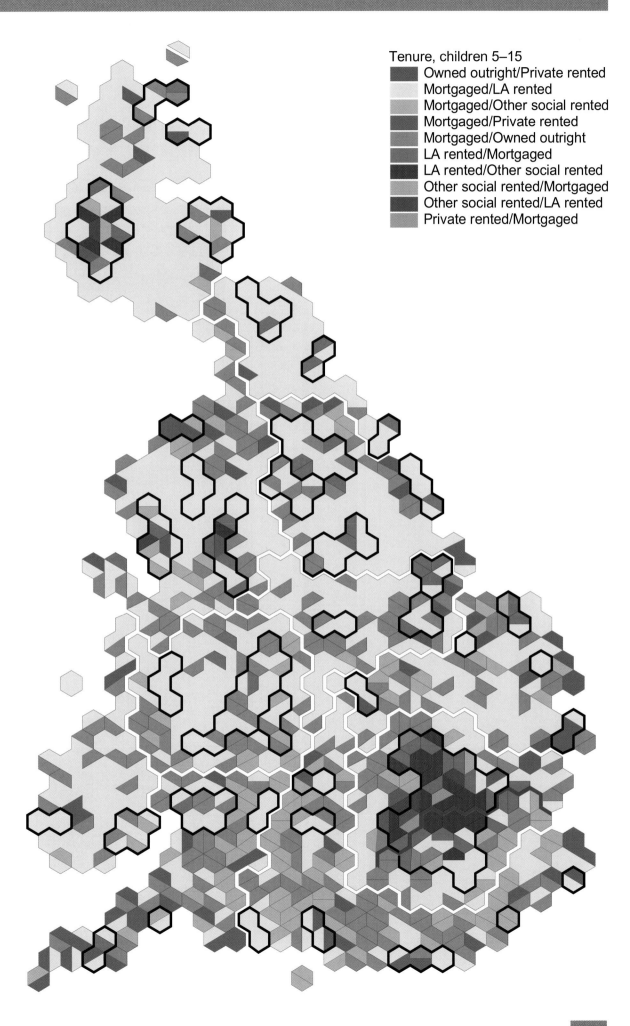

Tenure, children 5–15
- Owned outright/Private rented
- Mortgaged/LA rented
- Mortgaged/Other social rented
- Mortgaged/Private rented
- Mortgaged/Owned outright
- LA rented/Mortgaged
- LA rented/Other social rented
- Other social rented/Mortgaged
- Other social rented/LA rented
- Private rented/Mortgaged

3.11 What's a home worth? Wealth of dependent children

Tenure, of course, provides almost no clue as to the cost or value of the properties being bought or owned. Tenure gives no indication of the amount of rent, or whether the renter also owns or rents elsewhere. Tenure is a very crude indicator of the relationship to land and property.

In contrast, we can look at the amount of wealth held in housing and in the context of this chapter look at the value of that wealth if it were to be shared out among all children currently living in the neighbourhood. The picture would be even more unequal if that wealth had been more realistically shared out only between children living in partially paid-off mortgaged properties or those owned outright. The Land Registry releases the value of housing sold on the open market by type for small areas in England and Wales. Similar data are also available for Scotland. Using that and knowing the numbers of children living in each neighbourhood in housing of each tenure, we estimated housing wealth per child as it stood in recent years.[1] Figure 3.11 opposite shows the average housing equity in each neighbourhood if it were averaged across all children in the neighbourhood. This provides an indicator of future possible mean levels of inheritance. Note that many children in most neighbourhoods will receive no inheritance from housing assets as their parent(s) rent or will never pay off their mortgage.

As the table below shows, the average wealth within each category shown in the map can vary widely, especially for the most affluent tenth of neighbourhoods where mean wealth in the most affluent neighbourhood (Kensington again) is more than twice that found in the least wealthy of the wealthiest tenth of areas (Bramhall in Cheadle, Stockport).

Children's housing wealth in Britain

Neighbourhood wealth per child, held in housing (£s) (2003)		
Decile	Minimum	Maximum
1	4,000	15,000
2	15,000	20,000
3	20,000	24,000
4	24,000	29,000
5	29,000	34,000
6	34,000	40,000
7	40,000	46,000
8	46,000	54,000
9	54,000	67,000
10	67,000	146,000

[1] The data is for 2003; the report *Know your place* can be found at http://england.shelter.org.uk/policy/policy-825.cfm/plitem/160/ and also at www.sasi.group.shef.ac.uk/publications/reports/knowyourplace.htm

3.11 What's a home worth? Wealth of dependent children

Figure 3.11

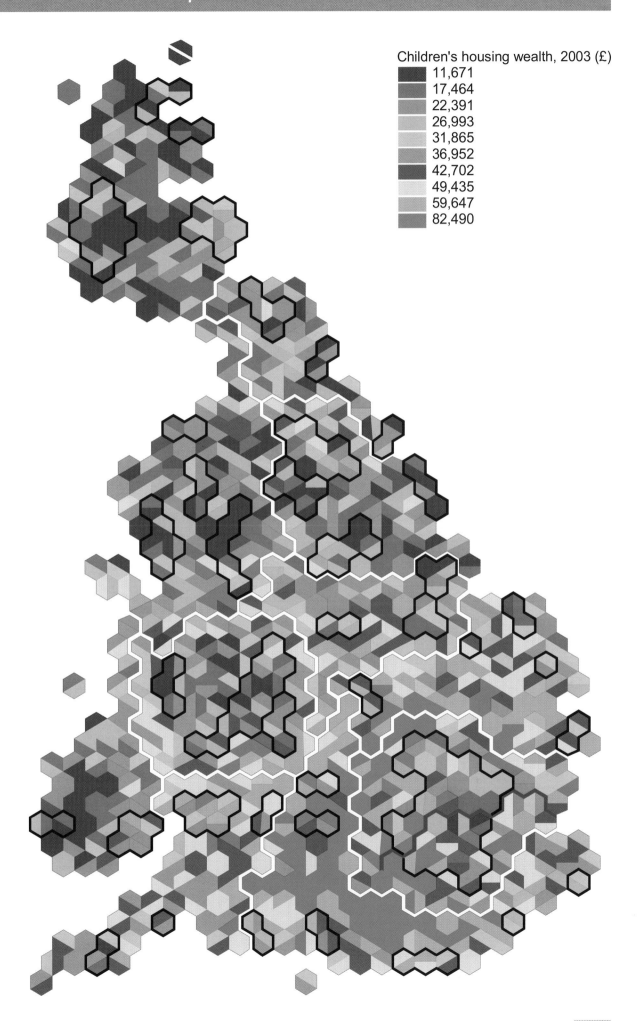

Children's housing wealth, 2003 (£)
- 11,671
- 17,464
- 22,391
- 26,993
- 31,865
- 36,952
- 42,702
- 49,435
- 59,647
- 82,490

3.12 Poverty: where children have least

There are many complicated measures of the proportion of children living in poverty. Often they are not available for all of Britain and usually they do not capture all of the meaning of poverty. Poverty is defined as not having access to the resources needed to live a life not excluded from the norms of society. However, in most cases what the families of poor children lack most is money and so a measure of the proportion of children who are income deprived captures most poor children in Britain in its remit. The measure used here is that calculated to produce the official index of deprivation indicator for children in England, shown in the map below.[2]

In order to include Scotland and Wales, and because again, in the majority of cases, income-deprived children are deprived of income for a simple reason, Figure 3.12 opposite simply shows the proportion of children in each neighbourhood living in families in receipt of key social security benefits. This information is available for all of England, Wales and Scotland, but only at parliamentary constituency level. Hence whole constituencies are coloured similarly in Figure 3.12.

Despite all the complexity surrounding the measurement of childhood poverty, a simple map of the proportion of children living in families receiving key social security benefits provides as good a picture as many more sophisticated methods. This is because the social security system is designed to identify families with children living in poverty and because the minimum wage and tax credit system, to a significant extent, now help to prevent many children whose parent(s)' earnings are low from living in absolute poverty.

Income deprivation, children (%)

	3.0 – 9.9
	10.0 – 19.9
	20.0 – 29.9
	30.0 – 39.9
	40.0 – 49.9
	50.0 – 70.4

[2] The Income Deprivation affecting Children Index for neighbourhoods was created from LSOA (Lower Super Output Area) data using the population weighted score from the Neighbourhood Statistics (NeSS) website at www.neighbourhood.statistics.gov.uk

3.12 Poverty: where children have least

Figure 3.12

Children of benefit claimants (%)

	4.1 – 9.9
	10.0 – 19.9
	20.0 – 29.9
	30.0 – 39.9
	40.0 – 49.9
	50.0 – 65.4

3.13 Grading: awarding qualifications to children

One way in which targets are raised over time is that qualifications become devalued over time as more and more higher level qualifications are expected. General Certificates of Secondary Education (GCSEs) were the passports that took a child on to a good job when the authors of this atlas were taking those exams (or, to be more honest about our ages, taking their precursor, 'O' levels). Back then, five or more grade A-C passes (A* did not exist) was quite a rare achievement and for a small minority this meant that they might carry on at school or go to a sixth form college. Now, most children are expected to, and do, achieve this level of qualification at ages 15 or 16, but achieving that is no longer a passport to probable educational and economic success.

Here we map GCSE and GNVQ (General National Vocational Qualification) results for England and Wales, and the broadly equivalent SCQF (Scottish Credit Qualifications Framework) level 5 results, based on pupils' residence rather than on where schools

are located. The Scottish educational system is significantly different from that in England and Wales and here it is only broadly compared at the five or more grade A*-C GCSE level. Note that the data are for 2003 for England and Scotland, and for 2004 for Wales, and only cover children attending maintained schools.

The most average place to live as a child in terms of your chances of gaining no qualifications at these ages in England is Eltham East in London where 5.0% gained no GCSEs in 2002/03; the distribution of no GCSE passes for all neighbourhoods is shown below right. Data for this category are only available for England. Note that the two neighbourhoods in England for which data are missing on this map are the two where almost all children gained five or more passes at grades A*-G.

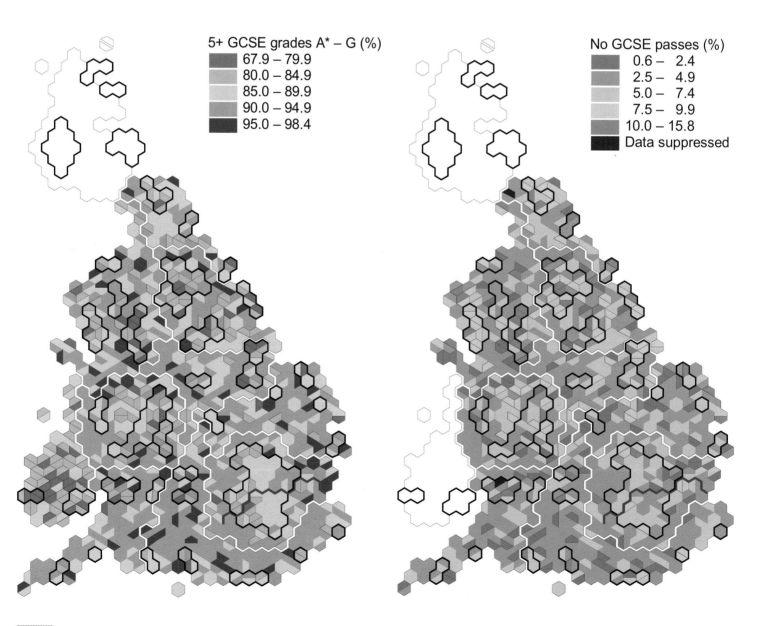

5+ GCSE grades A* – G (%)
- 67.9 – 79.9
- 80.0 – 84.9
- 85.0 – 89.9
- 90.0 – 94.9
- 95.0 – 98.4

No GCSE passes (%)
- 0.6 – 2.4
- 2.5 – 4.9
- 5.0 – 7.4
- 7.5 – 9.9
- 10.0 – 15.8
- Data suppressed

3.13 Grading: awarding qualifications to children

Figure 3.13 shows the mosaic of five or more grade A*-C GCSE passes (or the Scottish equivalent) for England, Wales and Scotland. In the median neighbourhood of residence in England by overall success (Bournemouth Central on the south coast), some 55.5% of children achieved this level in the academic year 2002/03. The median neighbourhood when English neighbourhoods are ranked by the wider measure of proportion of children living in them gaining at least five grade A*-G GCSEs is Cramlington in Northumberland where 91.7% did so; the map on page 81 below left shows the national distribution of five grade A*-G GCSEs for England and Wales.

Note that because data are only consistently available for England, that all the examples in this text are taken from England.

Figure 3.13

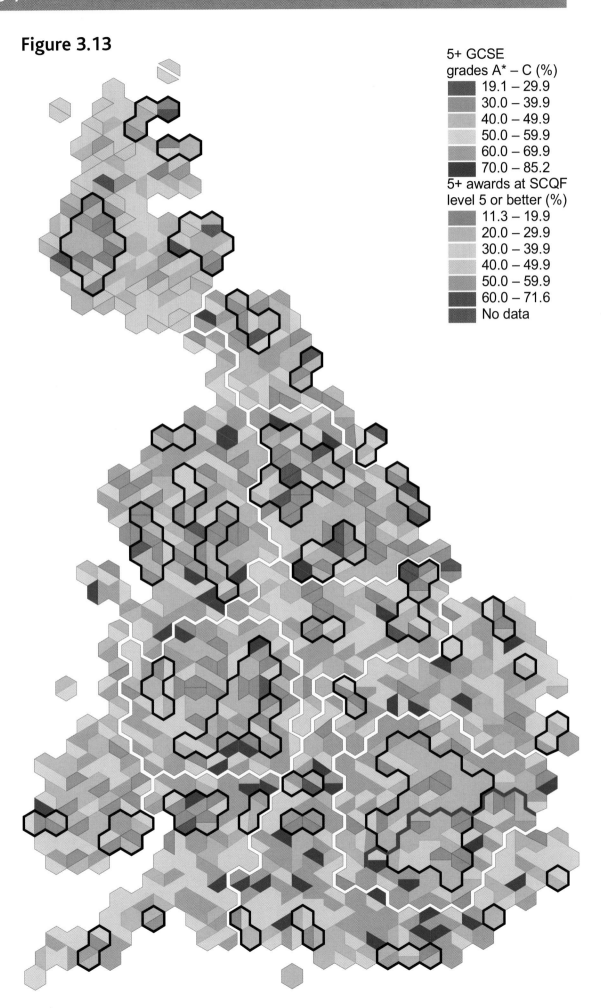

5+ GCSE
grades A* – C (%)
- 19.1 – 29.9
- 30.0 – 39.9
- 40.0 – 49.9
- 50.0 – 59.9
- 60.0 – 69.9
- 70.0 – 85.2

5+ awards at SCQF
level 5 or better (%)
- 11.3 – 19.9
- 20.0 – 29.9
- 30.0 – 39.9
- 40.0 – 49.9
- 50.0 – 59.9
- 60.0 – 71.6
- No data

3.14 Class mixing in childhood

As with infants, children's social class is determined by the status of the Household Reference Person. Just as with those aged under five, children aged 5-15 who are the offspring of 'higher managers' and are in the majority or largest minority in a neighbourhood mix mainly with children of 'lower managers'. Nowhere are children from another social class their most likely geographical playmates. There are some subtle changes to the map of mixing shown opposite (Figure 3.14) when compared with its equivalent for younger ages shown on page 41, but it is the continuity that is most apparent when these two maps are compared of the social class context to younger and older children's neighbourhoods. The map below shows to which class the majority of children aged 5-15 are allocated and the table provides a list of examples of those jobs done by their parents.

Example occupations and National Statistics Socioeconomic Classification (NS-SeC)

NS-Sec	Description	Example
1	Higher managers: higher managerial and professional occupations	Employees in large organisations; professionals such as chemists, software writers; school inspectors; solicitors; clergy; town planners; management accountants
2	Lower managers: lower managerial and professional occupations	A stores manager in goods warehousing in charge of stores and one person; teachers; nurses; journalists
3	Intermediate: intermediate occupations	Paramedics, police, lower civil servants
4	Small employers: small employers and own account workers	Park rangers
5	Lower supervisory: lower supervisory and technical occupations	Train drivers
6	Semi-routine: semi-routine occupations	Dental nurses; care assistants; electroplaters
7	Routine: routine occupations	Kennel maid working in dog kennels looking after dogs
8	Never worked: never worked or long-term unemployed	
9	Not classified: not classified	

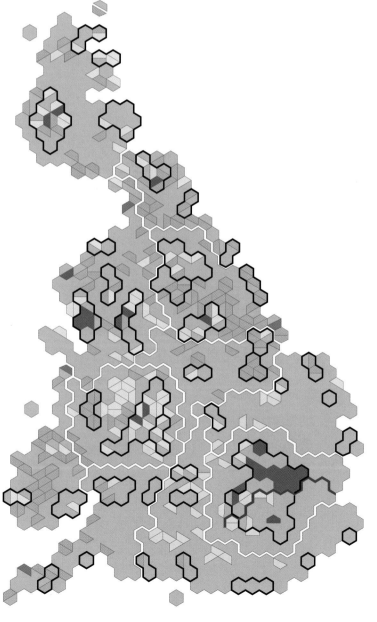

NS-SeC of Household Reference Person, children 5–15
- 1. Higher managers
- 2. Lower managers
- 4. Small employers
- 5. Lower supervisory
- 6. Semi-routine
- 7. Routine
- 8. Never worked

3.14 Class mixing in childhood

Figure 3.14

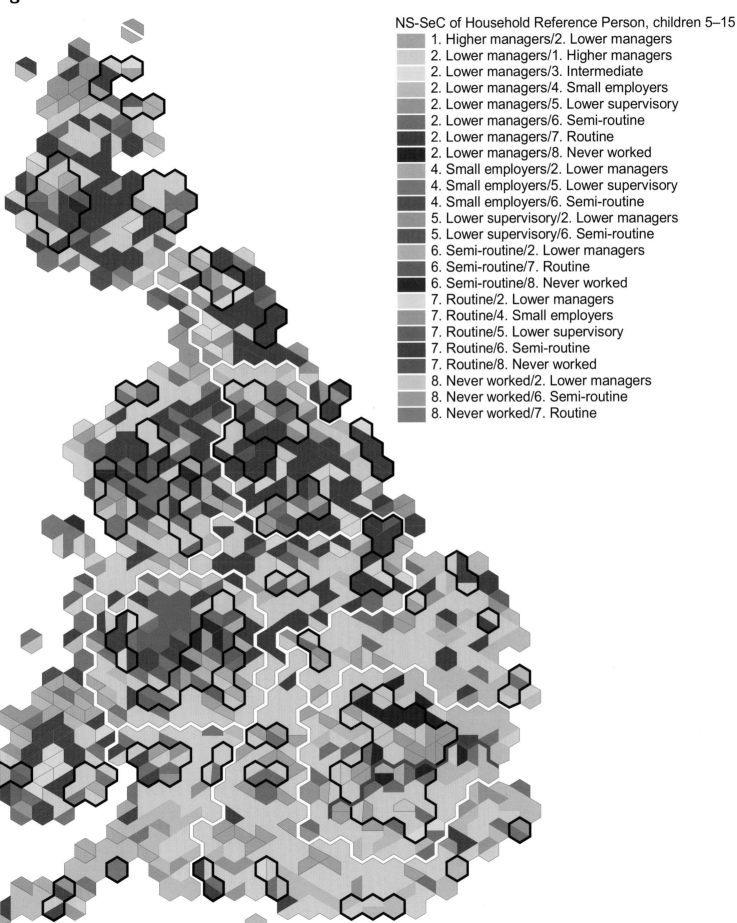

NS-SeC of Household Reference Person, children 5–15
1. Higher managers/2. Lower managers
2. Lower managers/1. Higher managers
2. Lower managers/3. Intermediate
2. Lower managers/4. Small employers
2. Lower managers/5. Lower supervisory
2. Lower managers/6. Semi-routine
2. Lower managers/7. Routine
2. Lower managers/8. Never worked
4. Small employers/2. Lower managers
4. Small employers/5. Lower supervisory
4. Small employers/6. Semi-routine
5. Lower supervisory/2. Lower managers
5. Lower supervisory/6. Semi-routine
6. Semi-routine/2. Lower managers
6. Semi-routine/7. Routine
6. Semi-routine/8. Never worked
7. Routine/2. Lower managers
7. Routine/4. Small employers
7. Routine/5. Lower supervisory
7. Routine/6. Semi-routine
7. Routine/8. Never worked
8. Never worked/2. Lower managers
8. Never worked/6. Semi-routine
8. Never worked/7. Routine

3.15 Children who care

Some 108,544 children are carers, almost all for their ill parent or parents. Although this amounts to only one child in every 74, the map of where they are most commonly found shows a pattern that should by now be familiar, as it shows where parents more often than not are poor and hence are more likely to be ill at ages young enough for their progeny to still be children. In the areas where higher than average numbers of children care, the ratio is one in 54 being a carer and it falls to less than one in 116 where caring is more rare. The table below shows the numbers and proportions of children caring in the above average, below average and average areas and how many care for up to 19 hours a week, up to 49 hours a week, or 50 hours a week or more in each of the three parts of the country shown in Figure 3.15 opposite. On average, 1.4% of children care and the areas labelled 'average' are where between 1.0% and 1.6% care.

Numbers and proportions of children in Britain that care by areas so typified

Area	Category	Children	Percentage
Above average	Caring 50 hours a week or more	2,805	0.2
	Caring 20-49 hours a week	3,122	0.2
	Caring 1-19 hours a week	26,963	1.5
	The remainder of children	1,741,197	98.1
Average	Caring 50 hours a week or more	4,665	0.1
	Caring 20-49 hours a week	4,819	0.1
	Caring 1-19 hours a week	55,971	1.1
	The remainder of children	5,015,338	98.7
Below average	Caring 50 hours a week or more	556	<0.1
	Caring 20-49 hours a week	633	0.1
	Caring 1-19 hours a week	9,010	0.8
	The remainder of children	1,176,791	99.1
Caring 50 hours a week or more		8,026	0.1
Caring 20-49 hours a week		8,574	0.1
Caring 1-19 hours a week		91,944	1.1
The remainder of children		7,933,326	98.7

3.15 Children who care

Figure 3.15

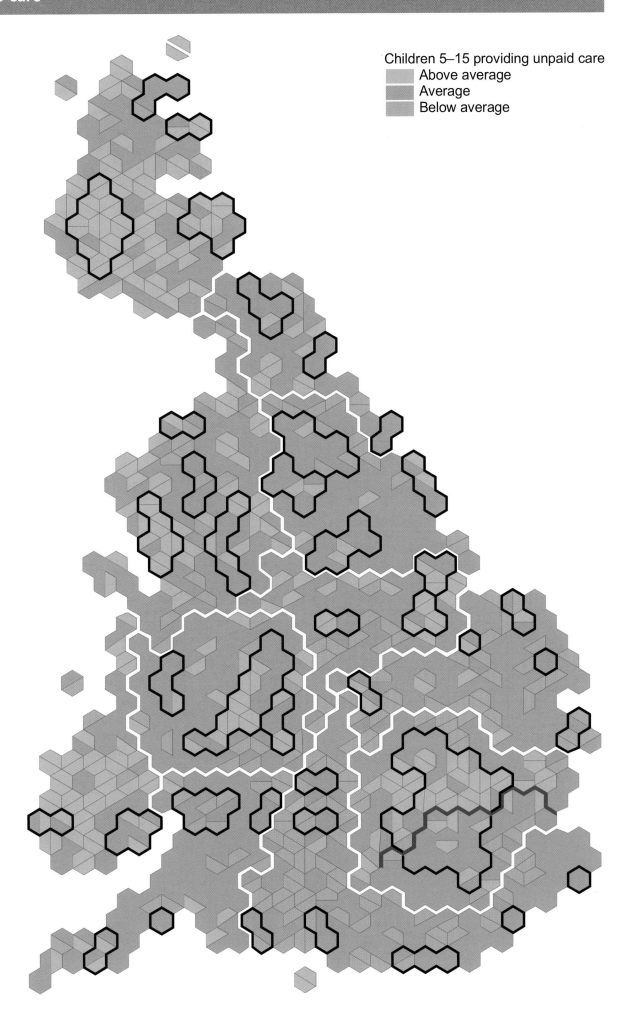

Children 5–15 providing unpaid care
- Above average
- Average
- Below average

3.16 Conclusion: the schooling years

It is during the years of schooling that children first properly become aware of where they live and perhaps a little more aware of where they do not live. Up until the age of four, the boundaries of home and family are far more important than those of neighbourhood, city and region. Of course, where you are born is likely to influence your mother's age and that in turn will greatly influence the nature of the family into which you are delivered. It will determine how financially warm or cold a climate you are born into and hence the nature of your home and of the adult or adults and possible siblings you will share it with, whether your home is over- or under-crowded, whether you are taken out of it in a car or on the bus, and whether your parent has come home from a job that saps the imagination or one that has brought you the perks of a materially luxurious early childhood (if not so much attention).

Who your parents mix with and can mix with will have influenced who you mix with and is determined by the geography of who is available; but as yet you have had little opportunity to assert your own identity. That, your birthplace, ethnicity and even in many cases your religion have been given to you. You have been where you are, moulded by those to whom you were given. However, in the schooling years that begins to change.

True, you are dependent on your parent(s) (or guardian) financially. True, the fate of their love lives will change or retain your family, but you can make life easier or harder for them and especially for anyone new they try to introduce, and more so as you get older. True, they may send you away to school but then they have little say left over what you become (although they have paid for the standard model that most get). Yes, if you have a religion it is most probably your parents', but then they tend to

fill the form in that tells us, the researchers, what you believe and so it may well not be so true. Yes, they decided to move when it was least convenient for you, but you have the rest of their lives to remind them of that. Their home is your home, rooms in it are yours, it adds to your identity as much as to theirs. And the back of their car(s) (if they have one) is almost certainly your space. And you begin to realise that you have a share in what they own, or do not own. But because like lives so often near to like, it may take you a little time to realise just how much you have, or do not have, or perhaps just how average you are.

Most children think they are normal, and a few are. Most of you are nothing special. You just did what we would expect of children from where you lived. Mostly you have just done what we have shown you to have done through these maps of where you grew up. If you did not do that, then most of you did what was next most common. And what was next most common is so often so similar to what the majority did as to be nothing special either. Areas are stereotyped for a reason. You should not be surprised by what you see of where you live, but you have little reason or opportunity to know how where you live fits into the overall mosaic.

The mosaics of childhood are like images of those parts of a beehive where the larvae grow. Change the environment slightly and the larva will emerge a little different. However, although the analogy of the beehive may be attractive, children's lives are not so strictly prescribed. The hundred thousand children caring for parents show that. But each child's chance of being among that hundred thousand is predetermined, even if the exact fate of each is so very far from certain.

4 And then the lover: ages 16-24

... and then the lover,
Sighing like furnace, with a woeful ballad
Made to his mistress' eyebrow;

4.1   Introduction

If childhood encompassed the years in which we grow, larva-like, in our neighbourhoods, the nine years from 16-24 are a metamorphosis.

At these ages, most move from the security/insecurity of their families through a series of usually more insecure tenures, relationships and occupations. A few years spent doing this and then a few spent doing that. Aside from those who are mothers (but not fathers) very few can say with much certainty at 18 what they will be doing by age 21. These are the ages at which original family background appears, superficially at least, less vital.

Teenagers' and young adults' lives are steered by more than that which makes younger children's environments so much more predictable. Later, by area at least, we will see that most revert to form and begin to live lives and, for the majority, bring up children not unlike the way they were brought up, albeit with the difference a generation makes. But doing that is so far from the minds of most 18- to 24-year-olds that in some cases it is almost an anathema. Ask first-year university students in an elite university, a group conforming more than most of their cohort, what they expect to be doing in their late twenties or even late thirties and suburbia, the office job and the family are not what they tend to reel off. So what is on the minds of this age group? Well you might have your suspicions and so we will begin by feeding your expectations with two maps of sex.

First, however, for you to have a balanced understanding of the rest of this chapter we need to show (see the map below left) the extreme clustering of those in young adulthood who can account for anything between not quite a twentieth and almost a half of the population of neighbourhoods at the most extreme. It is almost as if our youngest adults desire to live together in clusters. Alternatively, it may well be that the rest of us do not want to live with them. Whatever it is, and universities play a large part now, this age group, almost more than any other, clusters. The map left shows clearly where those clusters are most acute.

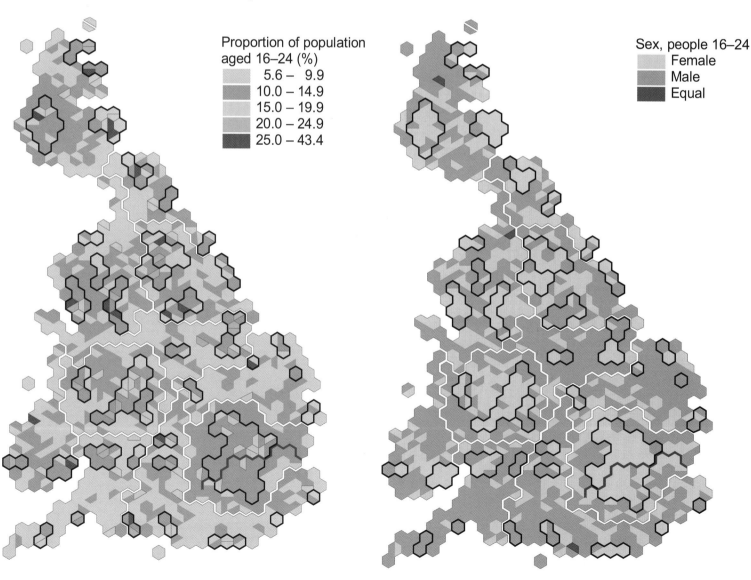

Proportion of population
aged 16–24 (%)

 5.6 – 9.9
10.0 – 14.9
15.0 – 19.9
20.0 – 24.9
25.0 – 43.4

Sex, people 16–24
Female
Male
Equal

4.1 Introduction

Sadly, neither the census, nor any other reliable survey, includes any question as to whether the interviewee or any member of their household is sighing like a furnace, but it does record that simplest of variables: biological labelling. Women are in the majority in a minority of places (shown opposite right, with the proportions mapped in Figure 4.1) partly, because, at least at the beginning of these years, men still outnumber them. However, young women are also a little more clustered in some cities, away from the remoter rural areas from which they out-migrate in greater numbers.

However, as this chapter goes on to show, young adults are divided in many more ways than by sex: by how they choose to live together (for those that do), by education, by work, by what kind of housing they inhabit, and by much we cannot easily map, such as whether they still live with their parents, or have returned to them, and by everything from sexual orientation, to political belief, favourite take-away food, and good or bad looks.

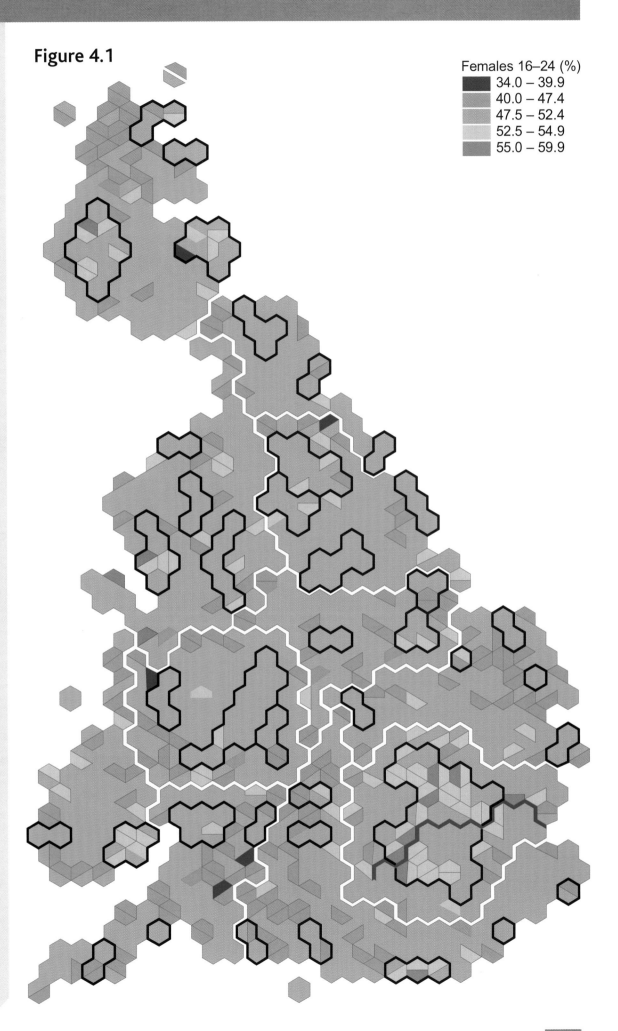

Figure 4.1

Females 16–24 (%)
- 34.0 – 39.9
- 40.0 – 47.4
- 47.5 – 52.4
- 52.5 – 54.9
- 55.0 – 59.9

4.2 Setting up home, first marriages, young widows in young adulthood

The large majority of young adults do not marry and nowhere are the married in a majority. Marriage is (literally) a religious act for many people, possibly more so for the youngest of adults who indulge in it and are least likely to have had issues of pensions rights, child access or inheritance tax on their minds during the happy day. However, compare the map of children's religion shown in the previous chapter with the distribution of first marriages below and the coincidence is not as strong as you might suppose. Neither is it very coincident with birthplace abroad, although over a sixth of infants in Mildenhall (see the map on page 45) are born outside the UK, mainly in the USA, and a sixth of young adults there are married. The other two clusters in Birmingham and across the Pennines relate to migration from the East rather than the West but in similar circumstances of poverty that lead to young North Americans joining their armed forces and coming here with their young families.

Mildenhall, however, does not feature on the map opposite (Figure 4.2). When young North Americans are widowed they presumably return home. In contrast, in Hodge Hill and Erdington in Birmingham and around the immigration assessment centre in Croydon as many or more than one in one hundred young adults have already lost their husband or wife.

Squint a little at Figure 4.2 and you begin to see that elsewhere the chances are far from even, even if almost everywhere else they are low. At least two orders of magnitude less likely than marriage, if you are young and widowed there are places in Britain where you will not be the only one to have loved and lost so soon. The table below shows the proportion of young people who are single, married (including remarried and separated), divorced and widowed.

Young and committed in Britain?

Age	Single (%)	Married (%)	Divorced (%)	Widowed (%)
16	99.5	0.3	0.1	0.1
17	99.4	0.5	0.1	0.1
18	99.0	0.8	0.1	0.1
19	98.0	1.8	0.1	0.1
20-24	91.9	7.8	0.3	0.1

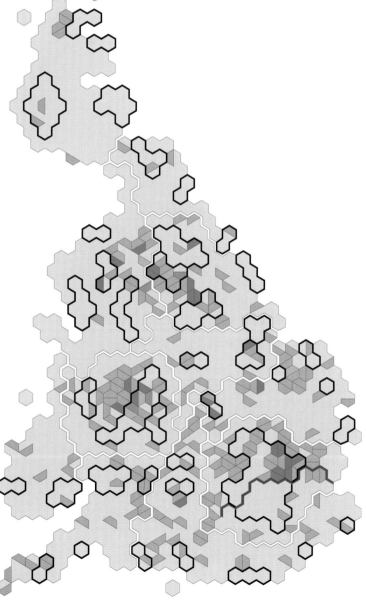

First marriage, people 16–24 (%)

	0.6 – 4.9
	5.0 – 9.9
	10.0 – 14.9
	15.0 – 19.9
	20.0 – 24.1

4.2   Setting up home, first marriages, young widows in young adulthood

Figure 4.2

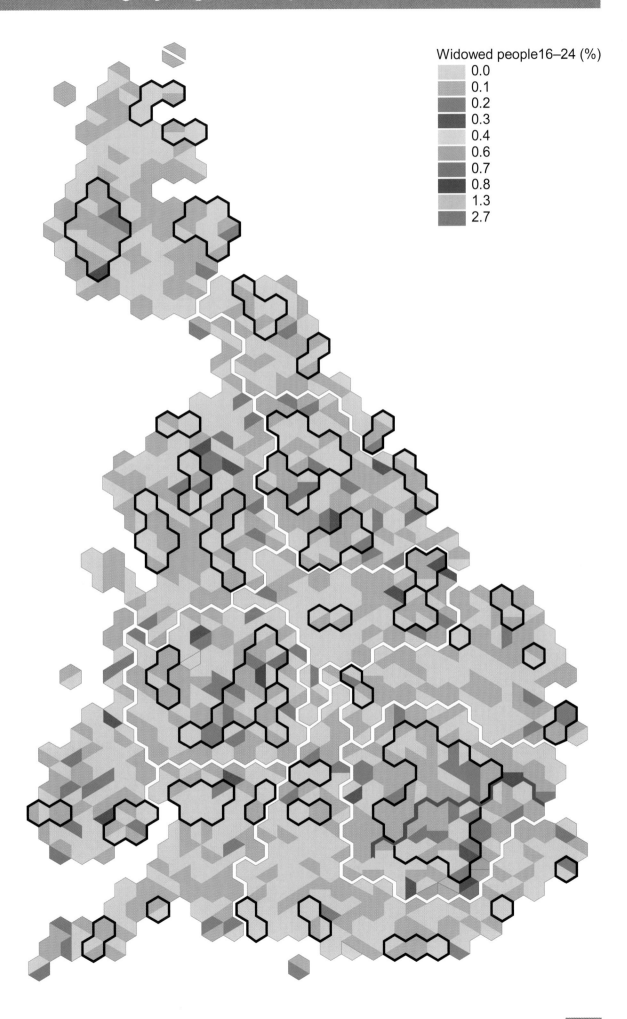

Widowed people16–24 (%)
0.0
0.1
0.2
0.3
0.4
0.6
0.7
0.8
1.3
2.7

4.3 Married young, living apart and cohabiting in young adulthood

Widowhood is, of course, far from the most common reason why young married people are no longer together. Many are divorced or separated as a result of their relationship ending, but still more live apart presumably from necessity; their work, study, childcare or other responsibilities mean that the young couple cannot live together and may not even be living in the same city or country. Figure 4.3 opposite shows, for those young adults who are married in each neighbourhood, the proportion who are not living with their husband or wife. In many places these separated lovers constitute over a fifth of young people who are married but are not living together. Contrast that with the distribution shown below of the proportion of all young adults who are living together but not married, that is, cohabiting (left). Almost everywhere at these ages, if couples are living together, the majority are cohabiting (right).

To recap, the map below left is of the proportion of all young adults cohabiting. That below right is of where the majority of young couples living together are either married or cohabiting; and that opposite is of the proportion of married or remarried young adults who are not living together.

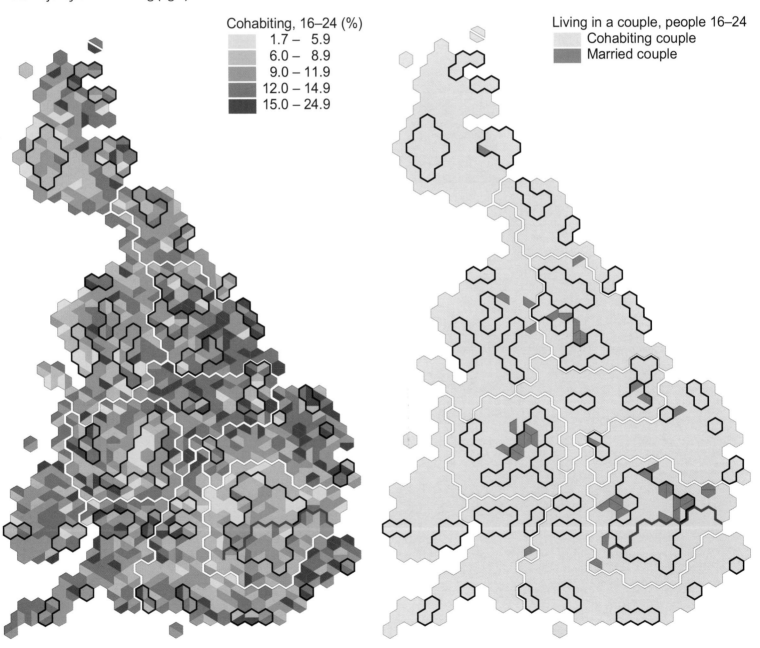

Cohabiting, 16–24 (%)
 1.7 – 5.9
 6.0 – 8.9
 9.0 – 11.9
12.0 – 14.9
15.0 – 24.9

Living in a couple, people 16–24
  Cohabiting couple
  Married couple

4.3   Married young, living apart and cohabiting in young adulthood

Figure 4.3

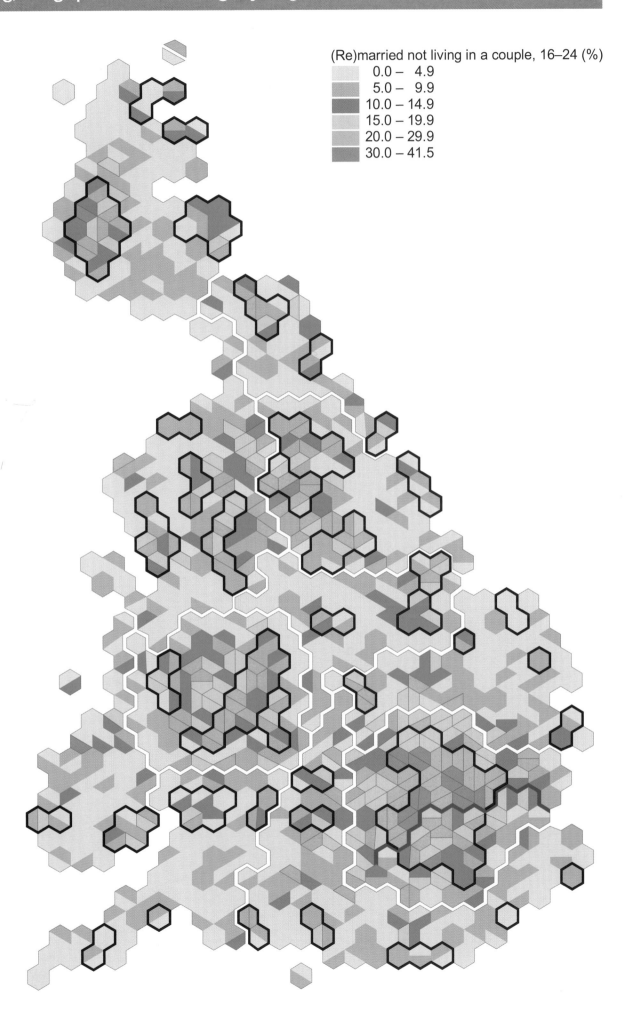

(Re)married not living in a couple, 16–24 (%)

	0.0 – 4.9
	5.0 – 9.9
	10.0 – 14.9
	15.0 – 19.9
	20.0 – 29.9
	30.0 – 41.5

4.4 What are you doing with your life in young adulthood?

Possibly the most annoying question to ask young people of today is what they are doing with their lives, although this may rank just under 'have you taken drugs?' and just before 'are you sleeping together?'. The census does not yet ask either of the latter two but is happy to probe on the former.

Only just over a third of this age group are employed full-time, although possibly a few of these are also studying. Over a quarter are full-time students or part-time students not otherwise employed and a further seventh are full-time students who are also working. The concept of full-time in the lives of this age group is deceptive. It tends to imply what they are doing for eight hours of a possible 12-hour working day. Exclude students and, as can be seen right and below, full-time employees are in the majority everywhere, followed most frequently by part-time, unemployed carers and the 3.4% who said they were engaged in

some 'other' activity into which they did not wish the state to enquire. Figure 4.4 opposite shows the full range of possibilities, and those unspecified others are nowhere in the majority or largest minority.

Proportion of people in Britain aged 16-24 according to their main economic activity

Activity	%
Employee full-time, possibly also studying part of what would otherwise be leisure/home time	37.0
Student not also working (either full-time or part-time)	26.3
Full-time student also working	14.7
Employee part-time, possibly also studying part-time	6.1
Unemployed	5.9
Family carer	3.7
Other	3.4
Self-employed full-time	1.3
Sick or disabled	1.1
Self-employed part-time	0.3
Retired	0.1

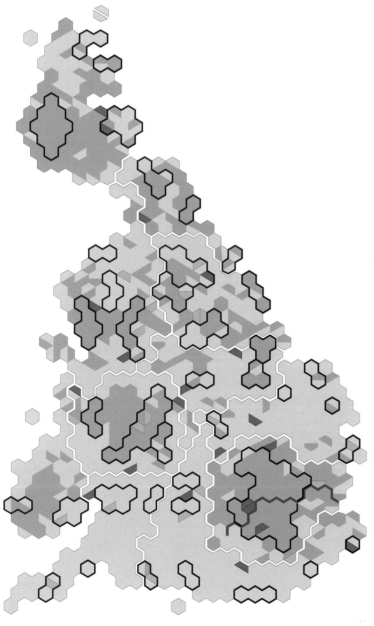

Economic activity 16–24 excluding students
 Full-time employee/Part-time employee
 Full-time employee/Unemployed
 Full-time employee/Caring for family
 Full-time employee/Other

4.4   What are you doing with your life in young adulthood?

Figure 4.4

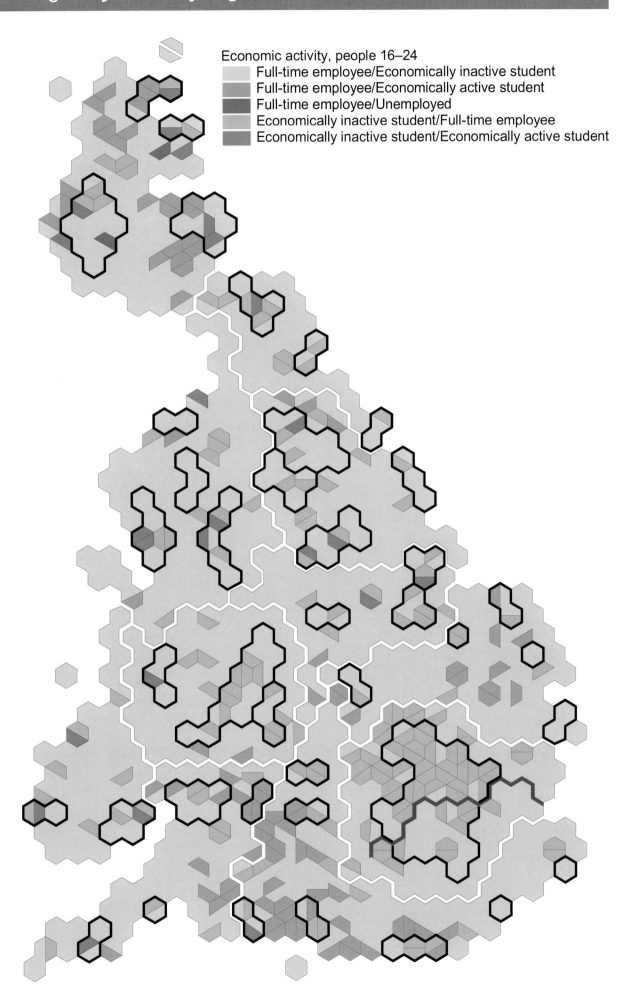

Economic activity, people 16–24
- Full-time employee/Economically inactive student
- Full-time employee/Economically active student
- Full-time employee/Unemployed
- Economically inactive student/Full-time employee
- Economically inactive student/Economically active student

4.5 Not in education, employment or training in young adulthood

'NEET', standing for 'not in education, employment or training', is not a nice acronym, but as it became harder to be able to say that you were unemployed, and as the government began to tighten the screws on younger mothers who tried to stay at home with their children, the NEETs evolved as a new social group defined by what they were *not* doing rather than what they *were* doing.

Almost everywhere a majority of young people aged 16-19 are students. In only a scattering of neighbourhoods are the majority of young people not students, as the map below left shows. Look carefully at this map and you see how London is unique in being a large city where almost everywhere most young people study. The NEET map (below right) is very much the mirror image of the student map and also very much the basis, for obvious

reasons, for the map of a wider age range of young people reliant on benefits shown in Figure 4.5 opposite. This map shows the proportion of young adults aged 16-24 reliant on and receiving one or more of the following forms of state social security in August 2005: Bereavement Benefit, Carer's Allowance, Disability Living Allowance, Incapacity Benefit, Income Support, Jobseeker's Allowance, Pension Credit and Widow's Benefit. Those reliant solely on Housing Benefit, Council Tax Benefit or Industrial Injuries Benefits are not included here. Note that although the map of NEETs and those living on benefits are similar, it is clear from these images that a high rate of young people in education, employment and/or training in an area does not necessarily mean fewer on benefits a few years later.

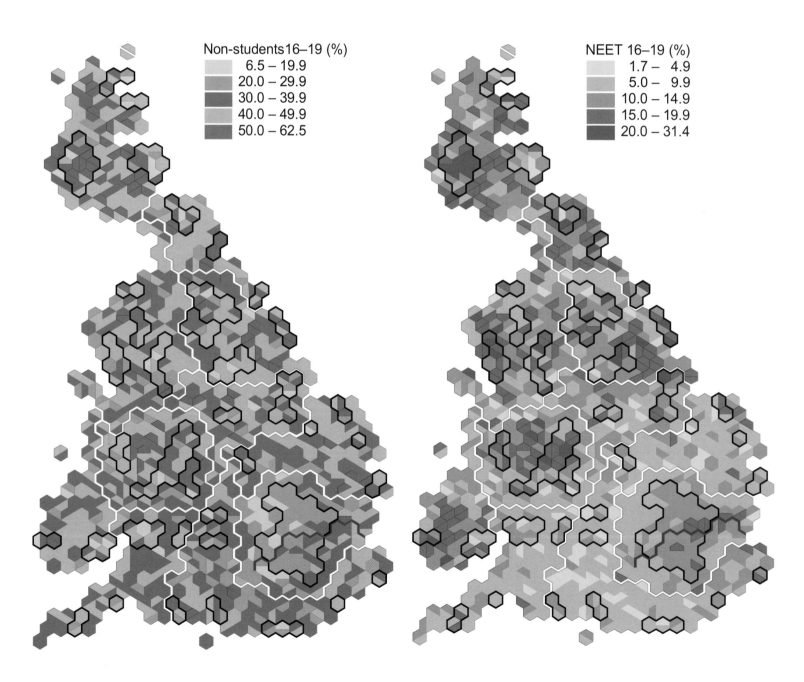

4.5 Not in education, employment or training in young adulthood

Figure 4.5

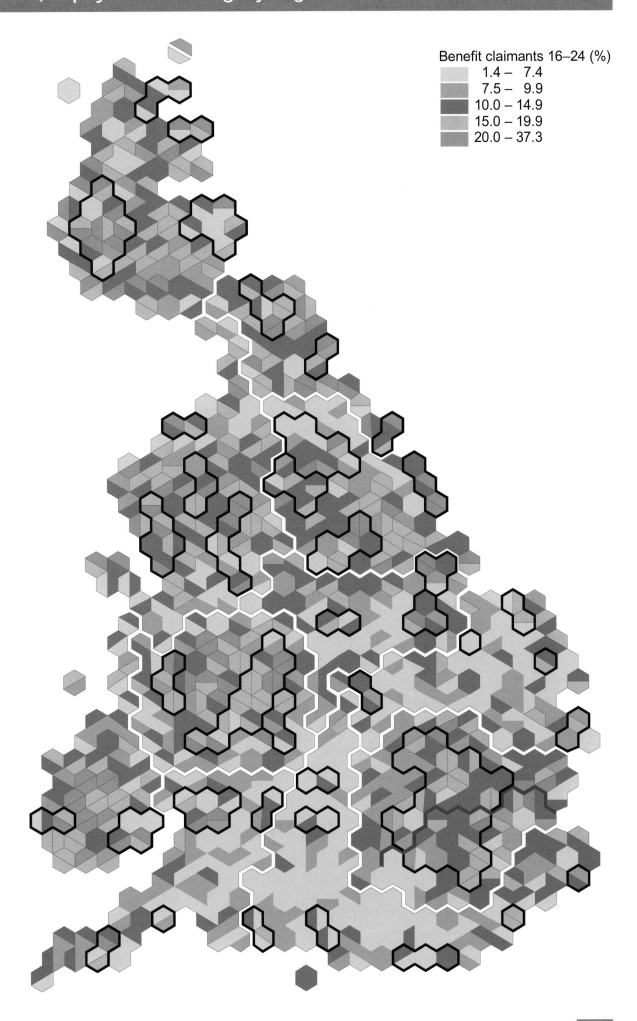

Benefit claimants 16–24 (%)
	1.4 – 7.4
	7.5 – 9.9
	10.0 – 14.9
	15.0 – 19.9
	20.0 – 37.3

4.6 Certificates, diplomas and degrees in young adulthood

By the age of 18 almost all young people in Britain are expected to have at least one qualification: a single grade G certificate in the most obscure of subjects counts. And there are places where almost all 18-year-olds do possess such a thing. Usually these are areas the names of which are synonymous with better-off student lands to the side of cities where the prevailing winds only brought fresh smelling air when the housing was first built: topping the list is the Ecclesall suburb of west Sheffield (98.4% hold those pieces of paper there). Then the Headingley suburb of north west Leeds, Clifton and Redland in north west Bristol, Cambridge West and Oxford West (97% each). In contrast, the other set of places where high number of adults aged 18-24 have no qualifications are highlighted in Figure 4.6 opposite.

The map of who has the highest qualifications is not simply the opposite of that of who has the least because gaining high qualification, outside of Scotland, usually involves and often requires migration, and further migration after gaining a degree. Thus the highest levels of qualifications among those aged 18-24 are found where most did not grow up, that is, in London, as shown on the map below.

After your eye is first drawn to London on the map below left, note that the next most concentrated clustering of areas with highly qualified young adults is found in Scotland. There migration is not the normal route to high-level pieces of paper. This has been the case for many decades and, in the case of a lucky few, for centuries.

Quite why the advantages of going to your local university have not been realised south of the border is an interesting question to contemplate, especially if you begin to ask whether many of the maps that follow would look like they do if 16-24 were not also the ages of mass migration for so many.

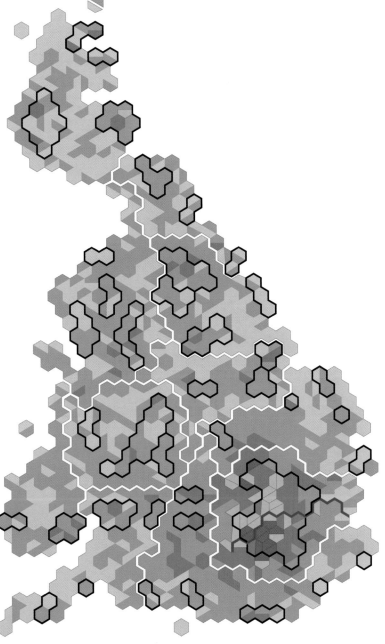

Higher level qualifications,
people 18–24 (%)

	2.8 – 9.9
	10.0 – 19.9
	20.0 – 29.9
	30.0 – 39.9
	40.0 – 53.0

4.6   Certificates, diplomas and degrees in young adulthood

Figure 4.6

No qualifications, people 18–24 (%)
- 1.6 –   9.9
- 10.0 – 14.9
- 15.0 – 19.9
- 20.0 – 24.9
- 25.0 – 34.3

4.7 Who gets to go to university in young adulthood

By neighbourhood, as few as 6% (Hunslet in Leeds) and as many as 71% (Kensington in London) of 18- and 19-year-olds get to go to university in a year. To be precise, these are the proportions of all children reaching the age of 18 starting study within two years in a higher education institution between 1994 and 2000. Note that the figures include higher education delivered in further education institutions.

Divide all neighbourhoods into 10 decile groups, from those containing the tenth of children least likely to go (decile 1) to those containing those odds on to go (decile 10) and you get the map shown opposite (Figure 4.7). The data used here are among the highest quality shown in this atlas. Why then does the pattern look a little 'shaky'? Well, remember that each neighbourhood is a parliamentary constituency split in two, dividing the lower income side from the more affluent side? Look again at the map and see if you can spot not only where the money is nationally, but where it is locally. Money is far from the only determinant of who goes to university. Rates in poorer parts of London and Scotland would be lower if all that determined university access were affluence, but affluence is, of course, most of what matters.

The table below left shows that children who grew up in the most advantaged areas in terms of university access (decile 10) had a 51% chance of attending higher education by the age of 19, made up 17% of all students in higher education, 20% of those in an elite group of institutions, but just 5% of those attending the least sought after institutions.

The graph below represents the first column of data in the table below. Note how smooth and steep the incline is. Move from decile 1 to decile 5 and your chances of attending university are doubled, move again to decile 10 and they double again. These are simply the average changes for all children growing up in each decile of neighbourhoods. Almost no children make the hop and skip between these areas, areas that in many parts of London are simply a short walk apart.

University access

Decile	Chance of going (%)	All (%)	Elite (%)	Least popular (%)
1	13	4	3	18
2	18	6	6	13
3	22	7	6	12
4	24	8	7	11
5	27	9	9	9
6	30	10	10	9
7	33	11	11	9
8	37	13	14	7
9	42	14	14	7
10	51	17	20	5
Britain	30	100	100	100

Chance of attending university by decile of opportunity in Britain

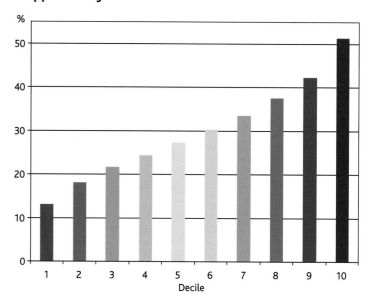

4.7   Who gets to go to university in young adulthood

Figure 4.7

Higher Education
participation by decile

1
2
3
4
5
6
7
8
9
10

4.8 Dreaming spires and other heart's desires in young adulthood

Not all universities are the same. That is well known; there are numerous rankings available that all differ slightly. As we are interested in access here, we use one characteristic of the areas that students come from to rank institutions. That characteristic is the mean rate of access to higher education as a whole for children from those areas. Thus the most elite universities are defined as those that take most students from areas where most go to any university. Here we have divided them into four groups.

Elite: those institutions that admit a tenth of students in total and admit the highest proportion from the highest participating areas. This group corresponds to the equivalent of the North American Ivy League and includes most of the ancient universities.

Over average: those admitting the next four tenths of students. These tend to be largely (when counting by student) those universities that have been in place in one form or another for around a century.

Under average: admitting the next four tenths of students, in other words, those from places where students tend to go to university but that are in the bottom half of the probability distribution.

Least favoured: the last tenth of students go to institutions that cater most for students from areas where access to university is least common. The majority of places offering higher education within further education institutions tend to be in this group.

The map on the left shows what proportion of children who go to university in each neighbourhood go to one of the elite institutions.

Note that partly because participation is so high in Scotland several of its institutions fall within the elite group defined as most likely to admit students growing up in areas most educationally privileged.

Figure 4.8 opposite shows to which type of institution the majority of children who do go to university get to and perhaps shows the basis for what could be the major future medium-term social divide: not if you go, but where you go.

Access to elite universities (%)

	0 – 5
	6 – 10
	11 – 20
	21 – 29
	30 – 53

4.8   Dreaming spires and other heart's desires in young adulthood

Figure 4.8

Higher Education entrants & university type
- Elite/Over average
- Over average/Elite
- Over average/Under average
- Over average/Least favoured
- Under average/Over average
- Under average/Least favoured
- Least favoured/Over average
- Least favoured/Under average

4.9 How old are you within young adulthood?

It is easy to feel out of place as a young adult. One minute you are just turning 18 in an area full of your contemporaries and the next year you are living in a social wasteland that everyone else has left. What is your home neighbourhood now feels like some nursery for adolescents. No one told you where the party was, or to be precise the three-year-long party for which the major entry qualification is that you come from the right place and that you are aged between 18 and 21. You can take a year out and come to the party at 19, but much later is not much tolerated.

Go to the party and stay still again, as you attain the old age of majority at 21, and again you may quickly begin to feel out of place and rapidly ageing. Every year another cohort of almost-children arrives and an equally large cohort of young adults leaves for the real world. Don't go and you may wonder what you are missing out on. This is, of course, only a story for the third of young people who go to university (the party) and only then for the majority who migrate there (from suburban and rural adolescent nurseries) and then from there to the real world of the advantaged, mostly found in London. However, through the flocking and swarming of this particular third of the cohort, the age-related territory for much of the rest is defined.

Figure 4.9 opposite shows the year group in the majority in each neighbourhood. For those not going to the party there is more space to stay at home, but if home is London, expect to be competing with some of the best paid and most demanding of your generation if you wish to stay in that space.

When first and second most common age band are studied (see map left) it becomes obvious that there is not much room for those aged under 19 in central London or in the hearts of a few other cities. In contrast, but often very near those places, 19- to 21-year-olds are most often missing from where they do 'best at school', and are found in the patchwork quilt of student lands where that age group dominates. In between these places are the suburban and rural nurseries of adolescence. These can again be divided by the likely age of the second most common band there. In the south of England and the commuter belts of the north that band is aged 22-24, because so many of the 19- to 21-year-olds are at university.

People 16–24

	Age 16–18/Age 19–21
	Age 16–18/Age 22–24
	Age 19–21/Age 16–18
	Age 19–21/Age 22–24
	Age 22–24/Age 16–18
	Age 22–24/Age 19–21

4.9   How old are you within young adulthood?

Figure 4.9

People 16–24
Age 16
Age 17
Age 18
Age 19
Age 20
Age 21
Age 22
Age 23
Age 24

4.10 Have you got a car in young adulthood?

Well, have you? Should you? See the map below for where most young adults of this age live in households with none, one or two plus cars and see Figure 4.10 opposite for how most who work travel to work (including travelling to study in Scotland). Of course, living in a household with a car does not mean that you necessarily have much access to the car. By law, no one at age 16 should be driving anyway, and there is that little matter of passing your driving test that helps make these years a little more challenging. Nevertheless, access to a car or cars is a precursor to use.

To understand car use, we have some idea about how this age group commutes to work when they work. Figure 4.10 shows the first and second most common methods in each neighbourhood. Commuting by car dominates, apart from London and parts of other cities, a reflection of the paucity of reasonably priced, frequent, reliable public transport services in many areas. Nowhere is cycling the dominant mode of commuting: the highest numbers of cyclists are found in Oxford, Cambridge and York. Many people commute over too great a distance to realistically be able to cycle, while few who have to carry heavy paperwork have the luxury of a chauffeur-driven car to transport it.

The plethora of solutions to moving around London that vary neighbourhood by neighbourhood highlight how choosing or being constrained to live in different parts of the capital at these ages determines how you are likely to spend a significant amount of your day travelling.

Light rail includes metro, underground and tram services. Places with such transport systems include Tyne and Wear, Glasgow, Merseyside, Blackpool, Manchester, Sheffield, West Midlands and London. Note that Nottingham's tram system did not commence operations until 2004 and so does not feature here.

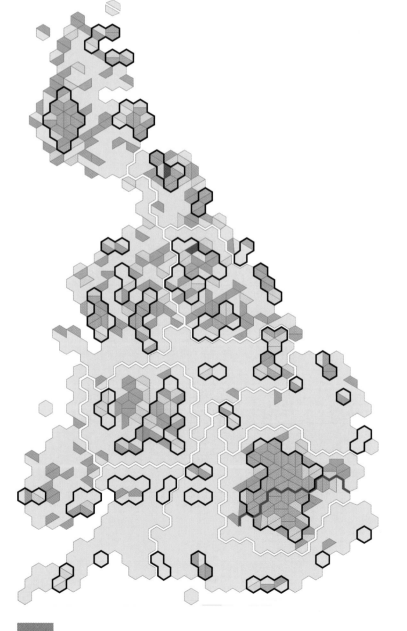

People 16–24 in households with
- No car/1 car
- No car/2+ cars
- 1 car/No car
- 1 car/2+ cars
- 2+ cars/No car
- 2+ cars/1 car

4.10 Have you got a car in young adulthood?

Figure 4.10

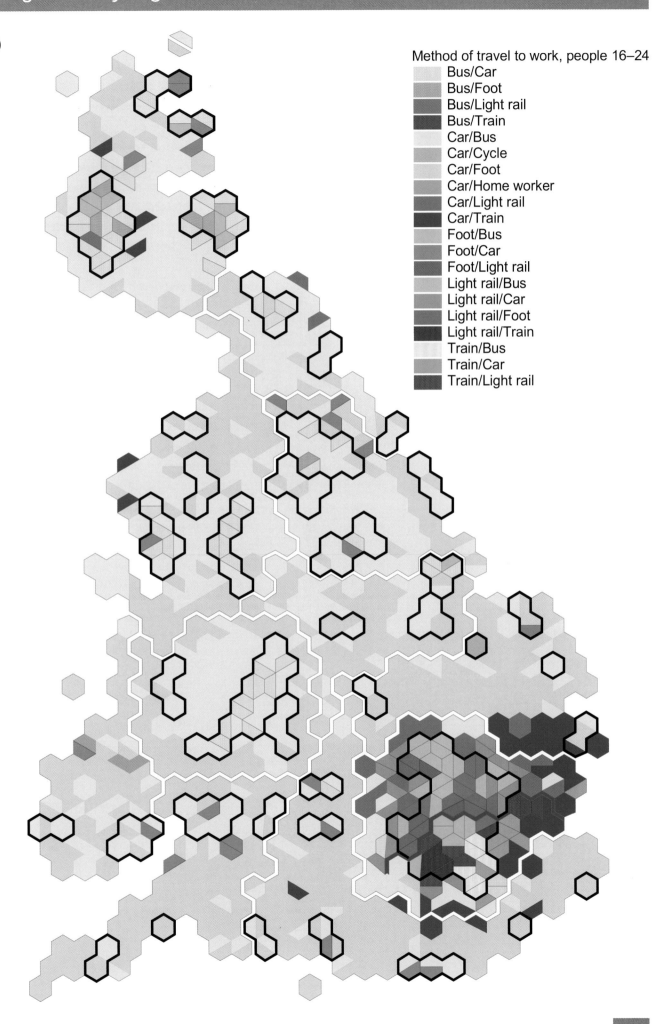

Method of travel to work, people 16–24
- Bus/Car
- Bus/Foot
- Bus/Light rail
- Bus/Train
- Car/Bus
- Car/Cycle
- Car/Foot
- Car/Home worker
- Car/Light rail
- Car/Train
- Foot/Bus
- Foot/Car
- Foot/Light rail
- Light rail/Bus
- Light rail/Car
- Light rail/Foot
- Light rail/Train
- Train/Bus
- Train/Car
- Train/Light rail

4.11 Where do you live and have you got children in young adulthood?

Where you live is not always an easy question to answer at these ages and certainly not simple to count. There is no simple estimate from the census of how many young people of these ages are living with their parents. What we can show is the tenure of the accommodation that they do live in and that gives quite a few clues as to whom those who are not married or cohabiting may be living with, and thus how their accommodation is provided.

Figure 4.11 opposite shows in which tenure this age group is most commonly and second most commonly housed in each area. Some of the tenures used earlier to describe the housing of children have been collapsed into a single category here to simplify the map. The category 'communal' almost always refers to living in halls of residence at these ages, but also includes prisons and military establishments. It is almost certainly the case that where the majority tenure is owner occupied (which includes 'mortgaged'), the owner is the parent or parents of the young adult and the majority of young adults there are still living at home (as almost all 16- and 17-year-olds will be everywhere).

One of the reasons why it is not simple to ascertain whether young adults are living with parents is that they themselves can easily be parents. Thus simply counting all households containing young adults and children will not only capture those still at home with their parents but also those who are parents themselves. These are the ages at which, up until very recently, it was usual to have children. Now, as the map on the left shows, much less than a tenth of young adults are parents in much of southern England. Nowhere are many more than a fifth of young adults parents.

To understand why these parents are where they are regionally requires remembering the patterns of access to education, migration and competition for space shown above. To understand more why they are where they are (and just as importantly are not) more locally, compare this map to Figure 4.11 of the most common tenures.

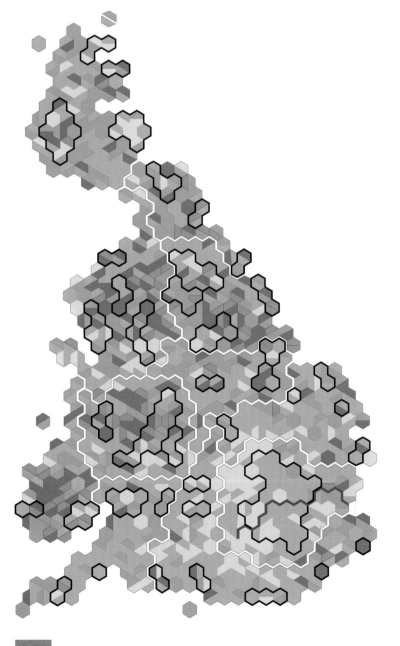

People 16–24 with children (%)

	0.6 – 4.5
	4.6 – 9.0
	9.1 – 12.0
	12.1 – 15.0
	15.1 – 21.0

4.11 Where do you live and have you got children in young adulthood?

Figure 4.11

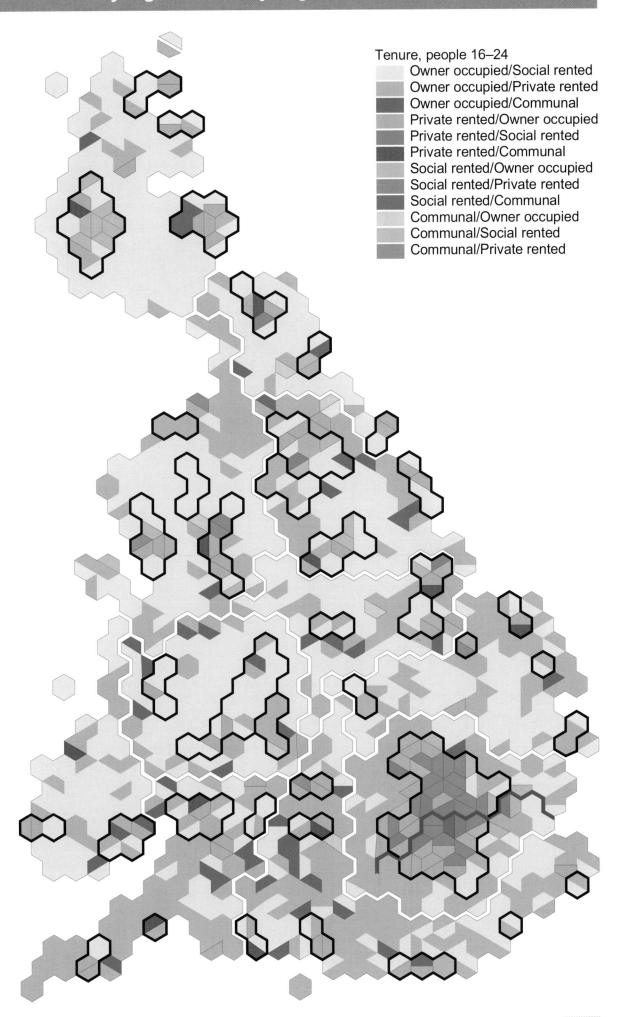

Tenure, people 16–24
- Owner occupied/Social rented
- Owner occupied/Private rented
- Owner occupied/Communal
- Private rented/Owner occupied
- Private rented/Social rented
- Private rented/Communal
- Social rented/Owner occupied
- Social rented/Private rented
- Social rented/Communal
- Communal/Owner occupied
- Communal/Social rented
- Communal/Private rented

4.12 Where do you come from and what do you believe in young adulthood?

Ethnic origin, what you feel your origin to be, is often assumed from looking at people. However, if you want to know where most 16- to 24-year-olds say their origins lie, when presented with a short series of options, then Figure 4.12 gives you the first and second most likely answers in each neighbourhood. More often than not, these are the answers actually given by the parent who fills out the census form. This is most often the case where most young people live with their parents, as indicated by the map of tenure just discussed. Nevertheless, the map of ethnic identity most likely captures the broad groups most young adults would use. Note that 'Other White' is a mix of those, mostly from Europe or North America, who do not feel themselves to be 'White British' and those born in Britain, with ethnic origin from Britain, but who dislike the implication of the label. Note also that this label was not used in Scotland (where

'Other White British' was used) and that a label of 'White Welsh' was not offered. In Scotland, classifications of ethnicity were only produced for zones meeting an ethnic diversity threshold of 50 White *and* 50 non-White residents.

Partly off-setting their ethnic anonymity, the Scots were offered a somewhat more imaginative set of religions to identify with than those of us living south of the border could align to (should we wish to: the question was thankfully optional). The same caveats apply over who fills the form in and what the labels chosen actually mean, but should you be interested in trying to guess correctly most of the time to what religion young people subscribe, that is shown on the map left. The picture in Scotland gives at least a clue as to how the picture in England and Wales might have looked more interesting had the 'Christian, I suppose' option not been the only one given for what, after all, includes the church imposed on these people by the state. Where young adults outside of Scotland have said they are Muslim, Jewish, Hindu or Sikh, or do not wish to state their religion, or have none, it is likely that they (or their form-filling parent) have thought a little more carefully over the answer given.

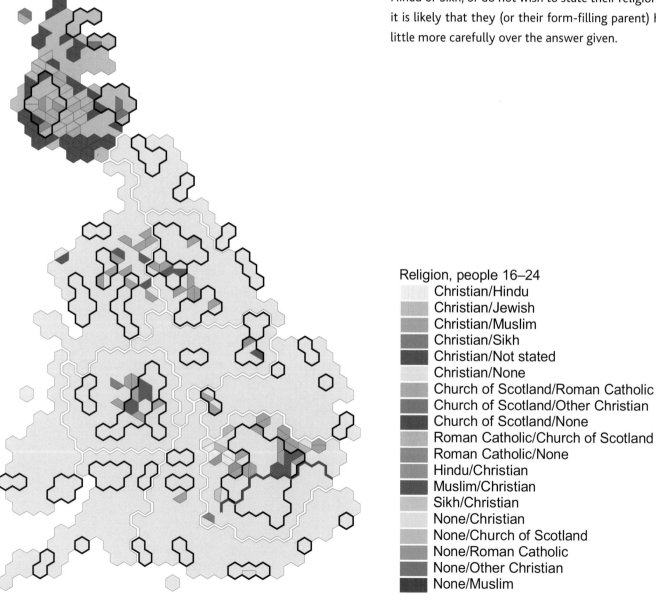

Religion, people 16–24
- Christian/Hindu
- Christian/Jewish
- Christian/Muslim
- Christian/Sikh
- Christian/Not stated
- Christian/None
- Church of Scotland/Roman Catholic
- Church of Scotland/Other Christian
- Church of Scotland/None
- Roman Catholic/Church of Scotland
- Roman Catholic/None
- Hindu/Christian
- Muslim/Christian
- Sikh/Christian
- None/Christian
- None/Church of Scotland
- None/Roman Catholic
- None/Other Christian
- None/Muslim

4.12 Where do you come from and what do you believe in young adulthood?

Figure 4.12

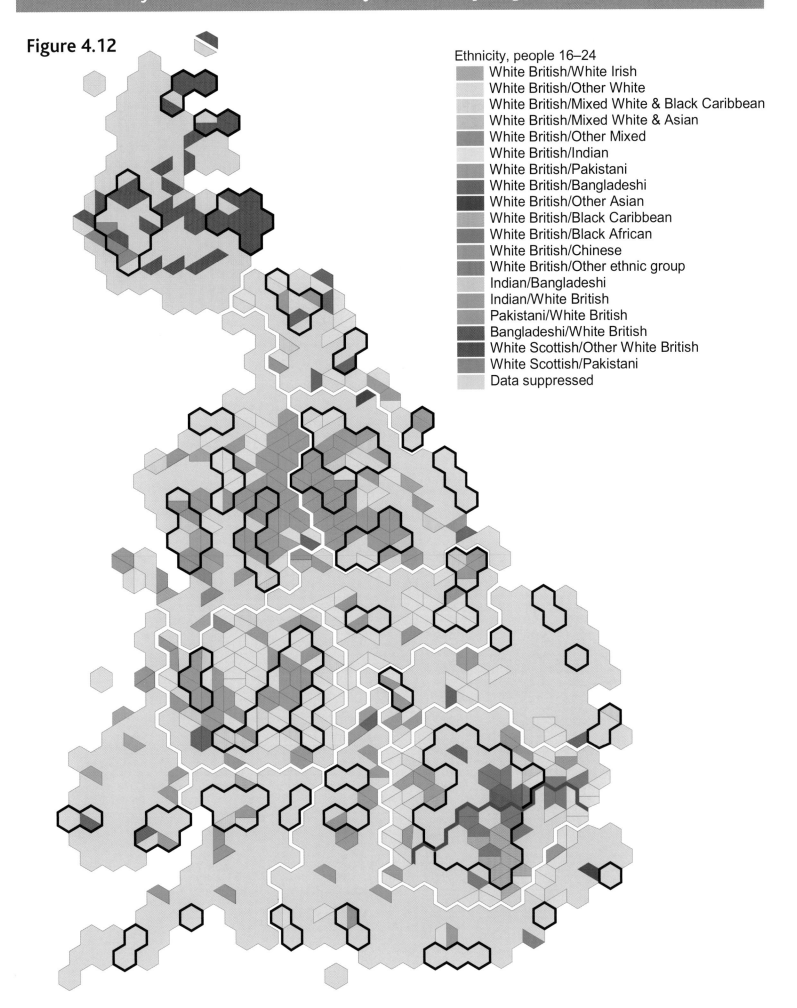

Ethnicity, people 16–24
- White British/White Irish
- White British/Other White
- White British/Mixed White & Black Caribbean
- White British/Mixed White & Asian
- White British/Other Mixed
- White British/Indian
- White British/Pakistani
- White British/Bangladeshi
- White British/Other Asian
- White British/Black Caribbean
- White British/Black African
- White British/Chinese
- White British/Other ethnic group
- Indian/Bangladeshi
- Indian/White British
- Pakistani/White British
- Bangladeshi/White British
- White Scottish/Other White British
- White Scottish/Pakistani
- Data suppressed

4.13 Where do you work and what do you do there in young adulthood?

We know quite a lot about how young adults live together or separately, about their educational achievements or 'lacunae', their access to possessions (cars) and shelter (homes) and even how those who work travel to work, but what is done when they get there? The primary and secondary activities of the workplaces of employed young people are shown in Figure 4.13 opposite. These are the industries that they work in. Retail dominates. In most places most of those who work are spending more time in shops and other retail outlets than in any other industry. Most people who get to say 'and would you like to go large with that?' are aged 16-24. There are places that are exceptions, but they are rare. Moral: don't joke about working in fast food outlets to the under-25s.

However, *where* people work does not necessarily define *what* they do in the workplace – supermarkets have managers as well as shelf-stackers. So what is actually occupying the time of these industrious young people? What are they actually being paid to do? What is their occupation? Well, at the broadest level of categorisation in most places for most young people they either work in sales or customer services, or at an activity deemed to be so elementary that it is labelled 'elementary'. Where this is and is not the case is shown in the map below left.

Only in one quarter of Oxford are a majority of young people in work 'professionals' (and there most young people are students so the majority does not include very many). Only in central London and a few other often similarly expensive locations can the largest group of young people expect to be labelled 'associate professionals'. Only in the remotest of places are most in a skilled trade. And study the map carefully before making any comments concerning secretaries when in Essex.

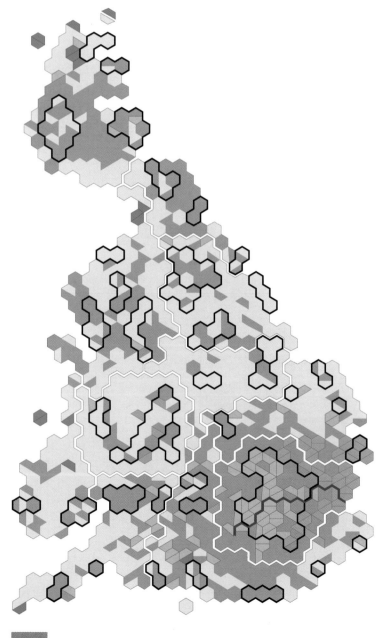

Occupation, people 16–24
- 2. Professional
- 3. Assoc Professional & Tech
- 4. Admin & Secretarial
- 5. Skilled Trades
- 7. Sales & Customer Service
- 9. Elementary

4.13 Where do you work and what do you do there in young adulthood?

Figure 4.13

Industry, people 16–24
- Education/Wholesale & Retail, Vehicle Repair
- Hotels & Restaurants/Wholesale & Retail, Vehicle Repair
- Manufacturing/Wholesale & Retail, Vehicle Repair
- Public Admin & Defence, Social Security/Wholesale & Retail, Vehicle Repair
- Real Estate, Renting & Business/Wholesale & Retail, Vehicle Repair
- Other/Wholesale & Retail, Vehicle Repair
- Wholesale & Retail, Vehicle Repair/Manufacturing
- Wholesale & Retail, Vehicle Repair/Transport, Storage & Comms
- Wholesale & Retail, Vehicle Repair/Construction
- Wholesale & Retail, Vehicle Repair/Agriculture
- Wholesale & Retail, Vehicle Repair/Real Estate, Renting & Business
- Wholesale & Retail, Vehicle Repair/Financial
- Wholesale & Retail, Vehicle Repair/Public Admin & Defence, Social Security
- Wholesale & Retail, Vehicle Repair/Hotels & Restaurants
- Wholesale & Retail, Vehicle Repair/Health & Social Work
- Wholesale & Retail, Vehicle Repair/Other

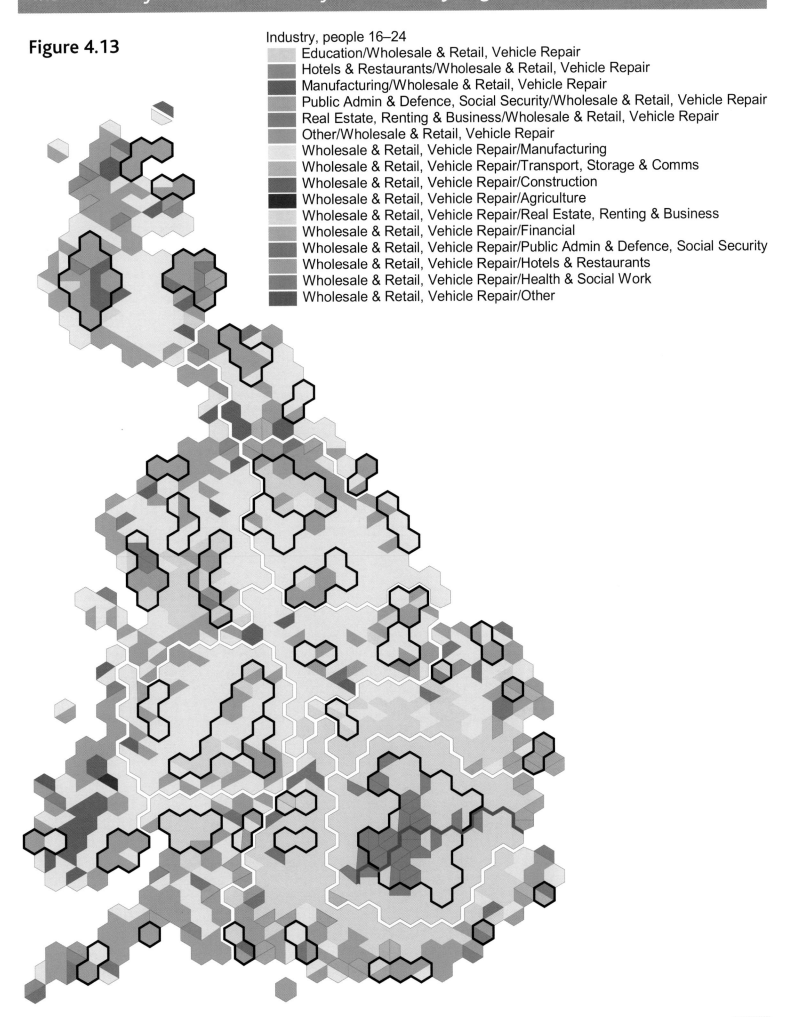

4.14 So what do you really do in young adulthood?

Saying you work 'in sales' does not give that much away. However, if you have an idea of what the second most common occupation of young people is, in an area where most work in sales, it might give you more of a clue as to the status of the former group.

In Figure 4.14, the most and second most common occupational groups are shown for young people in work in each neighbourhood. The pattern becomes a great deal more interesting as, at these ages by area, one occupational group blends geographically into another. Around the areas where the majority are most likely to be labelled 'associate professional' lies a band of areas where this is most likely to be the second most common group and 'sales' the most common; around them is found a band further from areas most expensive to live in where 'elementary' occupations take over as the most common largest minority occupation. Then 'elementary' takes over and 'sales' are in the minority until further out where 'skilled trades' emerge in many places as the second most likely job title. Just which jobs are assigned these eight labels, and the ninth that features nowhere, is made clearer in the table below.

Title in key	Major group	Sub-major group	Examples
1. Managers & Senior Officials	1. Managers and senior officials	11. Corporate managers	Chief executive, senior civil servant
		12. Managers and proprietors in agriculture and services	Farm manager, hotel manager
2. Professional	2. Professional occupations	21. Science and technology professionals	Physicist, engineer
		22. Health professionals	Doctor, psychologist
		23. Teaching and research professionals	Teacher, researcher
		24. Business and public service professionals	Architect, librarian
3. Assoc Professional & Tech	3. Associate professional and technical occupations	31. Science and technology associate professionals	Lab technician, draughtsperson
		32. Health and social welfare associate professionals	Nurse, dental technician
		33. Protective service occupations	Police sergeant, prison officer
		34. Culture, media and sports occupations	Journalist, football player
		35. Business and public service associate professionals	Train driver, sales representative
4. Admin & Secretarial	4. Administrative and secretarial occupations	41. Administrative occupations	Book-keeper, telephonist
		42. Secretarial and related occupations	Secretary, typist
5. Skilled Trades	5. Skilled trades occupations	51. Skilled agricultural trades	Farmer, fishing trades
		52. Skilled metal and electrical trades	Riveter, motor mechanic
		53. Skilled construction and building trades	Plumber, plasterer
		54. Textiles, printing and other skilled trades	Printer, butcher
6. Personal Service	6. Personal service occupations	61. Caring personal service occupations	Care assistant, childminder
		62. Leisure and other personal service occupations	Travel agent, hairdresser
7. Sales & Customer Service	7. Sales and customer service occupations	71. Sales occupations	Sales assistant, debt collector
		72. Customer service occupations	Call centre operator
8. Operatives	8. Process, plant and machine operatives	81. Process, plant and machine operatives	Sewing machinist, scaffolder
		82. Transport and mobile machine drivers and operatives	Bus driver, crane driver
9. Elementary	9. Elementary occupations	91. Elementary trades, plant and storage-related occupations	Labourer, packer
		92. Elementary administration and service occupations	Security guard, waiter

4.14 So what do you really do in young adulthood?

Figure 4.14

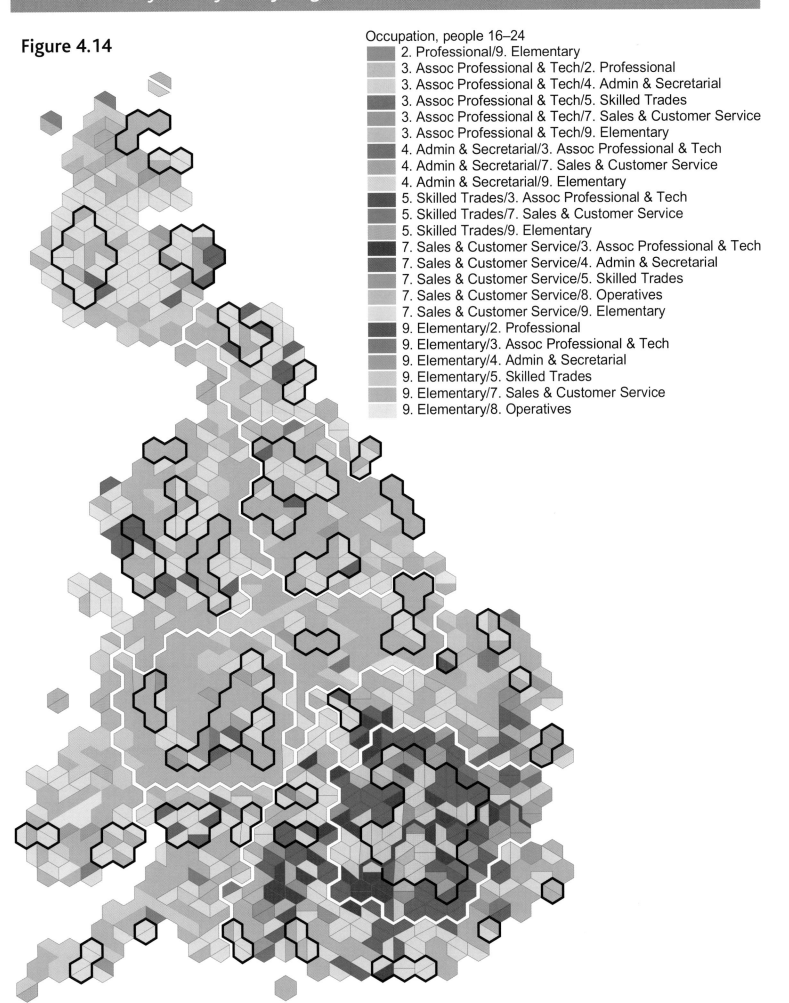

Occupation, people 16–24
2. Professional/9. Elementary
3. Assoc Professional & Tech/2. Professional
3. Assoc Professional & Tech/4. Admin & Secretarial
3. Assoc Professional & Tech/5. Skilled Trades
3. Assoc Professional & Tech/7. Sales & Customer Service
3. Assoc Professional & Tech/9. Elementary
4. Admin & Secretarial/3. Assoc Professional & Tech
4. Admin & Secretarial/7. Sales & Customer Service
4. Admin & Secretarial/9. Elementary
5. Skilled Trades/3. Assoc Professional & Tech
5. Skilled Trades/7. Sales & Customer Service
5. Skilled Trades/9. Elementary
7. Sales & Customer Service/3. Assoc Professional & Tech
7. Sales & Customer Service/4. Admin & Secretarial
7. Sales & Customer Service/5. Skilled Trades
7. Sales & Customer Service/8. Operatives
7. Sales & Customer Service/9. Elementary
9. Elementary/2. Professional
9. Elementary/3. Assoc Professional & Tech
9. Elementary/4. Admin & Secretarial
9. Elementary/5. Skilled Trades
9. Elementary/7. Sales & Customer Service
9. Elementary/8. Operatives

4.15 So, are you a posh young adult?

Well, that is a slightly different question to what your job title is. Up until the age of 15 social class title was determined by the status of 'Household Reference Person' (usually 'dad'). But from 16 onwards you can have your own. If you have never had a job, it will be 'never worked' but if you have a job, or have had any job in recent years, your class label will be based mainly on that, and also on whether you manage other people, the degree of autonomy you have to do your work and so on. We gave a few examples of who is allocated to each (new) socioeconomic classification earlier when plotting the maps for children by class. The map below highlights how it is 'semi-routine' classes that young people are most likely to be allocated to across most of the country, with a smattering of areas where 'routine work' or 'no work' dominates (both mostly in the north).

Almost all the neighbourhoods where young adults are mostly likely to be in 'intermediate' or 'lower managerial' or 'associate professional' work are in the South East. Nowhere are a majority 'higher managers' or 'professionals' by the National Statistics Socioeconomic Classification (NS-SeC) of their social and economic position.

Figure 4.15 opposite also shows the second most common class of young adults. When the second largest group is considered, it becomes apparent that there are a handful of places where this consists of higher managers and professionals. In every case for that handful the largest group is the next one down.

The highest group never mixes so obviously with any other class in a pattern that became familiar when we considered children but which we perhaps would not have expected for this so geographically mobile an age group. Also for this group, given that it is both the most and least affluent who most probably have never worked, it is those in routine occupations who are at the bottom end of this class system. There is just one neighbourhood where they are in the majority and 'lower managers' are the next largest group: Knutsford.

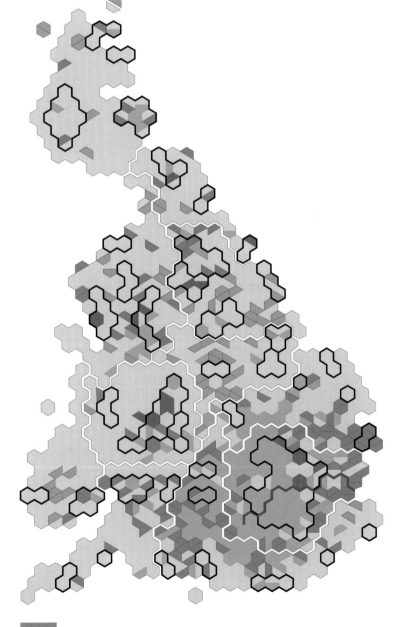

NS-SeC, people 16–24
2. Lower managers
3. Intermediate
6. Semi-routine
7. Routine
8. Never worked

4.15 So, are you a posh young adult?

Figure 4.15

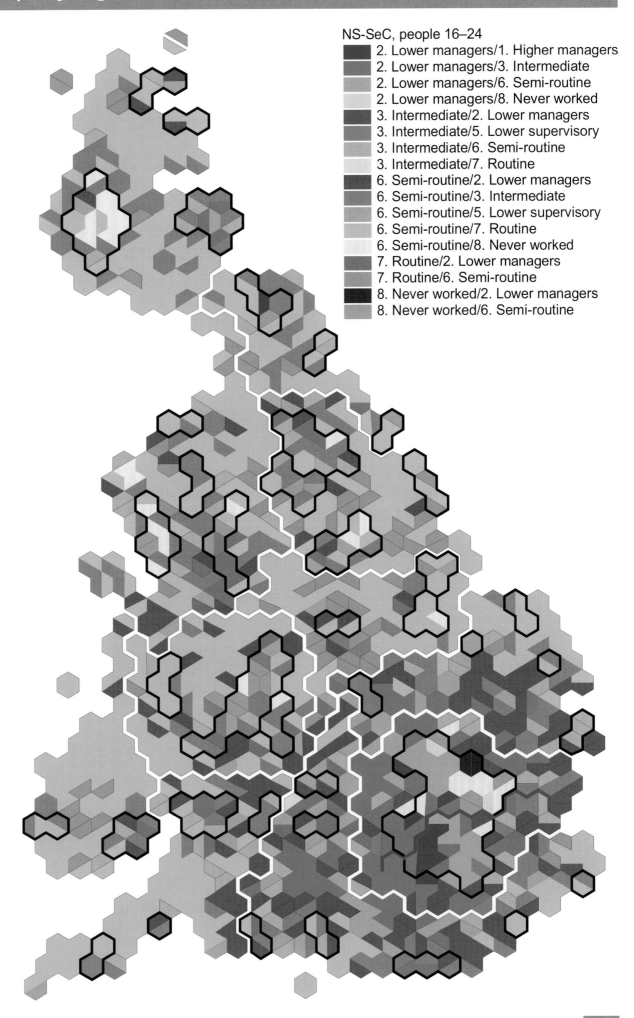

NS-SeC, people 16–24
- 2. Lower managers/1. Higher managers
- 2. Lower managers/3. Intermediate
- 2. Lower managers/6. Semi-routine
- 2. Lower managers/8. Never worked
- 3. Intermediate/2. Lower managers
- 3. Intermediate/5. Lower supervisory
- 3. Intermediate/6. Semi-routine
- 3. Intermediate/7. Routine
- 6. Semi-routine/2. Lower managers
- 6. Semi-routine/3. Intermediate
- 6. Semi-routine/5. Lower supervisory
- 6. Semi-routine/7. Routine
- 6. Semi-routine/8. Never worked
- 7. Routine/2. Lower managers
- 7. Routine/6. Semi-routine
- 8. Never worked/2. Lower managers
- 8. Never worked/6. Semi-routine

4.16 How about if we were to look at your class the way they used to for young adults?

There is much more to class than job title, responsibilities and degree of autonomy. Almost a century before the (new) socioeconomic classification was introduced we had an old one that slowly transformed into the marketing/political social classes known best as A, B, C1, C2, D and E (or in social epidemiology and human geography as I, II, IIINM, IIIM, IV and V). Again we have provided a table showing the social grades together with examples of occupations that are assigned to each grade. The map below shows which social grade (of the 'Household Reference Person') is most common at these ages; the pairing of most common and next most common is shown opposite in Figure 4.16. Note that grades A and B were combined in the source data because A is so rare.

There is a great deal to read from these maps, but just note one other thing: by this old system of classification none of those who actually mix in Knutsford gets their hands (or white collars) very dirty. Areas labelled 'AB' only ever mix with the nearest they have to (C1). How can Knutsford appear mixed by NS-SeC yet affluent by the social grade of the Household Reference Person? Well, it is not that easy an area to stereotype. More importantly, the class an area or person is allocated depends as much on who is designing the classification system as on the people being classified. It is only when areas and people are repeatedly assigned to the same groups under different criteria that you can have some certainty as to their nature.

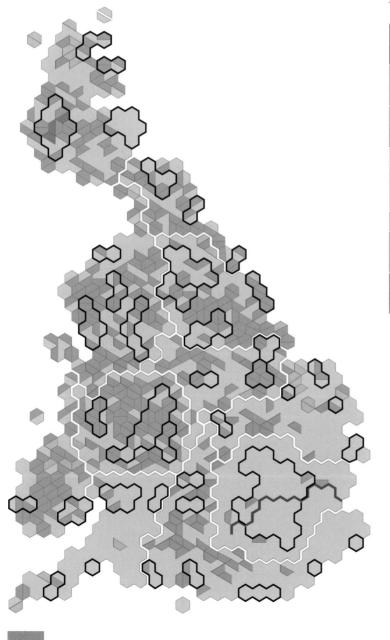

Social grade and example occupations

Social grade	Description	Examples
A	Higher managerial/ administrative/professional	Doctor, accountant
B	Intermediate managerial/ administrative/professional	Teacher, journalist
C1	Supervisory, clerical, junior managerial/administrative/ professional	Clerk, cashier
C2	Skilled manual workers	Carpenter, bus driver
D	Semi-skilled and unskilled manual workers	Machine operator, shop assistant
E	On state benefit, unemployed, lowest grade workers	Labourer, porter

Social grade, people 16–24
AB
C1
C2
D
E

4.16 How about if we were to look at your class the way they used to for young adults?

Figure 4.16

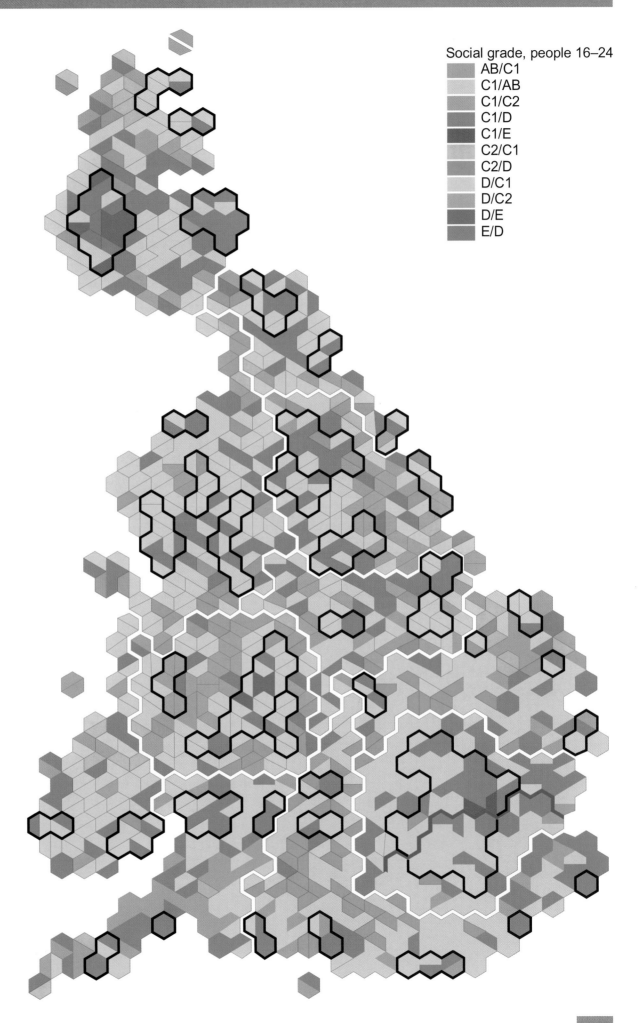

Social grade, people 16–24
- AB/C1
- C1/AB
- C1/C2
- C1/D
- C1/E
- C2/C1
- C2/D
- D/C1
- D/C2
- D/E
- E/D

4.17 So, is there anyone back at your place? Caring by, and health of young adults

Remember that some hundred thousand children provide unpaid care for ill or disabled parents? More than twice as many adults aged 18-24 do the same, again almost all for their parents (although some now for children who need special care). That is nearly 5% of this age group. For those ill adults there is someone back at their place to look after them, in 26,000 cases working unpaid for over 50 hours a week. Precisely where is shown in the map below. Around much of the Home Counties it is fairly safe to assume that most young adults you meet are uncommitted to an ill parent, but the proportion rises to just over a tenth in the worst-off neighbourhoods, where older adults are most often ill.

Not only are significant numbers of young adults caring for people who are ill, but more are themselves not in good health and/or are limited in what they can physically or mentally do, in the years labelled as being the prime of their lives.

The patterning of illness between the ages of 16 and 24 is shown opposite (Figure 4.17). Other than using your eyes, all you need to know to interpret this map is that nearly 6% of young people suffer from a limiting long-term illness (LLTI) or disability (one third of a million). And a million describe their health as either 'fair' or 'poor', rather than as 'good'.

In some places nearly as many young adults are providing some unpaid care for infirm parents or other older adults as are caring for children. Often these are the same carers. Also 28% who are caring at these ages are in 'poor' or only 'fair' health themselves. That, however, is far fewer than the proportions of carers at old ages who are not in good health (see page 244).

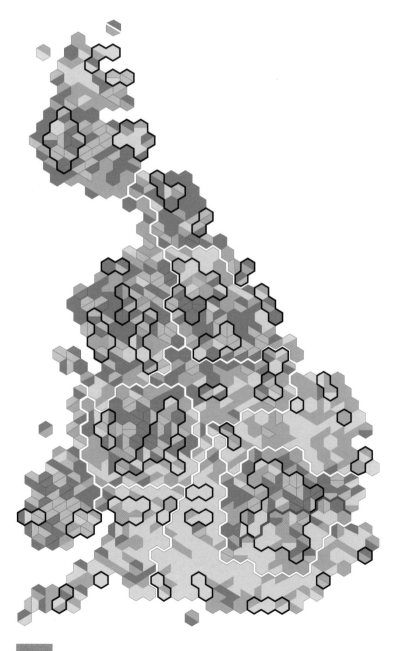

People 18–24 providing care (%)
- 1.8 – 3.9
- 4.0 – 4.9
- 5.0 – 5.9
- 6.0 – 7.4
- 7.5 – 10.6

4.17 So, is there anyone back at your place? Caring by, and health of young adults

Figure 4.17

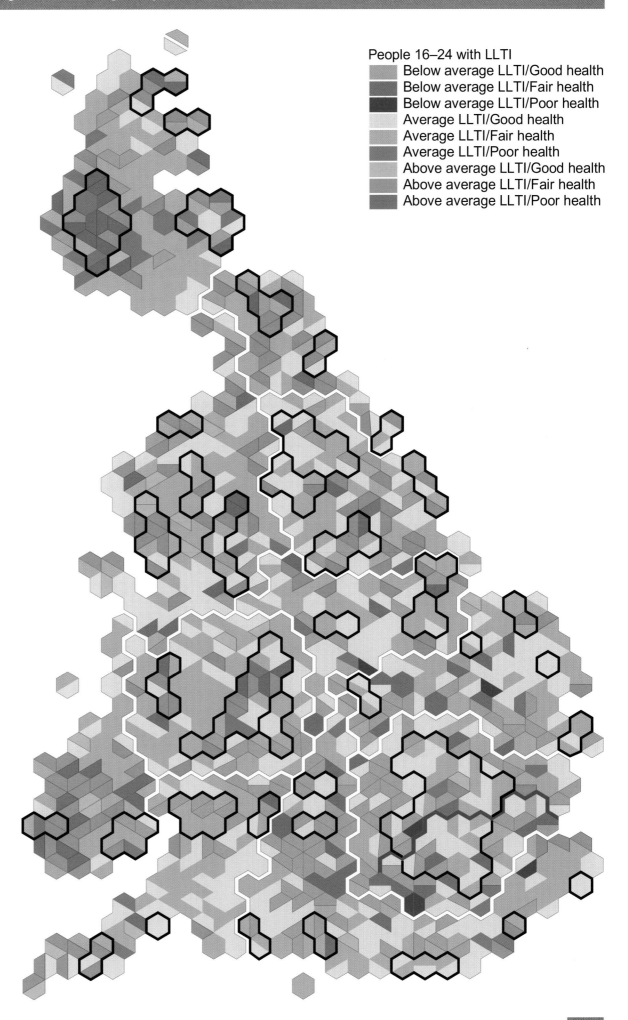

People 16–24 with LLTI
- Below average LLTI/Good health
- Below average LLTI/Fair health
- Below average LLTI/Poor health
- Average LLTI/Good health
- Average LLTI/Fair health
- Average LLTI/Poor health
- Above average LLTI/Good health
- Above average LLTI/Fair health
- Above average LLTI/Poor health

4.18 Conclusion: the years in between

The years in between the end of formal schooling and the often delayed beginnings of full-time working and family life are, for almost all, the years of greatest change. Before school, social environments are largely confined to the home and other very controlled environments. Different infants begin very different lives depending on where they were born, but those differences are almost all encompassed by the geographical influences on the circumstances of their families.

During the schooling years, the boundaries widen and the neighbourhood children are growing up in matters more. Many parents move to 'improve' their neighbourhood. Many who cannot afford to move, lament. Many who can afford a great deal also lament, especially those living around London. Their children, however, tend not to lament or smugly celebrate their advantageous positions, as they still have narrow horizons to compare themselves across. However, once the years in between childhood and midlife begin it becomes evident that the geographical world is changing, even for those who stay in their original family home in their original neighbourhood and even those who remain single and do not stray far for all nine years should begin to notice who near them does not do that and who else arrives (and from where, to get what, and with whom).

The years in between are the years in which people begin to make places by themselves rather than following the choices and constraints of their parents.

Short of showing you with whom each is likely to mix we cannot say much more about the subject of the title of this stage of life. The product of love and failed love is shown in the fall-out of marriages and separations, is consummated through cohabitation, or sustained despite living apart. While all this is going on we have tried to ask a series of questions about the mosaic of the lives of young people in Britain: what most are doing where, how they are being supported, rewarded with qualifications and places at college (especially at particular colleges), or punished and sustained with repetitive work and low incomes or benefits. We have tried to show how an innocuous series of simple questions can each be answered collectively to produce the detailed collective replies of a young nation as to how old they are, the cars they have, the homes they live in, their origins and beliefs, work, status, title and class, and whether they, or those with whom they live and care for, are well. Mostly rarely, we have shown those who have already loved and lost loved ones to death. Young widowhood is an experience most common in this country, the geography suggests, for those seeking asylum here.

We have tried to show just how strongly life chances are influenced by geographic origins and what, in turn, helps determine those origins. How going to university, and to which university, is so spatially predictable. We have tried to show the extent to which mixing may appear to happen in a few places but which on closer inspection is usually found to be less real. And we have tried to show how the divergent lives and geographies of young people set them up for living very different futures in the years after this in-between stage.

5 Then, a soldier: ages 25-39

... then, a soldier,
Full of strange oaths, and bearded like the pard,
Jealous in honour, sudden and quick in quarrel,
Seeking the bubble reputation
Even in the cannon's mouth;

5.1 Introduction

Below is the extremely distinctive geography of those in the middle (fourth) stage of life: the mid-years of 25-39 that can be just as clustered into particular enclaves of London as are their younger counterparts into university student lands as shown on page 88.

As you read on try to remember that there are differing numbers of people in their midlife in each place, although in most places between one and two fifths of the population are aged between 25 and 39. In the pages that follow we show what is typical and the rates for people of these ages, but these refer to far more people within London than almost anywhere else and only to a small minority of the population who spend these years of life in more coastal and rural environments.

If childhood and infanthood are the years before, and young adulthood the years in between, by ages 25-39 you have truly arrived. Welcome to the world. You are your own person and your life is soon half over.

We call these years the midlife. Most people become parents at these ages; more and more do not. Very few now live with or look after elderly relatives in their own home, but many are carers of others outside of their home. And these are also the first years in which age begins in earnest to catch up with you. In some places it catches up far faster than others. More than one in eight people in midlife in Glasgow, and only in parts of Glasgow, have a health status usually associated with old age. This is so stark that we highlight it first, in Figure 5.1 opposite, as it needs to be borne in mind throughout the pages that follow, and it also lays some foundations for what we later see in the next stage of life. Given the last maps shown in the previous life stage, it should perhaps not come as too much of a surprise to see the pattern in Figure 5.1, but note how the population continues to shift around to make patterns that were less stark in childhood and younger adulthood more solid now.

Below, is the health status of those in midlife that is most often reported by those suffering from a limiting long-term illness (LLTI) or disability. Note how in a very large minority of areas the majority say their health is fair. That large minority is where the fields of affluence are most fully occupied. There are even a scattering of very prosperous enclaves where the majority of those disabled say that they are enjoying largely good health.

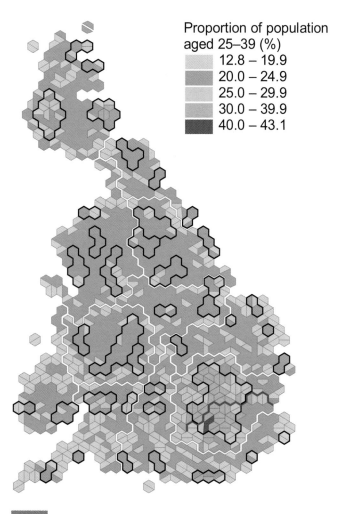

Proportion of population aged 25–39 (%)
- 12.8 – 19.9
- 20.0 – 24.9
- 25.0 – 29.9
- 30.0 – 39.9
- 40.0 – 43.1

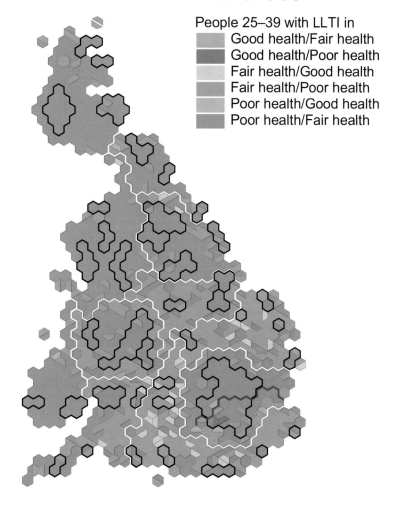

People 25–39 with LLTI in
- Good health/Fair health
- Good health/Poor health
- Fair health/Good health
- Fair health/Poor health
- Poor health/Good health
- Poor health/Fair health

5.1   Introduction

Figure 5.1

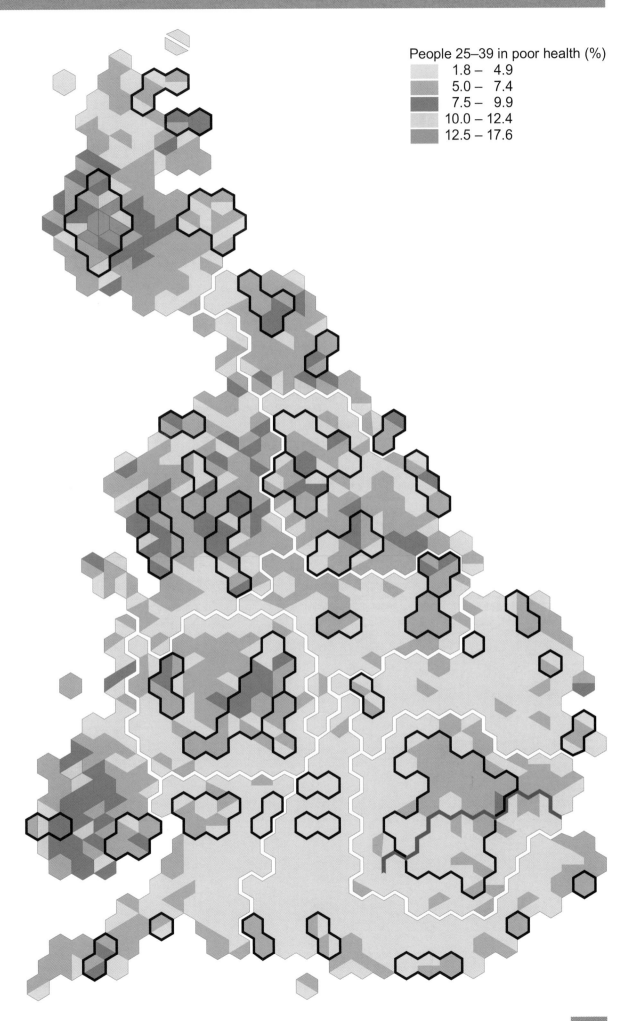

People 25–39 in poor health (%)
- 1.8 –   4.9
- 5.0 –   7.4
- 7.5 –   9.9
- 10.0 – 12.4
- 12.5 – 17.6

5.2 Accounting for the sexes: missing men in midlife

By the turn of the millennium, there were almost a quarter of a million more women of these ages, as far as could be counted, than men living in Britain. Many times more men die in these years than do women, but the numbers of deaths are all still far too low to account for all but a tiny fraction of this difference. Perhaps the men were hiding? Similar discrepancies were found at younger ages and had been found a decade earlier. Many more men than women may not want to be counted, may be hard to count, may have no fixed address, and may be less well linked to children and hence more mobile. This all makes them more easily missed. Thus many people, especially men of these ages and younger, were 'made up' and subsequently added to the official estimates. However, the original census estimates had already had hundreds of thousands of men imputed. It is possible that the authorities were over-estimating men's ability to evade enumeration, especially in the centre of London. The other possibility, and the one we highlight here, is that the men really were missing. More of them had, net, gone abroad than had women. Of those who had travelled abroad, more women had returned. Of those that were coming from abroad, more women were arriving than before. Britain imports a largely skilled workforce and women, worldwide, now make up the majority of those with degree-level skills.

There are at least three reasons to believe that it is possible that, for the first time in many decades, there are more midlife women than men in Britain. First, it has happened before. The event is not unprecedented. More men than women left these shores when Britain was a land of mass net emigration in the decades around 1880. A few left temporarily to help run the Empire, but many more simply left for good as there was more demand for them abroad than here. Second, if the men are here,

they are doing an excellent job of hiding. They are hiding not just from the census authorities but from those who count electors, register NHS patients and count dead bodies. Third, look at the places from where they appear to have left in greatest numbers. Could it be from where the work for men went first? There are 10 more women than men of these ages in every hundred in the Glasgow estates of Blairdardie, Castlemilk, Easterhouse, Milton, Nitshill and Parkhead, and in Birkenhead North-East. The men are missing in midlife from where you would expect them to have left most frequently had they entered the workforce between 1977 and 1992, as this cohort would mostly do. More could have left as older teenagers, or perhaps left after their first marriage ended, or when made redundant from their job. And of course, relatively higher numbers have died young there than almost anywhere else in Britain.

We will never know what happened to all the men who left and have not died. We just know that for men, in aggregate, there was less to come back for in the places shown to now contain more midlife women on the map (Figure 5.2). We also suspect that most of the exodus first reported by the millennial census really happened. The men are not in hiding. A final additional reason for suspecting this is that there are areas where there are more midlife men than women. These are found around the outer Home Counties where in general only couples can afford to live. On average the wives or girlfriends of men of these ages will be slightly younger than them. In areas from which such couples tend to leave before the man reaches 40 this will result in a higher proportion of men of ages 25-39 than of women. The census finds men, or successfully imputes them, when they are there.

5.2 Accounting for the sexes: missing men in midlife

Figure 5.2

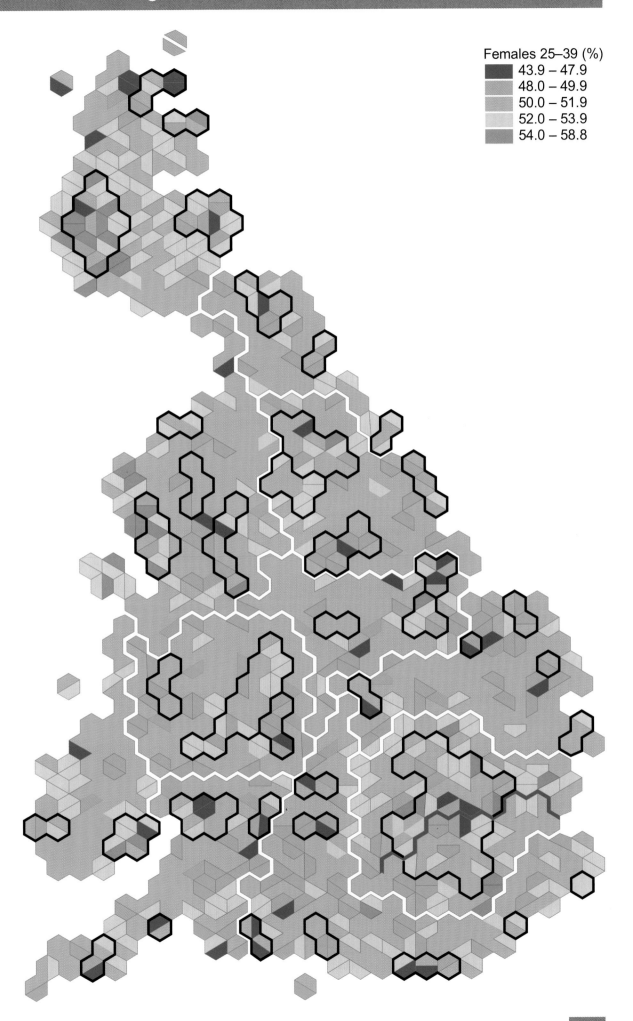

Females 25–39 (%)
- 43.9 – 47.9
- 48.0 – 49.9
- 50.0 – 51.9
- 52.0 – 53.9
- 54.0 – 58.8

5.3 Never married, first marriage and 'smug marrieds' in midlife

The significant absence of men was not the only novelty in these ages recorded by the first census of the millennium. That census was also the first to record a fraction more being single (42.8%) than being together in their first marriage at these ages (42.4%). In deference to the (albeit knife-edge) singleton majority, we show their midlife geography, enlarged, in Figure 5.3 opposite. Of these ages, those who are single and have never been married form the majority of the midlife population across most of our cities. They make up, however, only around a third of people of these ages, where either they cannot afford to be single, or where being single is still not well tolerated, and especially where such geographies of finance and prejudice coincide.

Being single and never married is also more common in places where fewer people are interested in the opposite sex.

In contrast, the geography to where midlife adults are most likely to have multiple cake knives and all the other paraphernalia that is part of the material debris from the modern (first) wedding ceremony, is shown below. In the majority for their age group in only a minority of places, the 'smug marrieds' (as they are sometimes referred to) tend to locate in the more self-satisfied regions of the country, suburbs and enclaves. The 'smug' descriptor thus partly refers to the fact they have got married, but perhaps also a little to where that then got them (or what got them that) or perhaps also, as we see next, to the fact that they are still married in that first marriage.

Increasingly, the map of first marriage is a map of who stays together as much as who marries in the first place.

First marriage, people 25–39 (%)

	15.5 – 29.9
	30.0 – 39.9
	40.0 – 44.9
	45.0 – 49.9
	50.0 – 62.7

5.3 Never married, first marriage and 'smug marrieds' in midlife

Figure 5.3

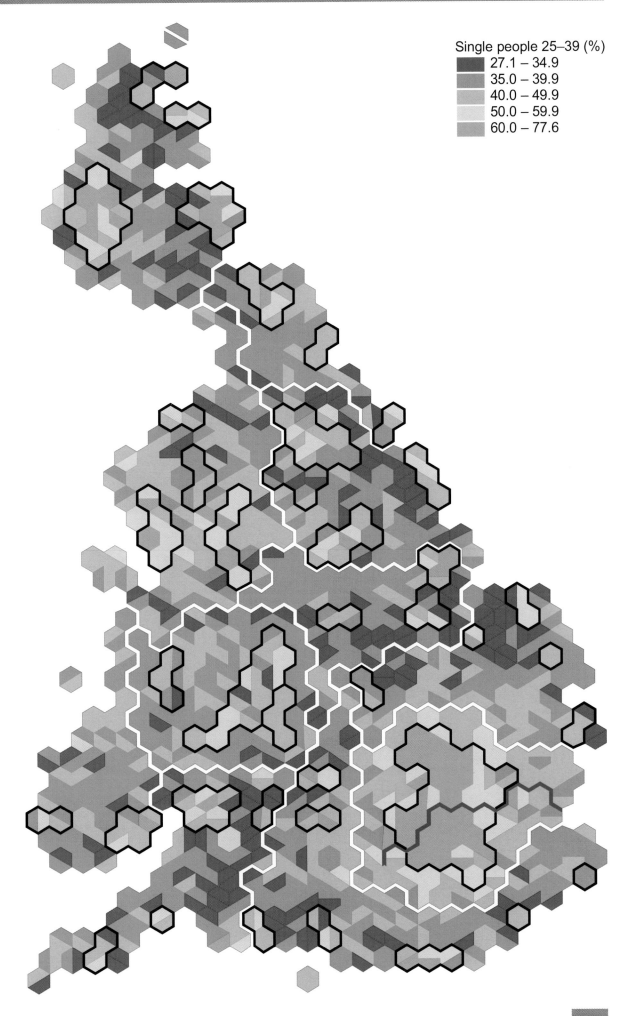

Single people 25–39 (%)
- 27.1 – 34.9
- 35.0 – 39.9
- 40.0 – 49.9
- 50.0 – 59.9
- 60.0 – 77.6

5.4   Remarried, separated or divorced: who already has a story to tell in midlife?

That the smug first marrieds and the singletons are the largest and second largest groups in midlife everywhere is made clear by the map of what is most common where, shown below. Those who are single are in the majority in neighbourhoods where some 7.7 million of those in midlife live, and those in their first marriage where some 4.9 million live. Nowhere is there a haven for the bulk of the rest who do not fall into these two camps: the 1.8 million 'remarried', 'separated' or 'divorced' people aged 25-39. Even when all three groups are combined, they are not even the second largest marital status-defined tribe in a single neighbourhood. Given this, it is not surprising that anyone anywhere of these ages who has a broken marriage behind them may feel a little out of the ordinary.

The coast is clearly something of an attraction to those that have loved once and lost, the five most popular neighbourhoods they relocate to being in Plymouth, Morecambe, Gosport, Lowestoft and Grimsby. Other places with similar military connections and where the living is a little easier on the purse also feature. However, this group includes many who have paired up again and sometimes married again, so their buying power is not necessarily diluted. In fact, compare the image opposite (Figure 5.4) of midlife adults who have had a previous marriage to that of step-children shown earlier on page 63 and the similarities should become apparent. Incidentally, should you wish to know where you are least likely to live should you fall into this group then look within Battersea, Fulham, Oxford West, Putney and Tooting. These are areas to be left well behind if things do not work out the first time.

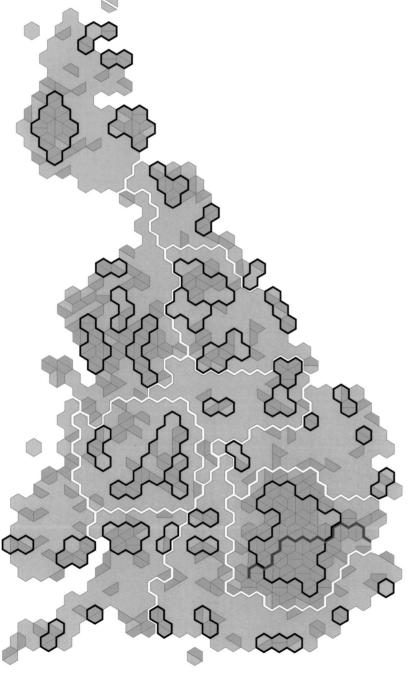

Marital status, people 25–39
First marriage/Single
Single/First marriage

5.4 Remarried, separated or divorced: who already has a story to tell in midlife?

Figure 5.4

Remarried, separated or
divorced people 25–39 (%)
5.2 –   9.9
10.0 – 12.9
13.0 – 15.9
16.0 – 19.9
20.0 – 23.8

5.5   Broken marriages and broken lives: separation and widowhood in midlife

Of every one who has ever been married in each neighbourhood how many in midlife are not now? The proportion ranges from just one in eight to over four in 10. The geographical map of where you need to be most circumspect at midlife dinner parties is shown below and the one that tries to really help you not put your foot in it at the dinner table is shown opposite (Figure 5.5). The map below differs subtly from Figure 5.4, which shows this group as a proportion of all their age group. There are places where marriage at these ages is now relatively rare, but where it does occur separation is unusually likely; parts of Glasgow now fit that description most closely. Conversely, across most of Greater London and the counties that border the capital the minority who do marry tend to stay married if they stay living there. The same is true in much of Birmingham and the West Midlands and in the pricier parts of the north and of Wales.

Widowhood in midlife is a very different kind of broken marriage, but also sadly still highlighting much of Glasgow as being a city of grossly disproportionate suffering in so many aspects of life and death. Widowhood is the rarest form in which a marriage can be broken for this age group and only occurs, of course, when people are married in the first place. Cohabit and never marry and you will be labelled 'single never married' if your partner dies. Thus Figure 5.5 only records a fraction of the stories of death at these still relatively young ages.

The stories are, however, beginning to show a pattern that is very different from widowhood in young adulthood shown on page 91. Although there is still an echo of the geography of deaths abroad being recognised through the widowed status of some who have sought asylum here, most people widowed at these ages were living with their husband or wife when they died in Britain. Thus this is the beginnings of a map of who is most likely to die young in this country by where they live, and by where their widows and widowers have moved to following their death. Below the age of 40 adults are most likely to die in the poorer estates of cities and so it is around there, and to where those widowed young might go, that rates are highest. And also, perhaps a few particular stories, of the kind where those that worked on a ship, or rig, that was lost at sea, mostly lived in, and were lost from, the same neighbourhood.

Broken marriages, people 25–39 (%)

- 12.5 – 19.9
- 20.0 – 24.9
- 25.0 – 29.9
- 30.0 – 34.9
- 35.0 – 42.7

5.5 Broken marriages and broken lives: separation and widowhood in midlife

Figure 5.5

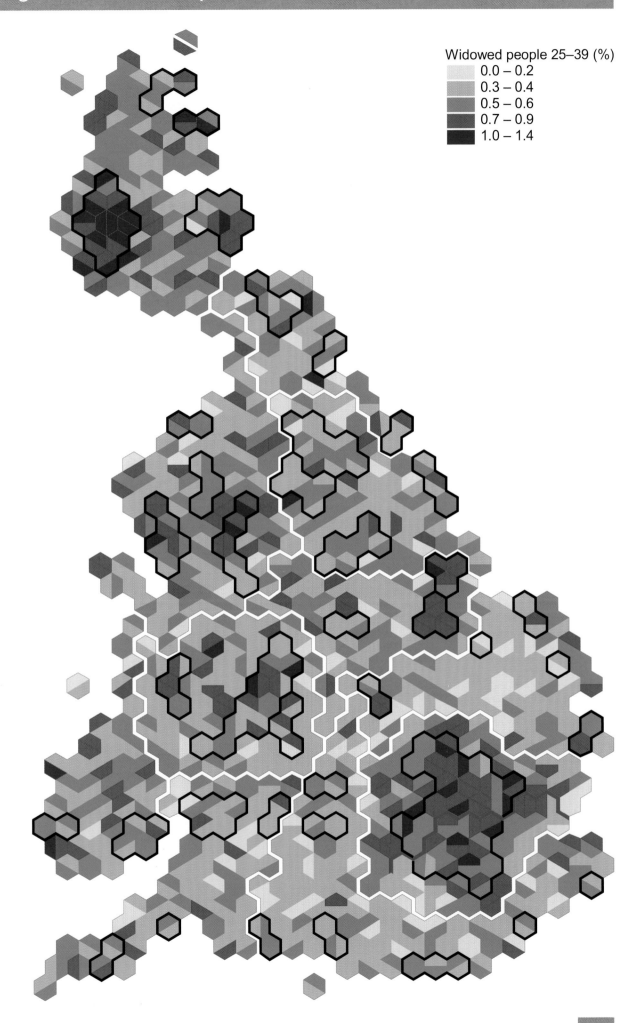

Widowed people 25–39 (%)
- 0.0 – 0.2
- 0.3 – 0.4
- 0.5 – 0.6
- 0.7 – 0.9
- 1.0 – 1.4

5.6 The household you live in (and who else is there) in midlife

For each age group, if you had to ask a single pertinent question, we have suggested what that question could be. For children it was the number of adults in paid employment in the household. How many bring home the bacon? For young adults it was sex. Not so much getting any, as who of which sex was doing what where you lived and how could you end up living with them. For those in midlife the pertinent question is 'Do you have children?'. When counted by whether they are living in a household that contains children, 6.5 million are and 6.0 million aged 25-39 are not. Note, however, that not every parent lives with their children. For every lone parent there has to be another parent, but there will not be quite as many estranged or never known parents as lone parents (you need to think about it for a bit; it all gets very messy very quickly).

In contrast, the map shown opposite (Figure 5.6) of the likelihood of someone in midlife living in a household with children is far from complex. There are some nuances, but, in general, move away from the centres of towns and cities and out of the south, and up to a maximum of two thirds of this age group are found living in households with children. In almost all cases these children are their biological children or their step-children.

In London and a few other parts of the South East those in midlife behave a little more like younger adults in their chances of having had children and how they choose or are able to live together. Conversely, in parts of Yorkshire and Wales especially, away from the bigger cities, the universities and the bright lights, by the age of 25 many have already settled down and the age group as a whole is behaving a little more like those a few years older than them nationally. Where you live is beginning to matter a little more than what your age means for how you live.

As to what kind of a family those in midlife live in, in almost all places the modal type is a married couple (even though almost nowhere are a majority in their first marriage). This is shown in the map left. All that makes the map interesting is a spattering of areas where a narrow majority are lone parents, and the well defined urban–rural division. That division here is between where the second most common family type in midlife consists of cohabitation, and where, if you are not in a married couple, you are most likely to be in lone parenthood. Note the three possibilities that feature nowhere in Britain. Two are accounted for because nowhere are a majority of those in midlife cohabiting. The third is because there is also no area where being in a married couple family is the least likely categorisation.

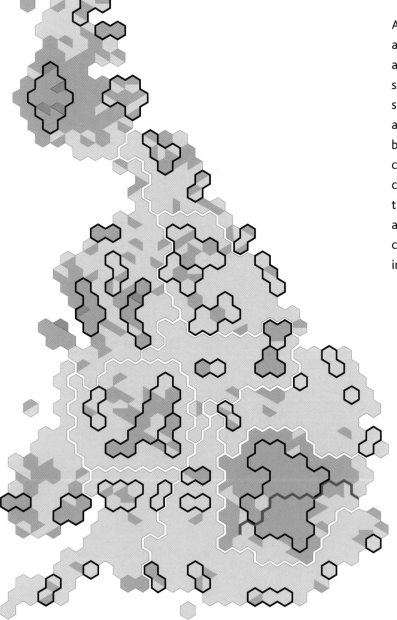

Family type, people 25–39
- Married couple family/Cohabiting couple family
- Married couple family/Lone parent family
- Lone parent family/Married couple family

5.6   The household you live in (and who else is there) in midlife

Figure 5.6

People 25–39 with children (%)
- 13.4 – 29.9
- 30.0 – 39.9
- 40.0 – 49.9
- 50.0 – 59.9
- 60.0 – 66.7

5.7   The family you are part of (and who still is not there) in midlife

Just as we saw for young adults (on page 93), there are still many adults who are married and not separated from their partner in spirit, but are in practice, as shown opposite (Figure 5.7). In much of the capital between a tenth and a quarter of all married midlife adults are not living with their spouse. Nor are they living with anyone else as a couple and nor do they say they are separated or divorced. By implication, then, these people are one half of a married couple, the other half of which may well also be shown elsewhere on the map, or may live abroad. It is even possible that the other half is living as a couple with someone else and does not feature on the map at all, but the person who does has not accepted that they have gone (or at least does not want to do so on a official form). As we have said before, things can begin to get quite tangled after at least a quarter of a century of life has passed. The point to be aware of is that within some places a ring on a finger does not imply a husband or wife always at home.

Although individual life trajectories can easily become complicated, neighbourhoods tend to be less complex. The two maps below show the few places where the majority of midlife people do not live in a couple household (on the left) and the tiny number of places where the majority who do live as a couple are cohabiting, when only couples are being considered (on the right). Thus, in some ways, in most places these are the years in which we begin to conform more and more to a single stereotype: most of us live together. If we do, we tend to be married. Regardless of that, most who live together have children. But only a narrow majority of those in midlife share their home with children.

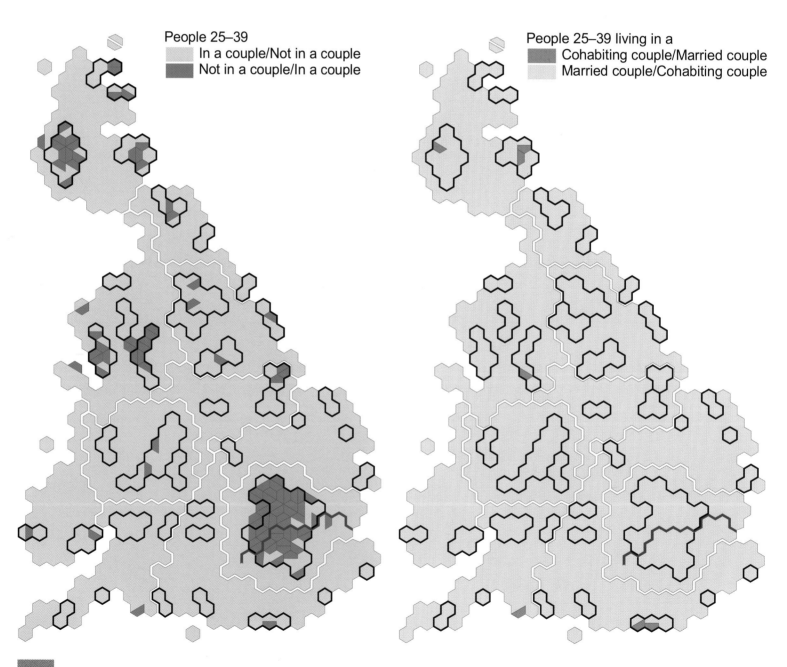

People 25–39
■ In a couple/Not in a couple
■ Not in a couple/In a couple

People 25–39 living in a
■ Cohabiting couple/Married couple
■ Married couple/Cohabiting couple

5.7   The family you are part of (and who still is not there) in midlife

Figure 5.7

(Re)married not living
in a couple 25–39 (%)
- 0.2 – 1.9
- 2.0 – 4.9
- 5.0 – 9.9
- 10.0 – 14.9
- 15.0 – 22.2

5.8   The families that share a neighbourhood: different ways of being midlife

So far, in looking at the mosaics of midlife lives we have not been too concerned with how they mix, save mixing with each other within the home. Here we start to look at neighbourhood mixing by whether the majority of those aged 25-44 (we have had to extend the age range by five years due to data availability) live in a couple or not, have children or not, and, if they have children, the age of the youngest of those children, shown in Figure 5.8 opposite. Are there places where those whose offspring are soon to leave the nest mix with what appear to be more newly established couples, and other areas where families with children live side by side to streets next best typified by the homes of single midlife households? The quick answer is no. And there is no leaving the nest occurring anytime soon anywhere at this stage in life anymore. If a midlife person lives in a household with children, and they ask you to guess the age of the youngest, wherever they live, guess aged under five.

In most cases, the modal group of midlife adults live in a couple and have no children. The second most common have children (or a child), the youngest of whom is aged under five. Sixty one per cent of neighbourhoods, coloured dark blue opposite, are typified by this combination. The most common group of those in midlife live in what might best be summarised as 'middle Britain', the land between the conurbations; a great deal of which, by the way, is in Scotland.

The next most common mix, accounting for a further 19% of neighbourhoods (half the remainder), are areas where the same two groups predominate, simply the other way round. Here couples without children are slightly rarer than the most common incarnation of midlife: living with a young family. We did warn you that things begin to get repetitive at this life stage! There is definitely a pattern to the slightly different locus of this ever so slightly different type of area in the mosaic. Neighbourhoods merge into areas that begin to beg to be stereotyped, but not before their cartographers lose interest in doing so and in further splitting such fine categorisations.

Of the remaining fifth of neighbourhoods, the majority (13% of all nationally) are again of one type: areas where the modal midlife person does not live in a couple nor with children, and the second most common arrangement is to live in a couple but again with no children. Such arrangements are almost always confined to cities. Then, of the remaining twelfth of neighbourhoods, almost all (6% of all nationally) are, in a not so uncanny repetition of the above, simply the inverse again: places where couples are slightly more likely than singles but neither with children. It should come as no surprise that such places are also mostly found in cities, but not so exclusively as before.

To bring this somewhat inevitably turgid story of midlife domestic arrangement to an end, we have to point out that there are two sets of neighbourhoods left on the map: those where couples with children are most common, followed by adults not in a couple with no children and, you've guessed it, their inverse. Although one group contains almost twice as many areas as the other, they are both near to 1% of the total; atypical, but hardly bohemian.

5.8 The families that share a neighbourhood: different ways of being midlife

Figure 5.8

Age of youngest child, people 25–44 (not) in a couple
- Couple, no children/Not couple, no children
- Couple, no children/Couple, youngest child 0–4
- Couple, youngest child 0–4/Couple, no children
- Couple, youngest child 0–4/Not couple, no children
- Not couple, no children/Couple, no children
- Not couple, no children/Couple, youngest child 0–4

5.9 What have you done with your life by midlife?

Now we know a little of how those in midlife live and with whom they live, we turn to what they do. In short, the answer is very much that they do what they are supposed to do. Long gone are they days when they could sit around, laze about and go out every night (or as young adults call it, 'study'). Neither too can they really afford not to work. Given the way that work-related benefits now operate, this is especially true if they have children.

Too young to retire or for many to be sick, too old to drop out or be otherwise engaged, the options of those in midlife are sparse and are taken up in some of the most predictable of ways. It is perhaps in these middle years, halfway through the play, that the player's lines are least original: neither the best nor worst of ages, and not doing far better (nor worse). Conformity is king.

Figure 5.9 opposite shows the activities that consume the time of the majority and the second most common group. Across most of the country most are engaged in paid full-time employment, and if not that, paid part-time employment (often this will be pairs of husbands and wives). The next most common type of neighbourhood substitutes the latter activity by the unpaid caring of children. The remaining three types of area are far rarer still.

Below, in an almost futile search for nuance, the equivalent maps to Figure 5.9 are shown but now for those in paid work (or seeking work) on the left and unpaid activity on the right. These maps show that there is more going on beneath the surface of the map opposite, but not that much more.

Economically inactive people 25–39
- Caring for family/Economically inactive student
- Caring for family/Sick or disabled
- Caring for family/Other
- Sick or disabled/Caring for family
- Economically inactive student/Caring for family
- Economically inactive student/Sick or disabled
- Economically inactive student/Other

Economically active people 25–39
- Full-time employee/Part-time employee
- Full-time employee/Self-employed full-time
- Full-time employee/Unemployed

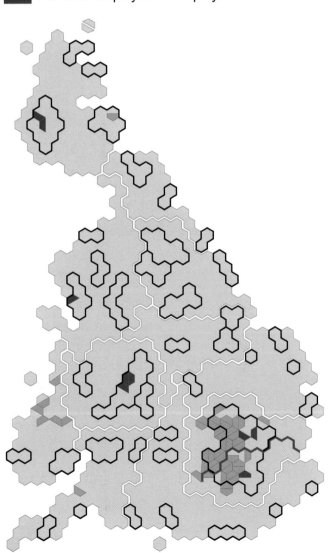

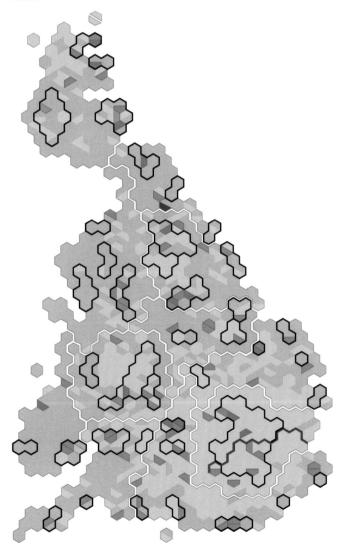

5.9   What have you done with your life by midlife?

Figure 5.9

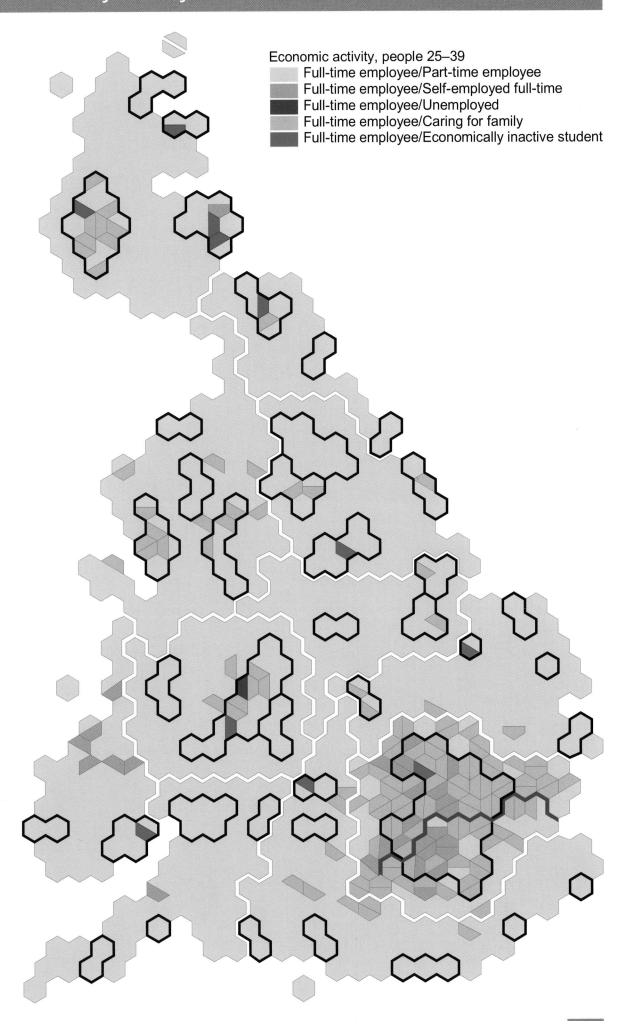

Economic activity, people 25–39
- Full-time employee/Part-time employee
- Full-time employee/Self-employed full-time
- Full-time employee/Unemployed
- Full-time employee/Caring for family
- Full-time employee/Economically inactive student

5.10 Were midlifers doing much too much, much too young?

The map of where those in midlife who are most reliant on benefits live, shown in Figure 5.10 opposite, covers the population above the usual age range of this chapter up to 44. In most areas less than an eighth of the population are in receipt of benefits at these ages. The benefits included here are Bereavement Benefit, Carer's Allowance, Disability Living Allowance, Incapacity Benefit, Income Support, Jobseeker's Allowance, Pension Credit and Widow's Benefit. Nowhere is there a neighbourhood where a majority are in receipt of benefits, but there are a dozen and a half places where over a third are. In general the places with the highest rates are surrounded by those areas with the next lowest and so on and on.

That this map is not simply a reflection of what people were doing when younger is illustrated by the relatively high rate of both claiming and qualifications within London. People almost all claim when they have to and tend to have to live in certain places when they have to claim. The chances of having to claim are strongly linked to where you grew up. In rural areas of near full employment it would be less likely for a person to claim benefits as a young adult and hence unlikely again in midlife. From the movements of the population it would be fair to assume that, if they had claimed benefits as a young adult, they would have been more likely to have left such areas and not to have later returned.

Below we show the qualifications gained (mostly earlier in life) by those aged 25-39: on the right, the proportion holding the highest (degrees etc), and on the left, those holding none. Note that although the two maps are not the mirror image of each other, there is no area where these two groups are the highest and second most numerous in a neighbourhood. Again, nowhere is there true mixing.

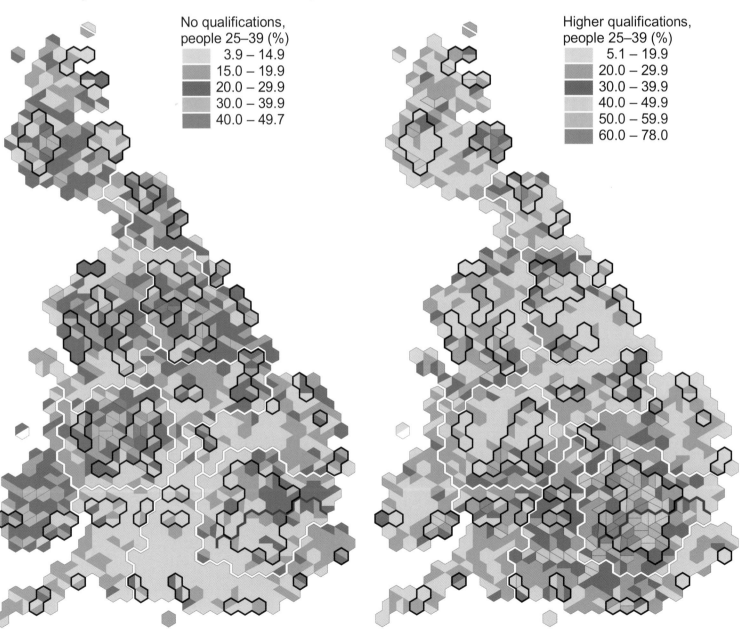

No qualifications, people 25–39 (%)
- 3.9 – 14.9
- 15.0 – 19.9
- 20.0 – 29.9
- 30.0 – 39.9
- 40.0 – 49.7

Higher qualifications, people 25–39 (%)
- 5.1 – 19.9
- 20.0 – 29.9
- 30.0 – 39.9
- 40.0 – 49.9
- 50.0 – 59.9
- 60.0 – 78.0

5.10 Were midlifers doing much too much, much too young?

Figure 5.10

Benefit claimants 25–44 (%)
- 4.0 – 9.9
- 10.0 – 14.9
- 15.0 – 19.9
- 20.0 – 29.9
- 30.0 – 41.3

5.11 Would it be rude to ask how old you are in midlife?

The mosaic of midlife itself is a thing of beauty. Simply by plotting (Figure 5.11 opposite) which single year of this age group is most numerous in each neighbourhood, you begin to see how people are moving around and why the experience of being in midlife is very different in the capital as compared with the coasts. Put most simply, those in midlife are much younger in London. True, towards the leafier parts of cities those in midlife are older. Then they form a kind of green belt, maxing out in their early thirties around the conurbations. As they progressively age (within the midlife age band) they move relentlessly towards the sea, causing all but a few, very select, resorts to be home to the more weather-beaten of this cohort. Thirty-six years before this snapshot was taken (2001) had been a bumper year for babies, but there is little evidence of such temporal concentrations of past events reflecting themselves in spatial concentrations in Figure 5.11. Rather it is the clumping together of people of similar vintage in similar locales that makes some colours stand out more strongly than others, especially towards the latter years of this life stage.

The settling together in midlife becomes even more obvious when modal and second most common age bands are enumerated, as shown below. In only five neighbourhoods where the youngest five years of this cohort are most or second most commonly found, are the oldest five years their partner. In contrast, in over two thirds of neighbourhoods the majority of those in midlife are in their late thirties and the next largest in their early thirties.

The midlife of 'man' is not a set of years that necessarily enjoy each other's company. Rather they are the years in which we begin to separate most clearly and deliberately, when we can choose to. No longer the years in between childhood and adulthood, these are the years where most are literally moving geographically towards (areas of) old age, as they, themselves, age.

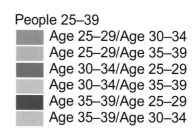

People 25–39

	Age 25–29/Age 30–34
	Age 25–29/Age 35–39
	Age 30–34/Age 25–29
	Age 30–34/Age 35–39
	Age 35–39/Age 25–29
	Age 35–39/Age 30–34

5.11 Would it be rude to ask how old you are in midlife?

Figure 5.11

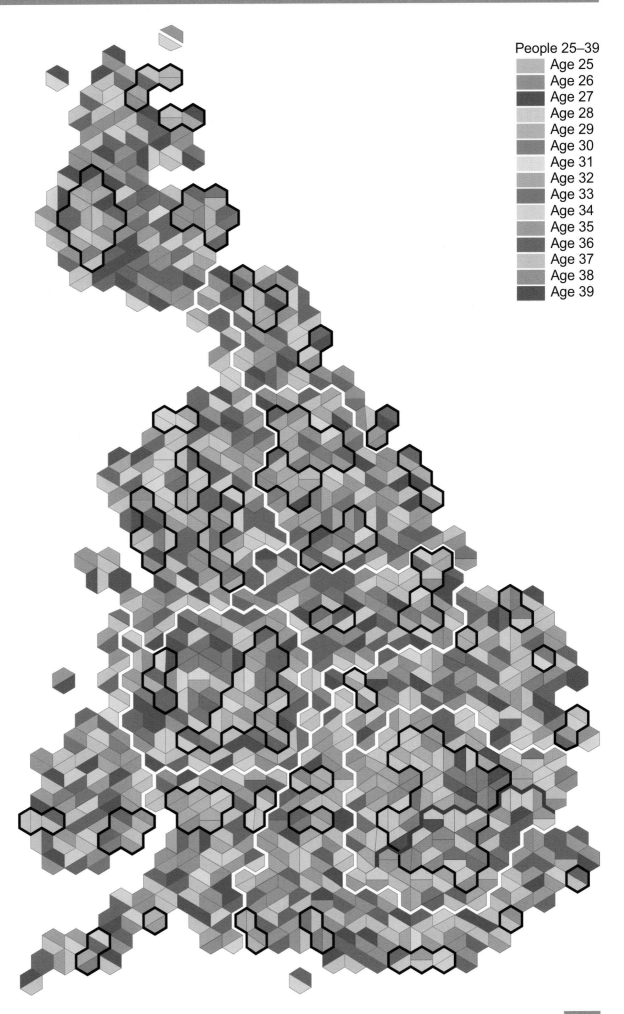

People 25–39
- Age 25
- Age 26
- Age 27
- Age 28
- Age 29
- Age 30
- Age 31
- Age 32
- Age 33
- Age 34
- Age 35
- Age 36
- Age 37
- Age 38
- Age 39

5.12 Do you drive? And other questions often not asked of those in midlife

One reason why those in midlife are able to separate themselves out so carefully geographically is because so many of them can both legally drive and have access to one or two or even three or more cars. Of course, not every one at these ages can drive, and even more do not have access to a car, but the general ubiquity of the automobile in midlife has to be seen to be fully appreciated.

Figure 5.12 shows how the majority and largest minority in midlife travel to work. In 95% of neighbourhoods the majority of those in midlife drive to work. That is worth saying again, but perhaps a little differently: outside of London there are only three neighbourhoods where the majority of the midlife population who work do not use a car. To save you eye strain in looking, two are in the centre of Edinburgh and one in Glasgow. The car has won. We could describe in detail the nuances of how else people travel and how public transport works best in London, but we

would not wish to divert you too much from the most basic and simple fact of midlife automobile hegemony.

Despite the fact that almost everywhere outside of London most people who work commute by car, there are still many neighbourhoods where the majority of people aged 25-39 do not have a car. Outside of London, however, these are largely places where high proportions of those in midlife are not commuting because they are not working.

The map below shows that in most of the south of England a majority of households have access to at least two cars, and the largest minorities within those areas also have a car. In most of the rest of the country the presumption in midlife is that you have access to one car, but if that is not the case you have access to two or more. By midlife we are swamped by cars. Given that, perhaps we should not have been so surprised to see how finely those in midlife are beginning to segregate themselves within themselves by age band.

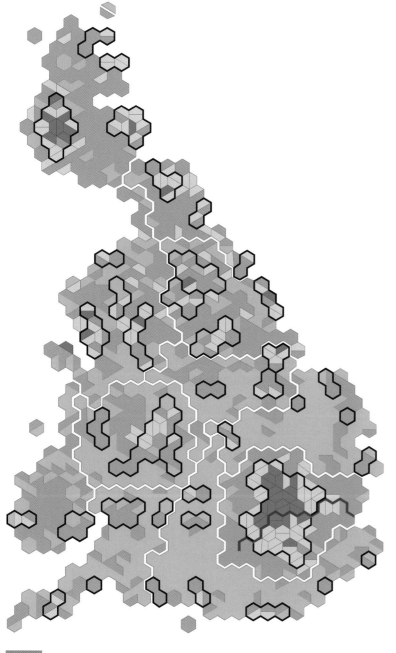

People 25–39 in households with
- No car/1 car
- 1 car/No car
- 1 car/2+ cars
- 2+ cars/1 car

5.12 Do you drive? And other questions often not asked of those in midlife

Figure 5.12

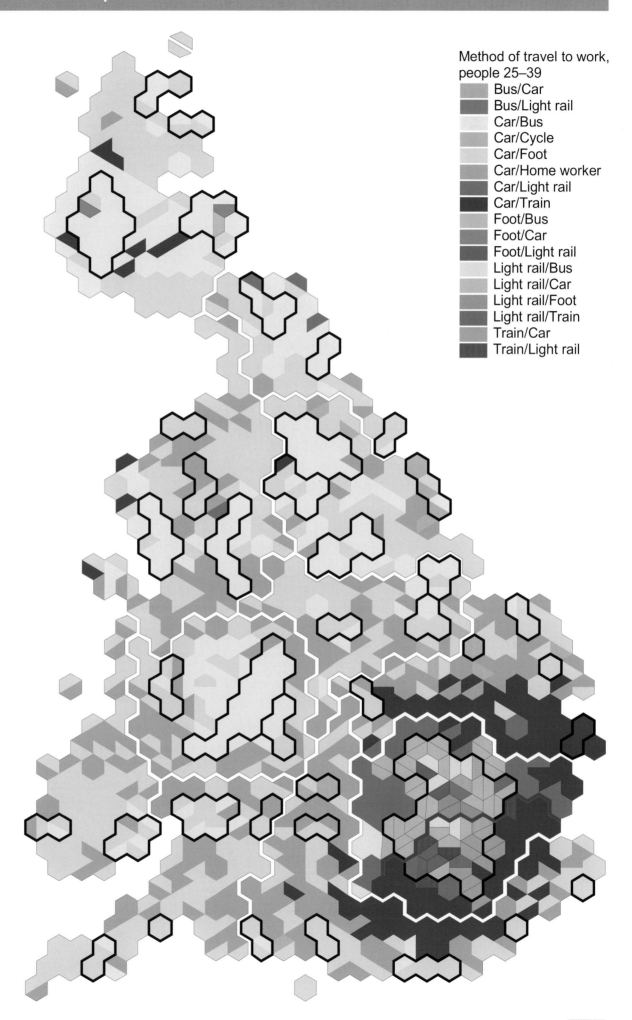

Method of travel to work,
people 25–39

- Bus/Car
- Bus/Light rail
- Car/Bus
- Car/Cycle
- Car/Foot
- Car/Home worker
- Car/Light rail
- Car/Train
- Foot/Bus
- Foot/Car
- Foot/Light rail
- Light rail/Bus
- Light rail/Car
- Light rail/Foot
- Light rail/Train
- Train/Car
- Train/Light rail

5.13 Got a mortgage? Continuation on a theme for those in midlife

Not all midlife people have a mortgage, just as not all have a car. Mortgages are, however, nearly as ubiquitous when neighbourhoods are compared. A narrow majority, some 56% of midlife people, live in a home that is mortgaged. In contrast, 96% of neighbourhoods are characterised, in midlife, by 'mortgaged' being the most common tenure. As Figure 5.13 opposite shows, the second most common tenure in the south and east of England (outside of London) tends to be 'private rented', whereas in the north of England it is 'local authority (LA) rented'. And almost all the colour is in London.

What is the tenure mix in neighbourhoods where those with mortgages live? The table below quantifies Figure 5.13 in terms of the 7.1 million of mortgaging midlife people. Most interesting are the cells that are blank and rows that are missing. These are combinations that simply do not occur. Nowhere do a majority of those in midlife own outright, for instance. The largest minority are in communal accommodation only where a majority are buying. Incidentally, if you are wondering where the midlife ashram of Britain is, we are afraid that we have to disappoint you. The neighbourhood where 3,998 mortgaged midlifers live, sharing their space with communal dwellers, is Helensburgh in Scotland. It is home to a naval base (HM Naval Base Clyde) within which the second largest cohort of this age group is housed.

Such nuances are not the reason for showing this table. That they exist at all among such uniformity is surprising. Instead, what the table is useful for is simply to confirm that the large majority of those in midlife with a mortgage live where most midlife people have a mortgage: these are some 6.9 of the 7.1 million people holding mortgages. There are very few 'urban venturers'. Most buy where it appears to be safe to buy, where most are already buying.

Number of people aged 25-39 in Britain in a mortgaged home according to tenure mix

People aged 25-39, mortgagees	Second most common tenure in the neighbourhood						
Most common tenure in the neighbourhood	Communal	Local authority rented	Mortgaged	Other social rented	Owned outright	Private rented	Total
LA rented			44,113			17,820	61,933
Mortgaged	3,998	2,229,454		211,375	1,917,236	2,573,402	6,935,465
Other social rented			4,623			1,766	6,389
Private rented		7,269	112,566				119,835
Total	3,998	2,236,723	161,302	211,375	1,917,236	2,592,988	7,123,622

5.13 Got a mortgage? Continuation on a theme for those in midlife

Figure 5.13

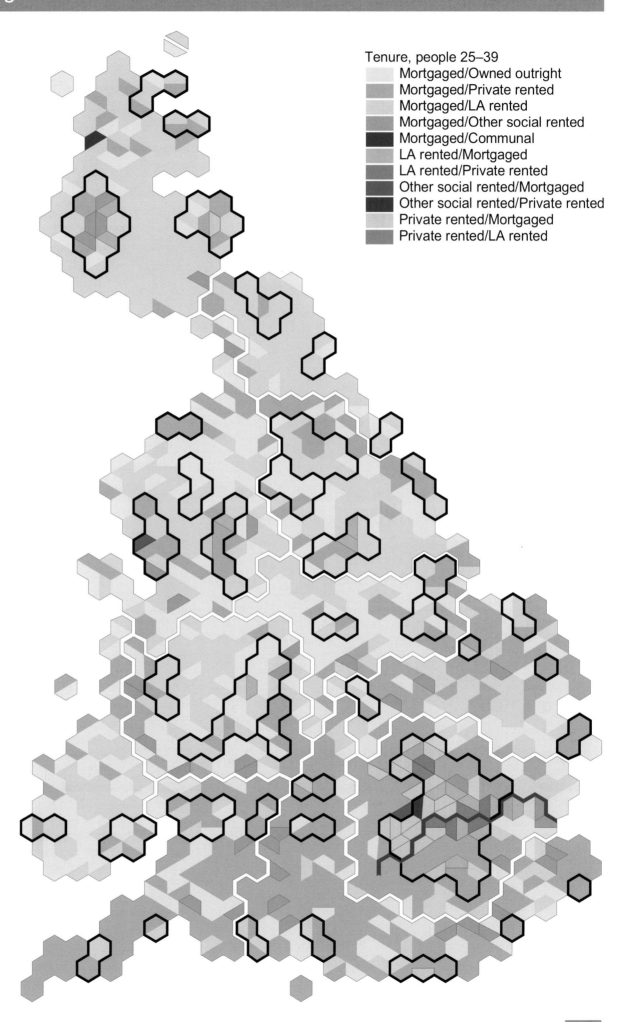

Tenure, people 25–39
- Mortgaged/Owned outright
- Mortgaged/Private rented
- Mortgaged/LA rented
- Mortgaged/Other social rented
- Mortgaged/Communal
- LA rented/Mortgaged
- LA rented/Private rented
- Other social rented/Mortgaged
- Other social rented/Private rented
- Private rented/Mortgaged
- Private rented/LA rented

5.14 Where do you come from and what do you believe in midlife?

Ethnicity in midlife is perhaps a little more interesting than you might have assumed. True, the majority of neighbourhoods in England and Wales are majority 'White British' and the majority–minority happens to be 'Other White', but 37% of neighbourhoods in England and Wales are not as bland as is shown in Figure 5.14 opposite. Of these, the largest sets are where 'White British' are in the majority and 'Indian' (8%) or 'Pakistani' (7%) the largest minority. Some 5% of neighbourhoods in England and Wales have a majority of those in midlife being 'Other White' and 'White British' as the largest minority, while 3% each have 'White Irish/White British' and 'White British/White Irish' as the most common combinations. Some 2% of areas are labelled 'White British/Black Caribbean' and 'Indian/White British' respectively. All areas in which a White group does not make up either the largest or second largest ethnicity midlife grouping account for less than half a per cent of neighbourhoods.

For Scotland the data were often suppressed when we sought to look at the full range of ethnicities that were asked on the form. However, of those areas where it was not suppressed, all but one had a majority 'White Scottish' and a minority 'Other White British'. The one exception was where 'Pakistani' was the majority–minority group. In Scotland religion is somewhat more interesting than ethnicity, as shown in the map below. Note that religion is shown only for those aged up to 34 because of the way that age groups are defined in the source for this information on our beliefs in midlife. Remember also that far more detail is asked of Christian denominations in Scotland than the catch-all used to imply such uniformity south of the border.

The patterns south are interesting, but mainly tell a tale that is better told in the detail of ethnicity shown in Figure 5.14. However, the patterns in Scotland are revealing in the light of so little information shown. Even where a majority of midlifers have explicitly said they have no religion in Scotland that is telling. Note, however, that it is easier for non-believers to be in the majority when Christianity is divided and also where religion of upbringing is asked so people can say what they once were as well as what they are. Religious identities change.

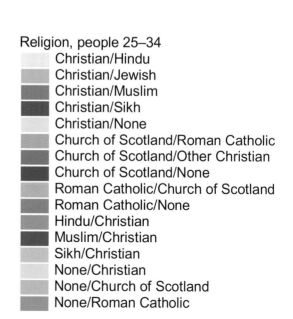

Religion, people 25–34
Christian/Hindu
Christian/Jewish
Christian/Muslim
Christian/Sikh
Christian/None
Church of Scotland/Roman Catholic
Church of Scotland/Other Christian
Church of Scotland/None
Roman Catholic/Church of Scotland
Roman Catholic/None
Hindu/Christian
Muslim/Christian
Sikh/Christian
None/Christian
None/Church of Scotland
None/Roman Catholic

5.14 Where do you come from and what do you believe in midlife?

Figure 5.14

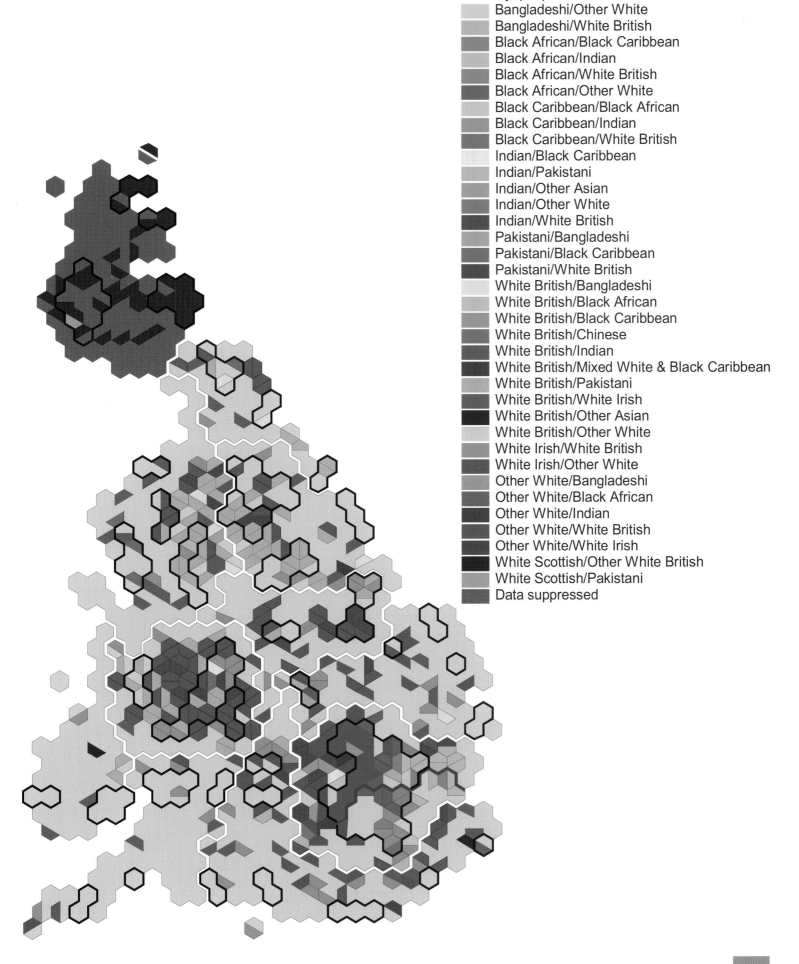

Ethnicity, people 25–39

- Bangladeshi/Other White
- Bangladeshi/White British
- Black African/Black Caribbean
- Black African/Indian
- Black African/White British
- Black African/Other White
- Black Caribbean/Black African
- Black Caribbean/Indian
- Black Caribbean/White British
- Indian/Black Caribbean
- Indian/Pakistani
- Indian/Other Asian
- Indian/Other White
- Indian/White British
- Pakistani/Bangladeshi
- Pakistani/Black Caribbean
- Pakistani/White British
- White British/Bangladeshi
- White British/Black African
- White British/Black Caribbean
- White British/Chinese
- White British/Indian
- White British/Mixed White & Black Caribbean
- White British/Pakistani
- White British/White Irish
- White British/Other Asian
- White British/Other White
- White Irish/White British
- White Irish/Other White
- Other White/Bangladeshi
- Other White/Black African
- Other White/Indian
- Other White/White British
- Other White/White Irish
- White Scottish/Other White British
- White Scottish/Pakistani
- Data suppressed

5.15 Middle management in middle England in midlife

It is true: across middle England the majority of those in midlife work in middle management. They are 'managers and senior officials'. This is perhaps clearest on the map below rather than on Figure 5.15 opposite. Middle England is, however, not the majority of Britain; thus, although the highest group typifies 30% of neighbourhoods, the third highest, 'associate professionals and technical grades', typifies 32% but is found further northwards (or in the heart of London).

As the key to Figure 5.15 shows, there is significantly more apparent mixing by social class in midlife than at younger ages. The reason we say apparent is that more jobs may be labelled 'senior' for people at these ages, to placate those who increasingly feel they are senior. It costs very little to change a job title. Calling someone under the age of 25 a 'senior manager' probably says much more about them. Nevertheless, the increased degree of mixing is noteworthy.

Perhaps those in midlife are willing to forgo a degree of segregation between social classes to allow them to increase their segregation from those younger than them? Better to live in a more socially mixed neighbourhood that is predominantly midlife than in an area popular with young people of your own class? What, after all, could be worse than having to hear the views of young professionals in your local pub when you could be with people who have lived a little?

It is also worth noting how many fewer areas are typified by the majority of people working in 'operative' or 'elementary' occupations at these ages compared with young adults. Far more frequently lower paid work appears as the largest minority occupation of those in midlife (Figure 5.15) rather than the majority occupation of this group (inset here). By midlife most people, and places, have become 'respectable'.

Occupation, people 25–39
1. Managers & Senior Officials
2. Professional
3. Assoc Professional & Tech
4. Admin & Secretarial
5. Skilled Trades
8. Operatives
9. Elementary

5.15 Middle management in middle England in midlife

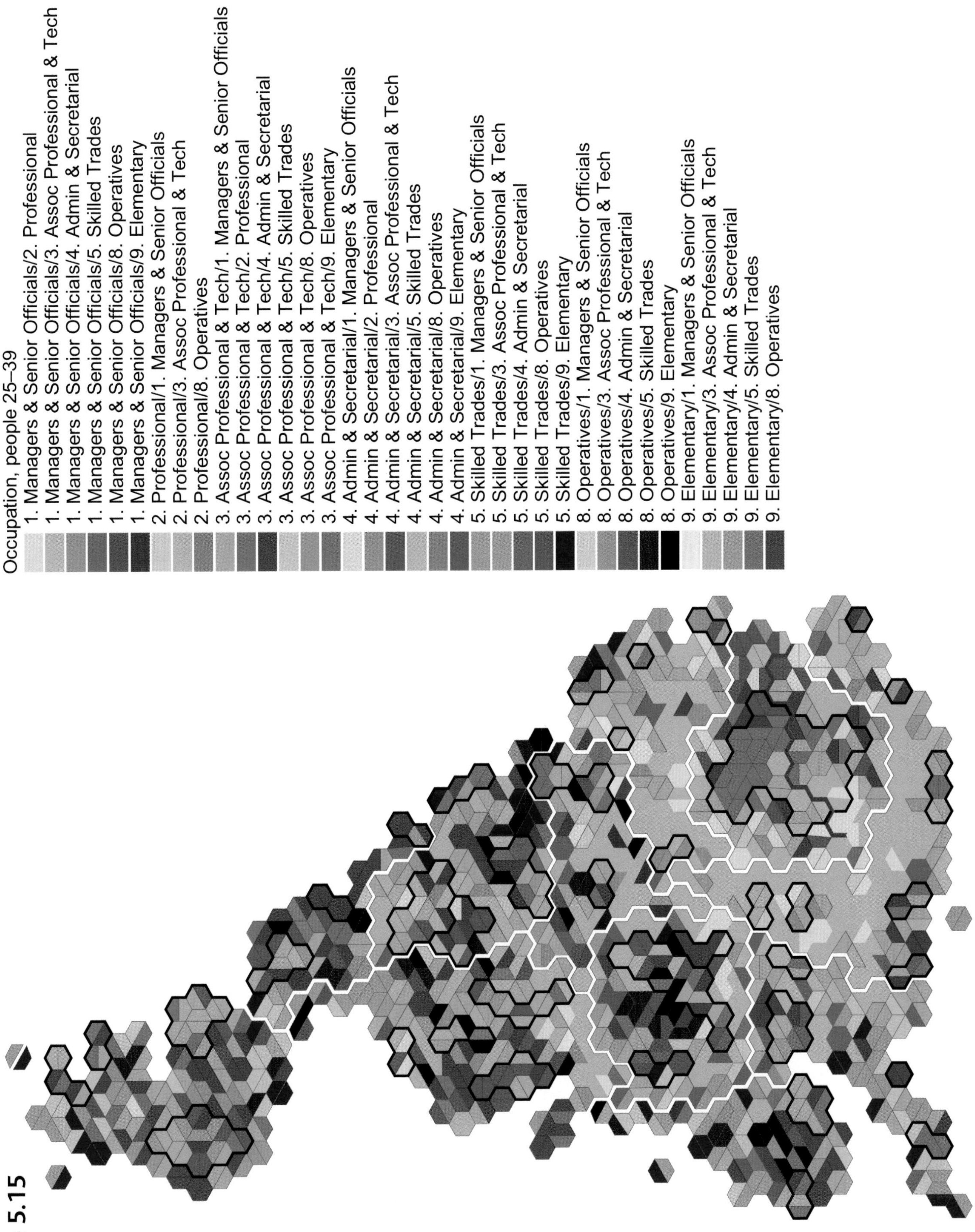

Figure 5.15

5.16 A nation of shopkeepers? Industry and midlife

To look at the map of dominant industry below and the mix of industries occupying the time of employed midlife people in Britain (Figure 5.16 opposite), you could well assume that we are a nation of shopkeepers, estate agents and garage mechanics; or at least the southern half of us are. Manufacturing still just about dominates most of Wales, Scotland and the north of England. In those places a majority still make some of the goods that the rest of us are so busy buying and selling. More esoteric industries, such as education, dominate only in odd places (such as Oxford West and St Andrews). Some old industries are now found dominant only in one, probably final, place: fishing in the rural parts of Eilean Siar, for instance.

Look opposite, however, at what is also second most common and a greater variety of places emerges. Far more distinct communities (such as Dover) and the second great activity of England, finance, become more obvious when no longer hidden by our first preoccupation (retail). However, although there is great variety to the map of industry, and certainly greater variety than there was for younger adults, most places are dominated by the same few service industries being in the majority or being second highest placed to manufacturing outside of the south. The unusual combinations are interesting because they are so unusual, and in some cases, unique to single neighbourhoods.

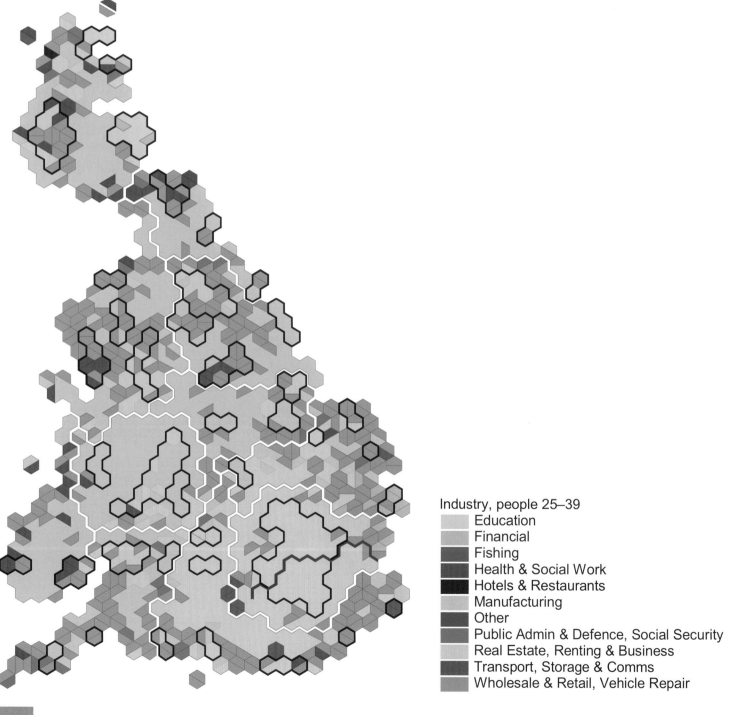

Industry, people 25–39
- Education
- Financial
- Fishing
- Health & Social Work
- Hotels & Restaurants
- Manufacturing
- Other
- Public Admin & Defence, Social Security
- Real Estate, Renting & Business
- Transport, Storage & Comms
- Wholesale & Retail, Vehicle Repair

5.16 A nation of shopkeepers? Industry and midlife

Industry, people 25–39

Education/Health & Social Work
Education/Manufacturing
Education/Real Estate, Renting & Business
Financial/Real Estate, Renting & Business
Financial/Wholesale & Retail, Vehicle Repair
Fishing/Health & Social Work
Health & Social Work/Agriculture
Health & Social Work/Education
Health & Social Work/Manufacturing
Health & Social Work/Real Estate, Renting & Business
Health & Social Work/Wholesale & Retail, Vehicle Repair
Hotels & Restaurants/Wholesale & Retail, Vehicle Repair
Manufacturing/Agriculture
Manufacturing/Construction
Manufacturing/Education
Manufacturing/Health & Social Work
Manufacturing/Public Admin & Defence, Social Security
Manufacturing/Real Estate, Renting & Business
Manufacturing/Wholesale & Retail, Vehicle Repair
Other/Manufacturing
Public Admin & Defence, Social Security/Health & Social Work
Public Admin & Defence, Social Security/Manufacturing
Public Admin & Defence, Social Security/Real Estate, Renting & Business
Public Admin & Defence, Social Security/Wholesale & Retail, Vehicle Repair
Real Estate, Renting & Business/Education
Real Estate, Renting & Business/Financial
Real Estate, Renting & Business/Health & Social Work
Real Estate, Renting & Business/Manufacturing
Real Estate, Renting & Business/Mining & Quarrying
Real Estate, Renting & Business/Other
Real Estate, Renting & Business/Public Admin & Defence, Social Security
Real Estate, Renting & Business/Transport, Storage & Comms
Real Estate, Renting & Business/Wholesale & Retail, Vehicle Repair
Transport, Storage & Comms/Public Admin & Defence, Social Security
Transport, Storage & Comms/Real Estate, Renting & Business
Transport, Storage & Comms/Wholesale & Retail, Vehicle Repair
Wholesale & Retail, Vehicle Repair/Construction
Wholesale & Retail, Vehicle Repair/Education
Wholesale & Retail, Vehicle Repair/Financial
Wholesale & Retail, Vehicle Repair/Health & Social Work
Wholesale & Retail, Vehicle Repair/Hotels & Restaurants
Wholesale & Retail, Vehicle Repair/Manufacturing
Wholesale & Retail, Vehicle Repair/Public Admin & Defence, Social Security
Wholesale & Retail, Vehicle Repair/Real Estate, Renting & Business
Wholesale & Retail, Vehicle Repair/Transport, Storage & Comms

Figure 5.16

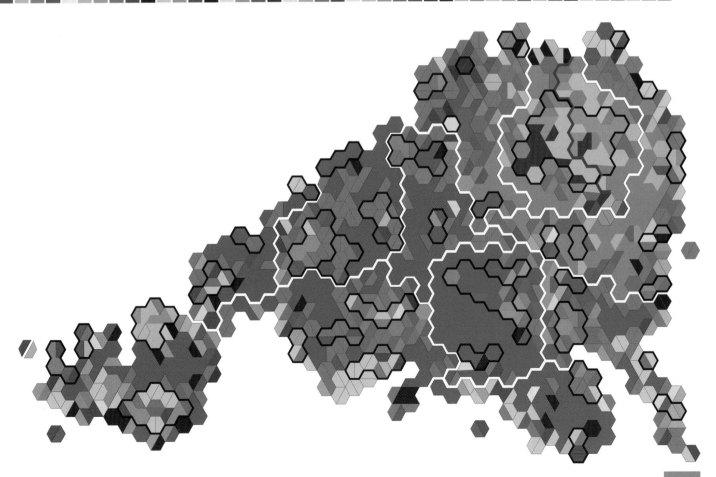

5.17 Knowing your place: class and lower management in midlife

There are those who think that Britain is a class-ridden society, and those who think it doesn't matter either way as long as you know your place in the set-up. (Miles Kington, 1989, Welcome to Kington, London: Robson Books)

Finally, by midlife, there is a place where most are posh. Not just one place, in fact, but six neighbourhoods where the majority of midlife people are higher managers. As Figure 5.17 shows, these places are: Oxford West, Edgbaston East, Edinburgh Morningside, Newcastle Jesmond and Cambridge (both East and West). Sadly it remains the case for those who are 'higher' that mixing is only with one's own or the class just beneath oneself. Lower managers mix with all, however, and are the ubiquitous majority

The table below tells us most about how little mixing there is when all the blank cells in the table are considered. Lower managers are very common by midlife and are found mixed with all other groups, albeit rarely with the most poor. The only other mixing that goes on is the 'semi-routine' with the 'routine' or 'never worked/long-term unemployed' groups, and one case of a neighbourhood (Bradford University) where the majority have never worked (or are long-term unemployed) at these ages, and the second most common group is those working in the most routine of occupations. Often the 'never worked' group is mostly

women who have been bringing up children in areas where it is still less usual for women to work. However, it is telling that a classification system designed by people working in universities should end up highlighting one university area at the bottom end of a spectrum and the six areas above, all closely related to elite higher education institutions at the other end of that spectrum.

Just as with younger adults, before taking this grading of areas by class in midlife as given, it is worth looking at how places are labelled if those in midlife are classed by older classification systems based on the Household Reference Person. In the case of many of the areas where many women have never worked their class will change, as often the man's name has been put first on the form and he has been, and usually is, working. The older class systems also appear a little less derogatory as we see in the next section, perhaps because less emphasis is placed on autonomy in work and who you are in charge of. Before turning from Figure 5.17 of people classed by themselves, it is worth pointing out just how clustered the colours become at these ages as areas take on the characteristics of their occupants and are labelled so much by what those in midlife in each place do. Thus it is not only that many people choose not to mix with others within neighbourhoods at these ages, but that very different neighbourhoods are less often found cheek by jowl, abutting within cities when characterised by the classes of their midlife residents.

Number of neighbourhoods by National Statistics Socioeconomic Classification (NS-SeC) mix of people aged 25-39

People aged 25-39	Second most common social class								
Most common social class	1. Higher managers	2. Lower managers	3. Intermediate	4. Small employers	5. Lower supervisory	6. Semi-routine	7. Routine	8. Never worked	Total
1. Higher managers		6							6
2. Lower managers	379		193	19	2	498	37	9	1,137
6. Semi-routine		52					39	8	99
7. Routine		9				21			30
8. Never worked		5				4	1		10
Total	379	72	193	19	2	523	77	17	1,282

5.17 Knowing your place: class and lower management in midlife

Figure 5.17

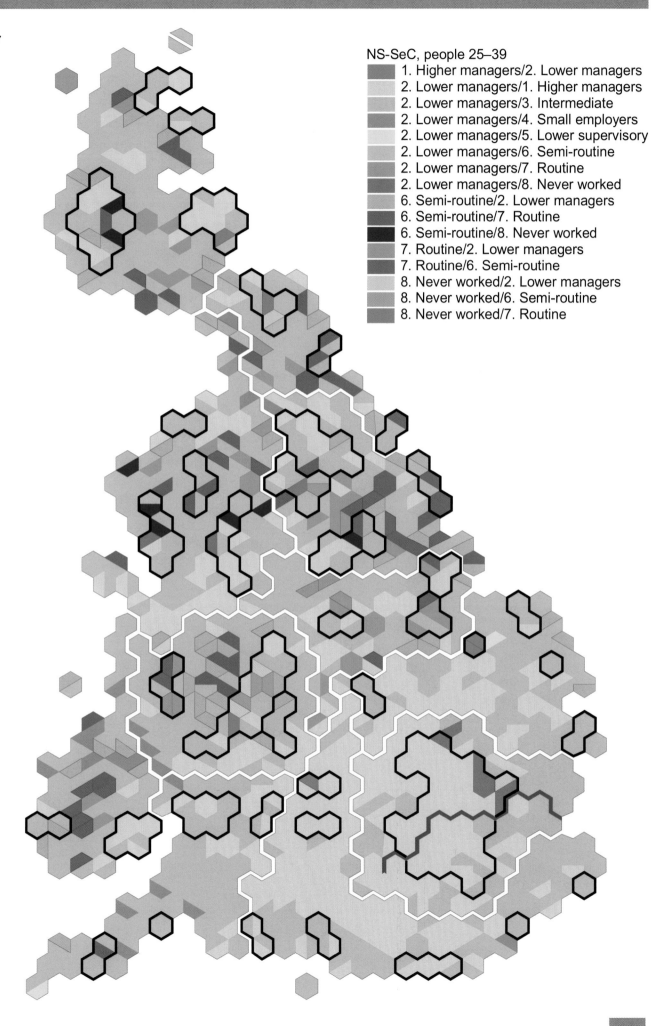

NS-SeC, people 25–39
- 1. Higher managers/2. Lower managers
- 2. Lower managers/1. Higher managers
- 2. Lower managers/3. Intermediate
- 2. Lower managers/4. Small employers
- 2. Lower managers/5. Lower supervisory
- 2. Lower managers/6. Semi-routine
- 2. Lower managers/7. Routine
- 2. Lower managers/8. Never worked
- 6. Semi-routine/2. Lower managers
- 6. Semi-routine/7. Routine
- 6. Semi-routine/8. Never worked
- 7. Routine/2. Lower managers
- 7. Routine/6. Semi-routine
- 8. Never worked/2. Lower managers
- 8. Never worked/6. Semi-routine
- 8. Never worked/7. Routine

5.18 Social grade: another way to partition those in midlife

For those confused by what a lower manager, intermediate or small employer is, the older system of just assigning six classes, three white-collar, three blue-collar, is much simpler to remember if perhaps now a little dated. Social grade is assigned to the individual purely on the basis of their Household Reference Person's job title or the title of the last job they held. The highest grade, A, is so rare that we combine it with the next, B as before (see page 118). Figure 5.18 opposite shows clearly how the areas most characterised in midlife as AB/C1 swarm in the south and are in turn surrounded most closely by those who are C1/AB. At the other end of the scale E/D (and D/E) is found only in Glasgow and D/C2 almost solely in the north.

It is perhaps simpler to see just how well the country is divided north/south when only the most common social grade is considered, as in the map below. As if to try to convince us to tilt the north–south divide north west–south east, the only place in the south where a majority are assigned class D is one of the quarters of Plymouth, the most westerly English city identified on our maps.

There is nowhere in London that is not dominated either by AB or C1 in midlife and only one such exception in the South East region. By midlife, people are largely sorted out in life. They have become what they were going to be. The idiosyncrasies and exceptions have been all but ironed out. Look to the midlife of a place to know most quickly at what kind of a place you are looking.

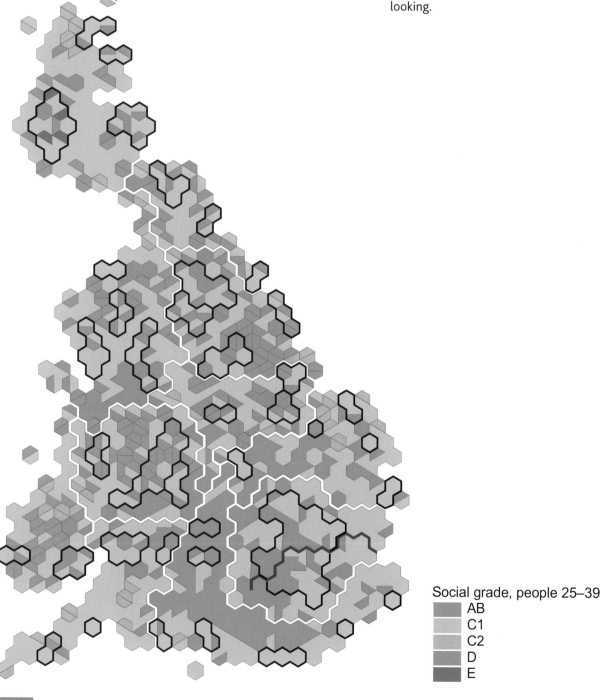

Social grade, people 25–39
- AB
- C1
- C2
- D
- E

5.18 Social grade: another way to partition those in midlife

Figure 5.18

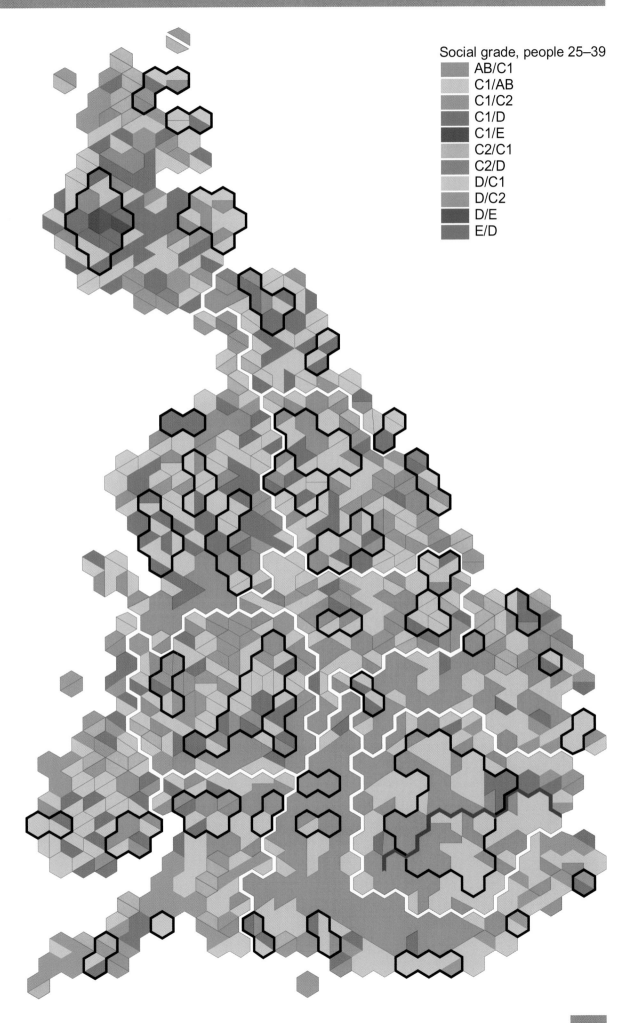

Social grade, people 25–39
- AB/C1
- C1/AB
- C1/C2
- C1/D
- C1/E
- C2/C1
- C2/D
- D/C1
- D/C2
- D/E
- E/D

5.19 Providing care: how else the midlifers live differently across the divide

Class, as defined by censuses, is all about paid work. But there is just as stark a class divide in unpaid work, although it has until recently been a part of our identity that has been ignored. That the midlife geography of the provision of unpaid care should paint such a clear image of a nation divided would be unexpected, unless you had seen the map below.

The years of being a soldier, full of strange oaths, have changed most over time for the poor in terms of geography of the weight of those above them in age, the need to care for them, and also (although thankfully less often required) to care for children in need of constant care because of illness.

A sprinkling of neighbourhoods in the south sees more than a tenth of this age group providing unpaid care, including that same quarter of Plymouth as was just commented on. But across most of the south, 7% or less of this age group are needed to care. In contrast, across all of the urban north, west central Scotland and the Welsh Valleys, over a tenth is providing substantial care. The midlife labour force in places is more than decimated in earning power through the extent to which its services are drawn on for free as carers of the ill and infirm.

The growing need to care makes up the first part of that decimation. The other half of the picture of the north–south health divide is shown opposite in Figure 5.19 and is well worth comparing with the same image for those aged a stage younger (on page 121). In contrast to the detailed mosaic shown then, in which good health featured in most places but all nine shades of possibility appeared, Figure 5.19 is dominated by four shades. Dominant now are places where health is poor and average or above average numbers have a disability; then almost as frequent are places where health is generally fair and average or below average numbers have a limiting long term-illness (LLTI). Only in a tiny number of neighbourhoods do a majority of those in midlife describe their health as good, and in all those places rates of disability are below average. Slowly, surely, a majority no longer feel so sure of their bodies, or do not wish to tempt fate by saying that their health is good.

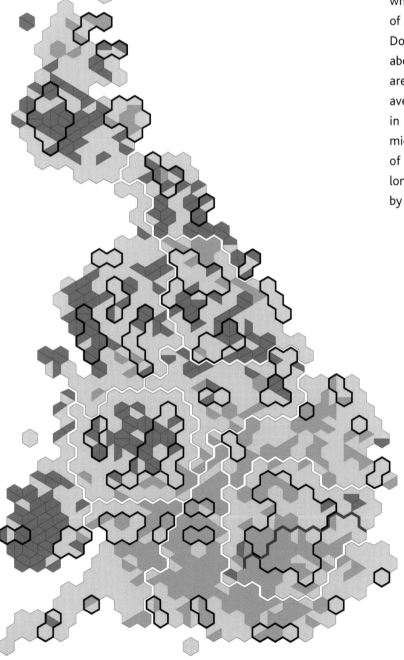

People 25–39 providing care
- Above average
- Average
- Below average

5.19 Providing care: how else the midlifers live differently across the divide

Figure 5.19

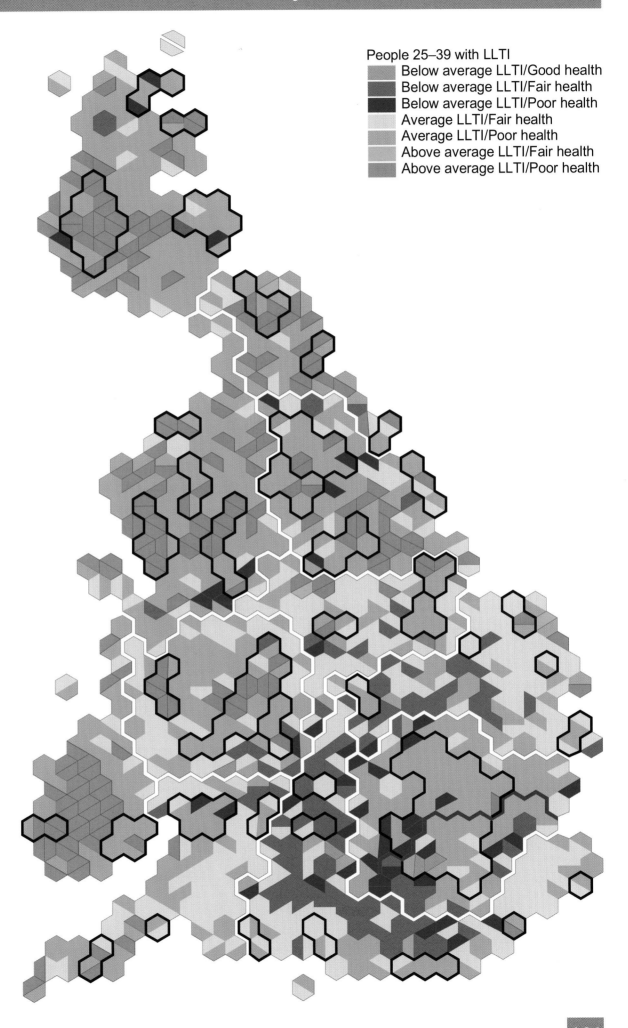

People 25–39 with LLTI
- Below average LLTI/Good health
- Below average LLTI/Fair health
- Below average LLTI/Poor health
- Average LLTI/Fair health
- Average LLTI/Poor health
- Above average LLTI/Fair health
- Above average LLTI/Poor health

5.20 Conclusion: the midlife years of conformity

The soldiers of midlife are, by a narrow majority, women, especially where men have done worse. A knife-edge majority are single and the single form a solid majority in cities, but a minority in the commuter land of the southern fringes. It is also mainly in those southern fringes that a majority are in their first marriage. Slightly further out is where you find the places where a fifth or more are already separated, divorced or in their second or subsequent marriage. Right in the centre of London are the places where up to a fifth are married, not separated but also not living with their husband or wife. There is thus no national model to how you are supposed to couple now in midlife, just a series of models of where you are supposed to be, or can afford to be, depending on who you are currently with and how you are with or without them.

At worst one in one hundred and at best one in one thousand are widowed, but in that, as with health more generally, we are beginning to see clear regional patterns emerging from what were at earlier ages specific and often unique stories of places and young adults, often of identity forged in persecution and in fleeing from persecution. In terms of who else they live with, midlifers are now split between the six million not living with children and the six-and-a-half million who do; again, not a life stage that can be so easily summarised, at least not by relationships.

By the time at least a quarter century of life has passed, the world of work is more predictable. At these ages almost everywhere is typified by a majority being full-time employees and the bulk of the rest in any place in midlife working part-time. In many places over a fifth are reliant on benefits, but almost nowhere does this proportion reach two fifths. Thus, because most have earnings (and vehicles are relatively inexpensive for this group and these times), almost everywhere a majority have access to at least one car.

Across most of the South East the norm is now two or more cars per midlife household. The effect of this mass mobility in midlife has been to allow the age group, and particularly its older members, to segregate more geographically. Practically everywhere outside of London most people of these ages drive to work, and they can drive some distance. Similarly, practically everywhere outside of London (and even in half of London) most of those in midlife have a mortgage, so have to work and need to drive to get to that work. They need to drive because almost all who buy will only try to buy a house where most people are already trying to buy and that often is not 'convenient' for where they are working.

At these ages there is segregation by life stage as well as by class, and many are moving away from where younger adults congregate. This is seen too by ethnicity where those in minority groups in midlife are a little more spread out than younger adults in the same minorities, and away from where the young are most numerous. There is still incredibly strong class segregation, but where, for younger adults, there were so many types of area mix that simply did not exist, there are now slightly fewer impossible combinations of class. Similar heterogeneity is found with possible combinations of modal and majority–minority industries. But, as always, by neighbourhood the higher managers of midlife mix only with their immediate subordinates. Lastly, when we assign social grade based on Household Reference Person the ubiquity returns and the South East in midlife becomes a sea of managers and professionals (lower and higher), As and Bs, those who more often than average do not have to care, unpaid, for others and where a majority are still in fair health and disability is rare. The urban north is the mirror image of this in midlife, and the lands in between the northern cities and southern commuter lands are slowly beginning to fix their identities too, as people move around more slowly and settle in midlife with their lot – in their place.

6 And then, the justice: ages 40-59

... and then, the justice,
In fair round belly, with good capon lined,
With eyes severe, and beard of formal cut,
Full of wise saws and modern instances,
And so he plays his part;

6.1   Introduction

Those in maturity at ages 40-59 are shown, below left, to constitute between a little more than an eighth and up to almost a third of the population, depending on where you look. When reading what follows and viewing each map, it also helps to try to remember where this age group is most and least common. In dramatic contrast to their younger peers, the centre of London, and to a lesser extent, Birmingham, are now an anathema to the 40-59 age group who in many cases crowded so willingly into the capital just a decade or two earlier. Now they are beginning to turn their backs on the bright lights and cluster most densely out of the city limits.

Years in between again, these older adult ages can be viewed either as the run-up to retirement – old age, the climacteric years – or as an extension of the new youthful midlife – the prime of life, the years in which many become free again of the responsibilities of being parents, the years when they have finally grown up, matured.

There is a great deal of sensitivity over the labelling, and exact demarcation, of this fifth stage of life, as with the last two that follow. For this reason, we have given these 20 years the label 'maturity'. We have chosen to try where possible to concentrate on those aged between 40 and 59 as these are the final years in which the majority are expected to work. They are also the years by which most that will have children have had them, and, as with infanthood, and young adulthood before them, these are years of transition. The previous transitions were infancy (into childhood) and young adulthood (into midlife). These mature years are the years of transition towards early old age, to being young retired (and then truly elderly) and thus we call them 'maturity' from here on. They are also the years beyond which the human body is not well designed to live.

Although three score years and ten were traditionally seen as our lot in life, from shortly before two score years our chances of shuffling off this mortal coil begin to rise exponentially and that rush to deterioration does not abate until death. These are the first years in which those changes are fully felt.

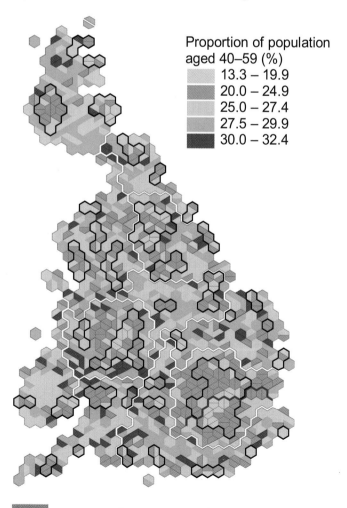

Proportion of population
aged 40–59 (%)
- 13.3 – 19.9
- 20.0 – 24.9
- 25.0 – 27.4
- 27.5 – 29.9
- 30.0 – 32.4

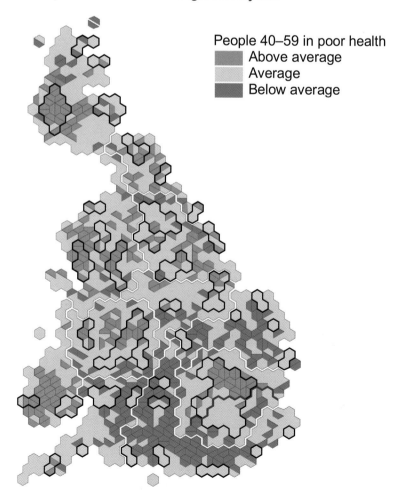

People 40–59 in poor health
- Above average
- Average
- Below average

6.1 Introduction

By the turn of the millennium, a 40-year-old man's chances of dying before he reached 41 in Britain were 600 to one against; 250 to one for a 50-year-old not reaching 51; and 100 to one for a 60-year-old of not reaching 61. For women, the respective rates at these same ages were: one in 1,000, one in 400 and one in 150. The ages at which women attain the mortality rates of 40-, 50- and 60-year-old men are 45, 55 and 65, respectively. In each case, this is almost exactly five years later. As Figure 6.1 shows, when compared with that drawn at the start of the last chapter for those in midlife (see page 125), rates of poor health have doubled everywhere and new areas of concentration emerge as people age. The map opposite, right, shows a simpler version of the distribution. Average rates are 8% to 15.9%.

Figure 6.1

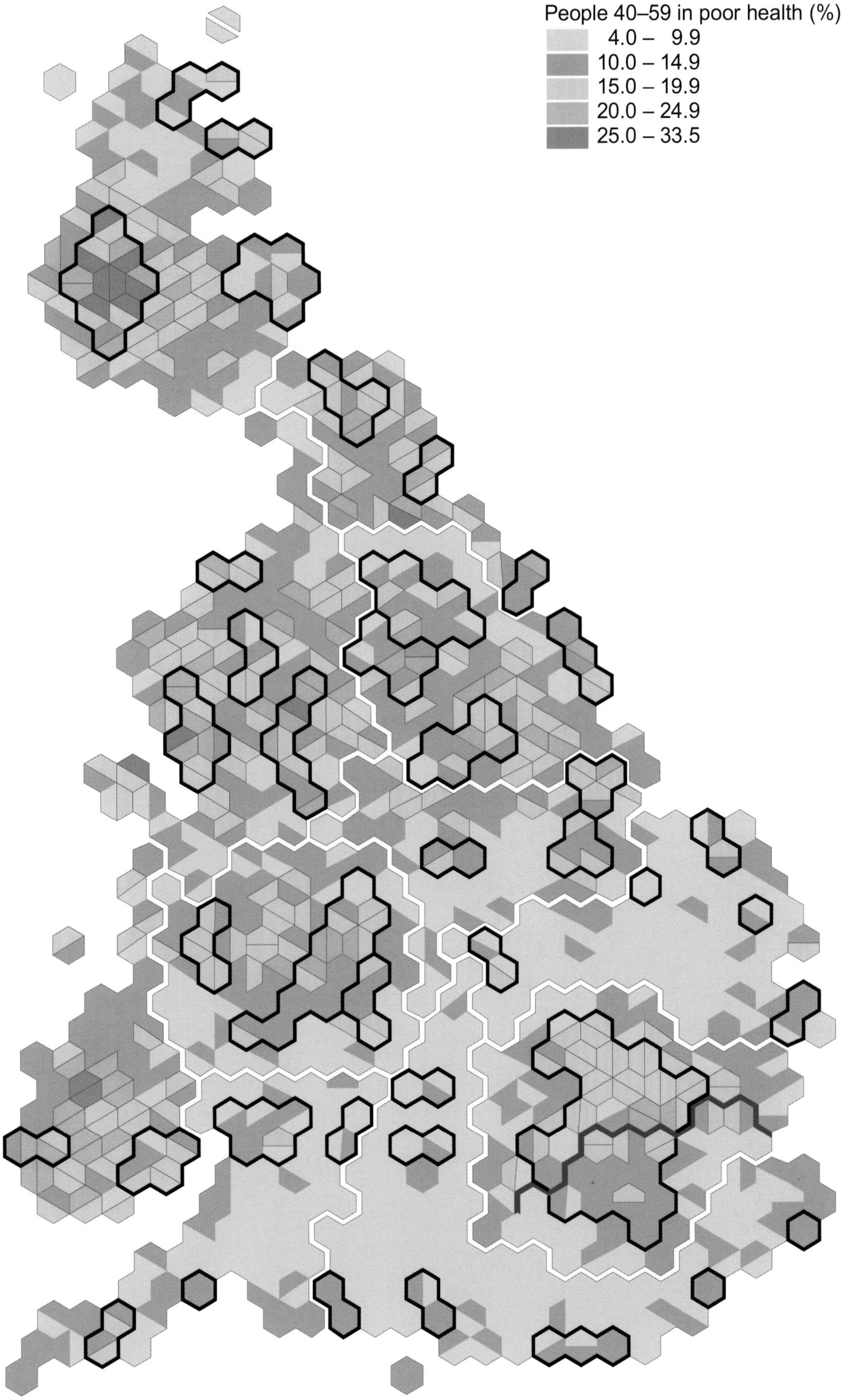

People 40–59 in poor health (%)

4.0 – 9.9
10.0 – 14.9
15.0 – 19.9
20.0 – 24.9
25.0 – 33.5

6.2 Sex ratios in maturity

For every 100 men aged 40-59, there are roughly 102 women living in Britain. Not an enormous discrepancy; far less, in fact, than that for the next youngest age group. However, whereas in midlife it was disproportionate male out-migration that led to the difference, by maturity it is disproportionate male premature mortality.

The age groups that reached maturity by the turn of the millennium had been born as early as the year when the course of the Second World War began to turn (1942) and some as late as not to have been around at the time of the Lady Chatterley trial (1960) but none after the release of the Beatles' first LP (1963). They most commonly entered the labour market at the age of 15 in the 20 years between 1957 and 1976, including when Britons had 'never had it so good' (as Harold Macmillan said of 1957 and as the New Economics Foundation said of 1976). Those mapped here as 'mature' have good reason to be 'in fair round belly with good capon' to eat (in fact, they were the first generation to enjoy factory-farmed chickens). Not knowing the future, and in sight of the past, these are not bad ages to be. But all is far from perfect in the history of this group, which becomes more obvious when we look at where there are more women than men.

In Figure 6.2 opposite there are as few as 82 women for every 100 men in maturity in the neighbourhoods at one extreme, and, at the other extreme, a majority of women in maturity in most areas in the south of England, Wales and Scotland. Two opposing trends result in places that are usually differently shaded being the same hues here. In London and the south it is the progressive in-migration of slightly more women than men, and women staying slightly longer than men (on average), that colours these areas so. In Wales and Scotland more men have left or died than women, while in-migration to these two countries has not been high.

Conversely, the areas that are now most male include some areas of recent immigration, sometimes more male-dominated, areas of economic prosperity, especially along the M4 corridor, and areas with army or navy bases. Again areas that would normally be coloured very differently are here often shaded the same. Regent's Park and Glasgow Easterhouse are both areas where women aged 40-59 are more likely to be found than men. This map is very similar to that shown for the ratios of those aged 25-39 on page 127 and so we can see that this is a pattern that has been built up slowly and as a result of the *differencing* of millions of individual decisions. By differencing we mean the net outcome, first of more baby boys being born, then of differential mortality chances in childhood and into older ages, and also of household and individual decisions and of differential propensities to split up, and migrate.

What you see opposite is the aggregate of all that. It occasionally results in neighbouring areas being at opposite extremes. Thus, despite geographical unevenness locally, should mature men and women aged 40-59 wish to meet, there are almost always opportunities within a short distance. Note also that areas may appear to be particularly unbalanced when there are unusual numbers of people of these ages with partners who live and work away much of the time. There are still high numbers of men from Liverpool and nearby (and around Glasgow) earning a living abroad or down south but with a wife and often children at home. There will be many women in London with husbands working overseas to whom they are still married. Where marriages do not survive, however, is part of where and how these patterns begin to get interesting.

6.2 Sex ratios in maturity

Figure 6.2

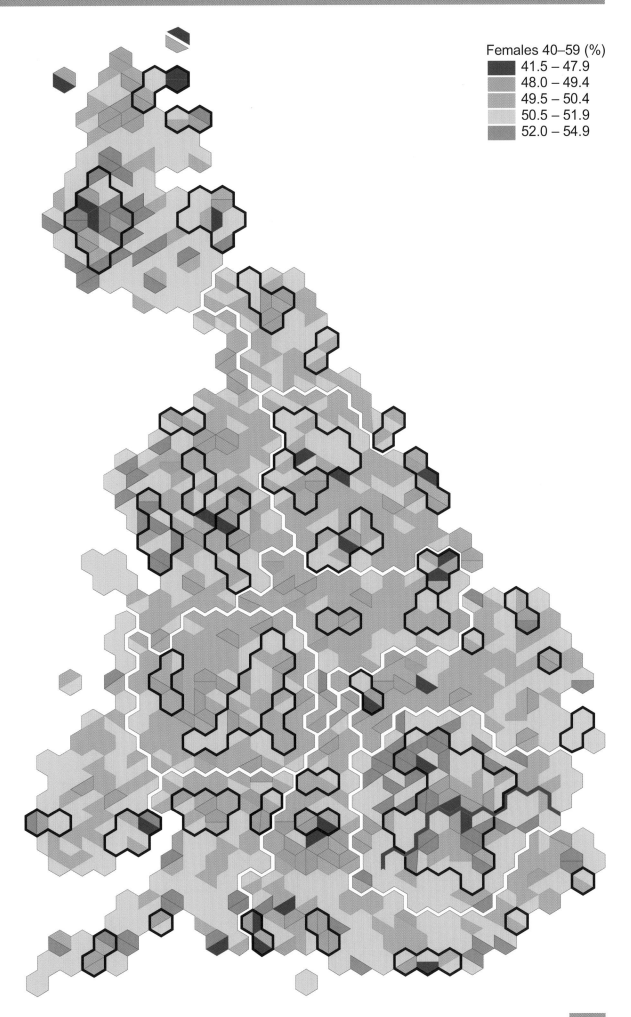

Females 40–59 (%)
- 41.5 – 47.9
- 48.0 – 49.4
- 49.5 – 50.4
- 50.5 – 51.9
- 52.0 – 54.9

6.3 Marriage in maturity

Marriage, *n. The state or condition of a community consisting of a master, a mistress and two slaves, making in all, two.* (Ambrose Bierce, 1967, *The Enlarged Devil's Dictionary*, London: Penguin)

Only 11% of people at this stage of life are single and have never been married. Again this is only partly a product of their ages. It is also a product of the years this group have lived through: of their cohort. People born when this group were born were expected to marry. Of the 89% who did, almost two thirds are still married to their original husband or wife. Of everyone of this age group, 14% are divorced, 13% remarried, 4% separated but not (or not yet) divorced and 2% widowed. Thus most people

of these ages not in a formal relationship were once married. However, in Figure 6.3 opposite we show the mosaic of those single and never married. Almost nowhere is more than a third (and only across almost all of Inner London more than a quarter) of this age group found to have been single and never married. That is quite rare in maturity across most of Britain. Thus, should you wish to find someone without a 'history', at least a legally recorded 'history', at these ages, you might need to travel a little further than the commentary above suggests.

The map of where most people of these ages are still in their first marriage, shown below, is largely the mirror image of Figure 6.3. Scotland is where the extremes are found. Only in two places are just less than a quarter (Edinburgh Holyrood), and just more than three quarters (Bearsden and Kirkintilloch South), of people in maturity in their first marriage. Outside of the cities of Britain almost everywhere a majority of people aged 40-59 are married and in their first marriage (in general, more so the further you move away from those cities). Were people in their first civil partnership also included, this map would change only slightly, as there have been too few partnerships yet recorded in Britain to have great effect in all but a smattering of places.

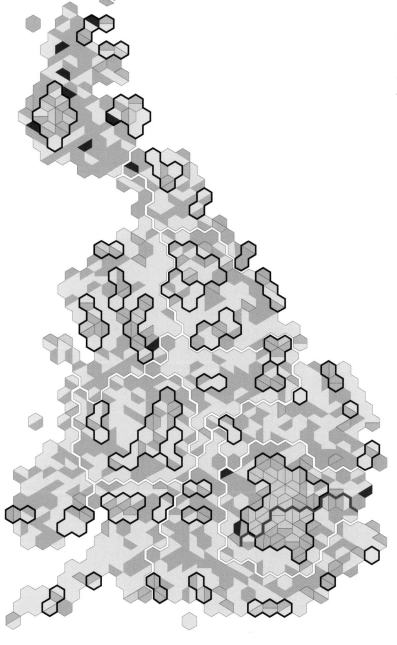

First marriage, people 40–59 (%)

	24.9 – 39.9
	40.0 – 49.9
	50.0 – 59.9
	60.0 – 69.9
	70.0 – 75.1

6.3 Marriage in maturity

Figure 6.3

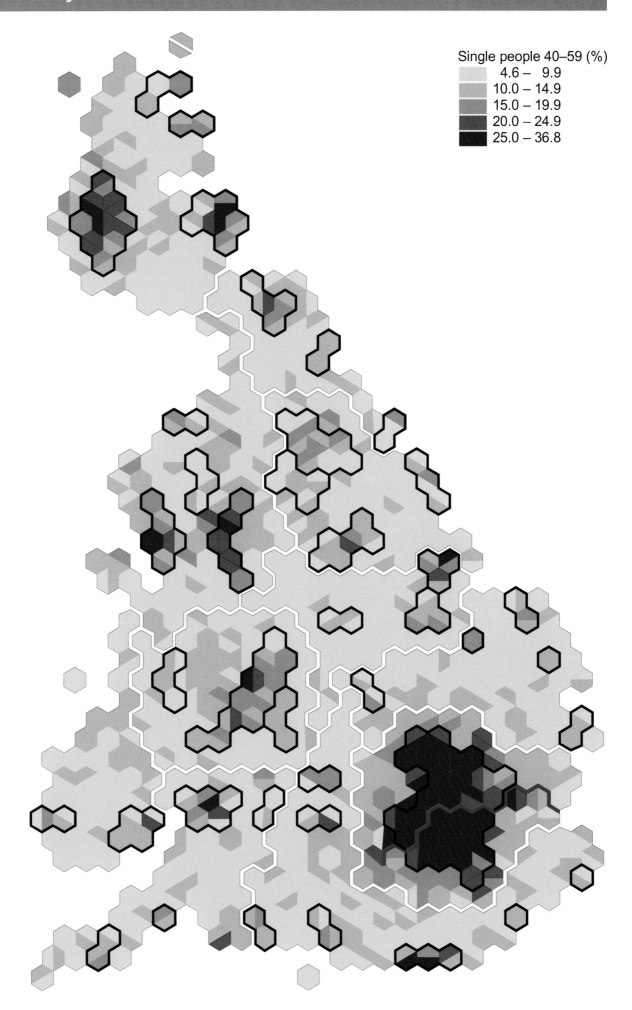

Single people 40–59 (%)
- 4.6 – 9.9
- 10.0 – 14.9
- 15.0 – 19.9
- 20.0 – 24.9
- 25.0 – 36.8

6.4 Separation, divorce and widowhood in maturity

The geography to the 31% of this age group who are remarried, separated or divorced is striking, as shown in Figure 6.4 opposite. The tendency to 'get away from it all' noted earlier in midlife, and for the parents of step-children, (see page 62), is very strong. The sea, especially the warmer sea, appears to draw those who have lost a marital partner. Some coastal towns are especially attractive, partly because it may be cheaper to live in these towns than elsewhere along the coast, and disposable income usually falls on separation. There are also many parts of Outer London and the more expensive quarters of other cities where those at least once separated are least often found. Here it is usually too expensive not to live as a couple and not far enough away from urban reminders for those who have separated either.

Outside of most of urban Britain, extol the values and sanctity of first marriage to someone of mature years, and often more than a third of the time you will be speaking to someone who has been there and done that. Across Britain nationally you would most securely begin digging yourself into a hole in only one such conversation out of fifty. These are the conversations where you will be talking to someone whose husband or wife has died but who has not remarried. This form of separation, that which brings the national total of broken first marriages up to almost exactly a third, usually has the opposite geography to the others, as is shown in the map below. We say 'usually' because the great exception, Glasgow, experienced high rates of remarriage, separation and divorce in maturity as well as widowhood. This map of where people are most likely to be a widow or widower aged 40-59 is a combination map of where they are first more likely to marry, and to die, and also to not remarry (at least not that quickly). A similar combination to consider in trying to understand this geography is that of religious belief, ill health and poverty.

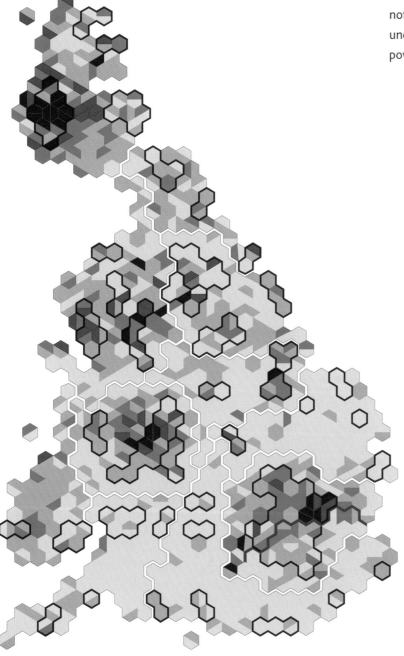

Widowed people 40–59 (%)

	1.4 – 2.4
	2.5 – 2.9
	3.0 – 3.4
	3.5 – 3.9
	4.0 – 5.4

6.4 Separation, divorce and widowhood in maturity

Figure 6.4

Remarried, separated or
divorced people 40–59 (%)
- 16.0 – 24.9
- 25.0 – 29.9
- 30.0 – 34.9
- 35.0 – 39.9
- 40.0 – 44.9

6.5 From married and living apart to cohabiting in the country in maturity

Although less rare by maturity than in midlife, in much of London and near the centres of many other cities, over a twentieth and occasionally more than a tenth of people of these ages are married but not living with their spouse or any other partner (and are not separated). The geography of this kind of physical separation is shown in Figure 6.5 opposite. There is a national, and very probably given the locations, often international, itinerant workforce where work location in most cases necessitates living apart much of the time. Of course, in some cases these may be couples about to split up, but then that is just as true for many married couples currently living together, and absence can also make the heart grow fonder.

Note, as the map below left shows, that these couples (together in marriage if not living together) help create majorities where it is usual to find people in maturity not living together. As the map below right highlights, this means there is only one neighbourhood where a modal majority of this age group are single never married, once the divorced are separated out as a group not in a couple. When that is done, it appears that everywhere else the majority are married couples and the neighbourhoods of Britain are best next differentiated in maturity by household constitution by whether the second largest group is single (in the cities), divorced (around the suburbs) or cohabiting (in the country), often as a prelude to second marriage.

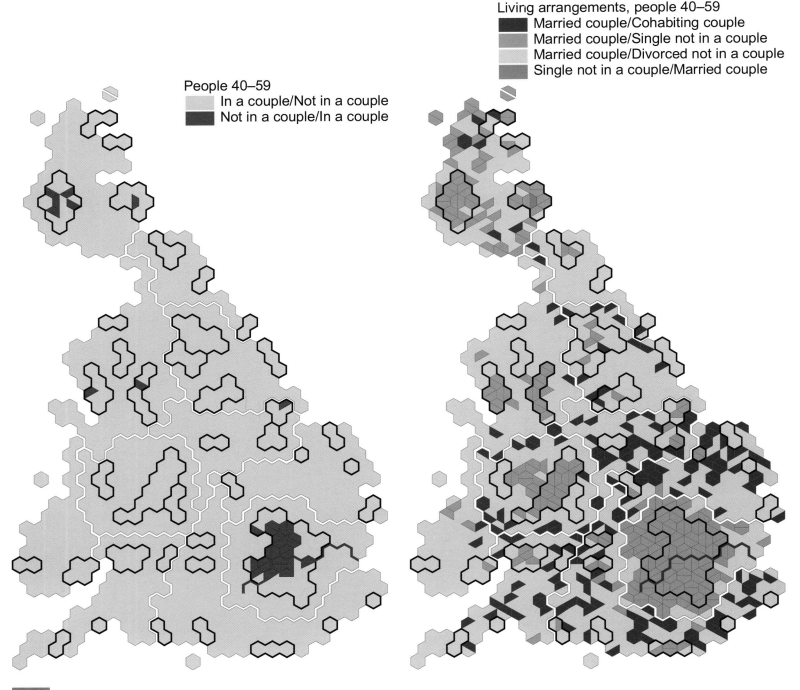

People 40–59
- In a couple/Not in a couple
- Not in a couple/In a couple

Living arrangements, people 40–59
- Married couple/Cohabiting couple
- Married couple/Single not in a couple
- Married couple/Divorced not in a couple
- Single not in a couple/Married couple

6.5 From married and living apart to cohabiting in the country in maturity

Figure 6.5

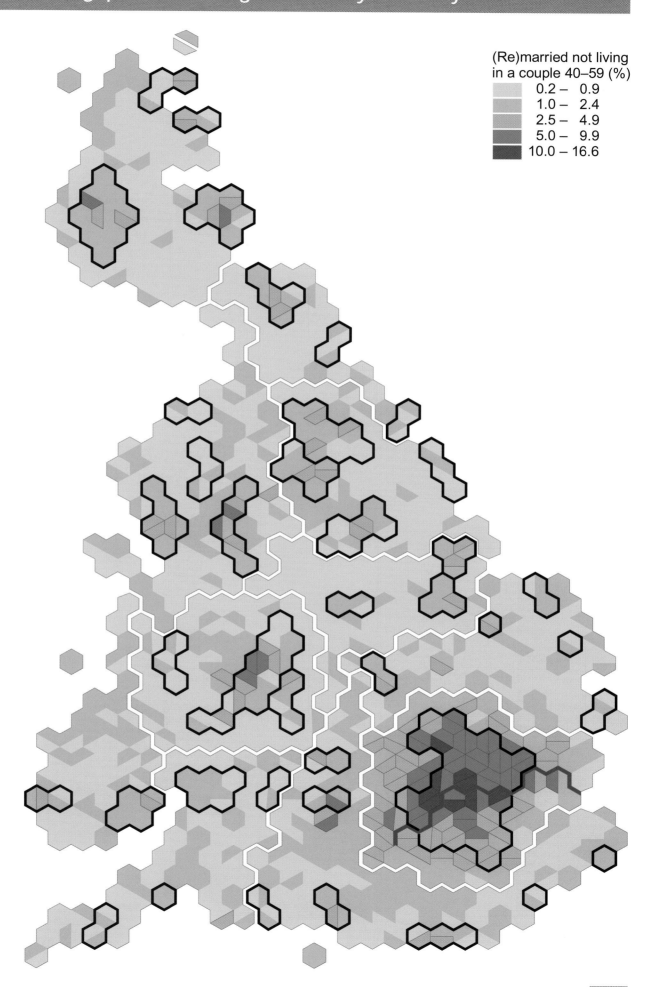

(Re)married not living
in a couple 40–59 (%)
0.2 – 0.9
1.0 – 2.4
2.5 – 4.9
5.0 – 9.9
10.0 – 16.6

6.6 With children where they are still at home in maturity

Everywhere at least one in eight (in the South East at least one in four) people in maturity live in households with children. In most cases these are their own children, but by these ages in an increasing number of cases they will also be other people's children or their step-children.

As Figure 6.6 opposite highlights, it is where mothers have had children latest that the highest numbers of adults in maturity live with children. Below left, we see that for those households everywhere the modal group live in a couple where the youngest child being cared for is aged 10-15. In parts of Glasgow and one neighbourhood of Liverpool the second most likely position for the mature carer of children to be in is on his (but more likely her) own. In the rest of the cities the second largest group comprises couples where the youngest child is aged under 10, while in the countryside they will more often be aged over 15.

The map below right shows that often less than a tenth, and at most only just over a third, of mature adults with children are not living as a couple (note, however, that they may well be married with mum or dad working elsewhere). The possible combinations can begin to make your head hurt, especially when statistical pedantry is added (note that the maps below and opposite are from age 45 up to pensionable age: at this time 59/64 depending on sex). Sometimes, no matter how hard we try, there is no simple way of describing in words what is so easy to see on a map – a good example of a picture being worth a thousand words.

Age of youngest child, people 45–pensionable age (not) in a couple with children
- Couple, youngest child 10–15/Couple, youngest child 0–4
- Couple, youngest child 10–15/Couple, youngest child 5–9
- Couple, youngest child 10–15/Couple, youngest child 16–18
- Couple, youngest child 10–15/Not couple, youngest child 10–15

People 45–pensionable age not in a couple with children, rate of all with children (%)
- 4.8 – 9.9
- 10.0 – 14.9
- 15.0 – 19.9
- 20.0 – 24.9
- 25.0 – 33.7

6.6   With children where they are still at home in maturity

Figure 6.6

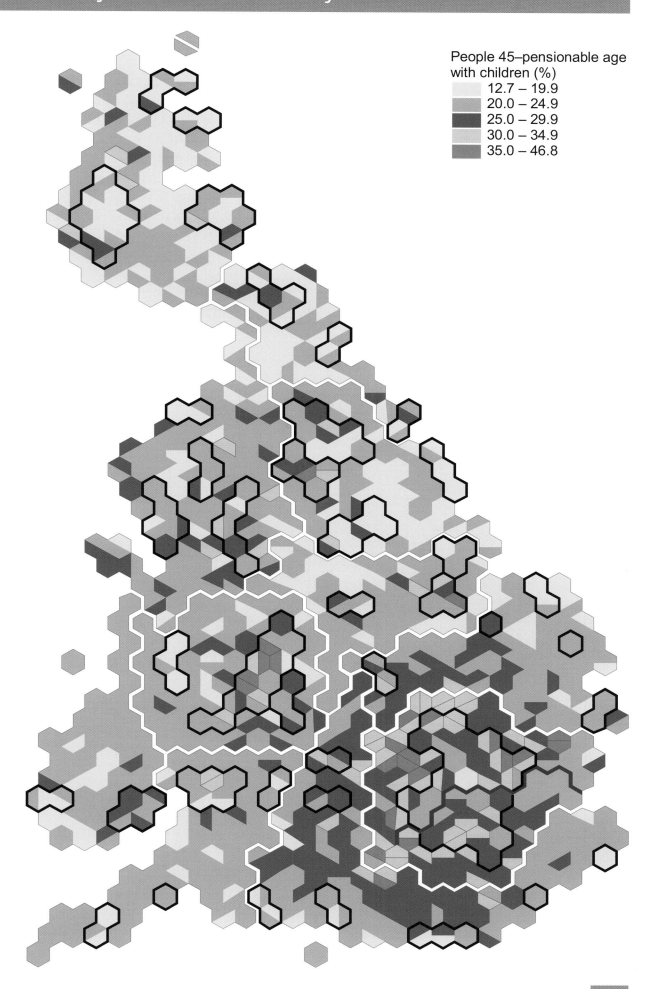

People 45–pensionable age
with children (%)

- 12.7 – 19.9
- 20.0 – 24.9
- 25.0 – 29.9
- 30.0 – 34.9
- 35.0 – 46.8

6.7 Keeping yourself busy at work and at home in maturity

In all but two neighbourhoods a majority of the mature are in full-time work. In the two exceptions, Liverpool Riverside North and Glasgow Milton, more are sick or disabled than are working full-time. In much of central and east London, south Wales, the west of Scotland and within many northern and midlands cities the reverse is true. The majority work full-time but the next largest group are sick or disabled. Next to these areas are found those where the second largest group describe their main economic activity as being full-time self-employed. Scattered in among them are the few districts where the largest minority are caring for their family. And surrounding all of these islands created by this typology is the hegemonic sea of uniformity where most work full-time and the next most work part-time. All this is made visible in Figure 6.7 opposite.

For those whose main activity is not work, a different patterning to the mosaic of economic labelling in maturity appears, as shown in the map below. In the north and in London the dominant activity of those neither working nor seeking work is to be sick and disabled themselves. In most of the south and the more affluent parts of the north it is to be caring for their family. Remember that it is mainly in the south that people of these ages often still have children living with them, and it is mainly in the north that enough fall ill or become so disabled that they cannot work.

It is also interesting to consider the not insignificant number of neighbourhoods, mainly encircling London, where the second most common activity of the 'inactive' is retirement. In the main you have to be wealthy to afford to retire so young. And there is only one area where the retired are second most commonly found to the sick or disabled: Poulton-le-Fylde in Lancashire.

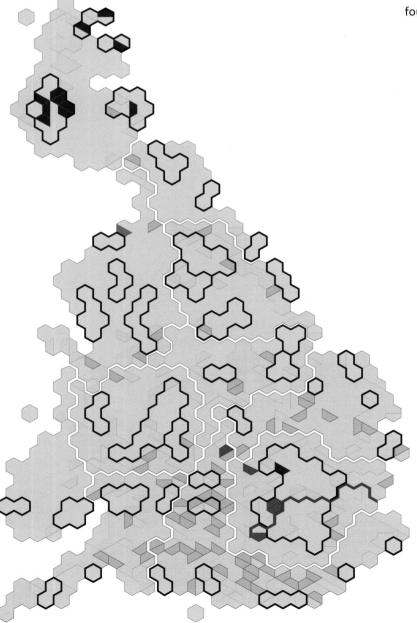

Economically inactive people 40–59

Caring for family/Sick or disabled
Caring for family/Retired
Caring for family/Other
Sick or disabled/Caring for family
Sick or disabled/Retired
Sick or disabled/Other

6.7 Keeping yourself busy at work and at home in maturity

Figure 6.7

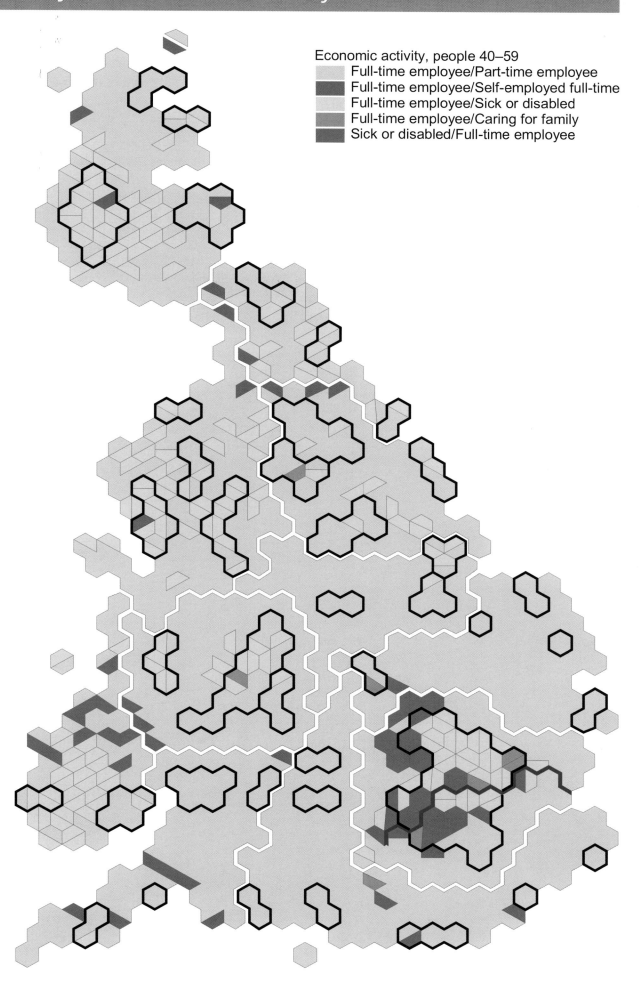

Economic activity, people 40–59
- Full-time employee/Part-time employee
- Full-time employee/Self-employed full-time
- Full-time employee/Sick or disabled
- Full-time employee/Caring for family
- Sick or disabled/Full-time employee

6.8 Sick, disabled, or otherwise incapacitated, reliant on benefits in maturity

One and one quarter million people between the ages of 45 and 59 rely on Incapacity Benefit and/or Severe Disablement Allowances to live in Britain. Nationally, between one in eight and one in nine of the mature are living on these benefits. Locally, more than a quarter in 32 parliamentary constituencies, more than a third in seven and almost half in one (Glasgow Shettleston) were reliant on such benefits around the time of the 2001 General Election. The areas shown in Figure 6.8 opposite are the neighbourhoods of Britain aggregated to the constituencies over which that election was fought. Scottish Westminster constituencies have subsequently been reorganised, but at that time Shettleston was the bulls-eye in the centre of the diamond of Glasgow shown in Figure 6.8. These two forms of benefit provide almost all the financial resources most there have to live on for the majority of mature people reliant on welfare.

Figure 6.8 shows the geography of lives damaged enough for the authorities to agree to pay slightly over the odds. They did not do this lightly, as these numbers and proportions of people unable to work due to ill health in Britain are unprecedented. Normally only around one in 20 people of these ages would be expected to be unable to work due to poor health, but these people did not live through normal economic times, especially in the places highlighted opposite. At the other extreme there are almost 50 constituencies that are now so expensive to live in that those who fall ill and require such benefits have to leave the area to afford to live.

When all those reliant on at least one form of benefit are included, in a few constituencies a majority of mature adults are in such a position of dependency. The number of neighbourhoods where this is the case, if local data were available, would be far higher. The map left shows the geography of all those reliant on at least one benefit to live. These are between one in five and one in six of this population nationally, but as low as less than a tenth in the Home County lowlands. Those too sick to work or otherwise unable to find work are often a minority, and so do not feature prominently on maps of economic activity, but they are a very large minority during years in which most people would expect to enjoy fair, if not good, health.

Benefit claimants 45–59 (%)

	5.8 – 9.9
	10.0 – 19.9
	20.0 – 29.9
	30.0 – 39.9
	40.0 – 49.9
	50.0 – 60.3

6.8 Sick, disabled, or otherwise incapacitated, reliant on benefits in maturity

Figure 6.8

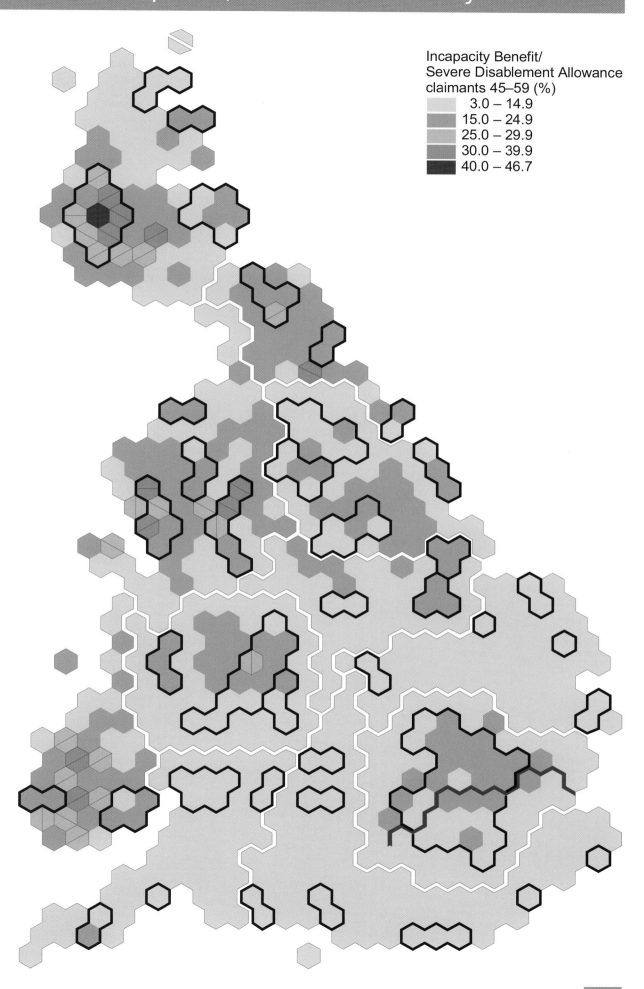

Incapacity Benefit/
Severe Disablement Allowance
claimants 45–59 (%)
3.0 – 14.9
15.0 – 24.9
25.0 – 29.9
30.0 – 39.9
40.0 – 46.7

6.9 Full of wise saws, modern instances, but not so many certificates in maturity

With almost two million of their number reliant on benefits of one kind or another, it is easy to forget that this is the generation that supposedly 'never had it so good'. However, this age group includes those who were among the first to benefit from the 1960s expansion of higher education (gaining a 'higher' qualification).

'Never had it so good' is something of an epitaph for this generation of the mature. In fact, most did not 'have it so good' and were not part of the education expansion and some had it much better than others partly as a result. Those that did go to university ended up particularly clustered geographically. Their concentration today is all the more extreme, as this secondary modern/technical/grammar school generation was 'creamed off' relatively geographically evenly compared with later generations. That is, a few went to university from almost everywhere (or at least a little less predictably by area than now).

The maps below show what proportion of those that went on to higher education ended up where, and what proportion in every neighbourhood left school with no qualifications and still have none. Figure 6.9 opposite shows the few places that the university educated actually came to dominate: the few suburbs of provincial towns they massed within and the larger parts of the capital they can now call their own. However, what is most striking about Figure 6.9 is that only to the west of Outer London are many places found where the majority have some qualifications, albeit for the majority these are qualifications lower than degree level. Elsewhere the majority have none. Only in a distinct slice of north east London do the majority have none and the largest minority have a degree or equivalent.

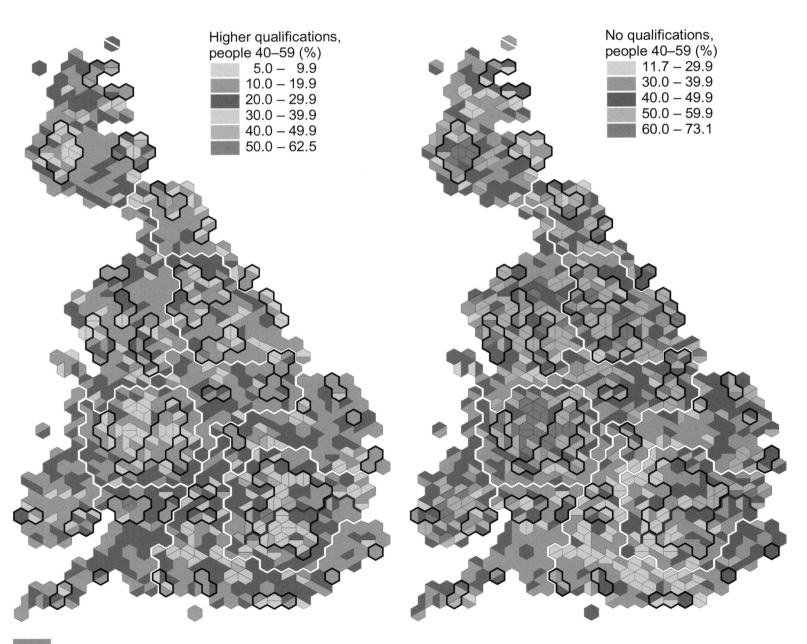

Higher qualifications, people 40–59 (%)
- 5.0 – 9.9
- 10.0 – 19.9
- 20.0 – 29.9
- 30.0 – 39.9
- 40.0 – 49.9
- 50.0 – 62.5

No qualifications, people 40–59 (%)
- 11.7 – 29.9
- 30.0 – 39.9
- 40.0 – 49.9
- 50.0 – 59.9
- 60.0 – 73.1

6.9   Full of wise saws, modern instances, but not so many certificates in maturity

Figure 6.9

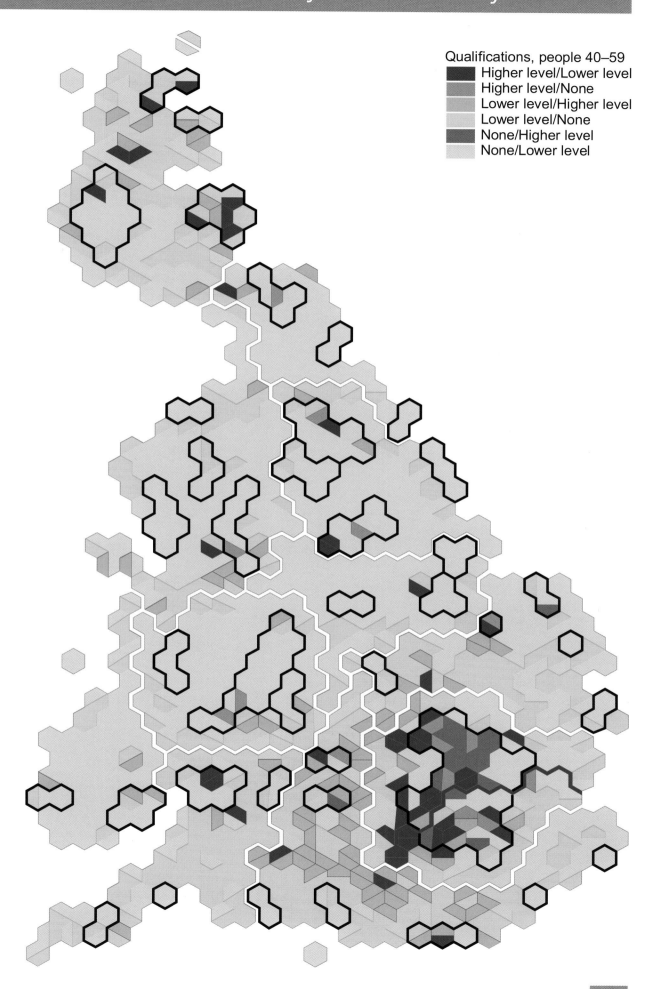

Qualifications, people 40–59
- Higher level/Lower level
- Higher level/None
- Lower level/Higher level
- Lower level/None
- None/Higher level
- None/Lower level

6.10 Places of preferences for those in maturity

The maps of qualifications just discussed are maps of both educational privilege and neglect. However, they also partly create, and to a lesser extent result from, patterns of age differentiation in these years. The same is true to varying degrees of all else that we have discussed above and will discuss below for this age group. Age differentiation has mattered for younger age groups and begins to matter more and more as calendar years of age grow in terms of biological import with maturity (you 'age' more proportionately each year that passes).

In terms of qualifications, the younger a person is, the more likely (s)he is to have higher qualifications and, as Figure 6.10 opposite shows, people at the younger end of these ages are more prone to city living. The map is dominated by the two colours representing (when this snapshot was taken) the ages

of 40 and 54. This domination is partly because of geographical polarisation as those who are older leave the cities more, but mainly the result of demographic history. Those aged 40 were the largest most recent birth cohort in this life stage being born at the beginning of the 1960s baby boom. Those aged 54 were born in the bumper years 1946/47, some nine months after most of the troops returned home from postings during the Second World War. It is also because so few babies were born in the war years that no neighbourhood has a majority aged 57, 58 or 59.

When five-year age groups are considered and the majority and largest minority identified, as is shown on the map left, some more subtlety is revealed. The cities are where the young mature mass. They in turn are all surrounded by suburbs where the youngest five-year group is most abundant and those aged 10 years older next so (the cohort containing the bumper birth years). Next the positions are reversed and those born in the mid to late 1940s bumper years dominate followed by the early to mid-1960s boomers. Finally, the south coast and much of Cornwall and mid- and west Wales are coloured the hues where the bumper years are still in the majority followed by those a little older. These are the lands of the early and semi-retired, found less in the north as slightly fewer people there reach these ages, and partly as a southward drift of the population in general occurred for this cohort, a drift most acute during the economic recession of the 1980s. Were we to be able to animate these patterns and turn days into seconds and years into minutes, the maps would flow with colour like an image of the annual migration of cattle on a savannah plain, except that this migration is not annual. It is a lifetime migration and for most, slowly and usually imperceptibly, the geographical trend is, like time, one-way.

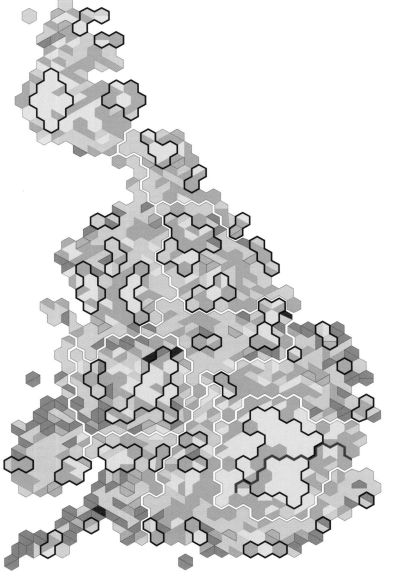

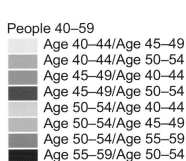

People 40–59

	Age 40–44/Age 45–49
	Age 40–44/Age 50–54
	Age 45–49/Age 40–44
	Age 45–49/Age 50–54
	Age 50–54/Age 40–44
	Age 50–54/Age 45–49
	Age 50–54/Age 55–59
	Age 55–59/Age 50–54

6.10 Places of preferences for those in maturity

Figure 6.10

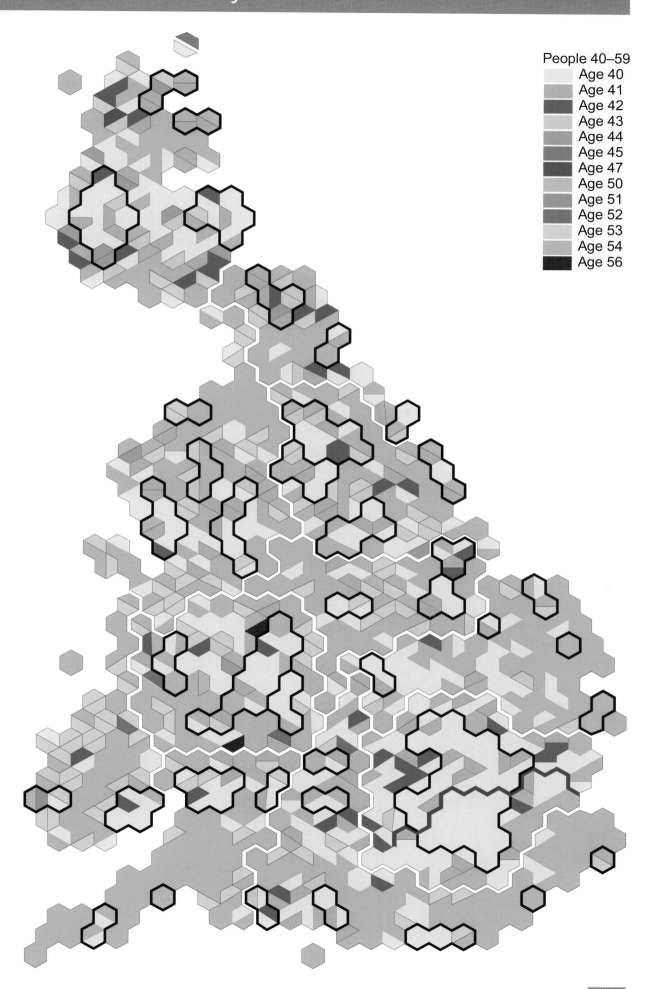

People 40–59
Age 40
Age 41
Age 42
Age 43
Age 44
Age 45
Age 47
Age 50
Age 51
Age 52
Age 53
Age 54
Age 56

6.11 Mobility in maturity

People flit around daily and this too obscures the slow mass migrations that occur over these years. However, travel to work patterns are noticeably different for this mature age cohort as compared with those a little younger in midlife (see page 147). It is in and around London that the difference occurs most obviously.

As Figure 6.11 opposite shows, there is much less diversity in approach to commuting than we saw at younger ages. Thus there are fewer categories in this map than there were for the younger generation. There is even more uniformity in car-dominated commuting at these ages than there was in midlife. This is interesting in that, when younger itself, this cohort group will have walked and cycled more than those that came after

them. It is notable also that there is still a significant smattering of areas where the largest minority cycle, but this smattering has reduced somewhat and it tends to be the flatter neighbourhoods where cycling is still done at older ages. Bones are becoming weary, people are a little happier to sit back and let the petrol engine take the strain, and perhaps also a little less willing to be crammed into commuter trains and light rail than are their younger colleagues.

This age group also has at least as much access to cars as those younger than them. The geography to that access, as shown in the map left, is also almost identical to that of their younger contemporaries and again there is nowhere mixed: having access to no cars or two or more cars are the two most likely positions to be in for the households in which those aged 40-59 years of age live.

Thus it appears that both for an adult of these mature years and of the midlife years just to live in many of these neighbourhoods for most can (and has to) be done with no car. This is where most have no car, either because they cannot afford one or because there is no parking. Around such neighbourhoods are areas where most can afford cars, can park, and carry out their everyday lives with one car. Around them are the places where in maturity, as in midlife, it is now usual to have at least two cars for members of the household to have access to. Where this is the case, it is as much (and usually more than) a product of local geography than of finances or teenager demographics.

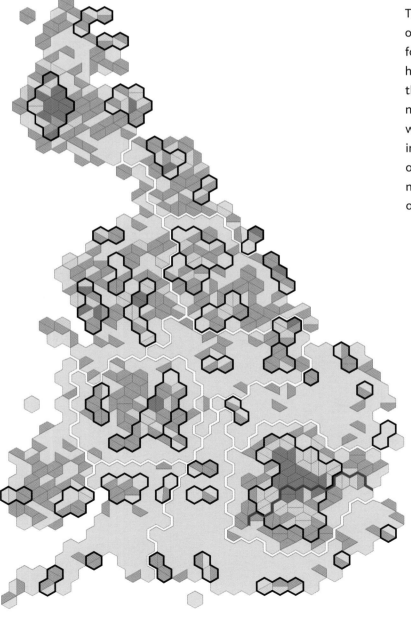

People 40–59 in households with
- No car/1 car
- 1 car/No car
- 1 car/2+ cars
- 2+ cars/1 car

6.11 Mobility in maturity

Figure 6.11

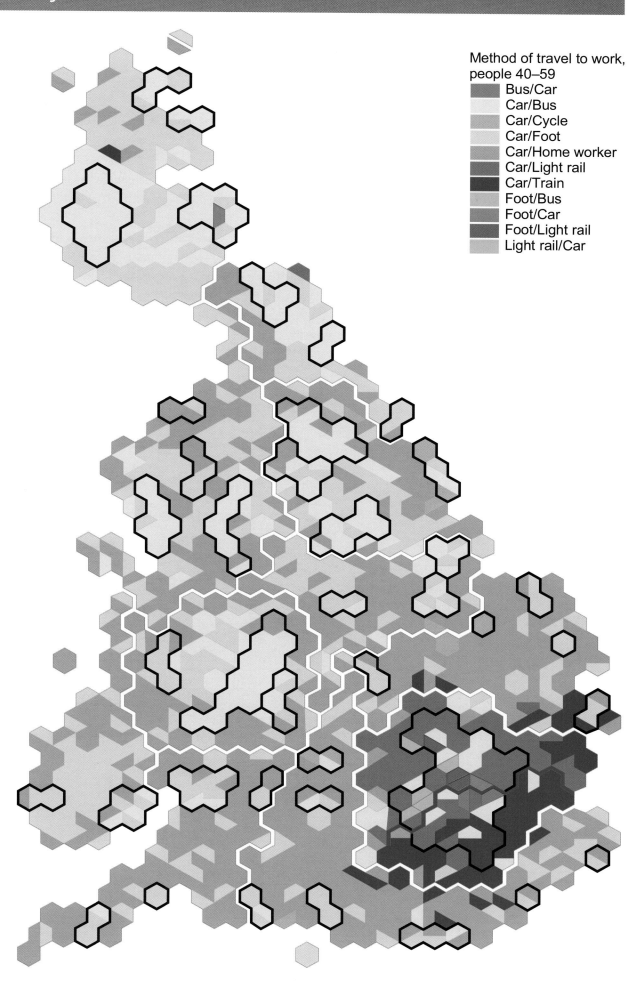

Method of travel to work,
people 40–59

- Bus/Car
- Car/Bus
- Car/Cycle
- Car/Foot
- Car/Home worker
- Car/Light rail
- Car/Train
- Foot/Bus
- Foot/Car
- Foot/Light rail
- Light rail/Car

6.12 Tenure and the mixing of neighbourhoods in maturity

By the years of maturity, the land is still a sea of conformity by tenure. The majority are still paying off those 25-year mortgages, or their second mortgage, or the mortgage they extended for a little equity withdrawal; there are many stories, but in most places most are still buying their home (see Figure 6.12 opposite). Perhaps unpredictably the places where a majority own outright are some of the most far flung and are often far from the most pricey; in both Orkney and the most rural half of Eilean Siar a majority own by these ages (note that crofting here continues, albeit with recent legal changes); a majority own also in the north of Rhondda, and the most rural parts of Ceredigion and Meirionnydd in Wales. All those houses in these five areas could be bought many times over, given the value of those in the other two neighbourhoods where a majority now own – Kensington and Chelsea – or the bank balances of many in the only neighbourhood where a majority of these ages rent privately – Hyde Park. Local authority (LA) and other social renting is dominant and in the largest minority in a shrunken set of places to those seen in earlier years by tenure.

If the table below is compared with that on page 148, we see that there are roughly as many mortgagees in Britain of mature years as in their midlife years. However, the huge difference between these stages of life is that by these years the very large majority are living in neighbourhoods where the second most common tenure is to own outright. Some seven million of the eight million mature mortgagees live in such neighbourhoods. There are also now a few neighbourhoods where a majority own outright, of which there are none in midlife.

Only three quarters of a million mature mortgagees live in neighbourhoods where the second most common tenure is renting from the council compared with two-and-a-quarter million of their equivalent in the midlife age bands. It would appear that if we compare the table below with its equivalent in the last chapter, people not only migrate away from cities as they age in Britain, but also drift up the tenure scale in terms of capital outlay and gain – out of renting into buying and out of buying into owning – thus making places where this is not the case for the majority or largest minority all the more unusual by these ages.

Number of people aged 40-59 in a mortgaged home according to tenure mix

People aged 40-59, mortgagees	Second most common tenure in the neighbourhood						
Most common tenure	Communal	LA rented	Mortgaged	Other social rented	Owned outright	Private rented	Total
LA rented			66,244	2,553			68,797
Mortgaged		764,680		31,187	7,141,449	4,953	7,942,269
Other social rented		4,806					4,806
Owned outright			19,160			3,225	22,385
Private rented			3,650				3,650
Total		769,486	89,054	33,740	7,141,449	8,178	8,041,907

6.12 Tenure and the mixing of neighbourhoods in maturity

Figure 6.12

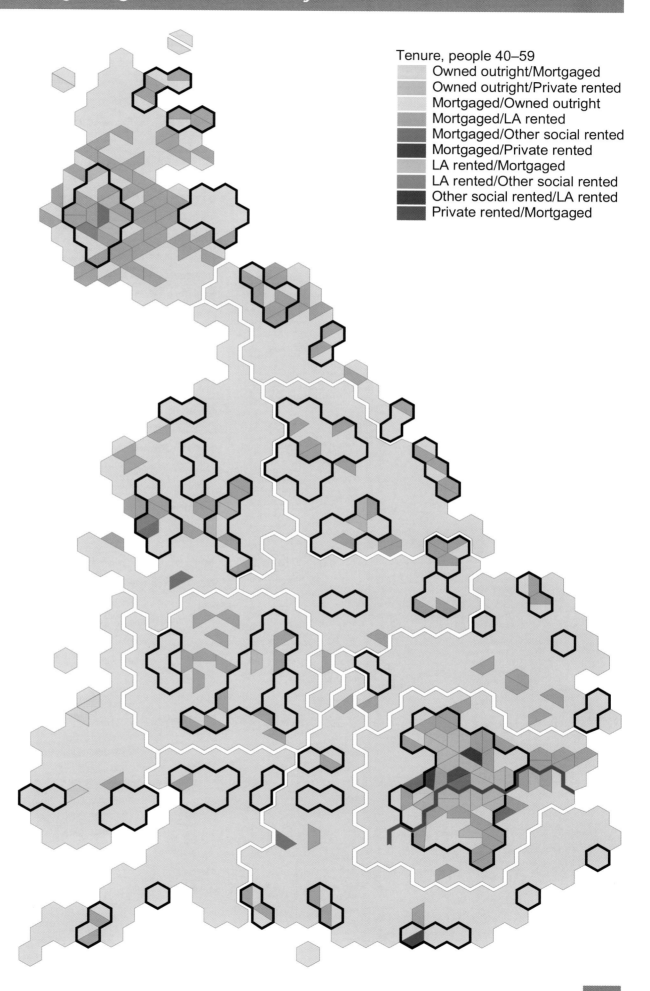

Tenure, people 40–59
- Owned outright/Mortgaged
- Owned outright/Private rented
- Mortgaged/Owned outright
- Mortgaged/LA rented
- Mortgaged/Other social rented
- Mortgaged/Private rented
- LA rented/Mortgaged
- LA rented/Other social rented
- Other social rented/LA rented
- Private rented/Mortgaged

6.13 Ethnicity, ancestry, religion and belief identities in maturity

A majority of those aged over 40 who do not identify themselves as some category of 'White' were not born in Britain. Thus Figure 6.13 opposite is as much a map of ethnicity as it is a map of where people of a particular age (who came here) came from and where they ended up as the largest minority or, very rarely at these ages, as the majority group. Note how few categories there are for people of these ages compared with the categories for those in their midlife (see page 151). Note too how the most widespread areas of minority representation are where 'White Irish' is the largest minority, or 'Other White British' in Scotland; only after these two does 'Indian' feature as the next most widespread minority ethnicity that people hold in maturity. Note also that at these ages very small numbers can change the shade of an area on the map opposite because so many areas are so 'White'.

Nationally, 90% of the mature age group claim to be 'White British' in England and Wales, and 4% some other kind of 'White'. Of the 6% left, two describe themselves as 'Indian', one 'Pakistani' and two 'Black' (of three kinds), with the final percentage being made up of all the remaining possibilities.

Our religious identities are only really substantially more revealing as markers of social and immigrant history in Scotland and there, at these ages, some clear patterns become visible as shown in the map below. The Church of Scotland is mostly in a majority. Roman Catholic comes second to the west, all around and in much of Glasgow and Catholic is in the majority in half a dozen neighbourhoods there. Elsewhere in Scotland a majority proclaim themselves to be of 'no religion' in only a few parts of the three largest cities. Note that responses in Scotland may have been influenced by the chance to declare religious upbringing as well as current religious tendency on the census form, unlike their brethren south of the border.

South of the border the picture is far less interesting: a few pockets of resistance to stating their religion where perhaps people did not want to be associated with the state church if they identified themselves as 'Christian'; a couple of 'Hindu' and 'Muslim' majority areas in maturity; one 'Sikh' enclave; and then not much more to report than could have been expected from what we see in Figure 6.13.

Note that, due to data limitations, the map of religion covers the age range 35-59.

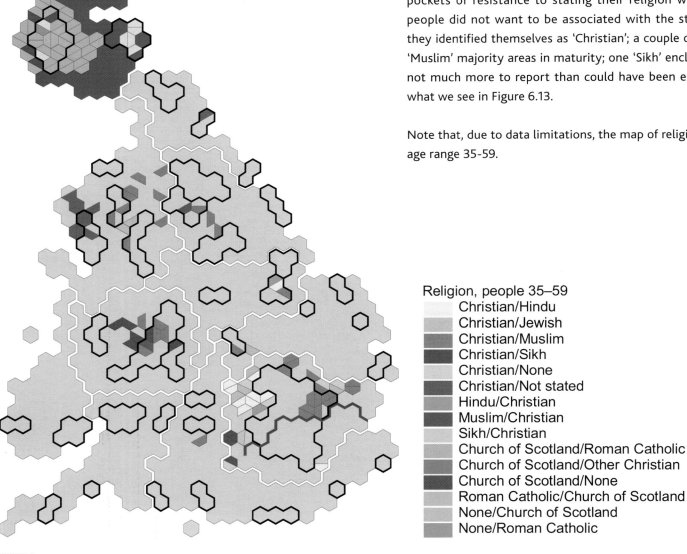

Religion, people 35–59
- Christian/Hindu
- Christian/Jewish
- Christian/Muslim
- Christian/Sikh
- Christian/None
- Christian/Not stated
- Hindu/Christian
- Muslim/Christian
- Sikh/Christian
- Church of Scotland/Roman Catholic
- Church of Scotland/Other Christian
- Church of Scotland/None
- Roman Catholic/Church of Scotland
- None/Church of Scotland
- None/Roman Catholic

6.13 Ethnicity, ancestry, religion and belief identities in maturity

Figure 6.13

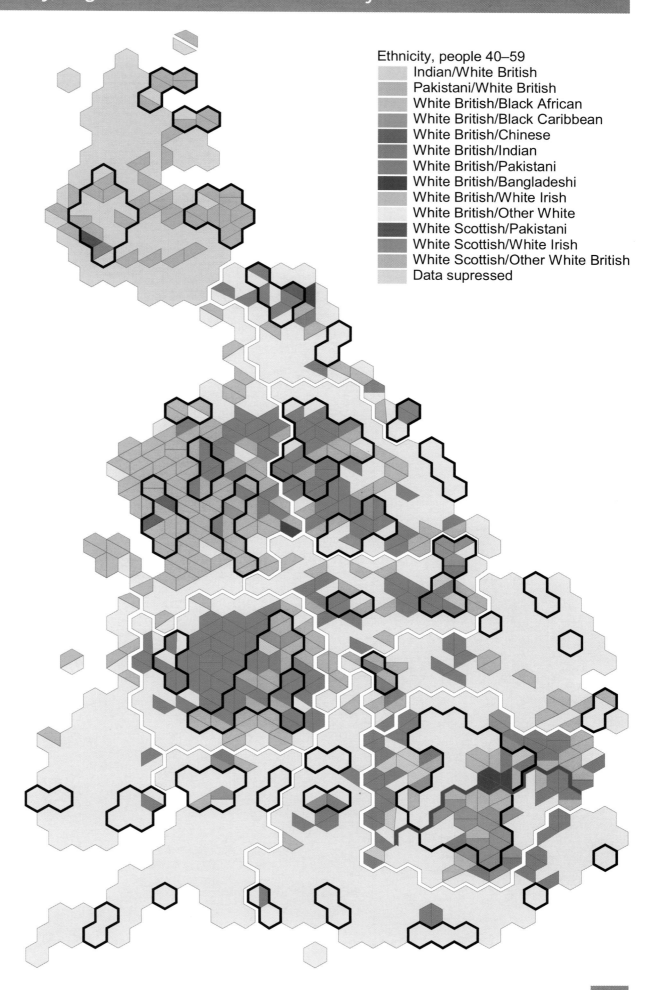

Ethnicity, people 40–59
- Indian/White British
- Pakistani/White British
- White British/Black African
- White British/Black Caribbean
- White British/Chinese
- White British/Indian
- White British/Pakistani
- White British/Bangladeshi
- White British/White Irish
- White British/Other White
- White Scottish/Pakistani
- White Scottish/White Irish
- White Scottish/Other White British
- Data supressed

6.14 The kaleidoscope of occupational identity in maturity

You *go to work to get the cash to buy the food to get the strength to go to work.* (Industrial Workers of the World)

Have you ever seen a map like Figure 6.14? Well, possibly earlier in this book, particularly the one concerning middle management in middle England in midlife a chapter ago (on page 153). But other than that we doubt you have. The psychedelic nature of Figure 6.14 is only tangentially related to the fact that these people were the children and teenagers of the 1960s. That tangential relationship is that this group is old enough to have gone into almost the full range of occupations that the classification of occupations was designed to distinguish. That is, there are not too dissimilar numbers of people of these ages in each of these groups. Also, as we noted for the younger cohort cross-referenced above, by later adult ages people appear to mix

a little bit more by occupational title, at least as they segregate more by age. Segregating both by age and class is still unusual in Britain (although common in gated communities of the affluent retired in the United States).

To aid interpretation of the cacophony of colour opposite, we also show below where each group is in a simple majority. Note that the two smaller groups are nowhere in the majority and also that people who have never worked or not worked in the past 10 years are not included as no occupation can be recorded for them.

Number of people aged 40-59 by occupation

Occupation	Number of people
Managers and senior officials	1,862,868
Professional occupations	1,338,571
Associate professional and technical occupations	1,375,927
Administrative and secretarial occupations	1,499,594
Skilled trades occupations	1,316,731
Personal service occupations	765,487
Sales and customer service occupations	631,748
Process, plant and machine operatives	1,062,737
Elementary occupations	1,223,087
All	11,076,750

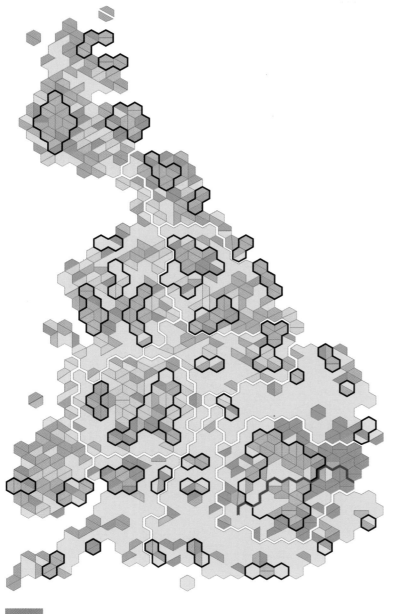

Occupation, people 40–59
1. Managers & Senior Officials
2. Professional
3. Assoc Professional & Tech
4. Admin & Secretarial
5. Skilled Trades
8. Operatives
9. Elementary

6.14 The kaleidoscope of occupational identity in maturity

Occupation, people 40–59

1. Managers & Senior Officials/2. Professional
1. Managers & Senior Officials/3. Assoc Professional & Tech
1. Managers & Senior Officials/4. Admin & Secretarial
1. Managers & Senior Officials/5. Skilled Trades
1. Managers & Senior Officials/8. Operatives
1. Managers & Senior Officials/9. Elementary
2. Professional/1. Managers & Senior Officials
2. Professional/3. Assoc Professional & Tech
2. Professional/4. Admin & Secretarial
2. Professional/5. Skilled Trades
2. Professional/9. Elementary
3. Assoc Professional & Tech/1. Managers & Senior Officials
3. Assoc Professional & Tech/2. Professional
3. Assoc Professional & Tech/4. Admin & Secretarial
3. Assoc Professional & Tech/5. Skilled Trades
3. Assoc Professional & Tech/9. Elementary
4. Admin & Secretarial/1. Managers & Senior Officials
4. Admin & Secretarial/2. Professional
4. Admin & Secretarial/3. Assoc Professional & Tech
4. Admin & Secretarial/5. Skilled Trades
4. Admin & Secretarial/8. Operatives
4. Admin & Secretarial/9. Elementary
5. Skilled Trades/1. Managers & Senior Officials
5. Skilled Trades/2. Professional
5. Skilled Trades/3. Assoc Professional & Tech
5. Skilled Trades/4. Admin & Secretarial
5. Skilled Trades/8. Operatives
5. Skilled Trades/9. Elementary
8. Operatives/1. Managers & Senior Officials
8. Operatives/2. Professional
8. Operatives/3. Assoc Professional & Tech
8. Operatives/4. Admin & Secretarial
8. Operatives/5. Skilled Trades
8. Operatives/9. Elementary
9. Elementary/1. Managers & Senior Officials
9. Elementary/2. Professional
9. Elementary/3. Assoc Professional & Tech
9. Elementary/4. Admin & Secretarial
9. Elementary/5. Skilled Trades
9. Elementary/8. Operatives

Figure 6.14

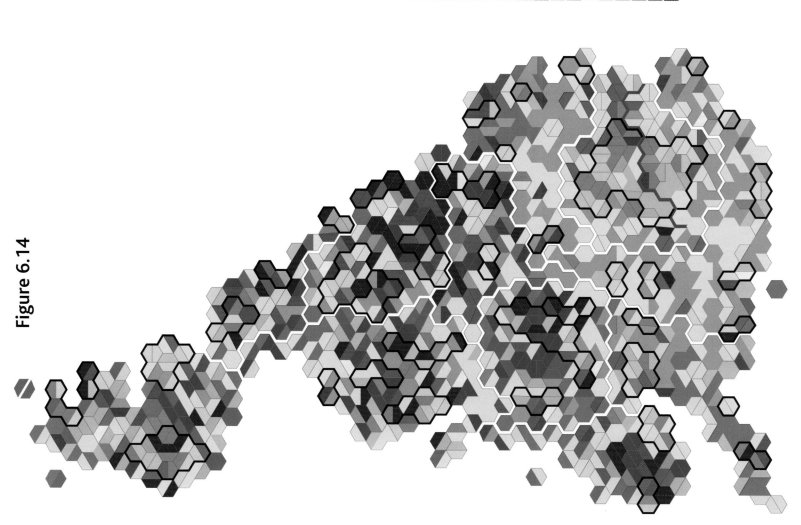

6.15 From real estate, renting and business to manufacturing: industry in maturity

In just under half of all neighbourhoods manufacturing pips other industries to the post as the main employer of those aged 40-59. That is, of course, because it has not been subdivided here into different kinds of manufacturing. Why manufacturing comes to dominate the maps is mainly because of how we classify and then group industries. That is partly why we show second most common as well as most common. Of the 11 million people being classified here, only 1.7 million work in manufacturing, but they are concentrated in particular (northern) neighbourhoods where other industrial activities are more evenly spread.

The combined service sectors of 'health and social work', 'real estate, renting and business' and 'wholesale and retail, vehicle repair' are the major employers in a narrow majority of neighbourhoods, and if we combined all services, they would, of course, be the majority employer everywhere. Even separated, one of these three is the largest minority industry in just over 1,000 neighbourhoods. Figure 6.15 opposite shows the full mosaic created by all the combinations that occur at these ages.

The map below presents the simpler picture of what is most dominant where. Note how almost exclusive to the London heartland is any dominance of business (including 'real estate, renting and business'). 'Wholesale and retail, vehicle repair' fills in much of the rest of the south, as does 'health and social work' in the north, in those 'urban holes' not dominated by manufacturing. 'Education' is found dominant only around the main universities; 'transport, storage and communications' around the Dover docks and southern airports.

Of the remaining possible forms of industry, only five neighbourhoods find any of them in a majority: public administrative work including defence and social security in Poulton-le-Fylde in Lancashire and Helensburgh in Scotland; hotels and restaurants dominate work only along the south shore of Blackpool and up on the Scottish west coast at Mallaig.

And, finally, 'agriculture' is now the dominant work activity only in one neighbourhood: the rural parts of Brecon. At ages 40-59 it is second most common only in four: Stranraer, Orkney, rural Penrith and rural Montgomeryshire. Note that construction is dominant nowhere and neither is finance when separated out from business more generally defined. It comes second to 'real estate, renting and business' combined only in the two neighbourhoods of Kensington and Chelsea.

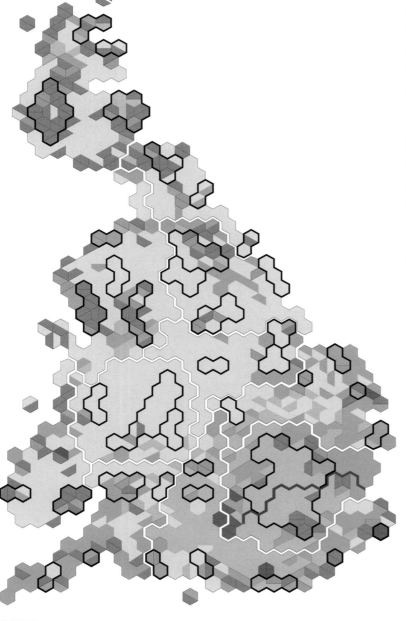

Industry, people 40–59
- Agriculture
- Education
- Health & Social Work
- Hotels & Restaurants
- Manufacturing
- Public Admin & Defence, Social Security
- Real Estate, Renting & Business
- Transport, Storage & Comms
- Wholesale & Retail, Vehicle Repair

6.15 From real estate, renting and business to manufacturing: industry in maturity

Industry, people 40–59

Agriculture/Health & Social Work
Education/Health & Social Work
Education/Manufacturing
Education/Real Estate, Renting & Business
Education/Wholesale & Retail, Vehicle Repair
Health & Social Work/Agriculture
Health & Social Work/Construction
Health & Social Work/Education
Health & Social Work/Manufacturing
Health & Social Work/Real Estate, Renting & Business
Health & Social Work/Transport, Storage & Comms
Health & Social Work/Wholesale & Retail, Vehicle Repair
Hotels & Restaurants/Health & Social Work
Hotels & Restaurants/Wholesale & Retail, Vehicle Repair
Manufacturing/Education
Manufacturing/Health & Social Work
Manufacturing/Public Admin & Defence, Social Security
Manufacturing/Real Estate, Renting & Business
Manufacturing/Transport, Storage & Comms
Manufacturing/Wholesale & Retail, Vehicle Repair
Public Admin & Defence, Social Security/Health & Social Work
Public Admin & Defence, Social Security/Wholesale & Retail, Vehicle Repair
Real Estate, Renting & Business/Education
Real Estate, Renting & Business/Financial
Real Estate, Renting & Business/Health & Social Work
Real Estate, Renting & Business/Manufacturing
Real Estate, Renting & Business/Other
Real Estate, Renting & Business/Public Admin & Defence, Social Security
Real Estate, Renting & Business/Wholesale & Retail, Vehicle Repair
Transport, Storage & Comms/Health & Social Work
Transport, Storage & Comms/Real Estate, Renting & Business
Transport, Storage & Comms/Wholesale & Retail, Vehicle Repair
Wholesale & Retail, Vehicle Repair/Agriculture
Wholesale & Retail, Vehicle Repair/Education
Wholesale & Retail, Vehicle Repair/Health & Social Work
Wholesale & Retail, Vehicle Repair/Hotels & Restaurants
Wholesale & Retail, Vehicle Repair/Manufacturing
Wholesale & Retail, Vehicle Repair/Public Admin & Defence, Social Security
Wholesale & Retail, Vehicle Repair/Real Estate, Renting & Business
Wholesale & Retail, Vehicle Repair/Transport, Storage & Comms

Figure 6.15

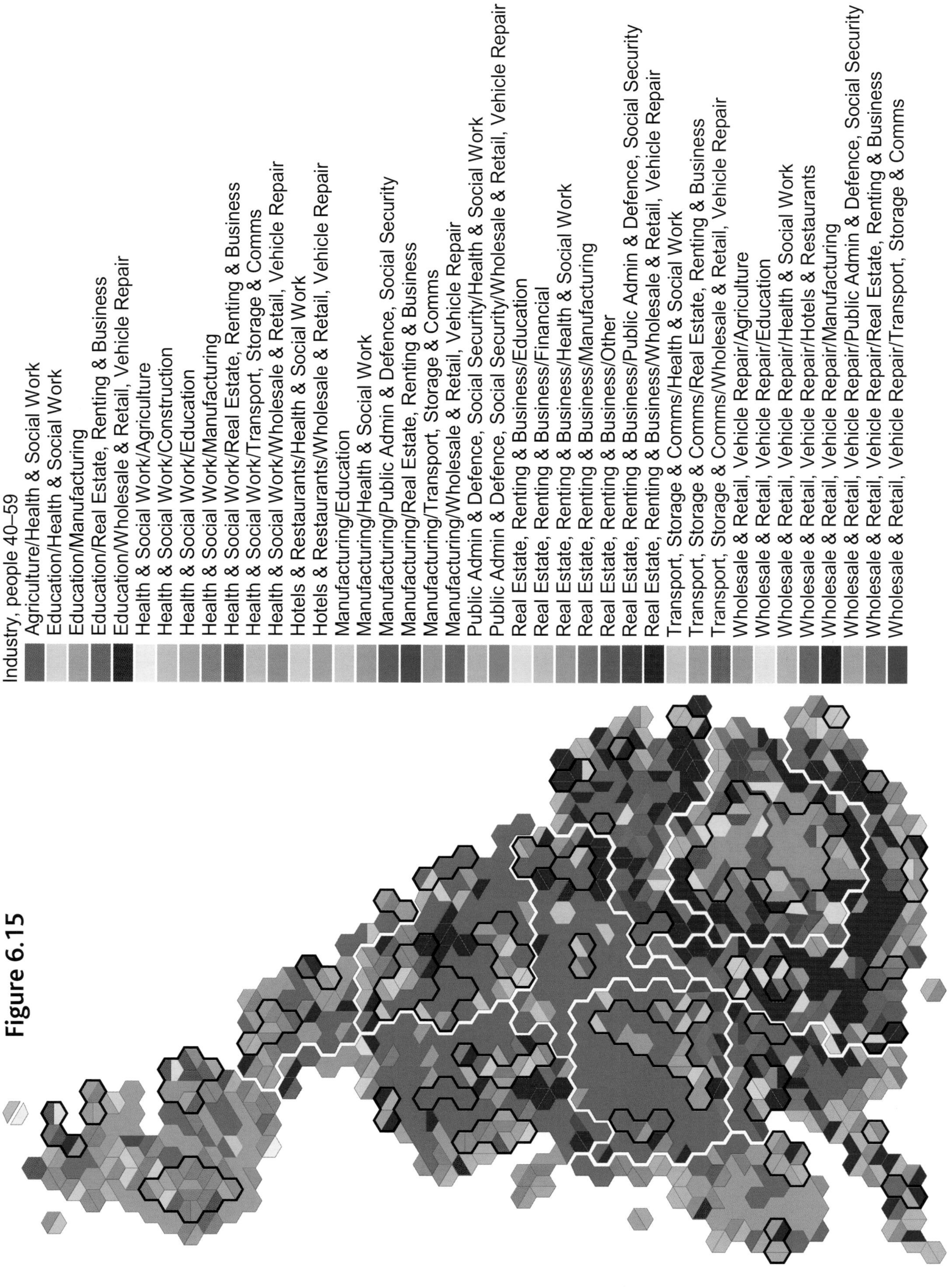

6.16 Remaining in your place: class and class mixing in the mature years

Whereas in midlife there were six neighbourhoods where 'higher managers' (according to the National Statistics Socioeconomic Classification [NS-SeC]) dominated, by maturity only one remains: Oxford West. Elsewhere those at the top have not, in general, lost their jobs; they are just dissipated out a little from their affluent enclaves – perhaps a few more are now commuting in from 'the country'. A few have also been able to retire early. However, as shown in the table below, two-and-a-half times more areas are also dominated by those in 'routine' work in maturity than was the case in midlife, as shown in the table on page 156. There are also 15 neighbourhoods by these mature ages where a majority are 'small employers'. There were no such neighbourhoods in midlife, and there were then just 19 areas where 'small employers' were the largest minority group (there are now 116 such places in maturity). Often found in rural areas, Figure 6.16 opposite shows that these small employers are not just farmers, but also people found clustered where small hotels dominate the coast and antique shops dominate the rural village: clearly a few are living their hotelier/shopkeeper dreams out in their more mature years.

Again it is worth noting how little mixing occurs how often. The table below shows that where they are in the majority, 'higher managers' mix only with 'lower managers' but 'lower manangers' mix with all other groups. 'Lower managers' are in the largest minority to all that make up a majority anywhere, but they are by far the largest group. Other than mixing with them, 'small employers' are only found in one neighbourhood mixing with anyone else: their 'semi-routine' employees in the hotels and restaurants of Blackpool's South Shore. The 'semi-routine' in turn are dominant only where, other than with the ubiquitous 'lower managers', those in 'routine' occupations are next most commonly found. They reciprocate that relationship except for one neighbourhood where those who have 'never worked' (mainly women looking after their homes in the Undercliffe neighbourhood of Bradford) are next most found. Note that the 'never worked' group includes many women at ages 40-59, especially from ethnic groups where it was unusual for women to work until recently, and also people who have not worked for at least 10 years.

Finally, the 'never worked' are in the majority, with 'lower managers' second in five London neighbourhoods – Stepney, Bow, East Ham, Poplar and Plaistow (in West Ham) – and in the inner Manchester neighbourhood of Gorton West. 'Semi-routine' workers are next most commonly found in the Birmingham neighbourhoods of Hodge Hill West, Ladywood (East and West), Handsworth, Fox Hollies and Sparkbrook. Those in 'routine' occupations as the second largest minority to those in maturity who have 'never worked' are found in Liverpool Riverside North, Bradford University and Blackburn East neighbourhoods.

Number of neighbourhoods by social class mix of people aged 40-59

People aged 40-59	Second most common social class								
Most common social class	1. Higher managers	2. Lower managers	3. Inter-mediate	4. Small employers	5. Lower supervisory	6. Semi-routine	7. Routine	8. Never worked	Total
1. Higher managers		1							1
2. Lower managers	301		60	116	1	549	37	8	1,072
4. Small employers		14				1			15
6. Semi-routine		49					52		101
7. Routine		26				51		1	78
8. Never worked		6				6	3		15
Total	301	96	60	116	1	607	92	9	1,282

6.16 Remaining in your place: class and class mixing in the mature years

Figure 6.16

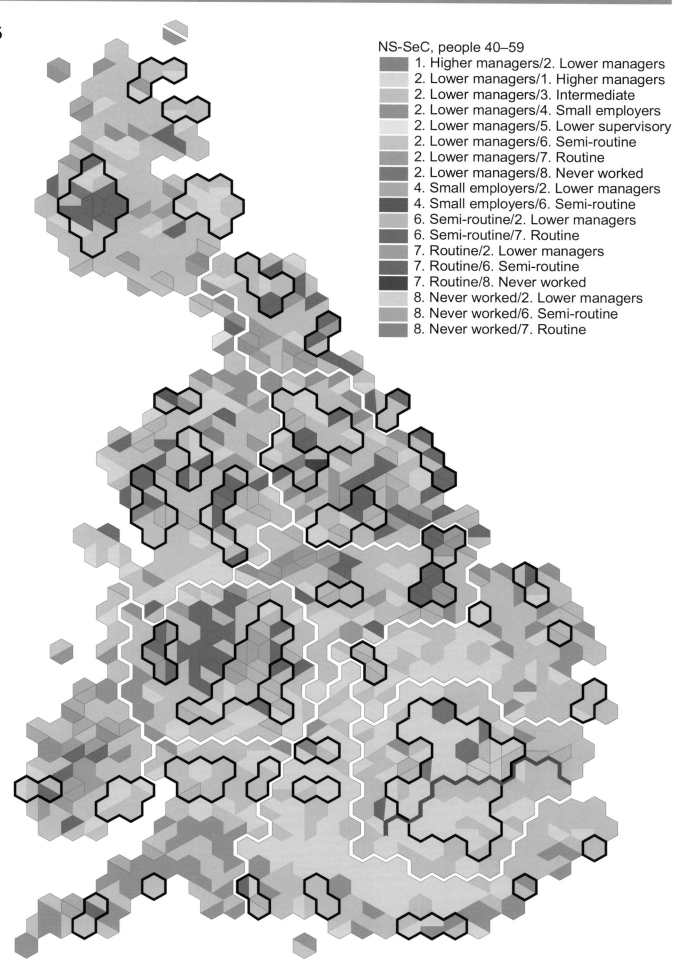

NS-SeC, people 40–59
1. Higher managers/2. Lower managers
2. Lower managers/1. Higher managers
2. Lower managers/3. Intermediate
2. Lower managers/4. Small employers
2. Lower managers/5. Lower supervisory
2. Lower managers/6. Semi-routine
2. Lower managers/7. Routine
2. Lower managers/8. Never worked
4. Small employers/2. Lower managers
4. Small employers/6. Semi-routine
6. Semi-routine/2. Lower managers
6. Semi-routine/7. Routine
7. Routine/2. Lower managers
7. Routine/6. Semi-routine
7. Routine/8. Never worked
8. Never worked/2. Lower managers
8. Never worked/6. Semi-routine
8. Never worked/7. Routine

6.17 Social grade and social climbing: from midlife to maturity

Social grade was the far simpler way by which people were categorised in the past and this method can still be used to subdivide them roughly now (see page 118 for the categories). Here we begin with something a little different and compare how many neighbourhoods are dominated by the same social classes at this stage in life as were in the last stage. The table shows that 1,030 neighbourhoods are identically stereotyped, whether by those aged 25-39 or those aged 40-59. Some 83 are classed 'up' a grade or more when the older age groups are used and some 169 'down' at least one. This downwards shift is to be expected as more people worked in more lower graded jobs and/or had less pompous titles in the past. However, the extremes of change are interesting.

Number of neighbourhoods by social grade at ages 25-39 and ages 40-59

Number of neighbourhoods	Neighbourhood classified by social grade of those aged 40-59					
Classified by those aged 25-39	AB	C1	C2	D	E	Total
AB	266	94		1	1	362
C1	19	607		63	6	695
C2		45	3	3		51
D		18	1	150	1	170
E					4	4
Total	285	764	4	217	12	1,282

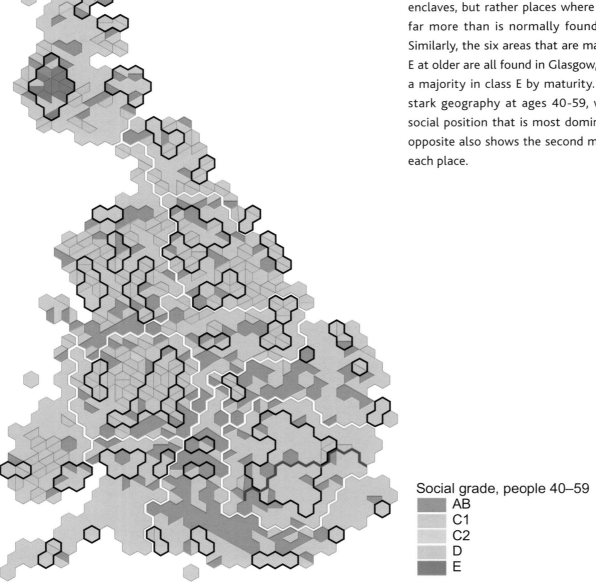

The two areas that drop from being AB at ages 25-39 to D and E respectively for older workers are Worcester East and the University neighbourhood of Glasgow. These are not gentrifying enclaves, but rather places where people of different ages tend, far more than is normally found, to do quite different work. Similarly, the six areas that are majority C1 at younger ages and E at older are all found in Glasgow, as are all the other areas with a majority in class E by maturity. The map left shows this very stark geography at ages 40-59, when class is counted by the social position that is most dominant in each place. Figure 6.17 opposite also shows the second most commonly found group in each place.

Social grade, people 40–59
- AB
- C1
- C2
- D
- E

6.17 Social grade and social climbing: from midlife to maturity

Figure 6.17

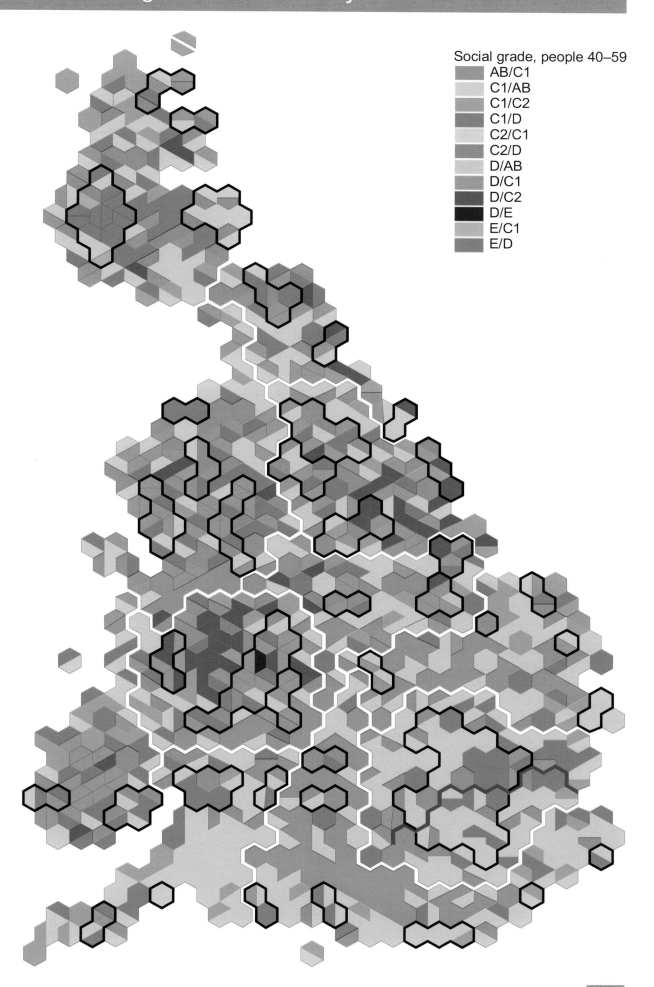

Social grade, people 40–59
- AB/C1
- C1/AB
- C1/C2
- C1/D
- C2/C1
- C2/D
- D/AB
- D/C1
- D/C2
- D/E
- E/C1
- E/D

6.18 Providing care in maturity

The map below can be compared with that for those in midlife on page 160, and one key difference immediately becomes apparent: by maturity people in Scotland are providing care at a rate similar to that prevalent across much of southern England. The same is not true for those in midlife and, as we see later, is not due to any sudden improvement in the health of Scots as they age. What accounts instead for the map below being significantly different to that for those aged 25-39 is that between 1991 and 2001 there was a large increase in the provision of local authority and independent care homes in Scotland that did not occur elsewhere. (The reasons for this are reported in detail in a study by Laura Banks and her colleagues published by the Joseph Rowntree Foundation in July 2006 and available in summary as *JRF Findings* no 412 at www.jrf.org.uk/knowledge/findings.) That work and the difference between the map below and that for younger ages shows that people do not need to provide unpaid care when illness rates are high. Such care can be paid for by those with the means to do so, while in Scotland it is free.

On the map below the proportions providing care are as low as 11.6% in Hyde Park, the average being between 16.0% and 20.0%, and as high as 25.7% in the south west of the Gower.

Opposite, the maps of proportion of the population as a whole, and of men and women separately providing care, are shown and contrasted. Note that different age bands have had to be used for some of these maps, but the same colour key is employed in all to aid comparison between them. The proportion of those who are providing that care, despite only being in fair health themselves, is also shown bottom right using the same shading. Note also that it is where least care needs to be given, where it is provided by the state, or where people tend not to be ill, that those whose health itself is not good do not so often also need to provide care to others.

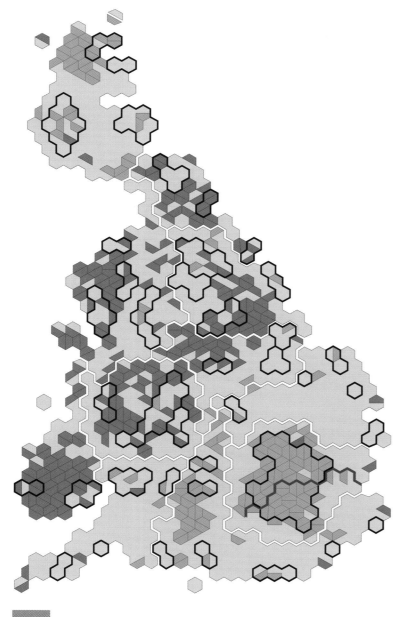

People 40–59 providing care
- Above average
- Average
- Below average

6.18 Providing care in maturity

People 40–59 providing care (%)
- 11.6 – 14.9
- 15.0 – 17.4
- 17.5 – 19.9
- 20.0 – 22.4
- 22.5 – 25.7

Women 45–59 providing care (%)
- 14.7 – 17.4
- 17.5 – 19.9
- 20.0 – 22.4
- 22.5 – 25.9
- 26.0 – 31.7

Men 45–59 providing care (%)
- 10.1 – 14.9
- 15.0 – 17.4
- 17.5 – 19.9
- 20.0 – 22.4
- 22.5 – 24.1

People 45–59 in fair health providing care (%)
- 15.5 – 17.4
- 17.5 – 19.9
- 20.0 – 22.4
- 22.5 – 27.9
- 28.0 – 32.2

6.19 Illness, disability and poor health in maturity

Illness *is not something a person has; it's another way of being.* (Jonathan Miller, 1978, *The Body in Question*, London: Jonathan Cape)

By the years of maturity, significant numbers of people are describing their health as 'poor' when asked. However, there is an eight-fold difference in the likelihood that this will be the case by areas, as the map shown on page 165 at the start of this chapter summarised. The maps of poor health rates separated for men and women (not shown here) are remarkably similar at these ages. Below we also show where the numbers that suffer from a limiting long-term illness (LLTI) are above or below average in the years of maturity, and in Figure 6.19 opposite we show the rate at which this population tends to suffer such limitations in

each neighbourhood. At these ages the average neighbourhood rates of LLTI are between 15.0% and 24.9% suffering from such conditions. The rate is highest at 46.0% in Glasgow Milton and lowest nearby in Scotland at 8.4% in Balerno (in Edinburgh).

Maps such as that below and Figure 6.19 can give the impression that illness is a product of place, or that what we are showing is simply a reflection of social class and disadvantage as reflected through places. These maps are in fact a bit of both and more as the eight images overleaf attempt to illustrate. Each of those eight is drawn on the same colour scale and shows the proportions of people of the ages within each social class who are also suffering poor health. Almost everywhere less than a tenth of 'higher managers' are so afflicted, whereas up to a quarter of those of these ages in 'routine' occupations have poor health. However, for those in 'routine' occupations, this depends mostly on where they live. Finally, for those who have 'never worked' (or not in the past 10 years) the geographical patterns are most stark. But in the most affluent parts of the south their rates of poor health are as low as for 'higher managers'. Note also that in all eight of these maps we take an age range that begins five years younger than usual due to limitations with the original data. The overall map of propensity to suffer poor health is the sum of these eight, each weighted by population in each class in each place. These eight maps show just one way in which the overall map opposite can be decomposed.

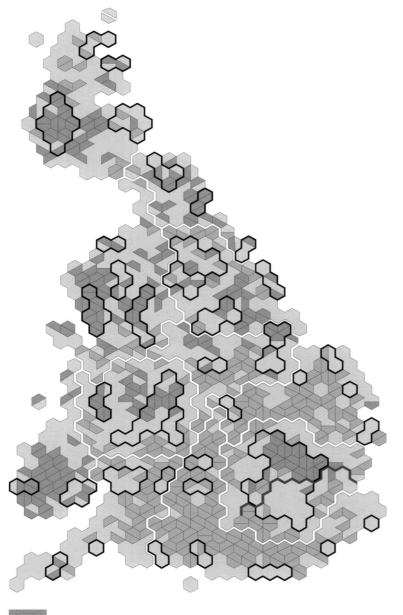

People 40–59 & LLTI
- Below average LLTI
- Average LLTI
- Above average LLTI

6.19 Illness, disability and poor health in maturity

Figure 6.19

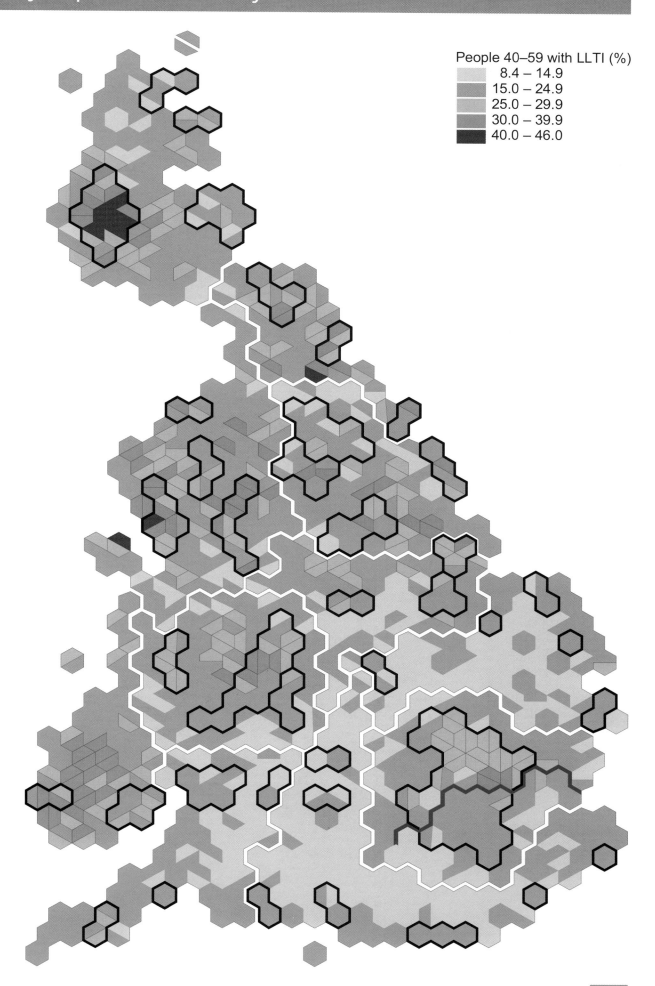

People 40–59 with LLTI (%)
- 8.4 – 14.9
- 15.0 – 24.9
- 25.0 – 29.9
- 30.0 – 39.9
- 40.0 – 46.0

6.19 Illness, disability and poor health in maturity

NS-SeC 1. Higher managers
35–59 in poor health (%)
- 1.0 – 4.9
- 5.0 – 9.9
- 10.0 – 13.6

NS-SeC 2. Lower managers
35–59 in poor health (%)
- 2.6 – 4.9
- 5.0 – 9.9
- 10.0 – 14.9
- 15.0 – 16.2

NS-SeC 3. Intermediate
35–59 in poor health (%)
- 2.4 – 4.9
- 5.0 – 9.9
- 10.0 – 14.9
- 15.0 – 15.4

NS-SeC 4. Small employers
35–59 in poor health (%)
- 2.6 – 4.9
- 5.0 – 9.9
- 10.0 – 14.9
- 15.0 – 17.8

6.19 Illness, disability and poor health in maturity

NS-SeC 5. Lower supervisory
35–59 in poor health (%)

- 2.3 – 4.9
- 5.0 – 9.9
- 10.0 – 14.9
- 15.0 – 19.9
- 20.0 – 20.2

NS-SeC 6. Semi-routine
35–59 in poor health (%)

- 3.1 – 4.9
- 5.0 – 9.9
- 10.0 – 14.9
- 15.0 – 18.4

NS-SeC 7. Routine
35–59 in poor health (%)

- 3.6 – 4.9
- 5.0 – 9.9
- 10.0 – 14.9
- 15.0 – 19.9
- 20.0 – 24.9
- 25.0 – 26.2

NS-SeC 8. Never worked
35–59 in poor health (%)

- 4.8 – 4.9
- 5.0 – 9.9
- 10.0 – 14.9
- 15.0 – 19.9
- 20.0 – 24.9
- 25.0 – 29.9
- 30.0 – 39.0

6.20 Concluding maturity: the years out of midlife and towards retirement

On your way from the varying life chances of midlife to the more well-fired mosaics of the certainties of where you have got to by retirement, the journey of these in-between mature years began here with a reminder of how age starts to catch up with you. These are the beginnings of the years in which poor health is no longer a novelty, although still rare across most of Britain; the years in which fewer men are found because more have died. As we turned to maturity, we began on the path down to the end, but most of us have, at least nowadays and in our rich nation, still some way to go.

Maturity includes the years by which time people have lived through enough for those experiences of the past to begin to be etched on their maps. A multitude of processes can be identified that have resulted in the subtle mosaic of variation in the ratio of mature women to men across the country. Even more complex are the histories that have come together in their millions to produce the maps we have shown of who is married, still married, married and together but living apart, remarried, single, cohabiting, has children and is still living with them, is living in a household containing their new partner's children, is separated, divorced or widowed.

These images are affected as much by the years these people have lived through, and what was expected of them when they were young in terms of having children and making friends, as they are patterns of maturity. They are in part patterns of the past. Similarly, too, the maps of economic activity are as much maps of the economic fortunes of areas over recent decades as they are maps of the current achievements and misfortunes of this generation.

At these ages we see for the first time large numbers, mainly of women, who have never been in the formal labour market (or at least as far as the counting goes, not in the past 10 years). Again, as much, if not more, a product of how people of these ages were brought up to behave, and what was possible and made available for most of them, this is a map mostly of choices or constraints of and in maturity. And all through these maps sickness begins to feature more and more in a way it has not before, with a clear geography to it that, as we have shown, has far more to it than just class or place. That extra is part of the geography to the history of the times this life stage has already acted out. That history, although current policy is changing as we write, has resulted in over a million of the people of these ages being reliant on Incapacity Benefit or Severe Disablement Allowances.

The history of this generation also explains the patterns of qualifications held by those in their mature years; why so many were born in particular years and hence now bunch at particular ages; why so few travel by means other than the car; why so many are buying their home and where an increasing minority own outright in most places; their religious and ethnic heritage, class, occupational and industry history and hence their current reality: whom they have to care for and whether they themselves require care, and if they get it, before they too retire.

A few are already retired. Mostly these are the lucky ones, those rich enough as a result of having benefited most from living through what many thought were the best of times. Many more are working in servile occupations in their older years, are reliant on state benefits and often made to feel worthless for so being, living where this age group have been in least demand. It is here, where their skills were least required in the past, or they were told that they did not have the skills that the world now needed, that the largest numbers are now already quite ill. For many of these people this may be their last stage of life, not their fifth. For most in the poorer parts of the country this is their penultimate stage and retirement will be short.

For many in the richer parts of the country these are by contrast very good years. Soon they will own their home outright and can move where they like, they have their cars and can travel, and are beginning to really enjoy life. Their children (that they had a little late in life) will be fleeing the nest in the not too distant future. It is not just that the affluent at these ages have so much more. It is almost as if they are not even of these ages. It is as if their wealth, their good jobs, and the advantages of their upbringing have brought them extended youthfulness; in maturity they at worst suffer the chances of poor health and other disadvantages that others face in midlife. By maturity some people can appear a stage younger in some places compared with others.

As we turn now to the sixth stage of life, it is worth remembering that people have aged at different rates in different places, especially as they have moved through their mature years, to produce the images we next see. Understanding these following mosaics would be impossible without first having seen this geographical differentiation extend itself through so many lives and places, through the years of maturity. Each stage differs greatly from that preceding, and each cohort's experience of each stage also changes over time, but less abruptly.

7 The lean and slippered pantaloon: ages 60-74

... the sixth age shifts
Into the lean and slippered pantaloon,
With spectacles on nose and pouch on side,
His youthful hose, well saved, a world too wide
For his shrunk shank, and his big manly voice,
Turning again toward childish treble, pipes
And whistles in his sound;

7.1   Introduction

A shift now to something different: turn 60 and your free bus pass awaits. Turn 60 and it's time to slow down, shift back a gear, retire, or at least get ready to retire.

No longer expected to look after children, to earn money, to have to pay off loans: for some, these are the easy years. Most of the generation above you in years have died. There are fewer people all round to look after, other than your partner, if you still have one. But even if, by the start of these later years, there is not much looking after to be done, there probably soon will be. For many others the looking after has already begun, or they still have to work just to get by and to heat their home, while their contemporaries who had different lives now frequently holiday abroad in the warmth when they fancy it.

These are the years when the social divisions can be seen as most stark between those who have been able to amass their wealth and those from whom (at home if not abroad) they have amassed it: those who still must struggle. Most bleakly, these are the years in which these differences are mostly played out in early death and widowhood for the many, and, at the other extreme, a relatively healthy old age for the few. 'Old age' and the 'older aged' are terms that slip out too easily to encapsulate these years. You can still be young in old age, or you may feel all the weight of your age in your bones, but these are the last years before we are truly elderly. Here we are considering the oldest ages that most now at these ages expected to live to (when they were young).

Left we show the geographies for those aged 60-74. As above at earlier life stages, this is the basic distribution to remember as you consider the various characteristics of people at these ages.

No longer living just outside towns, by old age the coasts and remoter countryside draw most strongly. Less than a tenth of the people in most central sites and much of London are in their old age. In contrast, two to three times more of the old are more commonly found in the areas where they are most likely to migrate to in retirement.

Note that as we shrink, put spectacles on our noses, watch our paunches grow, and for men, hear our voices break back high, we are changing quickly in these years. We know that almost none of us will have children again (for women at least), that we are very different specimens at the start of these years, on average, compared with the end. By the turn of the millennium, a 60-year-old man's chances of dying before he reached 61 in Britain was 100 to one against, 60 to one for a 65-year-old not reaching 66 and 30 to one by 72 of not reaching age 73. For women, the respective rates at these same ages were: one in 150, one in 100 and one in 50, and the ages at which women attained the mortality chances of 60-, 65- and 70-year-old men were 65, 70 and 75 respectively. If you didn't know better, you'd be led to believe there was a God and that she was a woman with a numerical penchant for leaving obvious signs of her sympathies.

Proportion of population
aged 60–74 (%)

	6.3 – 9.9
	10.0 – 12.4
	12.5 – 14.9
	15.0 – 17.4
	17.5 – 22.7

7.1 Introduction

Figure 7.1 is not one we could draw at the start of the last two chapters as the result would have been too dull, but here it sums up the divisions across the country for those in old age that underlie much of the rest of what this penultimate stage of life is about geographically. Where life has been and continues to be hardest are the few places where the majority in old age are in poor health and most of the rest only in fair health. These two health statuses are reversed in the rest of the poorest parts of Britain. Around them in turn are the neighbourhoods where fair health is most likely but good health next most so, and around them the areas where good health is mostly found followed by fair. The 'good' and the 'poor' never mix in old age in the neighbourhoods of Britain, just as we have seen so little mixing in earlier years.

Figure 7.1

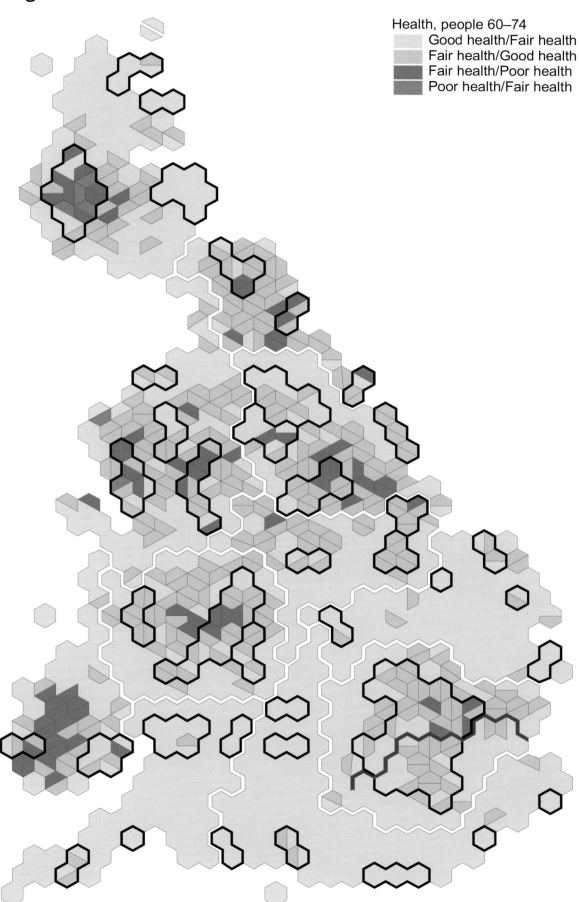

Health, people 60–74
- Good health/Fair health
- Fair health/Good health
- Fair health/Poor health
- Poor health/Fair health

7.2 Sex ratios in old age: places that age before and after their times

Figure 7.2 opposite shows just how uneven a mosaic of the ratio of women to men forms across the country at these ages. Migration plays a part in this formation. As more women survive, they make it to the retirement enclaves of the south coast in somewhat higher numbers than men. In this part of the pattern of sex ratios they leave in the picture part of the evidence of the last great migration of the autumn of our years. However, migrations much earlier in life, of more men out of particular northern and Scottish cities, and more importantly of men not moving there when there were no jobs for men, have also played their part. Similarly, the sex ratio is almost even and in a small number of areas tilted towards the older man in those places where, in general, two good wage packets were required to settle earlier in life.

For all its importance in creating the patterns we see in this mosaic (and those earlier in this atlas), by old age migration finally becomes the lesser factor determining what you see in Figure 7.2. The major factor in creating the mosaic is that for different neighbourhoods some men die, on average, many years earlier than in others. The national pattern to the sex ratio difference is attributable to inequalities in mortality at each age, and those inequalities are shown for these ages in the graph below. Because in some places 60-year-old men die at the rate of 70-year-olds elsewhere, and in other neighbourhoods 74-year-old men are faring better than 64-year-old men elsewhere, and because women's rates are so much lower and also do not have a geography that simply echoes men's at lower rates, there are places where there are now almost as few as only two old men living for every three old women alive.

The converse, in those places where men outnumber women, is not because women are dying more often than is normal. Where this is the case it is instead those few areas where there is a generation of men who came to Britain through immigration and not as many women followed them: the five neighbourhoods with more than 1% extra older men being Luton High Town, Stepney, Hackney North, Sparkbrook and Poplar. These are areas where in the past immigration from the Indian subcontinent and the Caribbean was high.

Annual mortality rates in Britain at older ages and resulting % female (60-74)

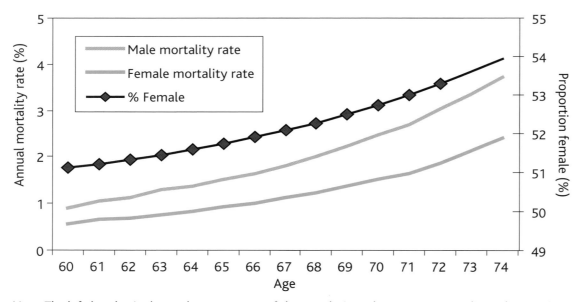

Note: The left-hand axis shows the percentage of the population who can expect to die each year given mortality rates in Britain (2002-04). The right-hand axis shows the growing proportion of the population who are female as a result of these differences in rates.

7.2 Sex ratios in old age: places that age before and after their times

Figure 7.2

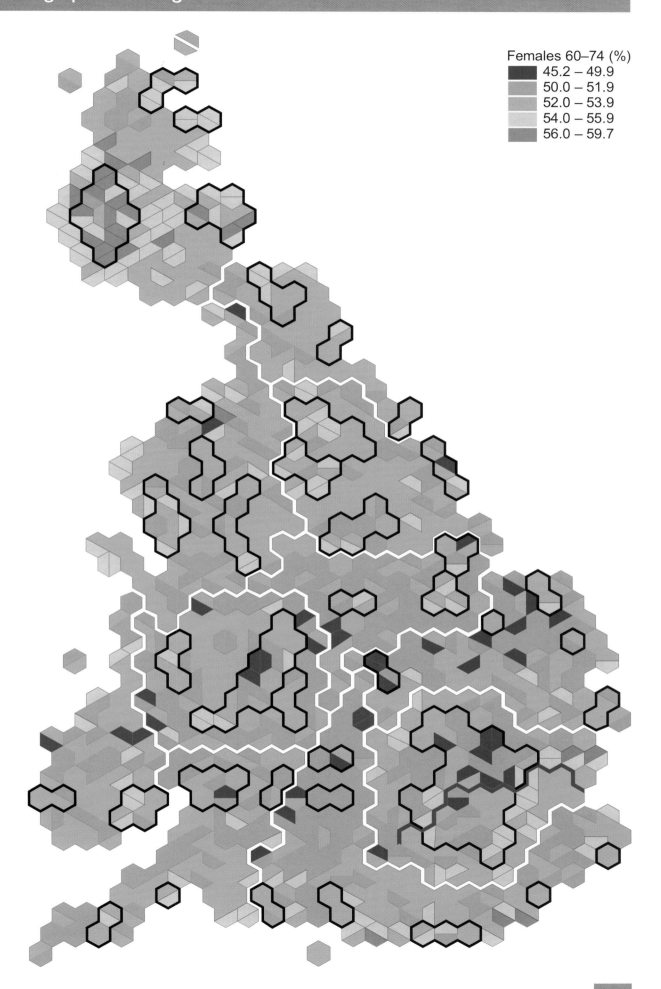

Females 60–74 (%)
- 45.2 – 49.9
- 50.0 – 51.9
- 52.0 – 53.9
- 54.0 – 55.9
- 56.0 – 59.7

7.3   Single and never married or still within their first marriage in old age

Just as death begins to play a more significant part in forming the mosaic of *where* different people are mostly to be found, so too does it begin to seriously affect *with whom* they are found in older ages. Almost as many people (16.5%) are separated from their married partner at these ages due to being widowed as due to having left them to become remarried, separated or divorced (18.9%). There are still a majority who are married and still in their first marriage (58.1%), leaving just a small group of people, one of the smallest for any cohort in British history, who remain single and have never married (6.5%). For that small group, especially unusual for their cohort, refuge was and still is most often found in the anonymity of living in cities and in particular the capital, shunned by many others of their age.

Figure 7.3 opposite highlights those neighbourhoods where the largest proportions of older people are 'single never married'. Note that there are usually few in old age in total in many areas where the proportion is high. Perhaps those that did not fit so well into the norms of their generation find it easier not to live where most in old age now live?

In contrast, the map shown below here is of the proportion in old age who are married and who are still living with their partner from that first marriage. The youngest of this generation were born during the Second World War and the oldest were children during it. Unlike the generation older than them, very few will have lost lovers due to war and have remained unmarried as a result. That fate fell most heavily on the generation of the parents of today's truly elderly as so many of their men were killed in the First World War. It is a fate echoed only now in Britain among a very small minority of those much younger who are refugees from the hundreds of smaller wars that have more recently swept the world (see page 91). As everything affects everything else, although near things more often than far, even maps of marriage can be partly maps of war and peace.

First marriage, people 60–74 (%)

	31.2 – 39.9
	40.0 – 44.9
	45.0 – 49.9
	50.0 – 54.9
	55.0 – 59.9
	60.0 – 71.7

7.3 Single and never married or still within their first marriage in old age

Figure 7.3

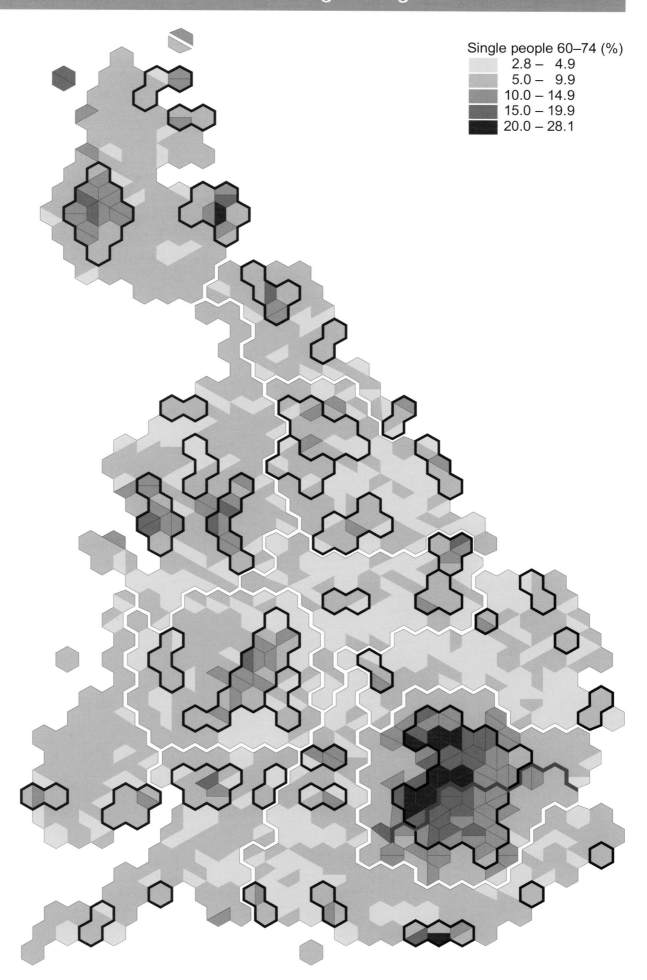

Single people 60–74 (%)
- 2.8 – 4.9
- 5.0 – 9.9
- 10.0 – 14.9
- 15.0 – 19.9
- 20.0 – 28.1

7.4 Widowed, remarried, separated or divorced in old age

The casualties of war within marriage take many forms and can only be counted here by what they currently are, not what they have been. To be remarried requires first having either been divorced or widowed. Thus not everyone who has been divorced is shown opposite (Figure 7.4), but they are included in at least one of the categories there, or are widowed, have left the country, or have died. Similarly, those 'separated' will only be a minority of all who have ever been married. They too will be widowed, separated, divorced, dead or emigrant in their turn. Snapshots from the wars within marriage are thus just that.

In this snapshot are shown 700,000 old people who are remarried, 630,000 who are divorced, but only 110,000 who are separated. Thus, at the time this snapshot was taken, of the 4.5 million of these ages still in their first marriage, just under one in 40 was separated. Of the 7.1 million ever married, 1.3 million are now widowed. The remainder, another 1.3 million, are remarried or divorced. These national counts, however, hide not just the marital states people have experienced to end up where they were when the snapshot was taken, but also the different geographical routes they took to cluster as they have now. Note just how attractive the southern coasts and Pennine hills are to those whose first marriage has broken up.

When those who are remarried, separated or divorced are shown as the proportion of all of these ages who have ever married, the rates appear higher and the pattern perhaps a little more distinct, as is shown left. At the least, by neighbourhood, just under a tenth of those in old age have had a broken marriage and at most, just over four tenths.

One correlation (that appears a little more clearly visually when the broken marriage rate is shown) is that those whose marriage has ended appear slightly more often to prefer to live near those who have never been married than do their counterparts still in their first marriage. Marriages made, or much more likely at least now settled in, the south of Bearsden and Kirkintilloch appear the least likely to break up. In contrast, the place where old people are most likely to have moved to after a broken marriage is central Brighton.

Broken marriages, people 60–74 (%)
- 9.7 – 14.9
- 15.0 – 19.9
- 20.0 – 24.9
- 25.0 – 29.9
- 30.0 – 40.6

7.4 Widowed, remarried, separated or divorced in old age

Figure 7.4

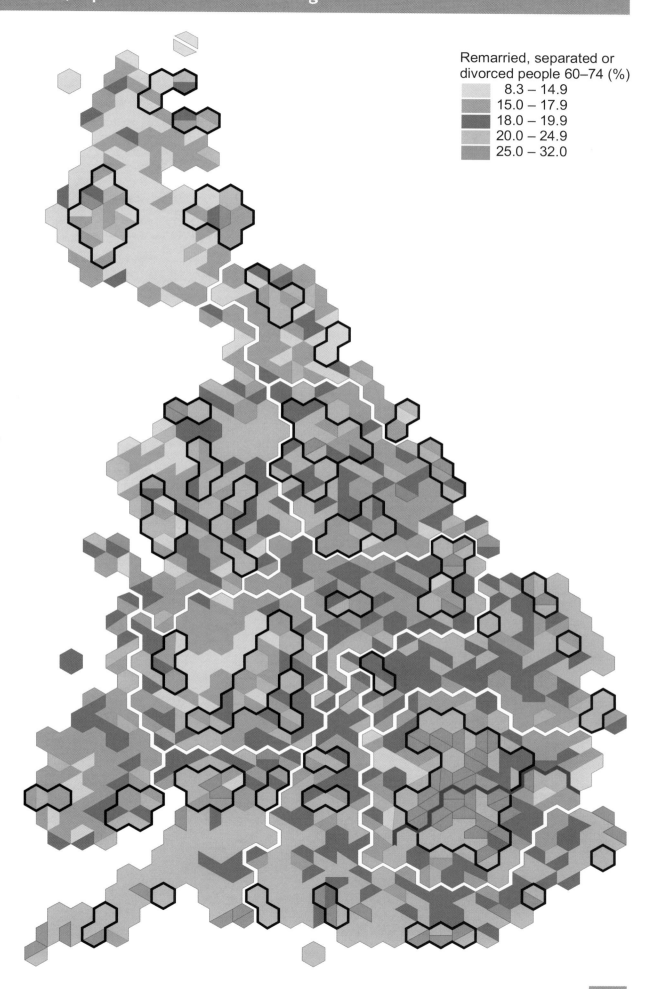

Remarried, separated or
divorced people 60–74 (%)
- 8.3 – 14.9
- 15.0 – 17.9
- 18.0 – 19.9
- 20.0 – 24.9
- 25.0 – 32.0

7.5   Widowhood in old age

Figure 7.5 opposite shows where, in old age, you are most likely to be living after your husband or wife dies. The one city, Glasgow, that stood out at earlier ages can still be seen to clearly suffer a different fate by the stories that can be told in it by these advanced years of age. Only there should you expect almost everywhere a quarter of people aged 60-74 to be widowed. Contrast that with rates only just over a tenth across much of the affluent south.

Widowhood is, however, a state much more common for women than for men. This is not just because many more men die at these ages and younger, but also because there are more women left for every man who remains and so remarrying for men who are widowed is, probabilistically if not in any other way, easier. This is exemplified by the fact that there is no overlap in the rates used to colour the two separate maps below of the chances for men and for women. Even where men are most likely to find themselves a widower, in Glasgow Easterhouse, they have a lower chance than where women are least likely to be widows (Hardwick in the south of Cambridgeshire).

There are many times when sex appears to matter more than geography, but the effects of geography can be longer lasting. It is thus also in Easterhouse that women are most likely to be widows by the time they are aged 60-74. There are a dozen similar neighbourhoods around Glasgow where over a third of women of these ages are widowed and a dozen other neighbourhoods scattered around the rest of the country with these very high rates. Men here, however, did not go to war; they simply lived and grew up in the wrong places.

The map for where women have died most early as revealed through where men are most likely to be widowed shows a similar geography, but with higher mortality rates for women most clustered where there were in the past mills working products such as jute. These were mills in which many women worked, and which killed many of them later in life, although still at a young age.

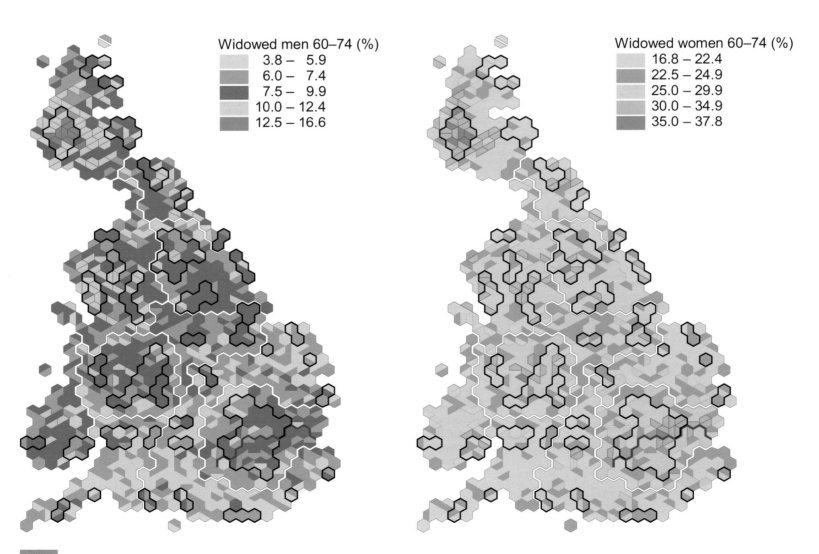

Widowed men 60–74 (%)
	3.8 – 5.9
	6.0 – 7.4
	7.5 – 9.9
	10.0 – 12.4
	12.5 – 16.6

Widowed women 60–74 (%)
	16.8 – 22.4
	22.5 – 24.9
	25.0 – 29.9
	30.0 – 34.9
	35.0 – 37.8

7.5 Widowhood in old age

Figure 7.5

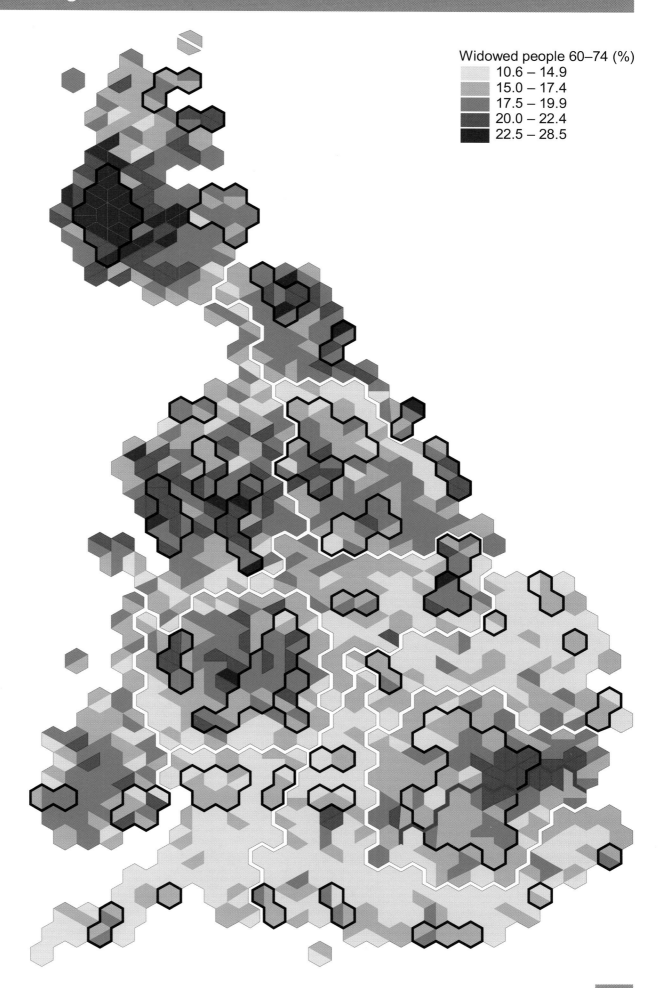

Widowed people 60–74 (%)
- 10.6 – 14.9
- 15.0 – 17.4
- 17.5 – 19.9
- 20.0 – 22.4
- 22.5 – 28.5

7.6   Living alone and other living arrangements in old age

Almost exactly two thirds (66%) of people in old age are living in a married couple family and in almost all cases they are that couple. Of the rest, only 67,000 are living in communal establishments (1%), just under 200,000 are cohabiting (2.5%), one quarter of a million are not living as a family, but there are other people in their household who they share with (3.5%), and almost 300,000 are living in lone-parent families (4%). Almost all of those consist of themselves and an older child or children who have not yet left home. This leaves by far the largest minority group of those in old age who are not living as a married couple – people living alone, 1.77 million at these ages (23%) – and their geography is mapped opposite (Figure 7.6).

Old people are least likely to live alone in the rural parts of South Norfolk and most likely to where exactly half do: in central London. Nationally, older women are twice as likely to be living alone as are men. Their separate mosaics of aloneness are shown below.

For the collector of geographic trivia we can report that the largest neighbourhood differences between the two maps below are to be found in Edinburgh Morningside where 40% of older women live alone, twice the male rate there, while for men, rates only exceed those for women in Deptford North and Moss Side. They are identical only in Birmingham Ladywood, the place to start that dating in old age agency should you think the local populace so inclined. Alternatively, should you be interested in where both cohabiting and lone parenthood are most common in old age, look no further than Kensal Town in the north (less exorbitantly expensive end) of Kensington.

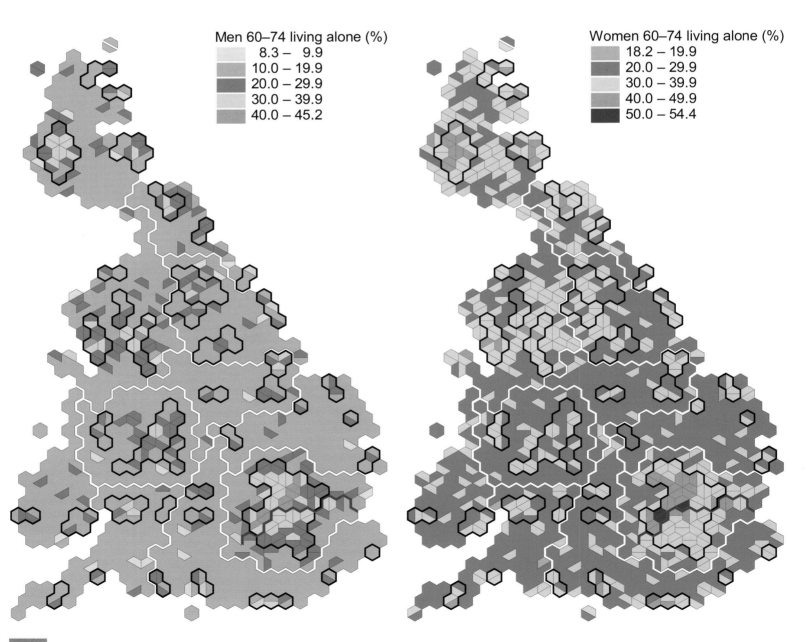

7.6 Living alone and other living arrangements in old age

Figure 7.6

People 60–74 living alone (%)
- 14.0 – 19.9
- 20.0 – 29.9
- 30.0 – 39.9
- 40.0 – 49.9
- 50.0

7.7   Retired, retired everywhere, or sick, disabled or working in old age

A life stage ago and all but a smattering of neighbourhoods were monopolised by those in work. Now, everywhere, a majority in old age are retired. It is in geographic variation in what is next most common that any pattern of differentiation across Britain is found. That is shown opposite (Figure 7.7) and the country can be seen split into two largely contiguous halves, depending on whether the largest minority in old age are still in full-time employment, or are sick or disabled. In both cases it will be the bulk of the younger men that fall into either of those categories as for them state retirement age is not until the age of 65. More often than not where these two halves of Britain meet are also found the few areas where another categorisation dominates in minority – self- or part-time employment – but such departures from the two main states are on the whole rare, although not impossible, as is any state other than retirement for the majority. In fact, as the key to the map below left hints, there is only one neighbourhood where an absolute majority are not retired, that being Hyde Park where 'only' 49.3% are retired.

The map below right breaks down dominant and majority–minority economic activity for all those who are still in the workforce at these ages. Note that nowhere does unemployment come even in third place. At these ages if you want work but cannot find it, you are retired, sick, or call yourself self-employed. Note also how the full-time/part-time hegemony still dominates at these ages albeit only for those in the labour market. Those in old age are not a reserve army who prefer to work part-time if they work at all. Finally, it is worth noting how remarkable it is that full-time is in the majority so evenly when, with 588,000 of the 'active' counted as such, it is not greatly more common than its part-time counterpart for the 428,000 so counted, or the 392,000 self-employed, even if it does dwarf the 58,000 unemployed or the 6,700 full-time students of these older years.

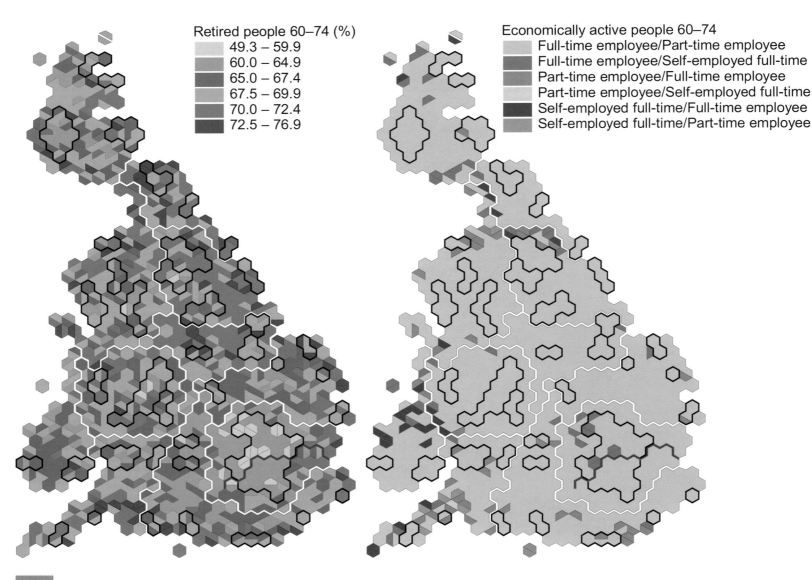

Retired people 60–74 (%)
49.3 – 59.9
60.0 – 64.9
65.0 – 67.4
67.5 – 69.9
70.0 – 72.4
72.5 – 76.9

Economically active people 60–74
Full-time employee/Part-time employee
Full-time employee/Self-employed full-time
Part-time employee/Full-time employee
Part-time employee/Self-employed full-time
Self-employed full-time/Full-time employee
Self-employed full-time/Part-time employee

Figure 7.7

Economic activity, people 60–74
- Retired/Full-time employee
- Retired/Part-time employee
- Retired/Self-employed full-time
- Retired/Sick or disabled

7.8   When did you last have a job in old age?

Of the 7.6 million people in Britain in old age, 5.2 million are retired, 0.6 million are sick or disabled, 0.2 million are 'other', 0.1 million are caring for their family, and of the rest who are economically active, rounding up adds a further 0.1 million who do not have a job. Of these 6.2 million old people not in paid work, 0.1 million had work until very recently, 0.3 million worked a year ago, 1.0 million before then but in the past five years, 2.1 million in the five years before that, 1.7 million in the 10 years before that, 0.9 million not for at least 20 years and only 0.1 million have never worked.

The 'never worked' never feature even as the second largest group on the map opposite (Figure 7.8), and not having worked for at least 20 years only marks out in largest minority one place on that map: Southwick in north Sunderland. The map again shows the clear mosaic of economic legacy, heightened in this categorisation where those currently working are in the majority when the bulk of the retired (and other economically inactive) are split by how long they have been out of work. The highest proportions currently working at these ages, all of over 30%, are to be found, in descending order, in Hyde Park, Chelsea, Golders Green, Oxford West, Highgate, Kensington, Newbury Rural, Fortis Green (in Hornsey) and Bushey (in Hertsmere).

There is a group, other than those in work who do not consider themselves retired, whose geography it is worth considering in relation to year last worked. Left is shown the proportion of the oldest women in this age group, those aged 70-74, who say that their main activity is looking after home/family. Retirement is, of course, only from paid work. Unpaid labour has no upper age limit, although interestingly it was mainly the older women of various environs of the county of Surrey and similar affluent and isolated neighbourhoods scattered elsewhere who had time enough to point this out. Practically no women in Bury, Bolton, Blackburn, and again many similar places, made the claim for that identity in their early seventies.

Women 70–74 looking
after home/family (%)

	0.0 – 1.9
	2.0 – 3.9
	4.0 – 5.9
	6.0 – 6.8

7.8 When did you last have a job in old age?

Figure 7.8

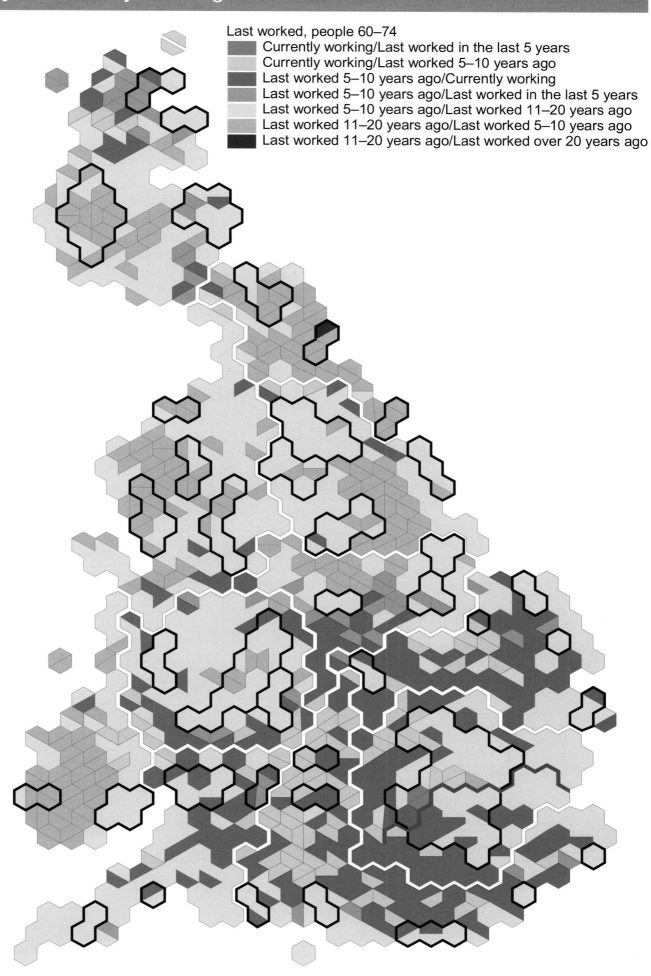

Last worked, people 60–74
- Currently working/Last worked in the last 5 years
- Currently working/Last worked 5–10 years ago
- Last worked 5–10 years ago/Currently working
- Last worked 5–10 years ago/Last worked in the last 5 years
- Last worked 5–10 years ago/Last worked 11–20 years ago
- Last worked 11–20 years ago/Last worked 5–10 years ago
- Last worked 11–20 years ago/Last worked over 20 years ago

7.9   Retirement by age and sex in old age

In this section the same colour scale is used to show how retirement increases relentlessly in likelihood with age, but is also less likely for some older people in particular neighbourhoods in some areas than for younger (old) people living elsewhere. The differences between the relative chances of men and women are also highlighted by how those differences are most stark below the age of 65. By their early seventies in most neighbourhoods, between 80% and 90% of people are retired. However, those who are not are not necessarily mainly in work as might misleadingly be implied by looking at the maps here. Often a large number identify themselves as sick or disabled, 'other', or looking after home or family as their next most common label (although the latter is most often reserved for leafier places).

The map below left shows the proportion of women aged 60-64 who are retired: nowhere are fewer than 40% in this category. The map below right shows the retirement rates for men of the same ages. As men's retirement age is 65 (apart from civil servants who are lucky enough to be able to retire with an occupational pension at 60), compared with women's current age 60, it is not surprising that men's retirement rates are far lower, with only one neighbourhood, Balerno in Edinburgh, having over 40% of retired men.

On the opposite page are the maps of retirement rates for women aged 65-69, men aged 65-69, and below, women aged 70-74 and men 70-74. Clearly, as this cohort ages more people of both sexes become retired in all places. Differences remain, with some older people without adequate pension provision feeling they have to continue working, some enjoying work too much to want to be consigned to a life of idleness, while some have opted for a life of retirement in the sun outside of Britain and hence are not counted here.

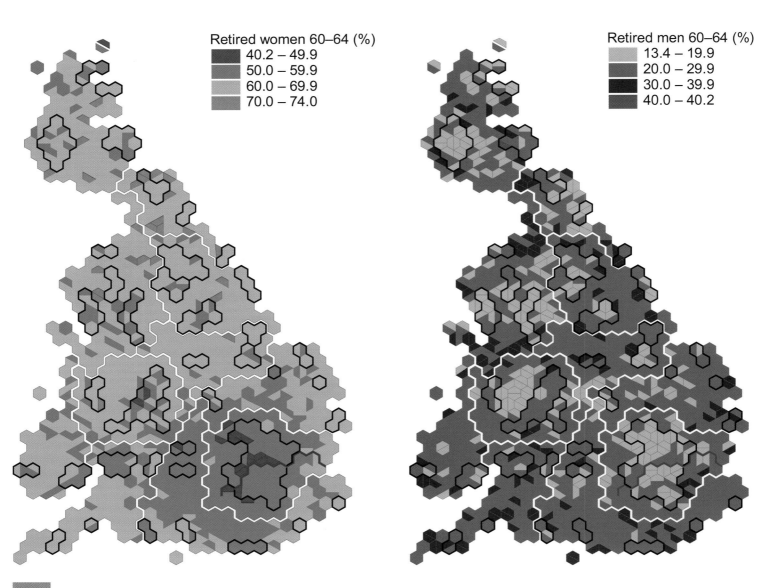

7.9 Retirement by age and sex in old age

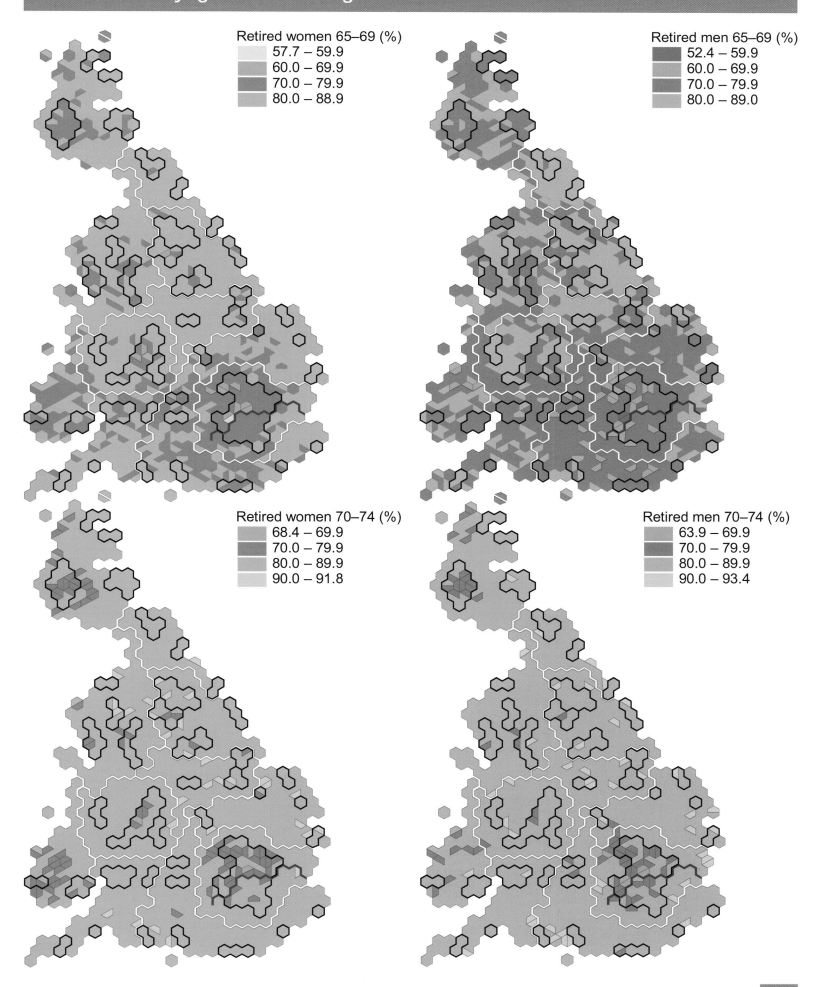

Retired women 65–69 (%)
- 57.7 – 59.9
- 60.0 – 69.9
- 70.0 – 79.9
- 80.0 – 88.9

Retired men 65–69 (%)
- 52.4 – 59.9
- 60.0 – 69.9
- 70.0 – 79.9
- 80.0 – 89.0

Retired women 70–74 (%)
- 68.4 – 69.9
- 70.0 – 79.9
- 80.0 – 89.9
- 90.0 – 91.8

Retired men 70–74 (%)
- 63.9 – 69.9
- 70.0 – 79.9
- 80.0 – 89.9
- 90.0 – 93.4

7.10 Benefits, Pension Credits and income deprivation in old age

There are many benefits that people become eligible to receive at various points during these years, depending on whether they are a man or a woman, and on how much paid work in Britain they have been involved in during their lives, and much else. These range from the full state pension, to eligibility for a bus pass or concessionary ticket to the cinema. Data on one particular means-tested benefit are available for all of Britain, although at these particular ages only at the parliamentary constituency level, and thus pairs of neighbourhoods are coloured identically in Figure 7.10 opposite.

Figure 7.10 shows the proportions of people of these ages in receipt of Pension Credit to bring their pensions up to a national minimum level. Note that Pension Credit is claimed on a household basis and therefore the number of people that Pension Credit helps is the number of claimants in addition to their partners for whom they are also claiming. Over half the older residents of the constituencies of Bethnal Green, Birmingham's Ladywood and Sparkbrook and Small Heath, and Glasgow Shettleston receive Pension Credits. It should be remembered that, according to Age Concern, some one-and-a-half million people eligible for Pension Credits have not claimed them.

To confirm that Figure 7.10 gives a good measure of where people of these ages are finding just getting by most difficult, the map left shows a general measure of poverty for all people aged 60+. Note that only England is included here, but data can be analysed at the neighbourhood level. These estimates of the proportions of old and truly elderly people living in income poverty were derived from part of the 2004 Index of Multiple Deprivation. Much the same places are identified here in Figure 7.10, partly because similar underlying sources are used, but also highlighting that the constituency approximation makes little difference here. The lowest rates of pensioner poverty are found in Ewell in Surrey (5%) and Hexham East in Northumberland (5.2%). Coincidently Hexham East is the place where the fourth highest proportion of women in their seventies are found who are not retired but are looking after the home and family (see page 220).

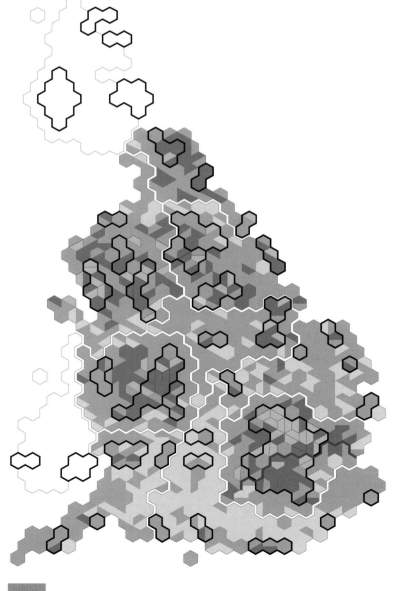

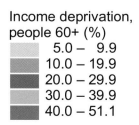

Income deprivation,
people 60+ (%)

	5.0 – 9.9
	10.0 – 19.9
	20.0 – 29.9
	30.0 – 39.9
	40.0 – 51.1

7.10 Benefits, Pension Credits and income deprivation in old age

Figure 7.10

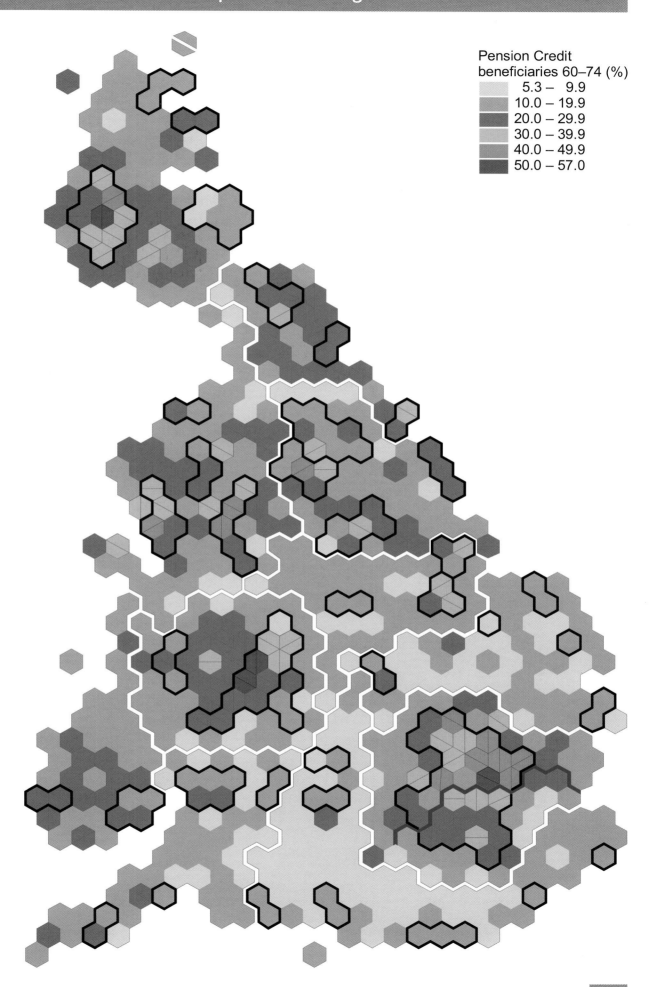

Pension Credit
beneficiaries 60–74 (%)
- 5.3 – 9.9
- 10.0 – 19.9
- 20.0 – 29.9
- 30.0 – 39.9
- 40.0 – 49.9
- 50.0 – 57.0

7.11 Qualifications in old age and the legacy of schooling half a century ago

As we mentioned on page 218, a few are still studying, but most people at these ages now have all the qualifications they will ever have. For a large majority, almost 70% of old people, their qualifications amount to nothing that is rated today, that is, nothing that is now the equivalent of a single school-leaving age qualification in any subject. This is the generation that was schooled exclusively under an apartheid education system that sorted them out, delayed Brave New World style, at age 11. Or they are the academic product of its even less forgiving predecessors. Some were schooled abroad under similar or even more unambitious educational regimes.

Figure 7.11 opposite shows mainly the effects of internal migration in the subsequent 45-60 years since the end of the set years of education for this generation. The concentration now in the fertile crescent from Surrey across to Somerset and up through Oxfordshire then over to St Albans is not there because a crescent formed of people who settled there on leaving school with qualifications, but one that they formed from eventually ending up there (if they had such qualifications). Simultaneously, it is a crescent that, once left, if you had no such education assets, you were unlikely to return to again by these ages. Elsewhere there are similar places, but they are pockets, not covering such a great swathe of land. The areas that the minority who were allowed to leave school holding any significant pieces of paper left, and did not return in great numbers to, are the much more extensive swathes where over four out of every five old people are unqualified.

However, from the pattern shown in Figure 7.11 you should not be fooled into thinking that at these ages the fertile crescent is awash with the well-educated old. It is just that many of the neighbourhoods there have a majority with some qualification. In most cases these are lower qualifications, the most basic of qualifications. The national proportion holding higher qualifications at these ages is an eighth, and only in a scattering of places does it exceed a third. The map left highlights where that scattering is. At the head of the well-educated oldies league table comes Oxford West (although still a minority there have a degree or equivalent, just). Next in Edinburgh are Balerno and Morningside; in London, Highgate, Fortis Green, Golders Green, Richmond North and Wimbledon North, Hyde Park and Chelsea; in Bristol, Clifton; Cambridge West; Stirling Rural and Milngavie in the west of Scotland; and the Ecclesall half of Hallam in Sheffield.

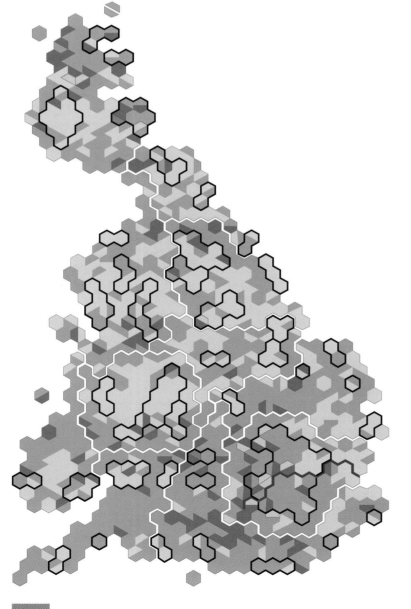

Higher qualifications,
people 60–74 (%)

	2.9 – 9.9
	10.0 – 19.9
	20.0 – 29.9
	30.0 – 39.9
	40.0 – 49.4

7.11 Qualifications in old age and the legacy of schooling half a century ago

Figure 7.11

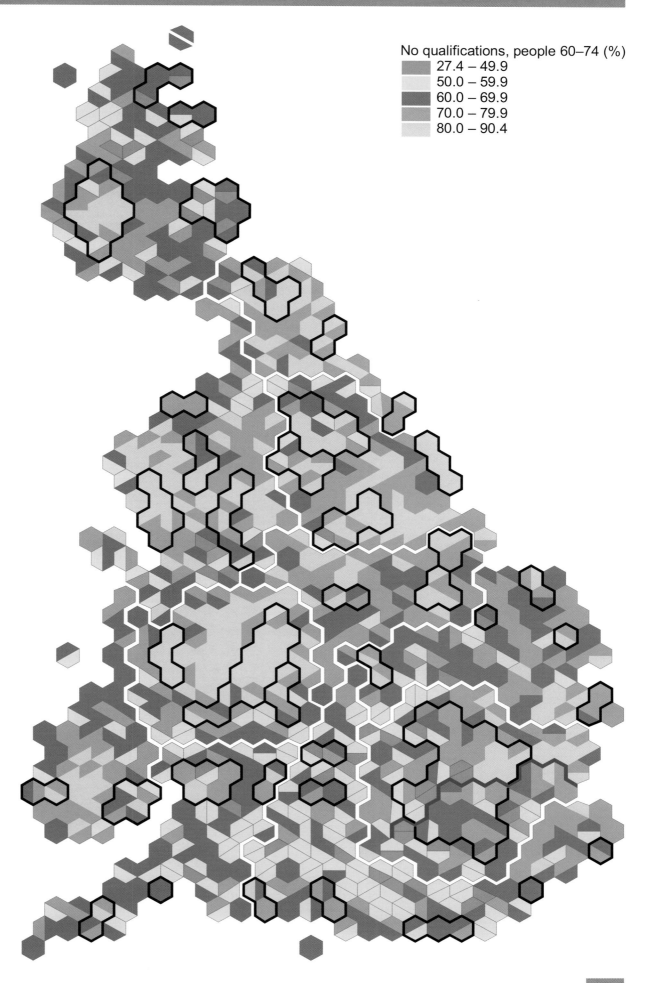

No qualifications, people 60–74 (%)
27.4 – 49.9
50.0 – 59.9
60.0 – 69.9
70.0 – 79.9
80.0 – 90.4

7.12 Age, cohort, sex and sorting within old age

At the start of this chapter we showed just how high by these ages the female proportion is in most neighbourhoods. Here we show the modal group opposite (Figure 7.12) by both five-year age band and by sex. Nowhere are males aged 70-74 the largest or even the second largest group in any neighbourhood. By their seventies everywhere there are fewer men. In fact men aged 65-69 are the largest five-year age group by sex only in one place: Nottingham New Basford. Quite what it is that preserves the 669 older gentleman especially in that part of that single city we do not know, other than to point out that the second largest group found there are women five years their junior (667 of them). In the largest number of neighbourhoods it is women aged under 65 who are in the majority in old age, with men of the same ages being the second largest group. Some 60% of neighbourhoods are dominated in old age by that combination, or its equivalent with the order of the sexes reversed.

As the map below shows, by single year of age the younger ages even more clearly dominate within this age band in Britain. However, more than three times as many neighbourhoods have a majority in old age aged 61 as are aged 60. That is mostly the effect of many men being abroad in 1940 and not in 1939. It is also partly the concentrating effect of retirement migration. Many retire when they are 60 but do not migrate until aged 61. At these ages the oldest neighbourhood in Britain is Cringleford to the south of Norwich, where the majority are aged 74 and the next most common age is 71. Two neighbourhoods in East Sussex currently vie neck and neck for the second and third place spots: Bexhill and Eastbourne West where 74-year-olds again form the largest single year of age groups, but are followed most closely by those in their 71st year (aged 70).

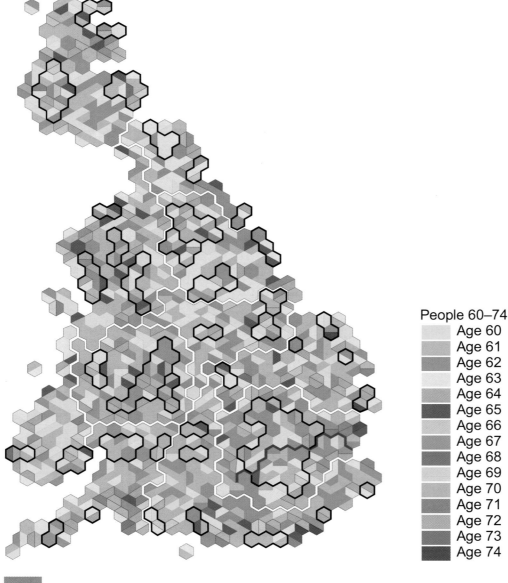

People 60–74
- Age 60
- Age 61
- Age 62
- Age 63
- Age 64
- Age 65
- Age 66
- Age 67
- Age 68
- Age 69
- Age 70
- Age 71
- Age 72
- Age 73
- Age 74

7.12 Age, cohort, sex and sorting within old age

Figure 7.12

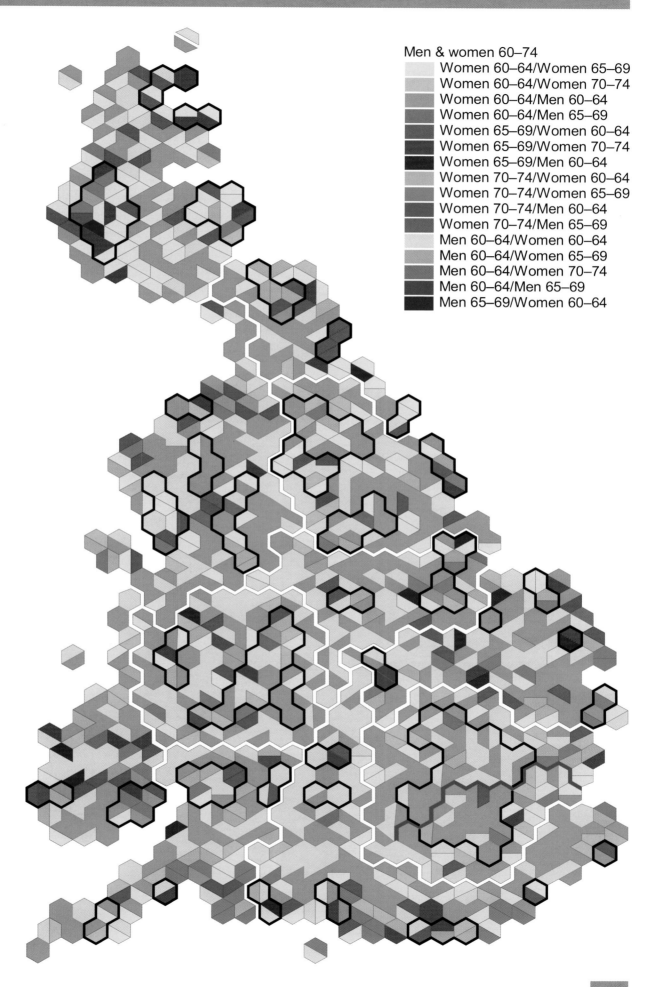

Men & women 60–74
- Women 60–64/Women 65–69
- Women 60–64/Women 70–74
- Women 60–64/Men 60–64
- Women 60–64/Men 65–69
- Women 65–69/Women 60–64
- Women 65–69/Women 70–74
- Women 65–69/Men 60–64
- Women 70–74/Women 60–64
- Women 70–74/Women 65–69
- Women 70–74/Men 60–64
- Women 70–74/Men 65–69
- Men 60–64/Women 60–64
- Men 60–64/Women 65–69
- Men 60–64/Women 70–74
- Men 60–64/Men 65–69
- Men 65–69/Women 60–64

7.13 Cars and means of travelling to work for those who still do in old age

If the number of cars available to the majority of people in each neighbourhood at these ages is counted separately for women and men, quite different images result, as shown below. Only in one neighbourhood do a majority of women in their sixties and early seventies live in households where there are two or more cars available to be driven (Walton in Surrey). It is not that women particularly dislike cars, or that there are some especially sad single old men hoarding cars as a substitute for company. Rather it is that women are a little more likely to be on their own at these ages as there are fewer men to go round. If you are on your own, what possible need is there to have more than one car? Further, the proportion of women who can drive at these ages is much lower than that of men. In 2001, 57% of women aged 60-69 had a full driving licence compared with 86% of men. For the over-seventies the divide is even starker, with only a quarter of women having a full driving licence compared with nearly 70% of men.[1]

Of the remaining 1,281 neighbourhoods in Britain excluding Walton, in 689 the majority of women live in areas where one car is the norm followed by two; 365 in neighbourhoods where one is most usual followed by none; and 227 where no cars is the norm followed by one. For men there are 65 neighbourhoods the equivalent of Walton; 734 where one is more common than two; 402 where one is more common than none; and only 81 where no car is the most common state (followed by one). There are thus three times fewer neighbourhoods, counting by men, where the majority of households with people of these ages have no car. There are sixty-five times more neighbourhoods counting by men rather than women where most have access to two or more cars.

[1] www.statistics.gov.uk/cci/nugget.asp?id=880

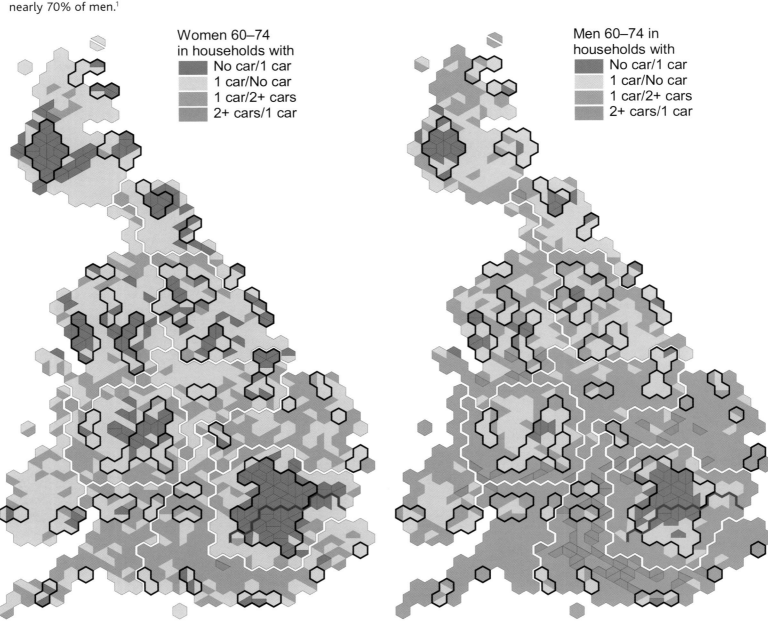

Women 60–74
in households with
■ No car/1 car
□ 1 car/No car
▨ 1 car/2+ cars
▨ 2+ cars/1 car

Men 60–74 in
households with
■ No car/1 car
□ 1 car/No car
▨ 1 car/2+ cars
▨ 2+ cars/1 car

7.13 Cars and means of travelling to work for those who still do in old age

Figure 7.13, of how that minority who are still in employment travel to work at these ages and how they choose or have to do so, is interesting compared with its counterpart already shown for the next youngest age group (on page 185). It is interesting mainly in how many fewer older people let the train 'take the strain' for them on the way to work from Outer London. Note also at these ages how working at or from home is the most common way of working for those in work, either in some of the remotest of rural areas or in the heart of the capital, but nowhere in between.

Figure 7.13

Method of travel to work, people 60–74

- Bus/Car
- Bus/Home worker
- Car/Bus
- Car/Cycle
- Car/Foot
- Car/Home worker
- Car/Light rail
- Car/Train
- Foot/Car
- Foot/Home worker
- Home worker/Car
- Home worker/Foot
- Home worker/Light rail
- Light rail/Home worker

7.14 Housing tenure and communal living in old age

At these ages a majority own their property outright in 1,218 of the 1,282 neighbourhoods; in the remainder a majority rent. Figure 7.14 opposite gives the impression that owning or buying dominates everywhere because renting is subdivided into three kinds. The map below left shows that if the three renting groups are combined as one, renting dominates in twice as many neighbourhoods and is the second most common (grouped) tenure at these ages in a majority of places.

Nationally, 60% of those aged 60-74 live in a home that is owned outright, 15% are mortgaged and so three quarters are in owner-occupation of one kind or another. Most who are mortgaged will own outright soon. An eighth, some 13%, rent from their local authority (LA), a twentieth, some 5% from another social landlord, a twenty-fifth, some 4%, rent in the private sector, 2% live rent free and 1% in a communal establishment.

Two thirds of those in communal establishments are housed in medical or care establishments and their geography is shown below right. The clustering around Glasgow is what is most striking here, that clustering being partly the product of demand (see page 207) and partly the product of supply (see page 198). However, nowhere do these medical and care establishments house more than 3.4% of the population at these ages and all communal establishments house no more than 5.3% in any neighbourhood. Thus in almost all the south of England outside of London most now own outright and in most places there the next largest group aged 60-74 is about to own outright soon. In London and many northern cities many rent, and where the majority own, the next largest group rents, and these people cannot expect to own a home at any point before they die.

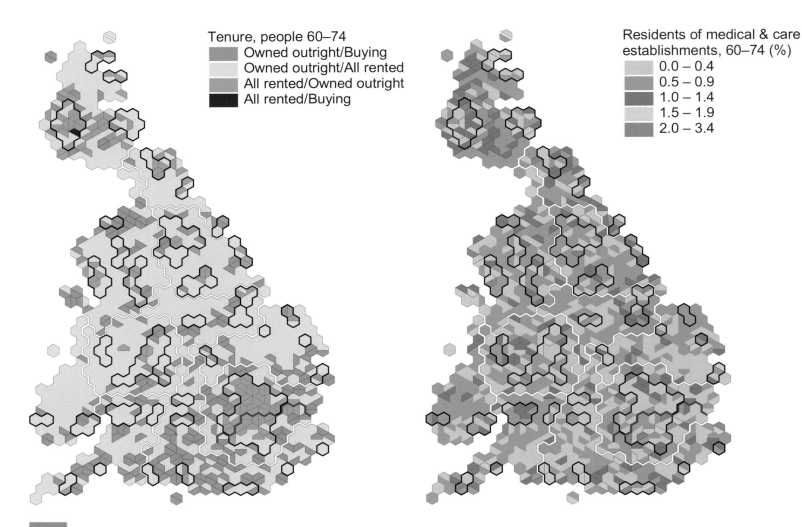

Tenure, people 60–74
- Owned outright/Buying
- Owned outright/All rented
- All rented/Owned outright
- All rented/Buying

Residents of medical & care establishments, 60–74 (%)
- 0.0 – 0.4
- 0.5 – 0.9
- 1.0 – 1.4
- 1.5 – 1.9
- 2.0 – 3.4

7.14 Housing tenure and communal living in old age

Figure 7.14

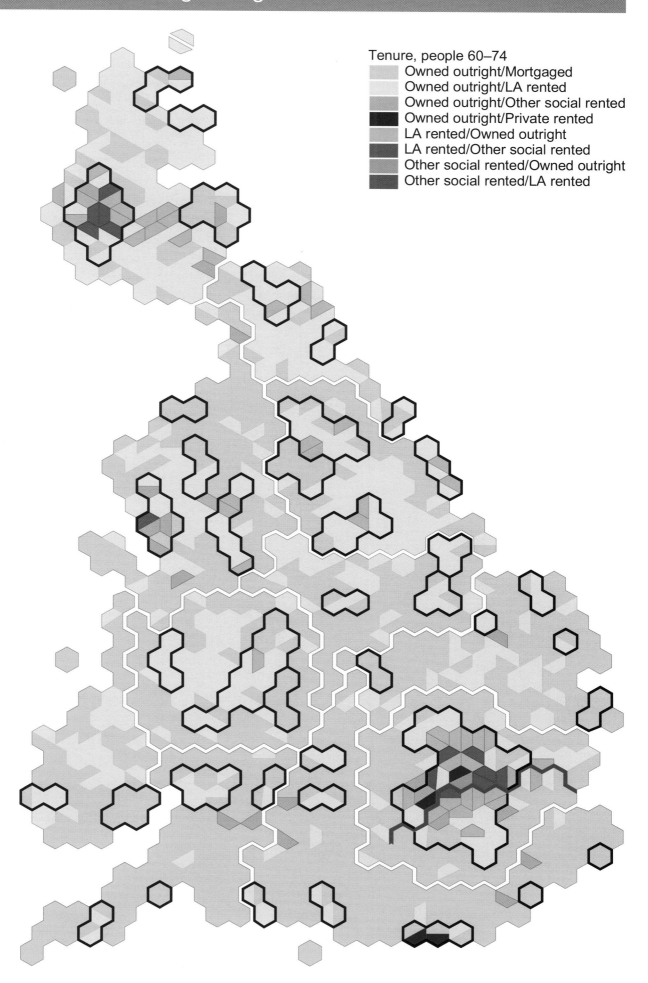

Tenure, people 60–74
- Owned outright/Mortgaged
- Owned outright/LA rented
- Owned outright/Other social rented
- Owned outright/Private rented
- LA rented/Owned outright
- LA rented/Other social rented
- Other social rented/Owned outright
- Other social rented/LA rented

7.15 State of housing and space in housing in old age

Few homes are now not heated through a central heating system, but the proportions that are not are higher for those in old age than for the population in general. This is especially true for those growing old in some of our older cities where up to almost half of those aged 60-74 are living in homes that are not well heated. Figure 7.15 opposite shows this concentration of housing poverty in old age. Rates of poorly heated homes are highest in the Harehills neighbourhood of east Leeds; in the western and southern halves of Liverpool's Walton, Wavertree and West Derby neighbourhoods; in the Undercliffe and University neighbourhoods of Bradford; in Erdington, Fox Hollies and Yardley in Birmingham; Cosham in Portsmouth; and Sutton in Hull. In all those neighbourhoods over 30% of people in old age go through the winter without central heating. Elsewhere, usually due mainly to the efforts of local authorities, rates are

as near to zero as makes no difference: in Scotland in Linlithgow and Motherwell; and in Washington, Morpeth, Jarrow, and Cramlington in the North East. There is no need for anyone to be living without central heating in old age if there is simply the local or national will to prevent it.

A contrasting picture to the concentration of housing poverty in old age in a few older and poorer urban areas is shown left when we consider the amount of space available to the majority of older people in their homes. Almost everywhere the majority of households with older members have at least two or more rooms than are deemed to be needed by such households and most of the rest have at least one extra room (see page 30 for the explanation of occupancy rating). Nationally, 4.7 million older people fall into the former category and 1.7 million into the latter. Only some 830,000 are living with as many rooms as are deemed necessary and some 208,000 with one room or fewer than they need to live in. High Wycombe is the only neighbourhood outside of London or Scotland where even the largest minority do not have surplus rooms.

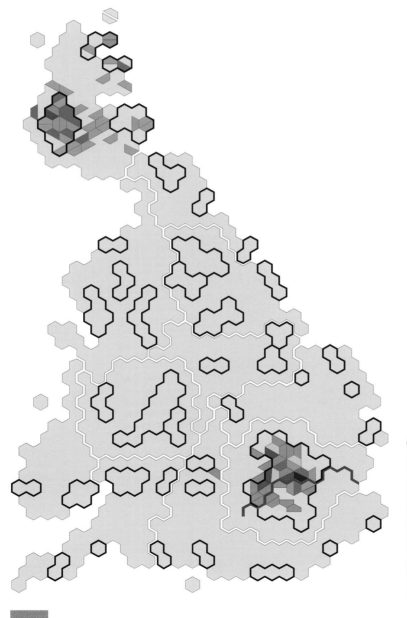

Occupancy rating, people 60–74

Occupancy rating +2 or more/Occupancy rating +1
Occupancy rating +2 or more/Occupancy rating 0
Occupancy rating +2 or more/Occupancy rating -1 or less
Occupancy rating +1/Occupancy rating +2 or more
Occupancy rating +1/Occupancy rating 0
Occupancy rating 0/Occupancy rating +2 or more
Occupancy rating 0/Occupancy rating +1
Occupancy rating 0/Occupancy rating -1 or less
Occupancy rating -1 or less/Occupancy rating 0

7.15 State of housing and space in housing in old age

Figure 7.15

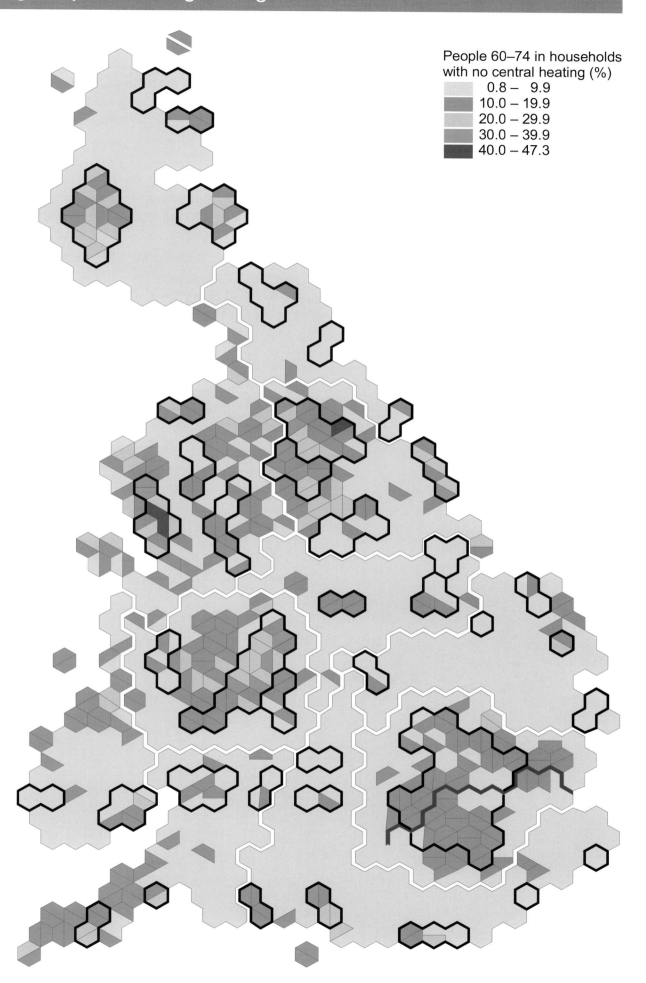

People 60–74 in households
with no central heating (%)
0.8 – 9.9
10.0 – 19.9
20.0 – 29.9
30.0 – 39.9
40.0 – 47.3

7.16 Ethnicity, past migrations, current stories, religious beliefs and non-beliefs in old age

The cohort aged 60-74 at the time the snapshot shown in Figure 7.16 opposite was taken will not be representative of the ethnicity of older people in years soon to come. That so much of the country is coloured by 'White Irish' as the second largest group in each area, and in London by 'Black Caribbean', highlights how often being shown here are the children, grandchildren, great-grandchildren or great-great-grandchildren of former migrants from what is now mostly the Republic of Ireland.

In the case especially of London, which people tend to leave after a couple of generations, many original migrants from islands in the Caribbean, who having crossed hundreds of miles of ocean in their youth, have in the subsequent three or four decades often moved only a dozen miles or so away from the place they first called home in Britain (for those still in Britain). The promised land (or at least a land not monopolised by any others)

for that one group turned out to be the streets of Harlesden in south Brent. Figure 7.16 is thus a map of tales of distance and times, as well as of places and often identities chosen from one parent or great-great-grandparent. Full information on ethnicity in Scotland is masked anywhere where there are not 50 'non-White' residents, which is quite a lot of that country.

In contrast to the paucity of information on ethnicity in Scotland, the country that created the label 'White Scottish' and then 'usefully' found that most people there fell into this category, the extra detail asked for in religion in Scotland brings out the colour there, as shown below. Again a monolith, in this case the Church of Scotland, dominates at these ages, but not everywhere, and the largely contiguous geography to the split in what is minority is clear, as are those pockets where other Christian denominations are significant enough to register other than the state and Catholic churches.

South of the border the propensity for older people in Wales and southern England to more often be in a larger minority if they identify their religion as 'None' rather than not stating their religion is what makes this image differ most when compared with those shown for younger adults. Perhaps by these ages people begin to think more carefully about what they believe in and do not mind being more open about it.

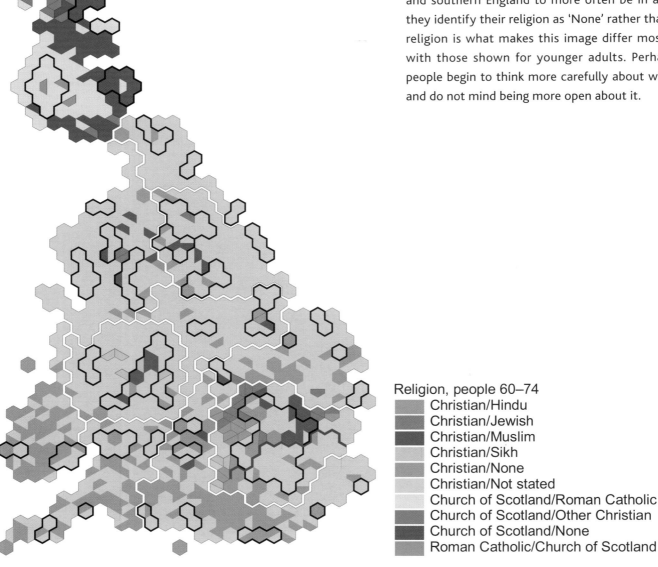

Religion, people 60–74
- Christian/Hindu
- Christian/Jewish
- Christian/Muslim
- Christian/Sikh
- Christian/None
- Christian/Not stated
- Church of Scotland/Roman Catholic
- Church of Scotland/Other Christian
- Church of Scotland/None
- Roman Catholic/Church of Scotland

7.16 Ethnicity, past migrations, current stories, religious beliefs and non-beliefs in old age

Figure 7.16

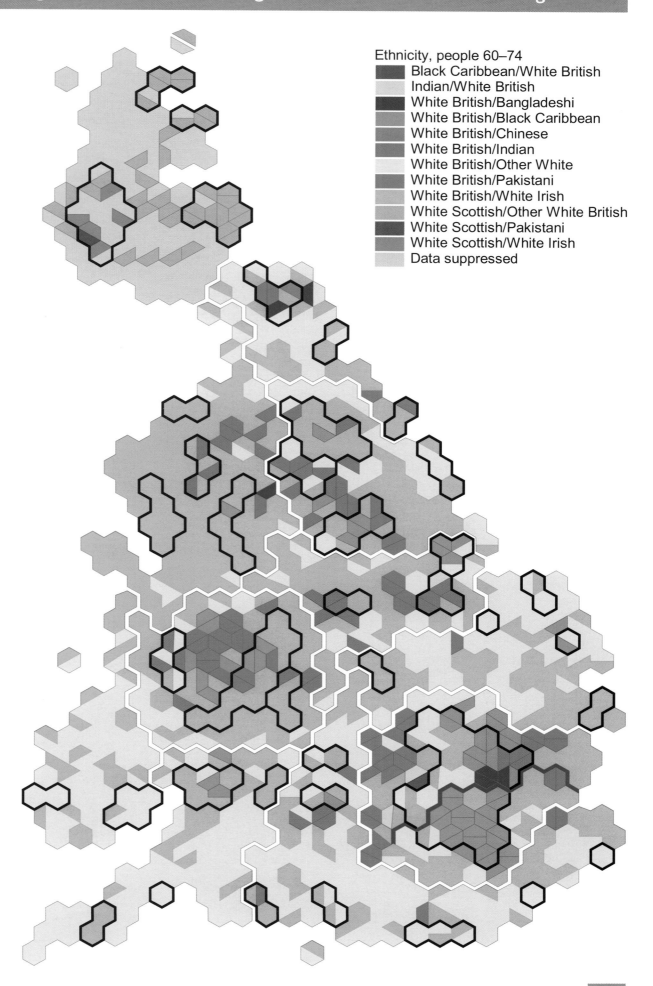

Ethnicity, people 60–74
- Black Caribbean/White British
- Indian/White British
- White British/Bangladeshi
- White British/Black Caribbean
- White British/Chinese
- White British/Indian
- White British/Other White
- White British/Pakistani
- White British/White Irish
- White Scottish/Other White British
- White Scottish/Pakistani
- White Scottish/White Irish
- Data suppressed

7.17 Occupations major and minor, and in combination in old age

The occupations of everyone still in work at ages 60-74 are shown in Figure 7.17 opposite, both for the most common and second most common major group. Although the patterns of younger years are still evident in Figure 7.17, as fewer and fewer people are involved, so the number of possible combinations appears to fall a little, but there are still some 33 shades shown in this mosaic. Most common is that for 'elementary' followed by 'operative' by which hue just under a fifth of neighbourhoods are shaded for those in work in old age. These are, in general, the lowest and next lowest paying groups of occupations. At the other extreme an almost equal number of neighbourhoods have 'skilled trade' and 'managers and senior official' occupations placed first and second, or second and first, shown by two hues in Figure 7.17.

The detail in Figure 7.17 can hide some of the basic detail that is shown in the map below left, of which major group of occupations is dominant in each neighbourhood among those in work aged 60-74. In almost exactly half of all neighbourhoods 'elementary' occupations dominate. 'Administrative and

secretarial' occupations dominate only in a ring around London, a relic of another age when every boss had 'his' secretary.

Figure 7.17 also conceals detail in that it only shows major groupings of occupations, albeit majority and majority–minority. When sub-major groupings are used instead, as shown below right, more detail emerges. There is only space to point out one cluster of old-age sub-major occupations. When the 'associate professionals and technical' group is divided into its constituent sub-groups (and all other major groups similarly subdivided), only one of the five possibilities emerges as a cluster. Those that are never dominant are old people working in science and technology, health and welfare, protective services, or business and public services. Instead it is old people who are 'associate professionals' in culture, media and sport who have their exclusive enclave: the adjoining neighbourhoods of Highgate and Holborn, Valhalla for those kings and queens of such arts. Behind most area stereotypes usually lies a little truth.

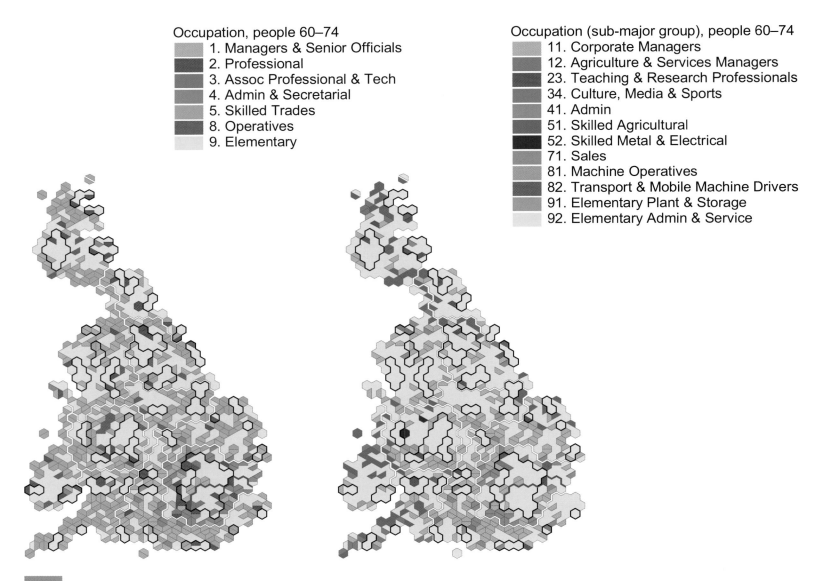

Occupation, people 60–74
- 1. Managers & Senior Officials
- 2. Professional
- 3. Assoc Professional & Tech
- 4. Admin & Secretarial
- 5. Skilled Trades
- 8. Operatives
- 9. Elementary

Occupation (sub-major group), people 60–74
- 11. Corporate Managers
- 12. Agriculture & Services Managers
- 23. Teaching & Research Professionals
- 34. Culture, Media & Sports
- 41. Admin
- 51. Skilled Agricultural
- 52. Skilled Metal & Electrical
- 71. Sales
- 81. Machine Operatives
- 82. Transport & Mobile Machine Drivers
- 91. Elementary Plant & Storage
- 92. Elementary Admin & Service

7.17 Occupations major and minor, and in combination in old age

Occupation, people 60–74

1. Managers & Senior Officials/2. Professional
1. Managers & Senior Officials/3. Assoc Professional & Tech
1. Managers & Senior Officials/4. Admin & Secretarial
1. Managers & Senior Officials/5. Skilled Trades
1. Managers & Senior Officials/9. Elementary
2. Professional/1. Managers & Senior Officials
2. Professional/3. Assoc Professional & Tech
2. Professional/4. Admin & Secretarial
2. Professional/5. Skilled Trades
2. Professional/9. Elementary
3. Assoc Professional & Tech/1. Managers & Senior Officials
3. Assoc Professional & Tech/2. Professional
3. Assoc Professional & Tech/4. Admin & Secretarial
4. Admin & Secretarial/1. Managers & Senior Officials
4. Admin & Secretarial/2. Professional
4. Admin & Secretarial/3. Assoc Professional & Tech
4. Admin & Secretarial/5. Skilled Trades
4. Admin & Secretarial/8. Operatives
4. Admin & Secretarial/9. Elementary
5. Skilled Trades/1. Managers & Senior Officials
5. Skilled Trades/2. Professional
5. Skilled Trades/4. Admin & Secretarial
5. Skilled Trades/8. Operatives
5. Skilled Trades/9. Elementary
8. Operatives/5. Skilled Trades
8. Operatives/9. Elementary
9. Elementary/1. Managers & Senior Officials
9. Elementary/2. Professional
9. Elementary/3. Assoc Professional & Tech
9. Elementary/4. Admin & Secretarial
9. Elementary/5. Skilled Trades
9. Elementary/6. Personal Service
9. Elementary/8. Operatives

Figure 7.17

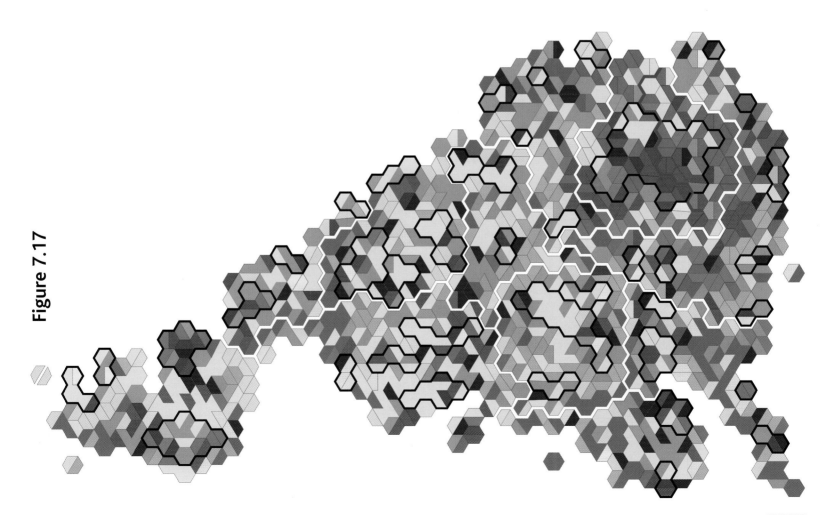

7.18 Industry and the neighbourhoods that typify each and are typified by each in old age

One industry remains as dominant at ages 60-74 as it was for younger people. As careful inspection of the colours and key of Figure 7.18 opposite reveals, manufacturing is dominant in over a third of all neighbourhoods and in most of those it is 'wholesale and retail, vehicle repair' that is the second most likely occupation of anyone still working in their sixties or early seventies. Unsurprisingly, given the age of these people and the nature of this work, this third of neighbourhoods is mainly found in the old industrial heartland of the midlands and northern England. Around that heartland are the neighbourhoods where selling is more popular than manufacturing as an industrial contribution in old age, and south of that, in London, is found a core of neighbourhoods where selling takes second place to talking about selling: providing premises for selling and trading things to sell (labelled 'real estate, renting and business').

The map below shows simply what is dominant where. It is included to make Figure 7.18 easier to interpret. Similarly, the table below shows the neighbourhood in which each industry employs the most older people in absolute numbers and what those numbers are. Note that these industries include those that failed to claim a single neighbourhood in the majority. They are starred in the table if they are also most common in the area they are most populous in. Note also that by these ages, even where workers in an industry are most clustered, we are only counting at most hundreds, and at least just a few dozen.

Neighbourhoods with most employees by industry of those aged 60-74 in Britain

Industry	People	Neighbourhood
Agriculture*	596	Penrith Rural
Fishing	40	Shetland
Mining and quarrying	55	St Austell
Manufacturing*	522	Gornal
Energy and water	41	Suffolk Coastal North
Construction	280	North Cornwall Rural
Wholesale and retail, vehicle repair*	530	Whittlesey
Hotels and restaurants*	309	Blackpool South Shore
Transport, storage and communications	238	Staines
Financial	198	Chelsea
Real estate, renting and business*	752	Hyde Park
Public administration and defence, social security	186	Salisbury Rural
Education*	535	Cambridge West
Health and social work	306	Finchley
Other**	349	Hyde Park

* Most industry common in area; ** second most common in area.

Industry, people 60–74

- Agriculture
- Education
- Health & Social Work
- Hotels & Restaurants
- Manufacturing
- Real Estate, Renting & Business
- Transport, Storage & Comms
- Wholesale & Retail, Vehicle Repair

7.18 Industry and the neighbourhoods that typify each and are typified by each in old age

Figure 7.18

Industry, people 60–74

Agriculture/Health & Social Work
Agriculture/Manufacturing
Agriculture/Wholesale & Retail, Vehicle Repair
Education/Health & Social Work
Education/Real Estate, Renting & Business
Education/Wholesale & Retail, Vehicle Repair
Health & Social Work/Agriculture
Health & Social Work/Education
Health & Social Work/Manufacturing
Health & Social Work/Real Estate, Renting & Business
Health & Social Work/Wholesale & Retail, Vehicle Repair
Hotels & Restaurants/Wholesale & Retail, Vehicle Repair
Manufacturing/Agriculture
Manufacturing/Construction
Manufacturing/Education
Manufacturing/Health & Social Work
Manufacturing/Hotels & Restaurants
Manufacturing/Real Estate, Renting & Business
Manufacturing/Wholesale & Retail, Vehicle Repair
Real Estate, Renting & Business/Education
Real Estate, Renting & Business/Health & Social Work
Real Estate, Renting & Business/Manufacturing
Real Estate, Renting & Business/Other
Real Estate, Renting & Business/Public Admin & Defence, Social Security
Real Estate, Renting & Business/Wholesale & Retail, Vehicle Repair
Transport, Storage & Comms/Health & Social Work
Transport, Storage & Comms/Manufacturing
Transport, Storage & Comms/Real Estate, Renting & Business
Transport, Storage & Comms/Wholesale & Retail, Vehicle Repair
Wholesale & Retail, Vehicle Repair/Agriculture
Wholesale & Retail, Vehicle Repair/Construction
Wholesale & Retail, Vehicle Repair/Education
Wholesale & Retail, Vehicle Repair/Health & Social Work
Wholesale & Retail, Vehicle Repair/Hotels & Restaurants
Wholesale & Retail, Vehicle Repair/Manufacturing
Wholesale & Retail, Vehicle Repair/Real Estate, Renting & Business
Wholesale & Retail, Vehicle Repair/Transport, Storage & Comms

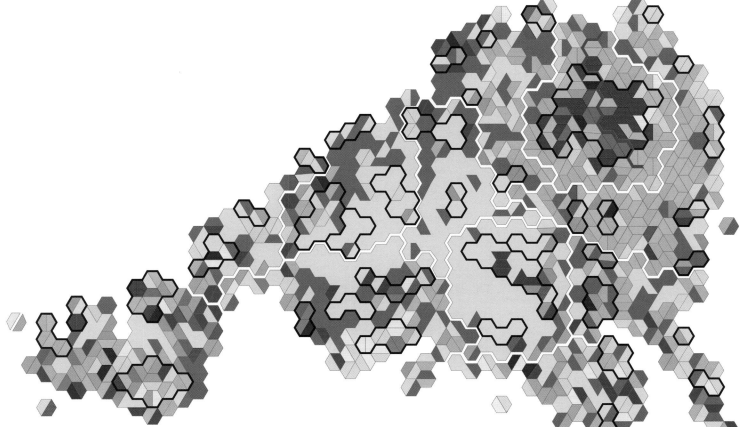

7.19 Class, dreams, aspirations, drudgery, routine and neighbours in old age

In midlife there were six neighbourhoods where 'higher managers' dominated; by maturity only one remained: Oxford West. However, by old age that favourite home of the ageing academic had been joined by two similar neighbourhoods: Jesmond in Newcastle and Cambridge West. And again, just as for the two age groups before them, 'higher managers' and 'professionals' mix only with the lower of their kind.

The table below shows the frequency of each type of neighbourhood mix and thus how, although 'lower managers' still dominate, they are not so ubiquitous as they were in maturity; this table can be compared with those for midlife (on page 156) and maturity (on page 194).

There are also twice as many areas where a majority of people at these ages have never worked compared with their younger counterparts. In many cases these places are so categorised because many women in those neighbourhoods did not undertake paid work when they were younger. It is not because people have managed to evade a job for at least 45 years, but where many are long-term unemployed they are included here.

Note also that the number of neighbourhoods denoted by 'old' rather than 'mature' ages where a majority are 'small employers' (such as hoteliers and shopkeepers) has risen from 15 to 152 (and that there were no such neighbourhoods in midlife). Clearly, people carry on in such occupations where they are in charge longer than others. Clearly, too, when Figure 7.19 opposite is consulted, these people have chosen to work mainly in places many others of their ages choose to retire to. For some such work may well be semi-retirement, especially if very few come through the antiques shop's door.

Almost as dramatic a difference between the table below and that shown earlier for those aged 40-59 is that there are now five times as many neighbourhoods where the majority of older people who work are employed in 'routine' occupations. Almost all of these places are to be found in the north of England, Wales and Scotland. For those over the age of 60 who are still working or who have recently worked, their lives bifurcate more towards a life of continued but relatively harder drudgery on older bones in 'routine', 'semi-routine' and 'lower technical' occupations (NS-SeC 5, 6 and 7), and an almost equal number classified as being in 'management' (higher or lower), the 'professions' or a 'small employer' or own account worker (NS-SeC 1, 2 and 4). Between these two are those few in the 'intermediate' class (NS-SeC 3, which dominates nowhere) and those who have 'never worked' or the 'long-term unemployed' (hardly useful groups to include in NS-SeC 8).

Number of neighbourhoods by National Statistics Socioeconomic Classification (NS-SeC) mix of people aged 60-74

People aged 60-74	Second most common social class							
Most common social class	1. Higher managers	2. Lower managers	3. Inter-mediate	4. Small employers	6. Semi-routine	7. Routine	8. Never worked	Total
1. Higher managers		3						3
2. Lower managers	52		14	225	216	66	6	579
4. Small employers		119			17	15	1	152
6. Semi-routine		40		6		107	2	155
7. Routine		63		6	278		14	361
8. Never worked		3			6	23		32
Total	52	228	14	237	517	211	23	1,282

7.19 Class, dreams, aspirations, drudgery, routine and neighbours in old age

Figure 7.19

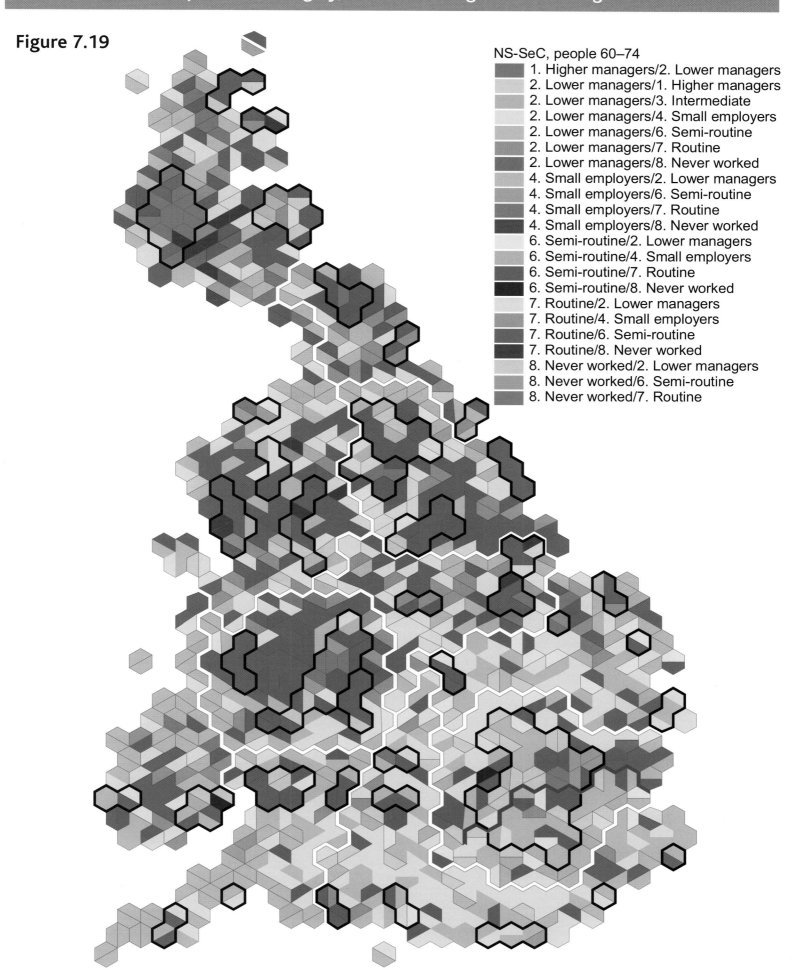

NS-SeC, people 60–74
1. Higher managers/2. Lower managers
2. Lower managers/1. Higher managers
2. Lower managers/3. Intermediate
2. Lower managers/4. Small employers
2. Lower managers/6. Semi-routine
2. Lower managers/7. Routine
2. Lower managers/8. Never worked
4. Small employers/2. Lower managers
4. Small employers/6. Semi-routine
4. Small employers/7. Routine
4. Small employers/8. Never worked
6. Semi-routine/2. Lower managers
6. Semi-routine/4. Small employers
6. Semi-routine/7. Routine
6. Semi-routine/8. Never worked
7. Routine/2. Lower managers
7. Routine/4. Small employers
7. Routine/6. Semi-routine
7. Routine/8. Never worked
8. Never worked/2. Lower managers
8. Never worked/6. Semi-routine
8. Never worked/7. Routine

7.20 Caring in old age

The maps opposite show the equivalent four images of the propensity to provide care in old age as were contrasted in maturity on page 199: the proportion of people aged 60-74 providing care, the proportion of those in fair health providing care, and the proportion of men and women providing care. In all four cases the rates of care giving tend to be lower at ages 60-74 than at younger ages. Initially, this may appear a little surprising as there will be more demand for care to be provided by the friends and relatives of this cohort, but there are a number of reasons why we should not be too surprised to see a little less care apparently being given.

In no particular order, the reasons are as follows: at these ages people may be less aware that what they are providing is unpaid care as they are not usually forfeiting earnings; people of these ages may also be more prone to see giving care as part of the 'job' of being a husband or wife; premature death leaves fewer people to care for (and to care); fewer of this age group may have children who require care; and fewer may be fit enough to

care, although of those who care, 57% are in fair or poor health themselves.

The mosaic top right opposite casts a little doubt on that last supposition as those in fair health giving care are generally fewer than those in fair health who are doing so at younger ages (although the meaning of 'fair health' changes also with age). From that mosaic in particular it is clear that less care is provided by older people in Scotland and London. That is confirmed by the map below left, included for completeness, with the comparison before maturity (here the average is 13.5% to 17.5% compared with between 16.0% and 20.0% there). Scotland has better state support and in London older people more often live alone, which makes caring for each other more difficult. However, the map below right shows that when people do care in the worst-off parts of Scotland and other poorer parts of Britain, they are more likely to provide a great deal of care rather than just a few hours worth a week.

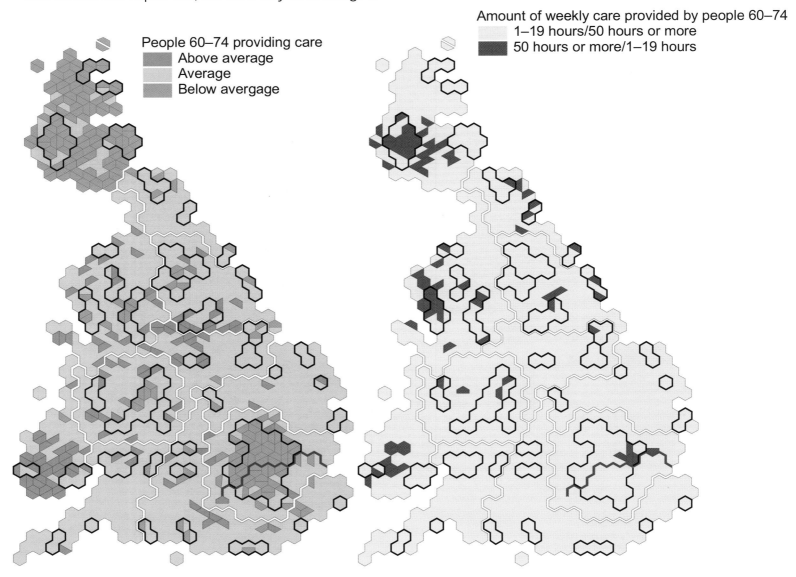

People 60–74 providing care
Above average
Average
Below avergage

Amount of weekly care provided by people 60–74
1–19 hours/50 hours or more
50 hours or more/1–19 hours

7.20 Caring in old age

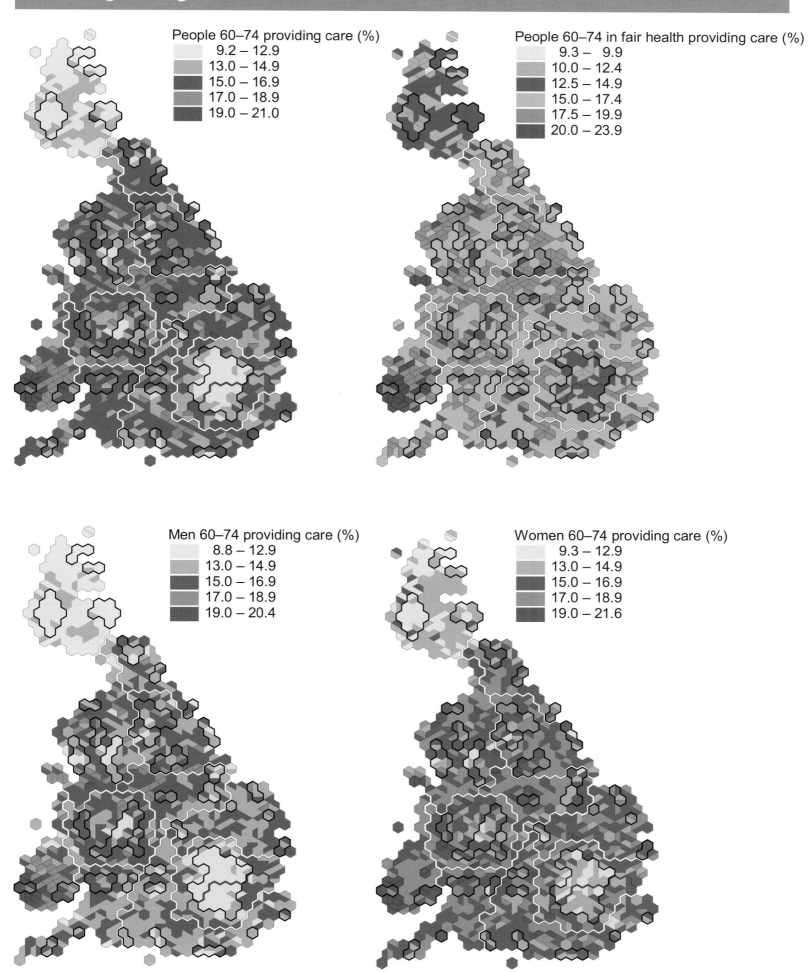

People 60–74 providing care (%)
- 9.2 – 12.9
- 13.0 – 14.9
- 15.0 – 16.9
- 17.0 – 18.9
- 19.0 – 21.0

People 60–74 in fair health providing care (%)
- 9.3 – 9.9
- 10.0 – 12.4
- 12.5 – 14.9
- 15.0 – 17.4
- 17.5 – 19.9
- 20.0 – 23.9

Men 60–74 providing care (%)
- 8.8 – 12.9
- 13.0 – 14.9
- 15.0 – 16.9
- 17.0 – 18.9
- 19.0 – 20.4

Women 60–74 providing care (%)
- 9.3 – 12.9
- 13.0 – 14.9
- 15.0 – 16.9
- 17.0 – 18.9
- 19.0 – 21.6

7.21 Health in old age: what you should expect depends on where you live

Life's *not just being alive, but being well.*
(Martial, Epigrammata)

The proportion of old people in poor health varies many-fold by neighbourhood as highlighted in Figure 7.21 opposite, which shows the basic rates of that population suffering across Britain. The island's old people are most sprightly in Balerno, Amersham, Henley and Leatherhead (where 9.1% or less experience poor health). They are mostly likely to be suffering poor health in the Glasgow neighbourhoods of Easterhouse, Milton, Parkhead and Ibrox (averaging two in five); and then in Rhondda, Merthyr Tydfil and Rhymney in south Wales, all at 38%. The reasons as to why these differences should be so acute have been rehearsed above many times (affluence/deprivation, migration/concentration, industrial legacy) but as age advances the differences become more stark and the numbers involved far more substantial.

The simplified version of this mosaic is shown below left, where average rates of poor health at these ages refer to rates of 13% to 25% of the older population. Underlying these spatial trends is a propensity for men to report slightly higher rates of suffering poor health than women, nationally. However, by area there are many neighbourhoods where women report a higher prevalence of poor health than men. Both types of area, and those where equality prevails, are shown below right and it is clear that the geographical pattern to sex differentiation is not random. Men are more likely not to be suffering poor health in the south of England and much of the midlands. Or, put another way, older couples are slightly more likely to remain in the south of England and the midlands while the man's health remains fair or good. This is even true of those parts of London where rates of poor health are above average, as are the living costs.

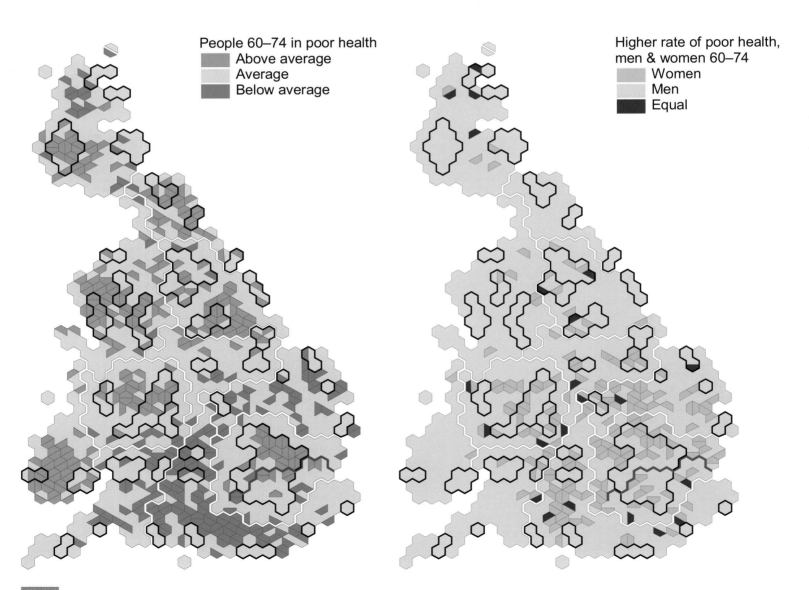

People 60–74 in poor health
■ Above average
■ Average
■ Below average

Higher rate of poor health, men & women 60–74
■ Women
■ Men
■ Equal

7.21 Health in old age: what you should expect depends on where you live

Figure 7.21

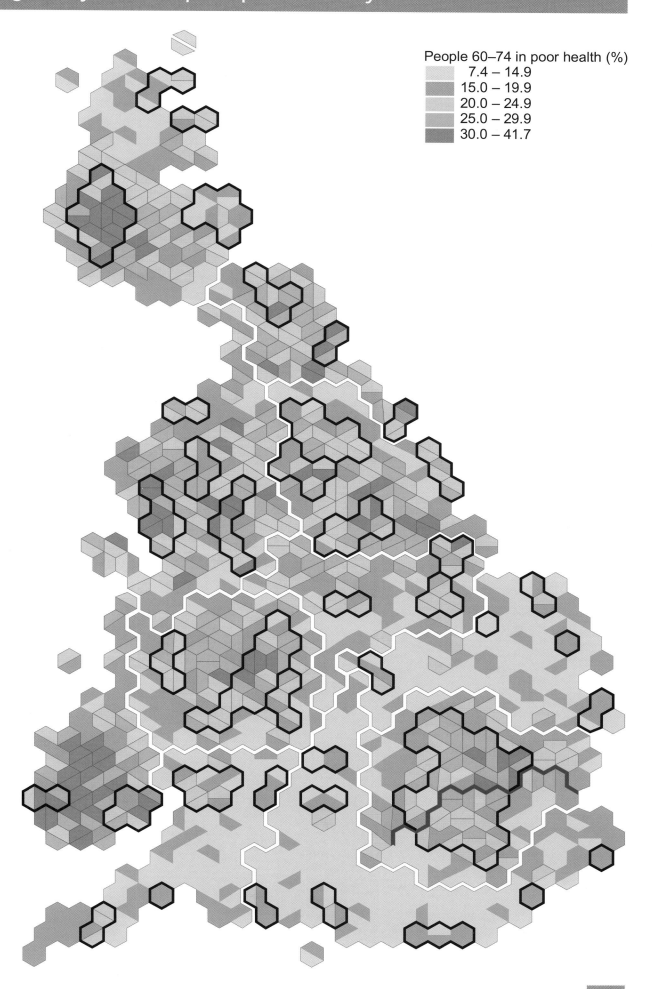

People 60–74 in poor health (%)
- 7.4 – 14.9
- 15.0 – 19.9
- 20.0 – 24.9
- 25.0 – 29.9
- 30.0 – 41.7

7.22 Living with a limiting long-term illness in old age

Balerno, Sevenoaks, Henley and Guildford Rural: sound familiar? Yes, two had the lowest rates of poor health while here they are the four neighbourhoods where older adults are least likely to be suffering from a limiting long-term illness (LLTI). Now, however, the rates are only just under a quarter of the population. No amount of selective migration, affluence or healthy living can prevent the slow progression of inevitable decline. By these ages, by area, at best you have a three in four chance of not suffering from a condition that limits your daily activities significantly. At worse your chances are only one in three of not suffering such limitation in Glasgow Parkhead and Easterhouse, and in the valleys of Rhondda, Rhymney and Merthyr Tydfil. Again familiar neighbourhoods, but LLTI rates for all the places in between are shown too, in Figure 7.22 opposite. And, if anything, disability of this kind at these ages creates an even clearer topology of opportunity and constraint from the lowland crescent centred just west of London, up to the peaks of misfortune within the old industrial cities of the north and the Welsh Valleys.

Again also, as the map below left illustrates, in most places rates are higher for men than for women, other than where the living is not financially easy, albeit with a few interesting exceptions. But, poor health and LLTI are far from being perfectly correlated as the map below right shows, contrasting areas where rates of LLTI are below average but the majority of people with LLTI are in fair health with five other combinations that occur and three that do not (nowhere are a majority of people with LLTI in good health by these ages). This map, dominated by four of those six shades, does, however, also show that by old age discrepant places become less common.

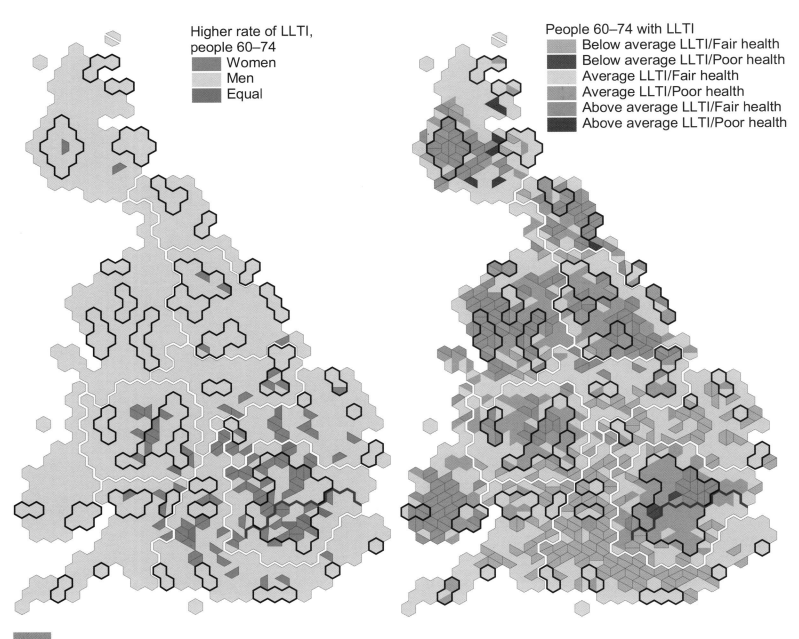

Higher rate of LLTI, people 60–74
- Women
- Men
- Equal

People 60–74 with LLTI
- Below average LLTI/Fair health
- Below average LLTI/Poor health
- Average LLTI/Fair health
- Average LLTI/Poor health
- Above average LLTI/Fair health
- Above average LLTI/Poor health

7.22 Living with a limiting long-term illness in old age

Figure 7.22

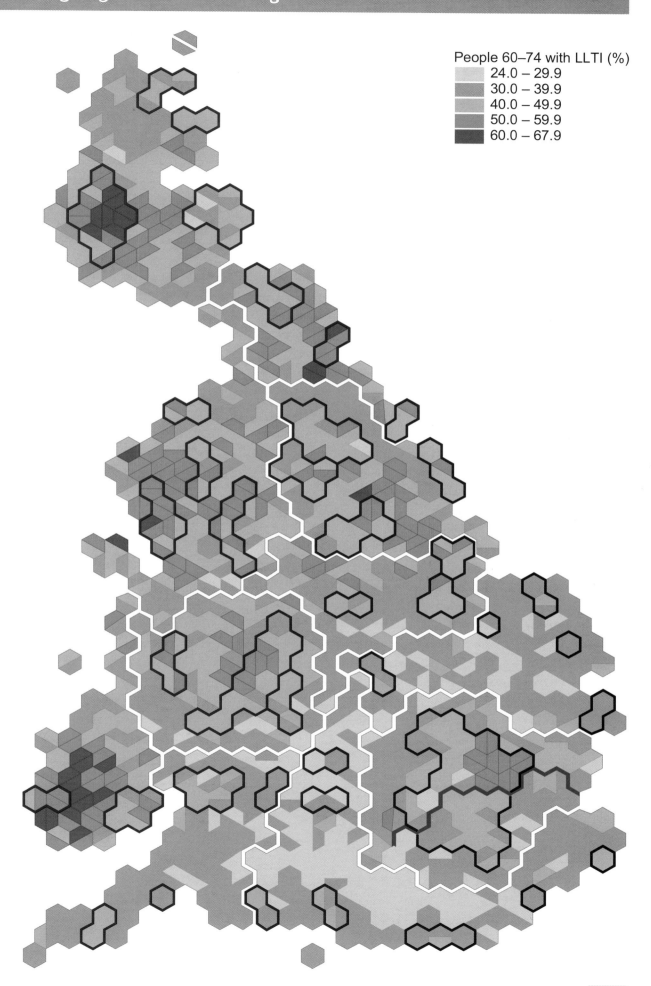

People 60–74 with LLTI (%)
24.0 – 29.9
30.0 – 39.9
40.0 – 49.9
50.0 – 59.9
60.0 – 67.9

7.23 Concluding old age: the penultimate act for most, the last for many

A quarter of women do not live past old age to become truly elderly; they die before they reach 75. A quarter of those did not reach 60. In comparison, one in nine men, at current death rates, does not live to see his sixtieth birthday in Britain, and over a third do not make it to 75. Thus for many men and women in Britain this is, or will be, their last, not penultimate, stage of life. That has been revealed all too clearly in the state of health of many, as well as in the patterns to the ratio of the sexes, with whom people live and/or are still married to and much else in this chapter.

By these ages, as many people have had their husband, or much less frequently wife, taken from them by death as have otherwise separated. Men in the worst-off areas have a lower chance of being a widower than women in the best-off areas have of being a widow. As a result, women in old age are twice as likely to be living alone as are men. There are many other ways in which the lives of men and women begin to become more differentiated by these ages, not just because they were more so when they were younger than are current younger generations, but also because women are so much more often single in old age. For instance, when looking at car access in this chapter it is clear that women are a staggering 65 times less likely to live in a neighbourhood where the majority have access to two or more cars than are men.

For the small minority passing through these years who are not retired, most of those in Wales, Scotland and the north are sick or disabled rather than in work. Those who do work in these places most often work in manufacturing. It is also almost exclusively outside of the South East where many neighbourhoods are found where most old people last worked between 11 and 20 years ago. And it is in a small subset of these places that a majority of older people are found to rely on Pension Credits to bring their pension up to a minimum, that some two in five are suffering poor health, and that up to almost two in three are living with a disability.

In contrast to those swathes of land where people in old age tend not to fare well is the contrasting fertile crescent within the South East where often only a minority lack any qualifications; where the majority of men at least live in households that have access to two or more cars; where most of those who do not already own their home in old age are about to; in (and to the south of) which a significant minority have no religion and are happy to say so; where most who still work are often managers and senior officials; where few people, and especially fewer men, are suffering poor health; and where those who retire tend not to do so for reasons of poor health.

Within places, but especially between places, the lives of those in old age in Britain bifurcate most clearly by age 60 into those that can identify with continued drudgery, poorly paid work and relatively few comforts to look forward to for the short time most, on average, have left, and those ending their working lives in charge of their jobs or businesses or of others, owning their own home, and looking forward to a relatively long and relatively luxurious older and then truly elderly age. The maps become simpler as we age. There are fewer oddities, fewer exclaves and fewer exceptions to the general geographical rules for where the living is easy and where it is not. However, equality begins to return again in some ways as we turn to the final years from 75 and beyond, and to those who are truly elderly.

8 To end this strange eventful history: aged 75+

... last Scene of all,
That ends this strange eventful history,
Is second childishness, and mere oblivion,
Sans teeth, sans eyes, sans taste, sans everything.

8.1 Introduction

And so to a final stage of transition, from old age to death, via the years of being truly elderly, which for statistical convenience more than biological import we label here from age 75.

These are the years in which almost nobody is in paid employment, in which almost nobody is caring for children, in which good health is not to be expected, and years that, until very recently, we almost all did not expect to reach. Now a majority of men (63%) at current mortality rates can expect to reach age 75 from birth. But of those who do make it to 75, a quarter are dead by 80, over half by 85, four out of five by 90, 95% by 95 and 99% by 99.

In contrast, three quarters (75%) of women at current rates can expect to make it to age 75 from birth. Of those, 20% are dead by 80, 40% by 85, two thirds (68%) by 90, 90% by 95 and 97% by age 99. Given these survival rates, the Queen should be sending almost three times as many birthday telegrams to women aged 100 as she does to men.

Below left we show the simple geography of those aged 75+. This is the last of our maps of the basic distribution of the seven ages of life. Note here, for the last time, the continued exodus to the coasts, but now especially the south coast, along the length of which the truly elderly, who are likely to survive a little longer than most, flock to. However, as the evidence from earlier years should make abundantly clear, it is not the clement weather that helps them live a little longer on the southern coast but privileges earlier in life.

The graph opposite continues the graph started on page 208. The left-hand axis shows the percentage of the truly elderly who can expect to die each year given mortality rates in Britain (2002-04). The right-hand axis shows the growing proportion of that population who are female as a result of these differences in rates. There is, of course, much more to these years than dying, but the shadow of death hangs over them throughout the maps and text that follow, and grows darker year on year as people age. As becomes quickly evident simultaneously through the images that follow, the differential size of this shadow makes the lives of truly elderly men and women ever more different as they age.

For men, most at these ages will end their lives with a wife looking after them. In contrast, most truly elderly women will have been living alone as they approach death. Men, more often living in couples, are more likely to still have access to a car, to be living in a house rather than a flat and not to be reliant on Pension Credits, and are less likely to be suffering a disability or to be in poor health, because on average they are much younger than the average truly elderly woman.

Proportion of population
aged over 74 (%)

	3.1 – 4.9
	5.0 – 7.4
	7.5 – 9.9
	10.0 – 14.9
	15.0 – 20.6

8.1 Introduction

Women have the advantage that in an increasing number of places they can expect to live into their late eighties, even if they simply have an average life span for those places. It is also they who will in the main end up the outright owner of most property on this island (if but for a few years before they pass it on), but despite that they are far more likely to be income poor. And it is they who best represent what it is to be truly elderly in Britain due to a sexual imbalance seen at no other life stage.

When you look at the mosaics for all people in the pages that follow you are looking at images that mainly reflect the lives of women. This is all because of the gap between the blue and pink lines on the graph opposite, which is no wider than a little finger's width, but which grows in impact like compound interest on savings, only in reverse, depleting years left to expect to live, or to expect to live together, rather than sums of monies to expect to accumulate or to later be able to share.

Annual mortality rates in Britain at truly elderly ages and resulting % female (75+)

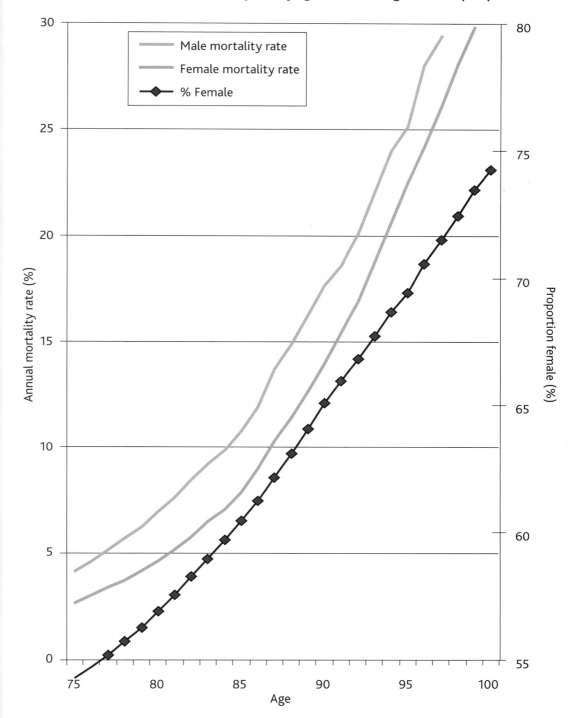

8.2 Which birthday cards should sell best in which places for the truly elderly?

The hundreds-and-thousands coloured map opposite (Figure 8.2) highlights who has survived in greatest and second greatest numbers to live in each neighbourhood in Britain by their late seventies onwards. If you do not know what hundreds-and-thousands are, ask a septuagenarian. In a third of places you find 75-year-olds in greatest numbers followed in second greatest numbers by 76-year-olds. We did warn you that death played a great role at these ages. Next most frequently is the next most likely, given mortality rates by age (76 then 75). Interestingly, there are fewer 78-year-olds than you might expect, given birth numbers 78 years ago, assuming immigration, and more importantly emigration, have been constant since then. Nevertheless, age smoothes out the most dramatic of demographic fluctuations and you would be hard put to spot that anomaly of those born in 1923 (turning 18 at the height of the Second World War) from the little evidence left in Figure 8.2.

The simplified map below left both makes that anomaly clearer and shows that nowhere are there more 82-year-olds (or over) than any single year's worth of those aged 75-81. Similarly, the places of preference within older age can be visually picked out, including the return to nursing homes in the cities and the strange hold that Sheffield has over some of its truly elderly people. Note, however, that numbers can be very low in particular neighbourhoods and much higher in others at these ages.

The map below right shows the variation in the proportions that are female. Again, rates are highest in some of the poorest and richest of areas, but lowest in a middling band roughly the distance from London that trains used to have to stop to refuel with coal during these people's childhoods, and within London, a place where those few truly elderly people who remain include disproportionate numbers of men, not found in the northern cities. Incidentally, the place to stock cards for 100-year-olds is the eastern side of the Isle of Wight.

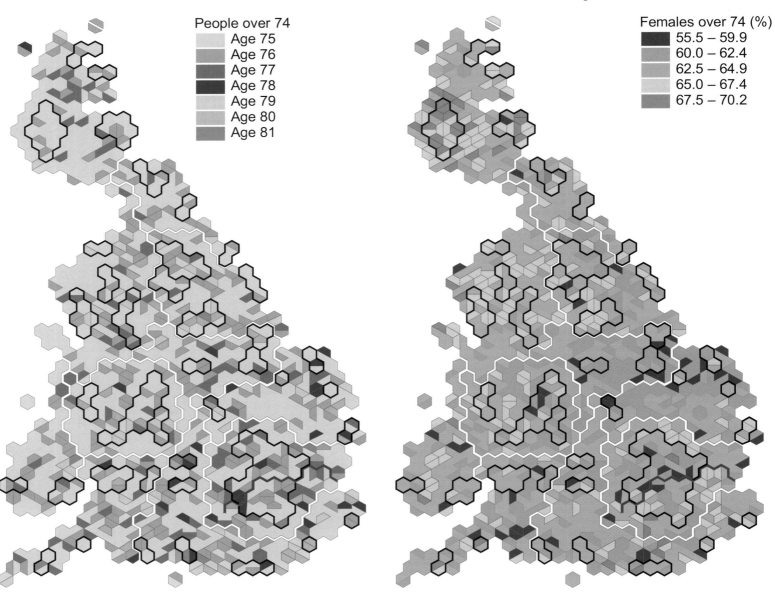

People over 74
- Age 75
- Age 76
- Age 77
- Age 78
- Age 79
- Age 80
- Age 81

Females over 74 (%)
- 55.5 – 59.9
- 60.0 – 62.4
- 62.5 – 64.9
- 65.0 – 67.4
- 67.5 – 70.2

8.2   Which birthday cards should sell best in which places for the truly elderly?

Figure 8.2

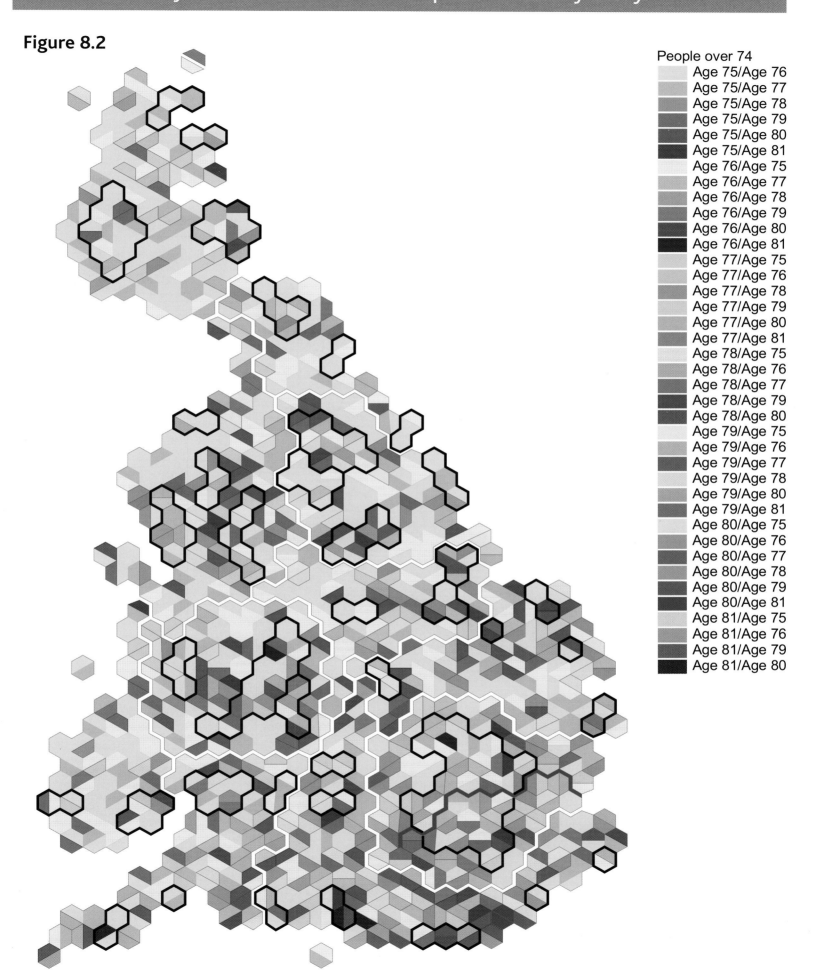

People over 74

- Age 75/Age 76
- Age 75/Age 77
- Age 75/Age 78
- Age 75/Age 79
- Age 75/Age 80
- Age 75/Age 81
- Age 76/Age 75
- Age 76/Age 77
- Age 76/Age 78
- Age 76/Age 79
- Age 76/Age 80
- Age 76/Age 81
- Age 77/Age 75
- Age 77/Age 76
- Age 77/Age 78
- Age 77/Age 79
- Age 77/Age 80
- Age 77/Age 81
- Age 78/Age 75
- Age 78/Age 76
- Age 78/Age 77
- Age 78/Age 79
- Age 78/Age 80
- Age 79/Age 75
- Age 79/Age 76
- Age 79/Age 77
- Age 79/Age 78
- Age 79/Age 80
- Age 79/Age 81
- Age 80/Age 75
- Age 80/Age 76
- Age 80/Age 77
- Age 80/Age 78
- Age 80/Age 79
- Age 80/Age 81
- Age 81/Age 75
- Age 81/Age 76
- Age 81/Age 79
- Age 81/Age 80

8.3 Single and never married for those who are truly elderly

Of those aged 75+ in Britain, 1% are separated, 3% are divorced, 5% have remarried, 7% are single, 33% are still in their first marriage and 51% are widowed. Nowhere are the first three states in a majority or even the largest minority and so we will ignore them from here on. The proportion of 'single never married' people is higher for this age group than it is for those a life stage younger, but the geography of where single people of these ages find themselves living and all the other marital statuses varies significantly in likelihood by sex. However, compared with the other possible marital states the proportion of men who are 'single never married' is not that much different than the proportion of women (it is a fraction lower). This is because it was when these men and women were much younger that the decision was implicitly (if not explicitly) taken never to marry. The Second World War resulted in the deaths of just enough potential husbands to account for the difference in the table below. Note, too, the subtle differences in the maps for single truly elderly men and women respectively. The two maps shown below combine disproportionately to produce the main mosaic shown opposite in Figure 8.3, disproportionately because although their rates are very similar, there are far more women alive of these ages than men. There are two single truly elderly women for every single truly elderly man.

Marital status for all and by sex for those aged 75+

Percentage people 75+	Separated	Divorced	Remarried	Single	First married	Widowed	Total
All	1	3	5	7	33	51	100
Men	1	3	8	7	53	28	100
Women	0	3	3	8	22	64	100

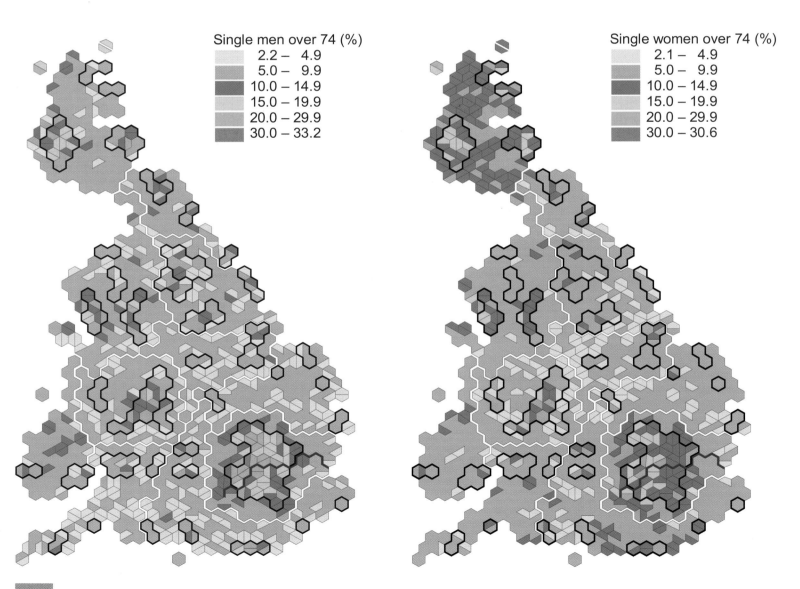

Single men over 74 (%)
- 2.2 – 4.9
- 5.0 – 9.9
- 10.0 – 14.9
- 15.0 – 19.9
- 20.0 – 29.9
- 30.0 – 33.2

Single women over 74 (%)
- 2.1 – 4.9
- 5.0 – 9.9
- 10.0 – 14.9
- 15.0 – 19.9
- 20.0 – 29.9
- 30.0 – 30.6

8.3 Single and never married for those who are truly elderly

Figure 8.3

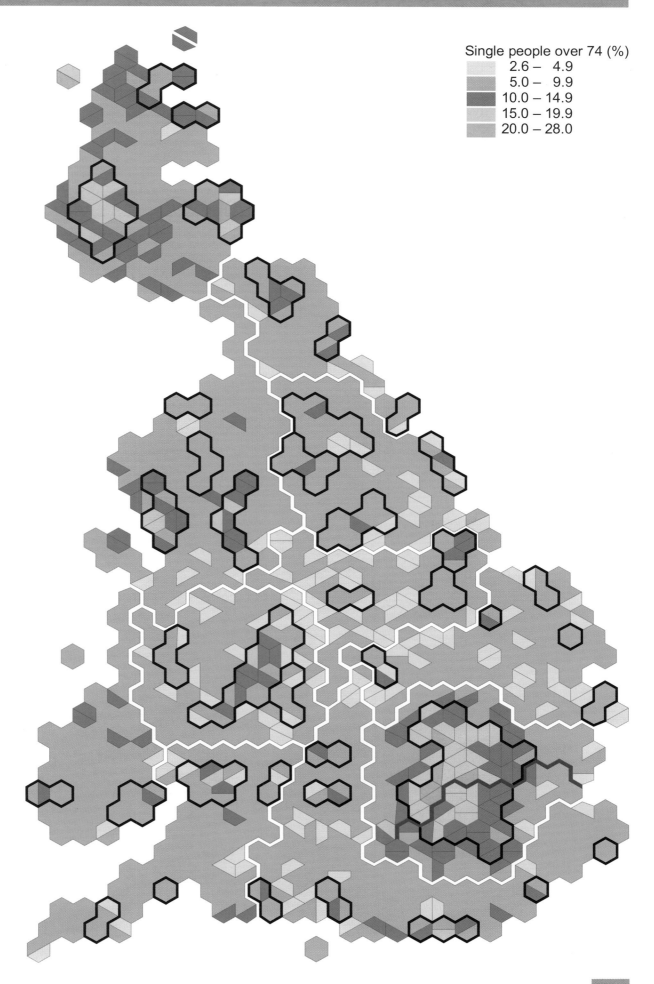

Single people over 74 (%)
- 2.6 – 4.9
- 5.0 – 9.9
- 10.0 – 14.9
- 15.0 – 19.9
- 20.0 – 28.0

8.4 Still in your first marriage when truly elderly

As the table on page 256 shows, a third of truly elderly people are married but that third is made up of a majority of men and less than a quarter of women of these ages. This is, of course, partly because men tend on average to marry younger women, but here it is also because there are fewer men that the proportions stack up in this way. In absolute terms 839,000 men and 593,000 women of these ages are in their first marriage, the discrepancy of some quarter of a million being due to men of 75+ being married to women aged under 75. Usually the age difference is of only a few years.

During economically bad times people tend to marry older and the age gap at marriage widens too. These people were old enough to marry first mainly in the 1940s and early 1950s, not the best of times. Rationing was in place for almost all of their young adult lives. Their children, in contrast, if they married, did so in the 1960s and early 1970s, far more prosperous times when most people did not wait very long before tying the knot. Their grandchildren married in the 1980s and 1990s, some still are marrying, and unprecedented numbers have not married, either by choice or by circumstance.

The maps below use the same shading scheme to highlight just how different the chances of still being in your first marriage are for men and for women at truly elderly ages. Most men of these ages end their marriage through their death, and most women through becoming a widow. Figure 8.4 opposite (of the rates still in first marriage for all) combines these two maps, using the same shades again, but is dominated as a result by yet another hue.

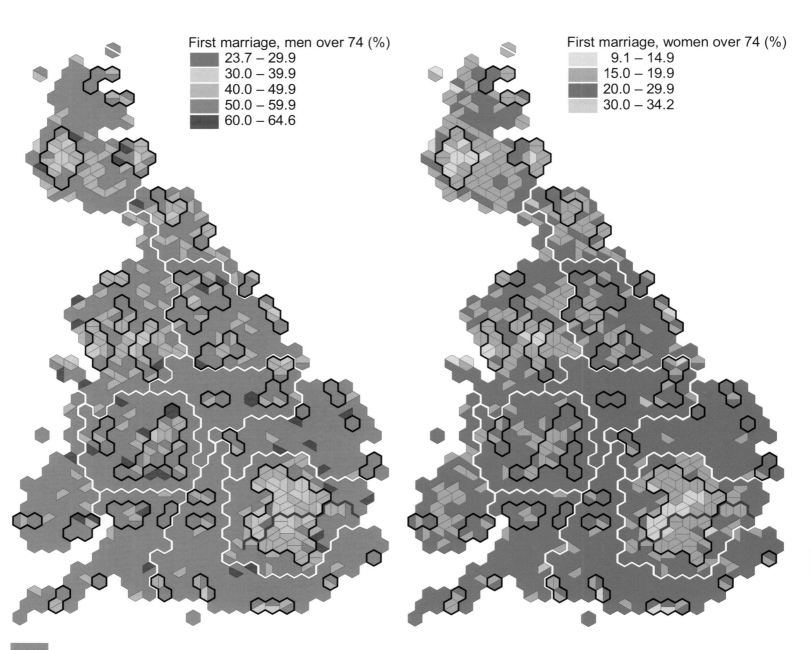

First marriage, men over 74 (%)
- 23.7 – 29.9
- 30.0 – 39.9
- 40.0 – 49.9
- 50.0 – 59.9
- 60.0 – 64.6

First marriage, women over 74 (%)
- 9.1 – 14.9
- 15.0 – 19.9
- 20.0 – 29.9
- 30.0 – 34.2

8.4   Still in your first marriage when truly elderly

Figure 8.4

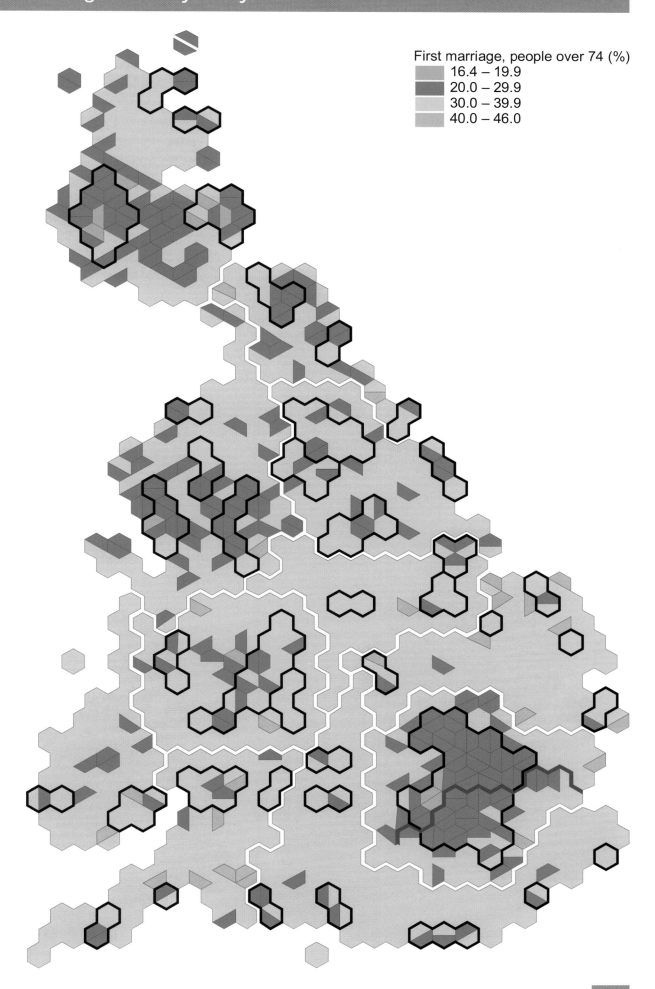

First marriage, people over 74 (%)
- 16.4 – 19.9
- 20.0 – 29.9
- 30.0 – 39.9
- 40.0 – 46.0

8.5 Widowed when truly elderly

Again, as for those a life stage younger, women in the best-off place (now Kensington) are more likely to be widowed than are men in the worst-off neighbourhood for them (Glasgow Easterhouse). Four times as many women are widowed when truly elderly than men. Although this is mainly due to women living longer, for those men who are widowed (perhaps much earlier in life) there is far greater opportunity to remarry than for women and that opportunity increases proportionately with age. Thus while the table on page 256 highlighted that almost two thirds of women and just over a quarter of men of these ages are widowed, it also reveals that men are more than twice as likely to be remarried at these ages compared with women. We have no way of knowing by area when that second, third or subsequent marriage took place, nor the age of the women to whom these remarried men are married, but clearly living longer has usually meant living more on their own for women of this generation.

Everywhere in Britain a majority of truly elderly women are widowed compared with the numbers who are single or still in their first marriage. In contrast, men of these ages are in the majority in their first marriage everywhere except Kensal Town (the only place where a majority of truly elderly men are single) and a majority are widowed in only 10 neighbourhoods: Chelsea (where the male pensioners of that name live), Canning Town in central London, Ardwick in central Manchester, Liverpool Riverside North, Birkenhead North-East, Linwood (see page 24), and the Glasgow neighbourhoods of Calton, Easterhouse, Ibrox and University. Below, the rates of being a widower or widow are shown and opposite (Figure 8.5) their combined effect. Again, a single shading scheme is used.

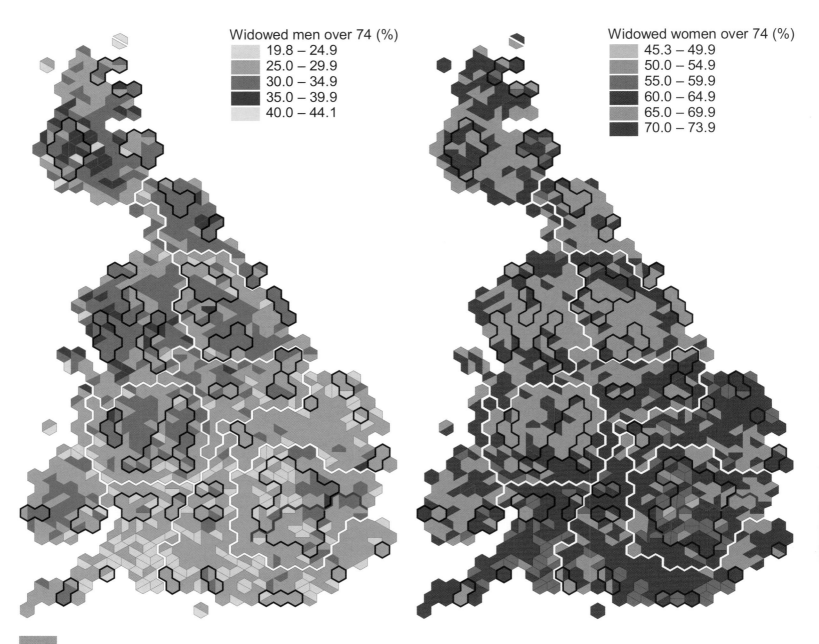

Widowed men over 74 (%)
- 19.8 – 24.9
- 25.0 – 29.9
- 30.0 – 34.9
- 35.0 – 39.9
- 40.0 – 44.1

Widowed women over 74 (%)
- 45.3 – 49.9
- 50.0 – 54.9
- 55.0 – 59.9
- 60.0 – 64.9
- 65.0 – 69.9
- 70.0 – 73.9

8.5 Widowed when truly elderly

Figure 8.5

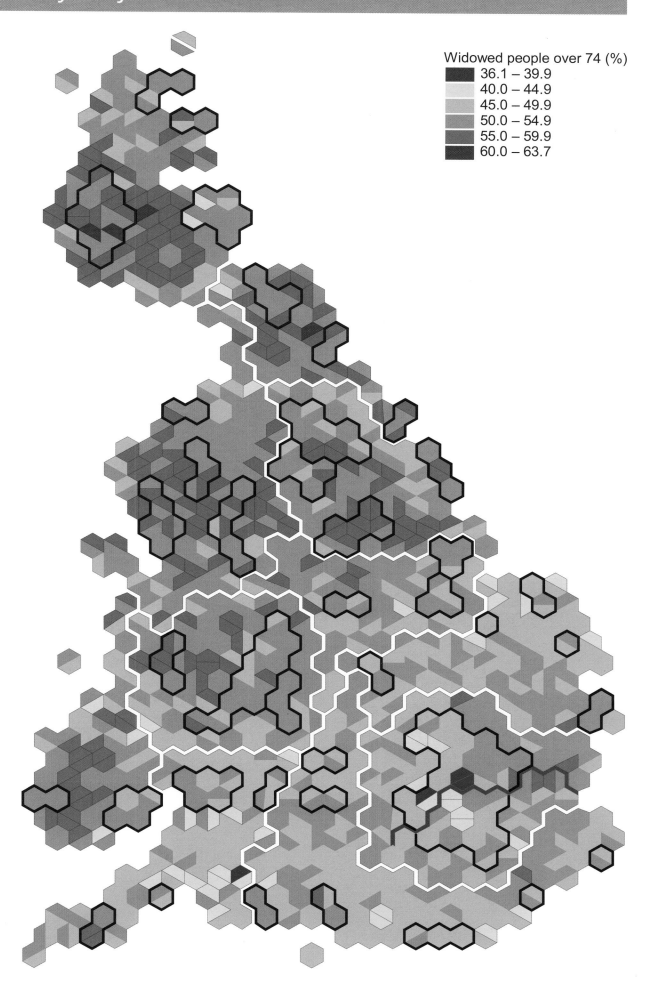

Widowed people over 74 (%)
- 36.1 – 39.9
- 40.0 – 44.9
- 45.0 – 49.9
- 50.0 – 54.9
- 55.0 – 59.9
- 60.0 – 63.7

8.6 Truly elderly living alone

In almost all of the north, in London, and in half of the rest of the south of England most truly elderly people live on their own, as is shown on the right. Nationally, 44% of truly elderly people live on their own compared with 1% who cohabit, 5% who live in a lone parent family (most often as the parent of the lone parent or as the only parent of their own grown-up child), 6% who do not live with a family but live with others, 8% who are in a communal establishment and 36% who are in a married couple family.

Below are shown the distributions for the 28% of men (on the left) and 53% of women (on the right) of these ages who live alone. Opposite (Figure 8.6), coloured exactly the same shade for each rate, are shown the rates for men and women combined. We are never so likely to live alone as when we are truly elderly.

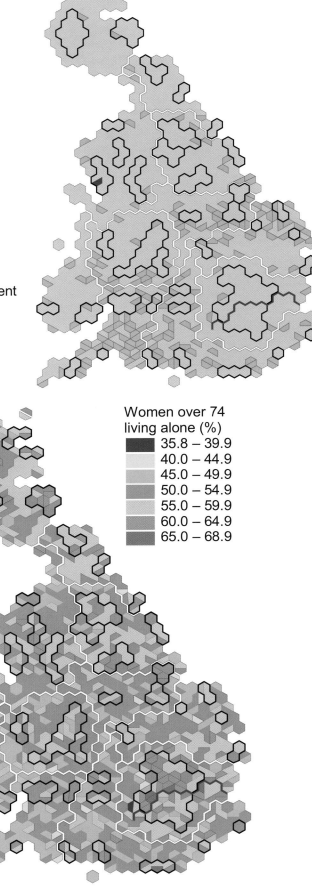

Living arrangements, people over 74
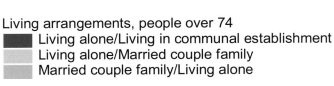
■ Living alone/Living in communal establishment
  Living alone/Married couple family
  Married couple family/Living alone

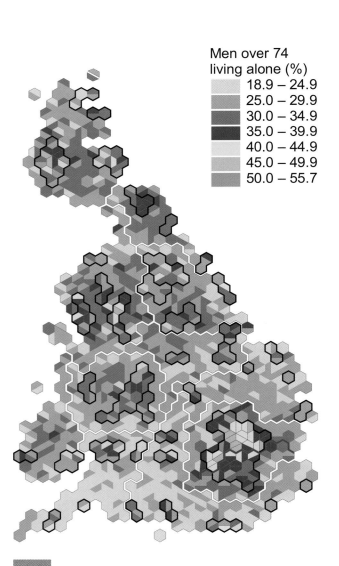

Men over 74
living alone (%)
18.9 – 24.9
25.0 – 29.9
30.0 – 34.9
35.0 – 39.9
40.0 – 44.9
45.0 – 49.9
50.0 – 55.7

Women over 74
living alone (%)
35.8 – 39.9
40.0 – 44.9
45.0 – 49.9
50.0 – 54.9
55.0 – 59.9
60.0 – 64.9
65.0 – 68.9

8.6 Truly elderly living alone

Figure 8.6

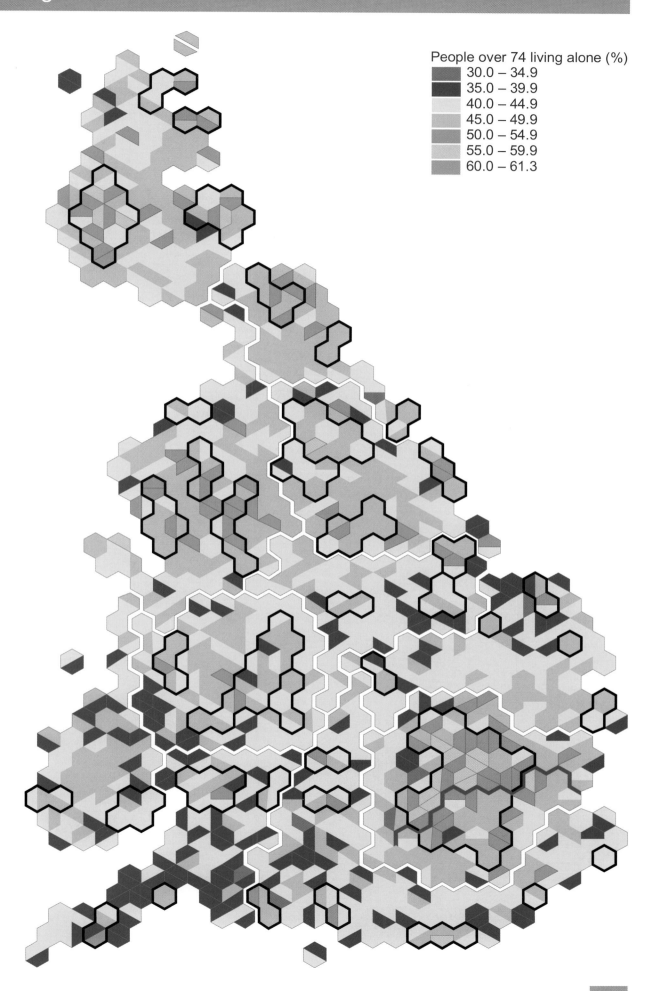

People over 74 living alone (%)
- 30.0 – 34.9
- 35.0 – 39.9
- 40.0 – 44.9
- 45.0 – 49.9
- 50.0 – 54.9
- 55.0 – 59.9
- 60.0 – 61.3

8.7 Tenure, communal establishments and the truly elderly

Figure 8.7 opposite shows the most and second most common tenure group in each place for the truly elderly. In 90% of neighbourhoods the majority now own outright and in all but two of the rest the majority rent from their local authority (LA). In the two remaining neighbourhoods they rent from another social landlord.

In no neighbourhood are the majority of the truly elderly living in communal medical and care establishments and, although nationally the proportion is 8%, it never reaches a quarter, as is shown on the right. The proportion living in communal accommodation is a little lower in London and the south, where people have on average had easier lives than their counterparts in the rest of the country and are as a consequence, fitter and where demand for buildings is more acute.

Below, the distributions of the two most common tenures, outright ownership (53%) and LA renting (17%), are shown. An additional 7% have a mortgage, 7% are social tenants of other agencies, 4% rent privately and 4% say they live rent free.

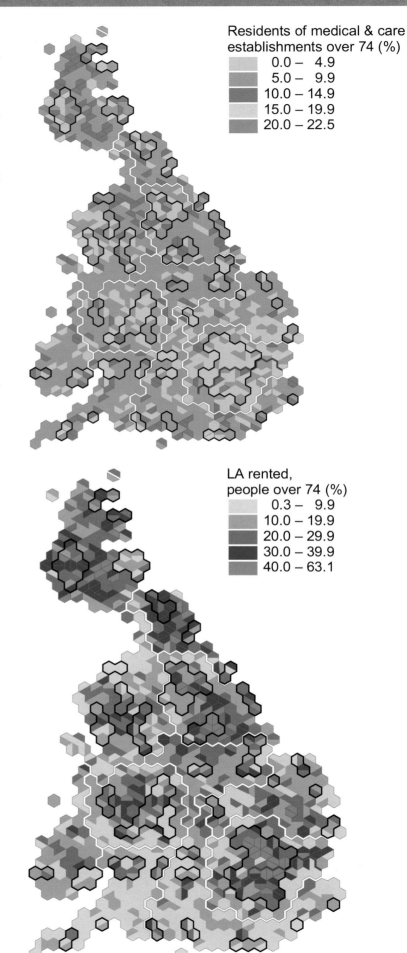

Residents of medical & care
establishments over 74 (%)
- 0.0 – 4.9
- 5.0 – 9.9
- 10.0 – 14.9
- 15.0 – 19.9
- 20.0 – 22.5

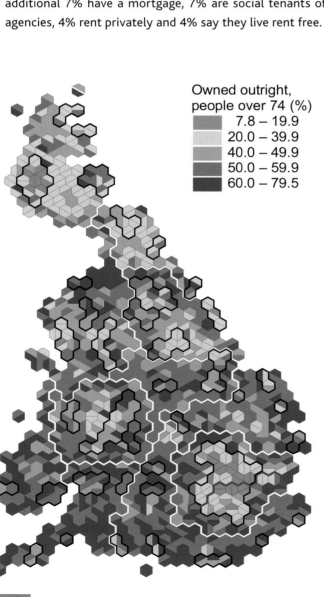

Owned outright,
people over 74 (%)
- 7.8 – 19.9
- 20.0 – 39.9
- 40.0 – 49.9
- 50.0 – 59.9
- 60.0 – 79.5

LA rented,
people over 74 (%)
- 0.3 – 9.9
- 10.0 – 19.9
- 20.0 – 29.9
- 30.0 – 39.9
- 40.0 – 63.1

8.7 Tenure, communal establishments and the truly elderly

Figure 8.7

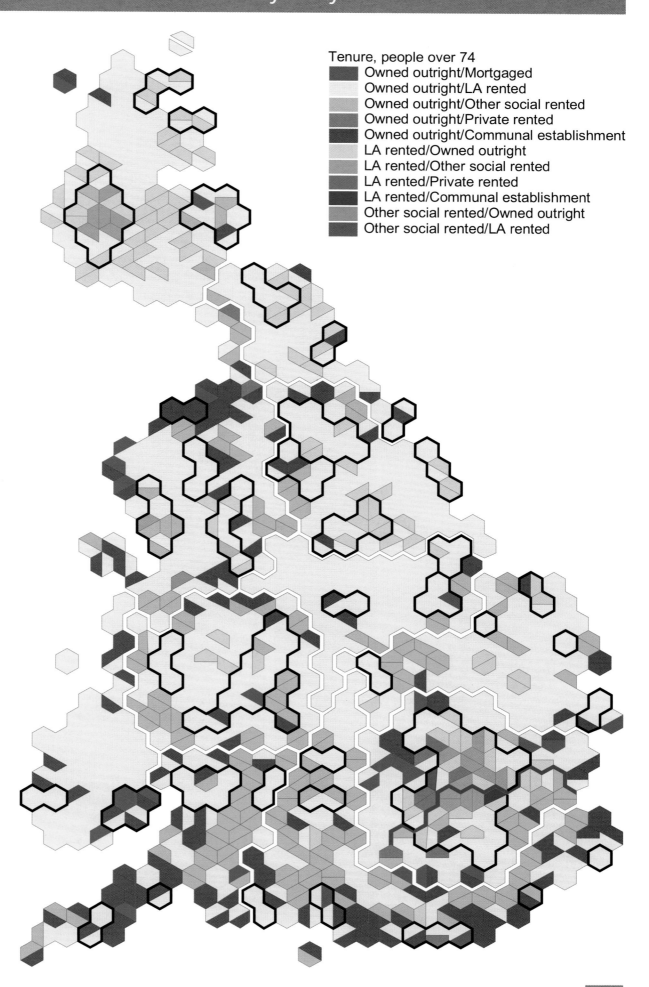

Tenure, people over 74
- Owned outright/Mortgaged
- Owned outright/LA rented
- Owned outright/Other social rented
- Owned outright/Private rented
- Owned outright/Communal establishment
- LA rented/Owned outright
- LA rented/Other social rented
- LA rented/Private rented
- LA rented/Communal establishment
- Other social rented/Owned outright
- Other social rented/LA rented

8.8 Stepping out and down or up: truly elderly living by floor level

Not all truly elderly people live in the country cottage with roses round the door and a view of the sea. One in eight lives in a flat where their entrance is above the first floor. One in seven of those lives above the second floor and 40% of those live on the fifth floor or above. Those 28,000 truly elderly people may have a nice view at least, although the map below left shows that that view is most likely of a skyline of other tenements or tower blocks in Glasgow or London. A further 55,000 people of these ages are living below the ground floor in a basement or semi-basement.

The map below right shows a cluster of significant numbers of truly elderly people living below ground level in parts of Bradford, Huddersfield and Halifax. It also shows where the 19,000 people aged over 74 who live in caravans or other temporary structures in Britain cluster most in North Bedfordshire, Rayleigh East in Essex and Sleaford West in Lincolnshire; although you do not get much elevation in a Lincolnshire caravan park you may at least have sea views.

Living in a caravan need not be poor living if it is well ventilated, well heated and spacious enough. Similarly, living in a basement can be perfectly acceptable, although again the views are rarely great so it helps to be mobile, especially for the stairs. Living above ground-floor level is not problematic in itself as long as there are lifts that work, and preferably do not smell too much. However, most of the housing in which truly elderly people now find themselves living above floor level was never designed with them in mind.

Lowest floor fifth floor or higher, people over 74 (%)

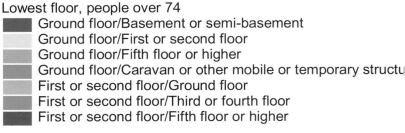

Lowest floor, people over 74
- Ground floor/Basement or semi-basement
- Ground floor/First or second floor
- Ground floor/Fifth floor or higher
- Ground floor/Caravan or other mobile or temporary structu
- First or second floor/Ground floor
- First or second floor/Third or fourth floor
- First or second floor/Fifth floor or higher

Lowest floor fifth floor or higher, people over 74 (%)
- 0.0
- 0.1 – 2.9
- 3.0 – 5.9
- 6.0 – 9.9
- 10.0 – 22.3

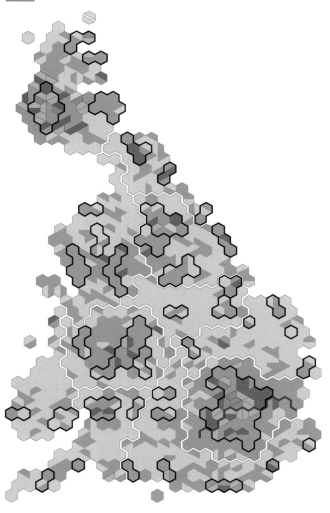

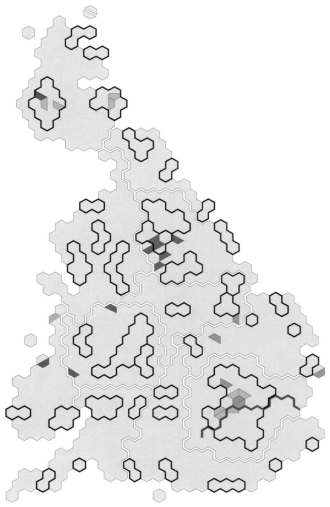

8.8   Stepping out and down or up: truly elderly living by floor level

Figure 8.8 shows where almost half a million people over the age of 75 live on the first floor and above. Much of such housing was built to squeeze poorer families into the cities of Scotland and into the boroughs of Inner London when they were expanding or their slums were being demolished. These are mostly not dwellings designed to house people in their seventies, eighties or nineties.

Figure 8.8

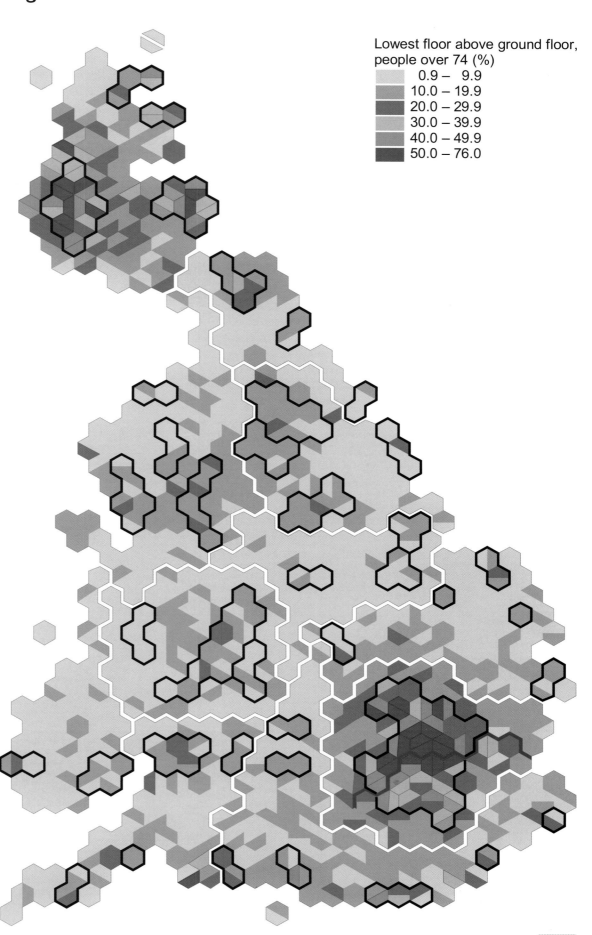

Lowest floor above ground floor, people over 74 (%)

	0.9 – 9.9
	10.0 – 19.9
	20.0 – 29.9
	30.0 – 39.9
	40.0 – 49.9
	50.0 – 76.0

8.9 Welfare benefits, central heating, under- and over-crowding for the truly elderly

The mosaic of the chances of truly elderly people living in homes with more or fewer rooms than they need is shown below left. Just as with those in old age, in the majority of neighbourhoods truly elderly people have at least two rooms spare and most of those that do not have at least one extra room. Many will have many more rooms that they do not need. At these ages they are also likely to begin to appreciate that they do not need them, find it harder to clean them, and so on. However, the large majority who own their large homes own them outright and are hanging on in them till the end.

There is nowhere where a majority of people of these ages have too few rooms to live in. Remember that almost half live alone so this is not surprising (although the nominal allocation for a married couple is not greater than that for a single person – the explanation of occupancy rating is on page 30).

A large minority of the truly elderly are over-crowded mostly only where large numbers also live above the ground floor (locations as shown in Section 8.8). However, having enough space to live in and a front door that does not open on to a stairwell are just the beginnings of what you might wish for when you are 75 or older. For instance, over a tenth of people of these ages live in homes without central heating. And as the map below right shows, that tenth is very clustered, mainly in areas of unimproved older housing held privately. Then, even if you have the heating, you need to be able to pay to run it and pay for everything else.

Occupancy rating, people over 74
- Occupancy rating +2 or more/Occupancy rating +1
- Occupancy rating +2 or more/Occupancy rating 0
- Occupancy rating +2 or more/Communal establishment
- Occupancy rating +1/Occupancy rating +2 or more
- Occupancy rating +1/Occupancy rating 0
- Occupancy rating 0/Occupancy rating +2 or more
- Occupancy rating 0/Occupancy rating +1
- Occupancy rating 0/Occupancy rating -1 or less

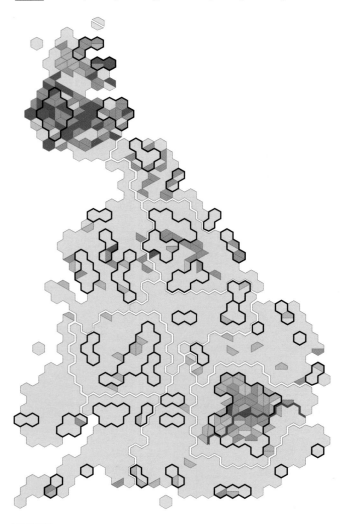

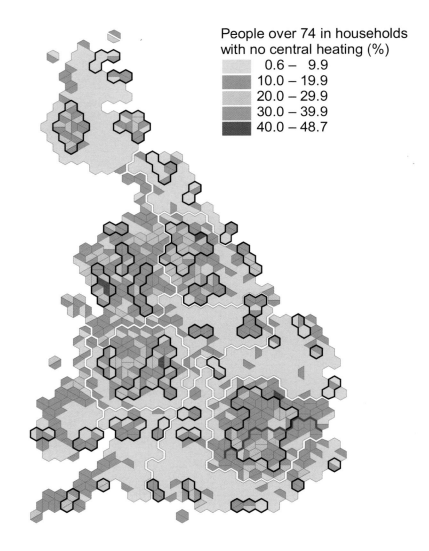

People over 74 in households with no central heating (%)
- 0.6 – 9.9
- 10.0 – 19.9
- 20.0 – 29.9
- 30.0 – 39.9
- 40.0 – 48.7

8.9 Welfare benefits, central heating, under- and over-crowding for the truly elderly

Shamed by the sight of truly elderly people in the dock for non-payment of their TV licences or found dead from cold in homes they could not afford to heat, the government pays higher heating allowances and exempts those over 74 from the licence fee – a free view at last, if only of a TV screen. Still, the government has had to make further payments of Pension Credits to over a quarter of people at these ages just to give them enough to survive on, living at a minimum, although the credits have to be applied for and less than 100% of those eligible do so. Figure 8.9 shows the places where most of those live whose passage into the good night is being prolonged by such hand-outs, thankfully at least now termed 'credits' rather than 'outdoor relief' (from a Poor Law that still existed in some of their childhoods). But 'credits' mean much the same as 'relief' when you begin to think about it a little.

Figure 8.9

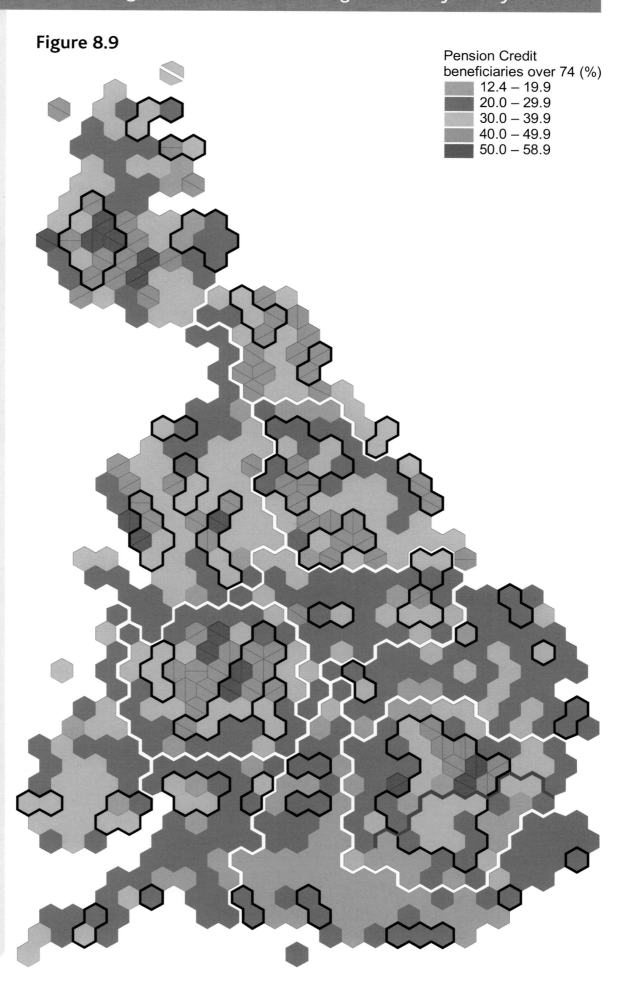

Pension Credit beneficiaries over 74 (%)
- 12.4 – 19.9
- 20.0 – 29.9
- 30.0 – 39.9
- 40.0 – 49.9
- 50.0 – 58.9

8.10 Access to cars and driving for the truly elderly

Truly elderly and want to continue driving? Then live in the South West. The majority of people over 74 there have access to a car as shown in Figure 8.10 opposite.

The rates of having no access to a car are shown on the right, and from these it is clear that the majority of those in their late seventies and eighties, and maybe even a few in their nineties, feel that it is a necessity outside of the cities to have a car. However, the two maps below show that men find such transport much more of a necessity (or are better able to afford it) than women in the countryside and there are still a smattering of neighbourhoods, mainly along the remoter rural regional boundaries, where the largest minority of men of these ages have access to two cars in their twilight years.

Desire, need, necessity, resource and perhaps a residual requirement for speed where it is most remote are all at play. Remember that only a quarter of women in their seventies have a full driving licence (see page 230).

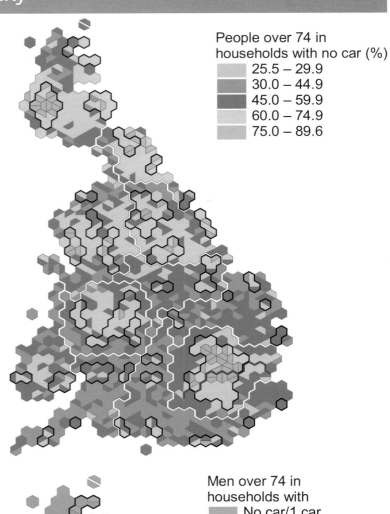

People over 74 in households with no car (%)
25.5 – 29.9
30.0 – 44.9
45.0 – 59.9
60.0 – 74.9
75.0 – 89.6

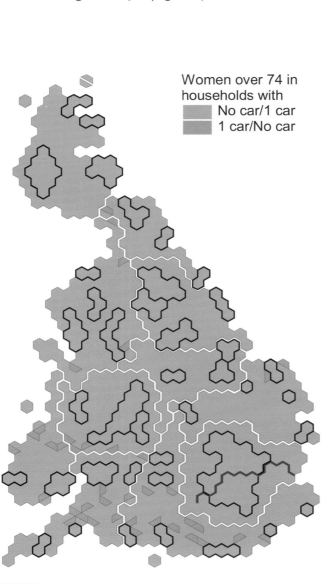

Women over 74 in households with
No car/1 car
1 car/No car

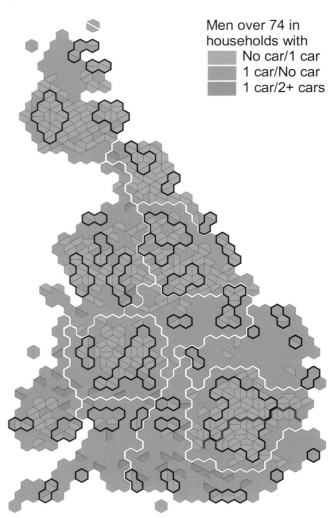

Men over 74 in households with
No car/1 car
1 car/No car
1 car/2+ cars

8.10 Access to cars and driving for the truly elderly

Figure 8.10

People over 74 in households with
No car/1 car
1 car/No car

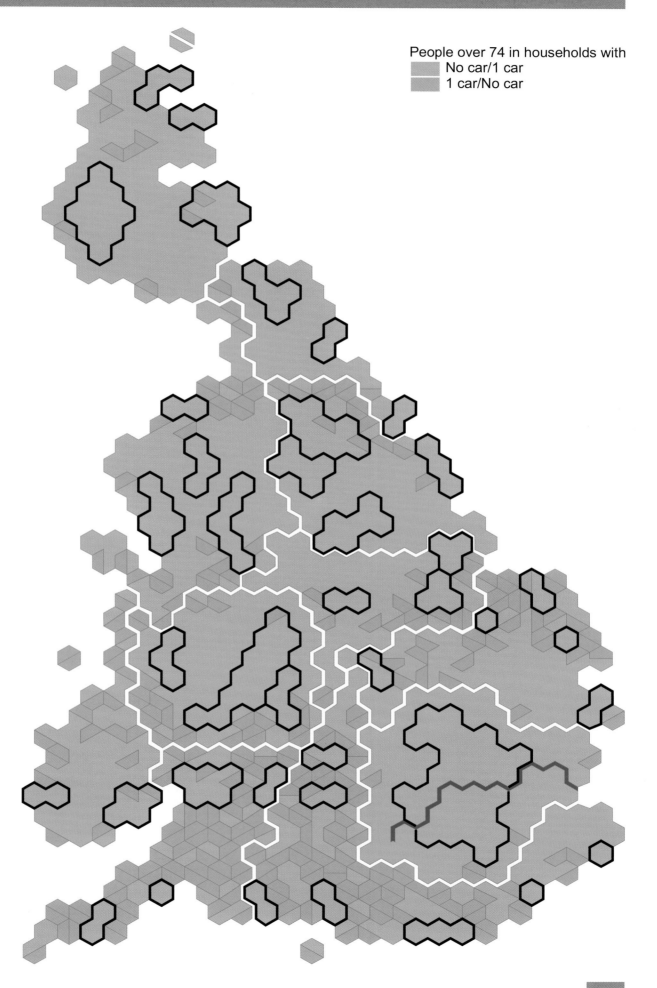

8.11 Ethnic identity and religious adherence among the truly elderly

Even in the oldest of life's stages there is colour and variety in the map of ethnicity shown opposite (Figure 8.11) and the mosaic of religion shown below. This is despite ethnic and religious identities such as German, Quaker, Huguenot, 55 varieties of Methodist and so on, which might mean more to people of these advanced years, not being asked in the last census. Because of such omissions, some 95% in England and Wales living in their last quarter century are left labelling themselves as 'White British'. Had 'English' been offered, most answers would have changed again, of course.

Ethnicity is as much a gift in the pen of those who design the census forms as in people's own imaginations of their origins and heritage (and the imaginations of others). Of the 5% not 'White British', when rounded, 2% each are 'White Irish' and 'Other

White', and 1% are 'Indian'. Less than four in a thousand people over 74 describe themselves as 'Black Caribbean'; less than two in a thousand as 'Pakistani'; less than one in one thousand as 'Chinese'; and less than one in two thousand as 'Bangladeshi'. Nevertheless, all these groups are somewhere in Britain the majority–minority for the truly elderly in at least a couple of neighbourhoods somewhere shown in Figure 8.11.

In England relics of older ethnicities can be seen in the map of religion below, where, for the first time since infancy and childhood (in these series of maps) there is an area where a majority are Jewish (Golders Green for those aged over 74) and there are now many places where that is the largest minority religion (including Giffnock in Scotland).

Only in Oxford West are even a majority of the minority in this last stage of life brave enough to say they have no religion! However, and as ever, it is in Scotland where this question is most revealing and the wider spreading of the Catholic minority across to the south east of that country in old age says more about retirement migration than beliefs in those places in earlier years. The one neighbourhood in Scotland with a majority of the truly elderly who are Roman Catholics is Calton in Glasgow. Note also how by both this division of ethnicity and religion Wales appears a homogeneous nation rather than the salad bowl of identities it more truly is.

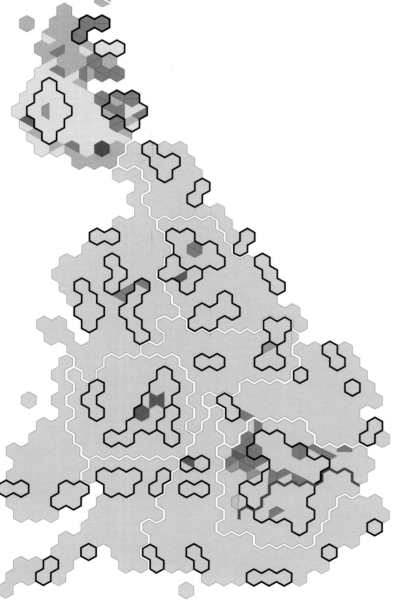

Religion, people over 74
- Christian/Hindu
- Christian/Jewish
- Christian/Muslim
- Christian/Sikh
- Christian/None
- Christian/Not stated
- Jewish/Christian
- Church of Scotland/Jewish
- Church of Scotland/Roman Catholic
- Church of Scotland/Other Christian
- Church of Scotland/None
- Church of Scotland/Not stated
- Roman Catholic/Church of Scotland

8.11 Ethnic identity and religious adherence among the truly elderly

Figure 8.11

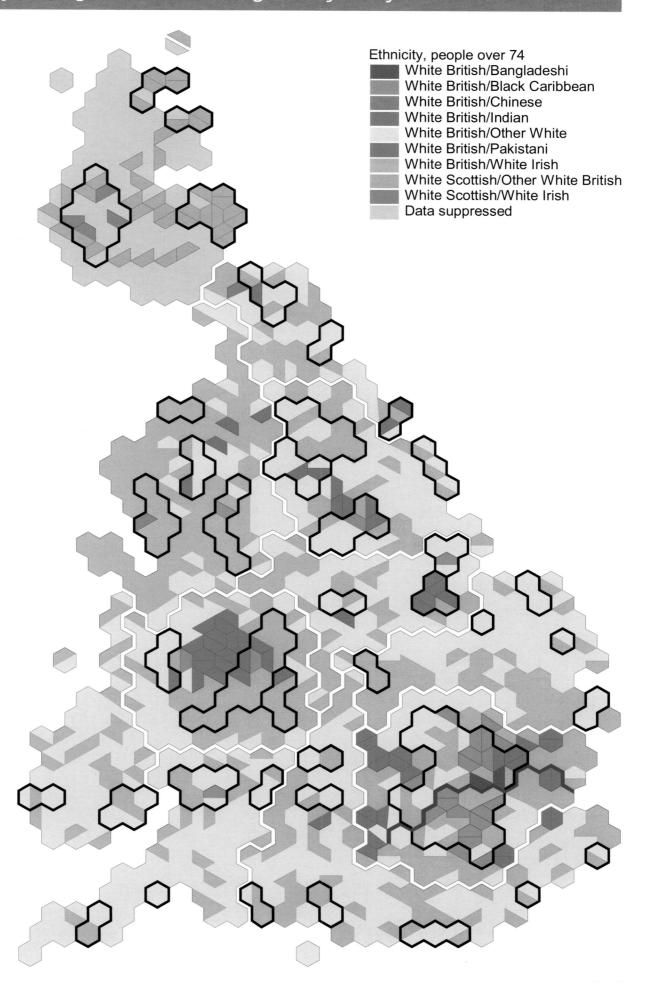

Ethnicity, people over 74
- White British/Bangladeshi
- White British/Black Caribbean
- White British/Chinese
- White British/Indian
- White British/Other White
- White British/Pakistani
- White British/White Irish
- White Scottish/Other White British
- White Scottish/White Irish
- Data suppressed

8.12 Health status of the truly elderly

The majority of people aged over 74 in Britain describe their health as 'fair', and they do this in most places, as is shown in Figure 8.12 opposite, which also gives second most common health status. In this sense what constitutes 'good', 'poor' and 'fair' health is relative, compared with what you would expect for your age. And note how the geographical divide is shown through what health status the majority of the minority live with. This is highlighted on the right where it is evident that the rate claiming poor health never quite reaches half the population. It is, of course, people dying that keeps the rate down.

The mosaic below left is a simplified version of that shown above right. In that mosaic average rates of poor health by place are any rate from 25% to 34% of the truly elderly population. Finally, the mosaic below right illustrates that by these ages more women than men in most places complain of poor health. Perhaps more of the men are just grateful to be alive!

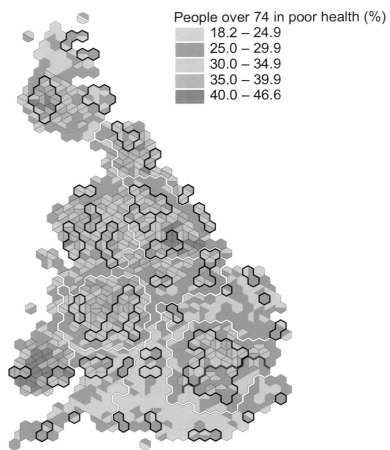

People over 74 in poor health (%)
- 18.2 – 24.9
- 25.0 – 29.9
- 30.0 – 34.9
- 35.0 – 39.9
- 40.0 – 46.6

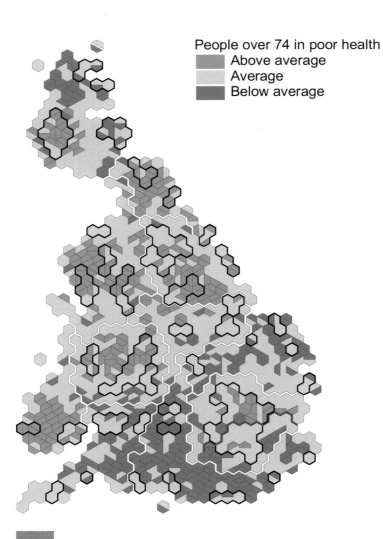

People over 74 in poor health
- Above average
- Average
- Below average

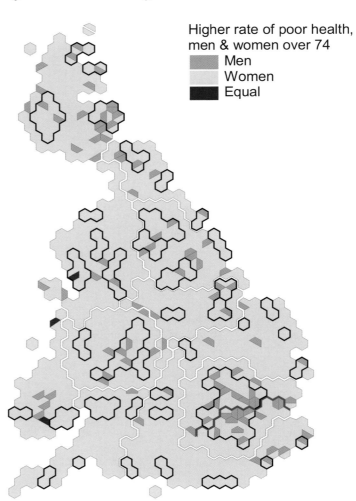

Higher rate of poor health, men & women over 74
- Men
- Women
- Equal

8.12 Health status of the truly elderly

Figure 8.12

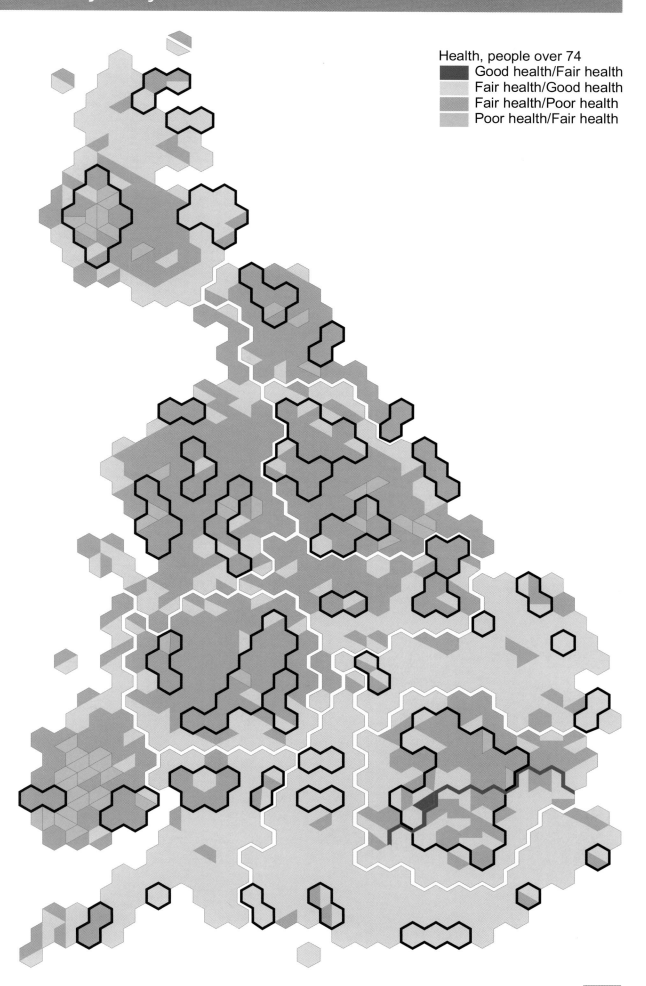

Health, people over 74
- Good health/Fair health
- Fair health/Good health
- Fair health/Poor health
- Poor health/Fair health

8.13 Disability and health status of the truly elderly

Add disability into the mix and the patterns become starker still. Whereas, as people might adapt to their general health status when they become truly elderly, and have a tendency to describe it as fair, when asked at these ages if there are things that they cannot do due to a disability (and encouraged to include problems that are due to old age) a more striking picture emerges.

Everywhere a majority of people of these ages suffer from a limiting long-term illness (LLTI), as shown below left. Simplify that map as to whether the rate in each place is below or above a national average band (of between 59% and 68%) and you get the map below right. Then look at how the majority and largest minority of those with LLTI of these ages describe their health and you see the mosaic on the right of a now far too familiar divide. And finally, include people without LLTI and use the average bands shown in the map below right and you get the detailed mosaic opposite (Figure 8.13) of what is most and next most common everywhere. The antecedents of these patterns lie in the pages and chapters above of the years before.

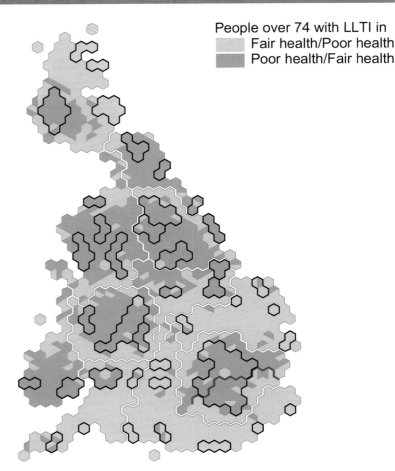

People over 74 with LLTI in
Fair health/Poor health
Poor health/Fair health

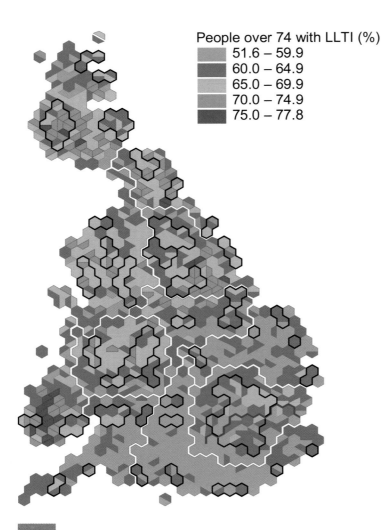

People over 74 with LLTI (%)
51.6 – 59.9
60.0 – 64.9
65.0 – 69.9
70.0 – 74.9
75.0 – 77.8

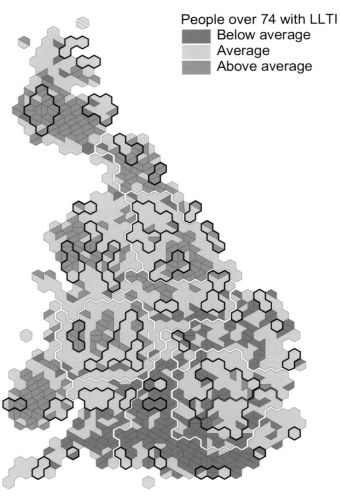

People over 74 with LLTI
Below average
Average
Above average

8.13 Disability and health status of the truly elderly

Figure 8.13

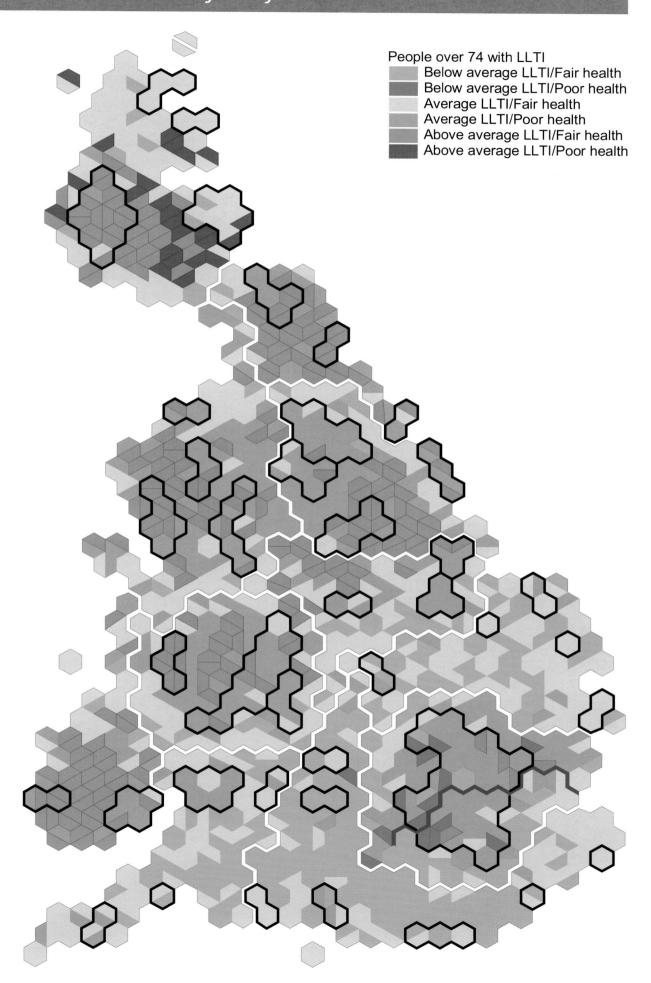

People over 74 with LLTI
- Below average LLTI/Fair health
- Below average LLTI/Poor health
- Average LLTI/Fair health
- Average LLTI/Poor health
- Above average LLTI/Fair health
- Above average LLTI/Poor health

8.14 Disability and health status by sex of the truly elderly

Rates of disability of men and women are sufficiently different to warrant mapping both, top left and right respectively. Those differences go a long way towards explaining the differences between the male and female versions of the mosaics bottom left and right of which individual health and disability status is most common at these ages. Combined, they in turn produce the overall summary of modal health status and disability shown opposite (Figure 8.14).

By now the reader hopefully knows how to read these maps. However, one thing worth pointing out is that, finally in the oldest of life stages, there is mixing within neighbourhoods by health and disability status, albeit only within London where those in poor health with LLTI are found in greatest numbers living alongside those in good health without disability.

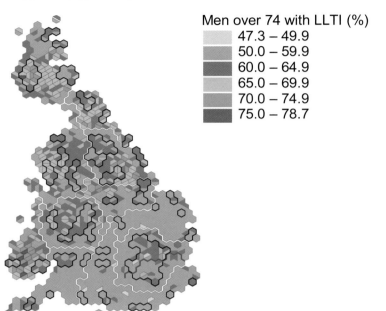

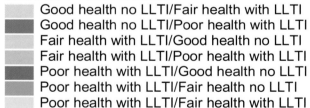

Men over 74 with LLTI (%)
- 47.3 – 49.9
- 50.0 – 59.9
- 60.0 – 64.9
- 65.0 – 69.9
- 70.0 – 74.9
- 75.0 – 78.7

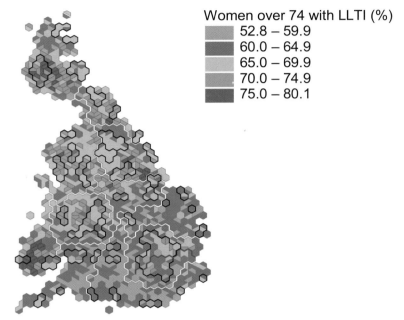

Women over 74 with LLTI (%)
- 52.8 – 59.9
- 60.0 – 64.9
- 65.0 – 69.9
- 70.0 – 74.9
- 75.0 – 80.1

Men over 74 LLTI & health
- Good health no LLTI/Fair health with LLTI
- Good health no LLTI/Poor health with LLTI
- Fair health with LLTI/Good health no LLTI
- Fair health with LLTI/Poor health with LLTI
- Poor health with LLTI/Good health no LLTI
- Poor health with LLTI/Fair health no LLTI
- Poor health with LLTI/Fair health with LLTI

Women over 74 LLTI & health
- Good health no LLTI/Fair health with LLTI
- Good health no LLTI/Poor health with LLTI
- Fair health with LLTI/Good health no LLTI
- Fair health with LLTI/Poor health with LLTI
- Poor health with LLTI/Good health no LLTI
- Poor health with LLTI/Fair health with LLTI

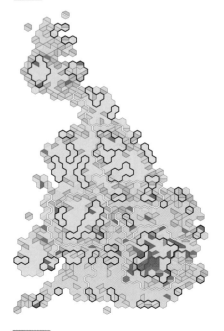

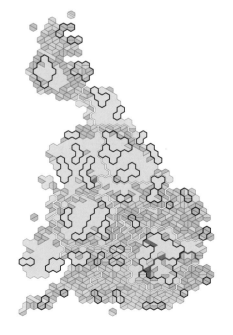

8.14 Disability and health status by sex of the truly elderly

Figure 8.14

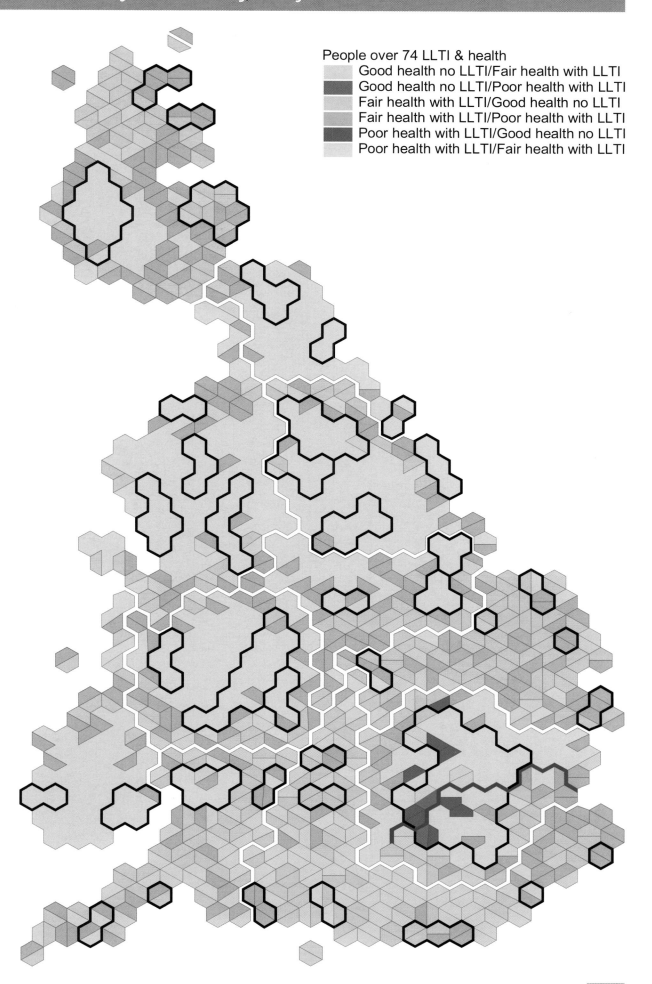

People over 74 LLTI & health
Good health no LLTI/Fair health with LLTI
Good health no LLTI/Poor health with LLTI
Fair health with LLTI/Good health no LLTI
Fair health with LLTI/Poor health with LLTI
Poor health with LLTI/Good health no LLTI
Poor health with LLTI/Fair health with LLTI

8.15 Most common age of death

And finally we turn to death. There is no neighbourhood in Britain where someone has not lived to at least 101 within the past 24 years, as shown on the map on the right. Our data here are of all deaths from 1981 to 2003.

What geographical pattern there is to extreme longevity is shown on the right. Figure 8.15 opposite shows the mosaic of modal age of death by five-year age band.

Below, the equivalent mosaics of modal age of death are drawn up for men and women separately, but using the same colour scale. For men there are a few places where most that die are not quite three score years and ten. Nowhere do most die over the age of 85. In contrast there are only two neighbourhoods where the majority of women who die are aged 71-74. And in affluent Britain most women who die are aged over 84.

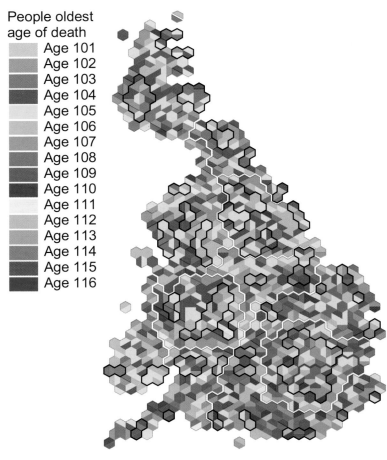

People oldest age of death

	Age 101
	Age 102
	Age 103
	Age 104
	Age 105
	Age 106
	Age 107
	Age 108
	Age 109
	Age 110
	Age 111
	Age 112
	Age 113
	Age 114
	Age 115
	Age 116

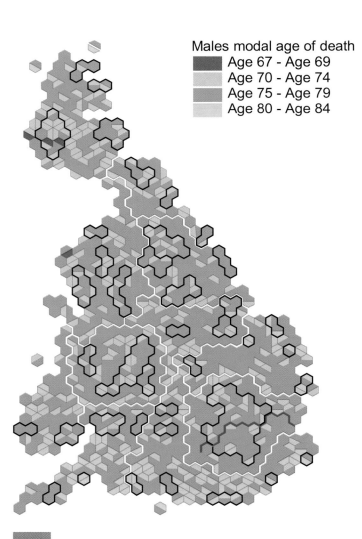

Males modal age of death

	Age 67 - Age 69
	Age 70 - Age 74
	Age 75 - Age 79
	Age 80 - Age 84

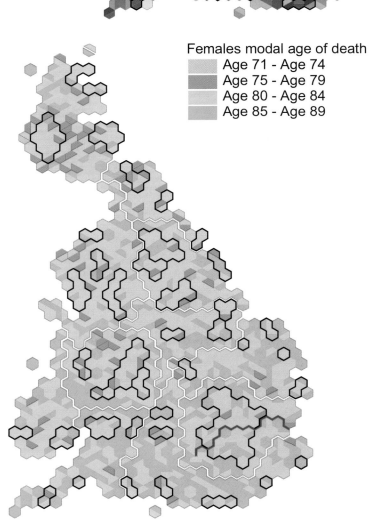

Females modal age of death

	Age 71 - Age 74
	Age 75 - Age 79
	Age 80 - Age 84
	Age 85 - Age 89

8.15 Most common age of death

Figure 8.15

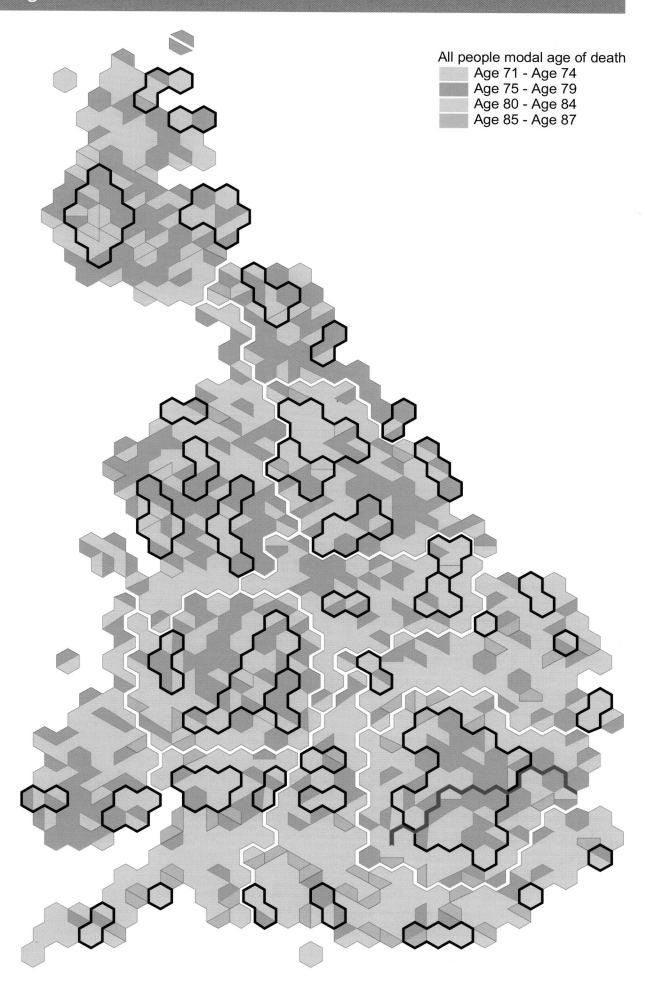

All people modal age of death
- Age 71 - Age 74
- Age 75 - Age 79
- Age 80 - Age 84
- Age 85 - Age 87

8.16 Conclusion: they have their exits – the final acts of life in Britain

In the introduction to this final chapter of life we began by pointing out that, while most men at these ages will end their lives with a wife looking after them, most women will be living alone as they approach death. In this chapter such fundamentals have been interspersed with trivialities. We have learnt where to find the most available truly elderly people for potential marriage; where centenary birthday cards should sell best; and where those over 74 are most likely to continue to have access to a car.

More seriously, this chapter has shown the subtle geographical differences between the similar areas where a majority of elderly women live alone and those where the minority of men who do so are most concentrated: in poor places. In much the same places a substantial number (occasionally a majority) are renting their home from the local authority and will have accumulated little in the way of wealth. In the same places, some 28,000 people over 74 live above the fourth floor, and almost half a million above the first floor, or below ground level, or in caravans or mobile homes. Here too are found those who are crowded into little space, most of the tenth going through winters without central heating and the quarter reliant on Pension Credits to boost their weekly incomes up to the minimum now deemed adequate just to get by.

They are also the places where the largest numbers are in poor health. However, in all cases these groups represent a minority of the truly elderly; often they are still the minority where they are most concentrated, but they are also often the majority of the minority groups here, and few would argue that such living is a good precursor to the dignified end of life.

Such poverty is tolerated because most people of these ages in these places die quietly, reasonably quickly and relatively young for the truly elderly: exiting the stage quickly and quietly muttering 'mustn't grumble', no doubt, rather than raging against the inequity of their premature death.

There are, of course, exceptions and so above it is shown how at least one individual has managed to live past 100 years of age in every single neighbourhood over the course of the past quarter century. But there are far more centenarians in some places than in others. When all the exceptions are brought together it is evident that they are collectively also following rules! But it remains true that you *can* survive to a century anywhere in Britain.

In contrast, the *modal* truly elderly pensioner does not have to rely on Pension Credits, owns his/her home outright and can heat it, and steps out from the front door to ground level. If he is a man, or a woman still living with her husband, in most places (s)he will still have access to a car and his/her health will be described as 'fair' (if not, it is more likely to be 'good' than 'poor'). On the flip side, however, (s)he will probably be suffering from a limiting long-term illness (LLTI) despite having fair health. That is part of the little bit of greater equality at these ages. But his/her chances of suffering such a disability are significantly less than those of his/her contemporaries living in the north of the country, in much of Scotland, in Wales, or within the poorer parts of London.

And when chances of living with poor health are also considered, it becomes apparent that an especially fortunate few live in locations within a band of counties from Sussex to Somerset where most truly elderly people who have retired there are in good health and without a disability, and the next largest group are in fair health albeit with a LLTI. Here are also found the enclaves where most people survive through to their eighties, and late eighties for the majority of women there. These will be the first places where soon some better-off women within them will begin to expect to live to 100 in not insignificant numbers.

Restrictions on information have made it impossible to look at the varying places of birth of this age group, or at their work histories and hence class identities. Also the information gathered on issues of care is not especially revealing as so many live alone, while many who live with a spouse or partner do not consider caring for their partner an activity that requires a tick on a form. After all, what did you expect to be doing for your husband or wife when you were both truly elderly? Also we cannot easily find out who cares for those truly elderly who need most care, but by looking at previous mosaics of caring done by younger people, and where they live, and between the generations, it all begins to match up across the spaces of these pages as well as across the map of Britain.

It is a modern miracle that so many people now become truly elderly, with teeth of some description (if false), and eyes often aided, if taste little impaired, but thankfully rarely *sans* everything. Perhaps it is partly because the survival of so many through to truly elderly ages is so new that we do not have the properly designed homes that many need to live in; that we have not worked out living arrangements that can preclude extensive loneliness; and that we allow such high proportions to still live in poverty at an age where most can do little to alter their circumstances (and who will have lived lives much harder than the vast majority of younger people now do).

It seems unlikely that as those below them age, they too will accept similar economic privations and social arrangements in their final years. They – you – may well think that. But, by then, who will listen to them – or to you?

9 Conclusion: merely players?

Let observation with extensive view,
Survey mankind, from China to Peru;
Remark each anxious toil, each eager strife,
And watch the busy scenes of crowded life.

(**Samuel** Johnson, *The Vanity of Human Wishes*, in Niall Rudd, ed,
1981, *Johnson's Juvenal: London and the vanity of human wishes*,
Bristol: Bristol Classical Press)

9.1   Introduction

Britain is a land of clichés, stereotypes and presumptions. There is some truth in most and we have not tried to dismiss many here. We may well be augmenting many and adding new ones. After all, after Shakespeare, Samuel Johnson is one of the most quoted of English writers, so we are continuing quite a few traditions. There are many limitations to stereotyping and we will list a few next, but very few people (to stereotype) have, or can have, a wide grasp of both the variety and monotony of the human geography of this country simply from having experienced it through actual travel.

Our sources of information may be limited to a few administrative files and a short form completed by most households at the turn of the millennium, but it is surprising to find how many people, especially academic geographers, do not know who else most commonly lives where they live or where they study; think that they are normal when they are often very much better rewarded than the average person; and think that things, such as social mixing, occur much more than they actually can and do.

Thus while there is some truth in most clichés and stereotypes, some understandings of the current busy, crowded life in Britain, let alone China or Peru, are badly misinformed. Different things are also true for different people in different places. What might be a good area to grow up in as an infant can easily be the dullest of villages to experience as a teenager, out of your price bracket and imagined environment of desire as a young adult, to be aspired to later in life and then rejected again even later. The same places can look very different when seen through the eyes of people in different life stages, from the point of view of men or of women, and depending on their personal, household and family circumstances in turn. We have tried to show a little of this variety by considering each life stage in turn.

Our subdivisions of life into seven quite rigid stages are, of course, to a large extent arbitrary. Nevertheless, these stages provide a series of extensive views over years that typically encompass very different experiences of life, if not so neatly demarcated to start for all at ages 0, 5, 16, 25, 40, 60 and 75. Similarly, our subdivision of areas into 1,282 large neighbourhoods is to an extent arbitrary. It might be rewarding to look at a more flexible delimitation of space and also for age. Just as for different people life stages start and end in practice at different times, so in different areas neighbourhoods vary much more in population. Most obviously, quarters of cities tend to be larger in larger cities. Thus within London we delimit within the inner city, and elsewhere the inner city may be encompassed within one of our neighbourhoods. Neighbourhoods also vary in shape and size as people age, and with much more. Approximated primary school catchment areas would not be a poor starting point were you to be thinking about the next level of detail down, for the young and their parents at least.

Criticism could also be levied at our subdivisions of the population in general, which boxes we have put people into where, which methods we have chosen to colour areas, even the colours we have chosen and the visual abilities we presume of the viewer. All this and more we would accept, save that although there are infinite ways in which this island of humans can be sliced, there is only one island, and the more you look at it, even as you increase the variety of ways in which you look at it, the less surprised you are perhaps by what you see. First, however, a comment on life's stages.

9.2 Life's stages from infancy to the truly elderly

Different numbers of people of different ages live in each neighbourhood. When viewing the maps throughout this book this needs to be borne in mind. The reader should also take into account that it is far from simple to consider patterns of age while simultaneously contemplating another pattern within a particular age group.

Below left we show respectively the spatial distributions of the majority of five-year age groups. Using 10-year bands rather than five-year bands produces a simpler picture to the geography of how people are distributed by age across Britain, as is shown below right.

In Figure 9.2 opposite, we show which 10-year age group is most and next most commonly found in each neighbourhood. Note that it is those that cluster most that have the most distinct geographies. Where there are either too few people of an age or they are too evenly spread across the country that group will not tend to form a majority in many areas.

Figure 9.2 also highlights how it is in the adult years before old age that we tend to clump the most. More people were born who are now of these ages than in more recent years of lower fertility, of course, and more are still surviving (compared with those born more than 60 years ago).

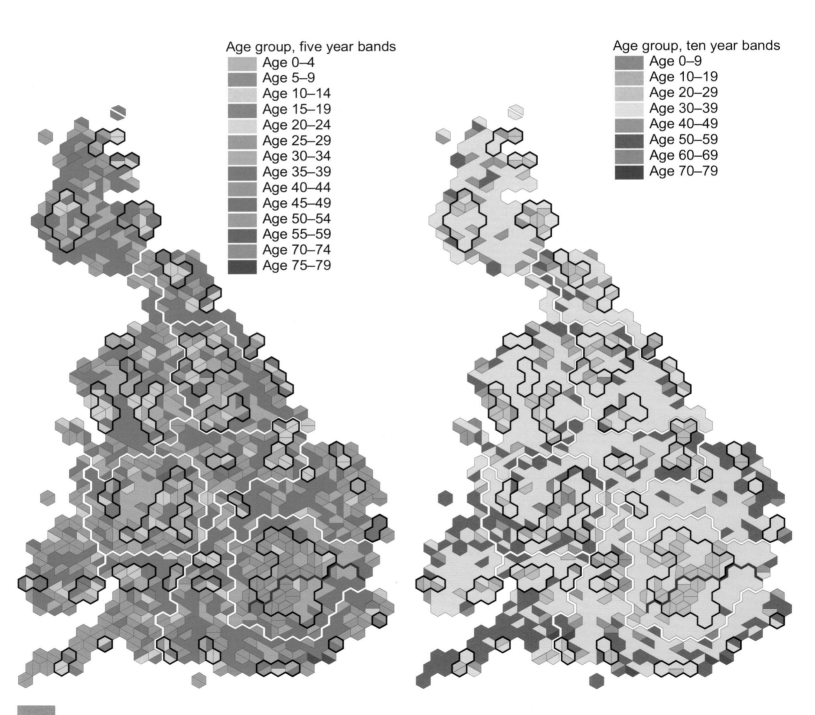

Age group, five year bands
- Age 0–4
- Age 5–9
- Age 10–14
- Age 15–19
- Age 20–24
- Age 25–29
- Age 30–34
- Age 35–39
- Age 40–44
- Age 45–49
- Age 50–54
- Age 55–59
- Age 70–74
- Age 75–79

Age group, ten year bands
- Age 0–9
- Age 10–19
- Age 20–29
- Age 30–39
- Age 40–49
- Age 50–59
- Age 60–69
- Age 70–79

9.2 Life's stages from infancy to the truly elderly

Figure 9.2

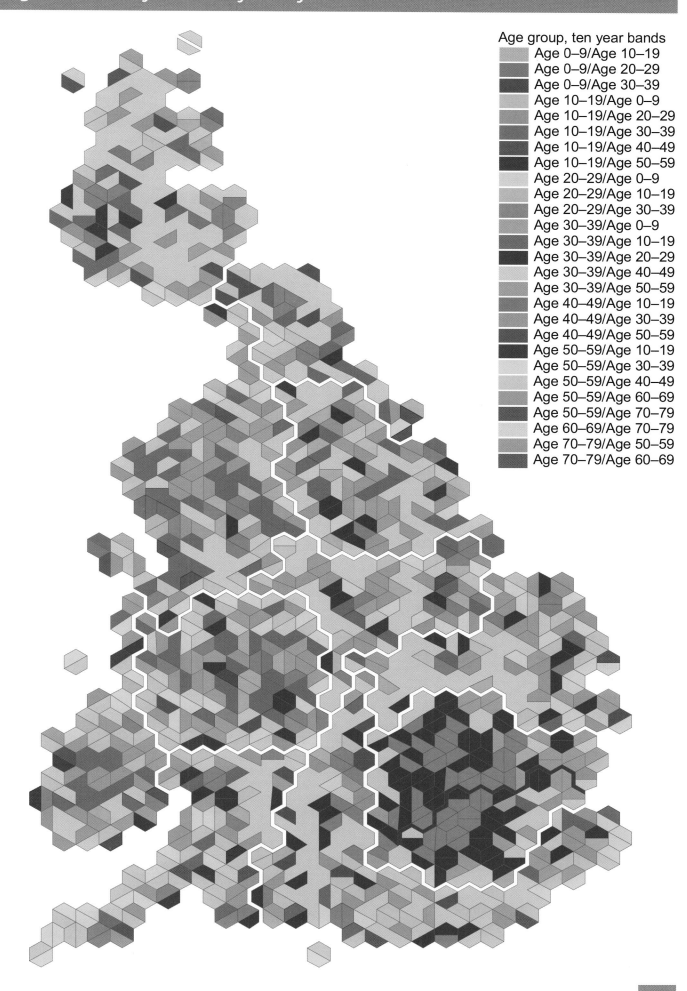

Age group, ten year bands
- Age 0–9/Age 10–19
- Age 0–9/Age 20–29
- Age 0–9/Age 30–39
- Age 10–19/Age 0–9
- Age 10–19/Age 20–29
- Age 10–19/Age 30–39
- Age 10–19/Age 40–49
- Age 10–19/Age 50–59
- Age 20–29/Age 0–9
- Age 20–29/Age 10–19
- Age 20–29/Age 30–39
- Age 30–39/Age 0–9
- Age 30–39/Age 10–19
- Age 30–39/Age 20–29
- Age 30–39/Age 40–49
- Age 30–39/Age 50–59
- Age 40–49/Age 10–19
- Age 40–49/Age 30–39
- Age 40–49/Age 50–59
- Age 50–59/Age 10–19
- Age 50–59/Age 30–39
- Age 50–59/Age 40–49
- Age 50–59/Age 60–69
- Age 50–59/Age 70–79
- Age 60–69/Age 70–79
- Age 70–79/Age 50–59
- Age 70–79/Age 60–69

9.3 Voting, abstaining, dissenting and political identity at ages 18+

Much of what constitutes the variety of human identity in Britain we have not been able to map, usually because the data are not available for the small areas we are showing. For instance, a map of the mosaic of second languages spoken across the land would be intriguing to see but only the numbers of people who can speak a couple of what are largely relic languages are officially estimated.

Often data on other forms of identity exist but cannot be disaggregated by age. Here we show just one example, of political identities, and those in turn as expressed at just one moment of time given a very limited number of options. Figure 9.3 shows the political party that received most votes and the runner-up in each constituency in the General Election held in the year of the last census. It is not hard to draw analogies with the identities held by particular age groups in particular neighbourhoods, as shown above. For instance, the spatial coincidence between those areas from Surrey to Somerset where old people moved to who were given an educational break in their youth and the places where the party that won this election, Labour, fell to third or lower place is very similar (see page 226). Those who got out of working areas often pulled a mental drawbridge up after them as they left politically, as well as leaving physically.

Below left is shown the simpler version of Figure 9.3, of simply which party's representative won where. Although which way an area swings is largely predictable from who lives there, occasionally the electorate are not merely players in terms of their political behaviour. Almost nothing in the maps previously shown could have been used to suggest that it would have been in Wyre Forest that a new form of dissent would emerge in 2001. In hindsight, given the unusual length to which men and women survived there (on average to 85 or older), for a not especially affluent area, there is perhaps a little prior evidence as to why Kidderminster hospital was so popular (see page 281).

No such tangential guesswork is needed in trying to account for the patterns evident in the map of turnout shown below right. However, for a single striking comparison turn to the map of those aged between 45 and 59 relying on Incapacity Benefit and/or Severe Disablement Allowances to live (page 179). Means-tested benefits do not encourage people to vote.

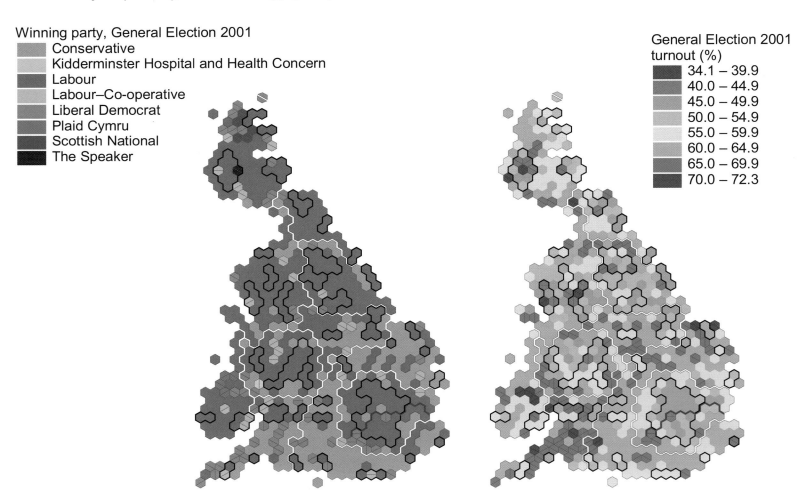

Winning party, General Election 2001
- Conservative
- Kidderminster Hospital and Health Concern
- Labour
- Labour–Co-operative
- Liberal Democrat
- Plaid Cymru
- Scottish National
- The Speaker

General Election 2001 turnout (%)
- 34.1 – 39.9
- 40.0 – 44.9
- 45.0 – 49.9
- 50.0 – 54.9
- 55.0 – 59.9
- 60.0 – 64.9
- 65.0 – 69.9
- 70.0 – 72.3

Figure 9.3

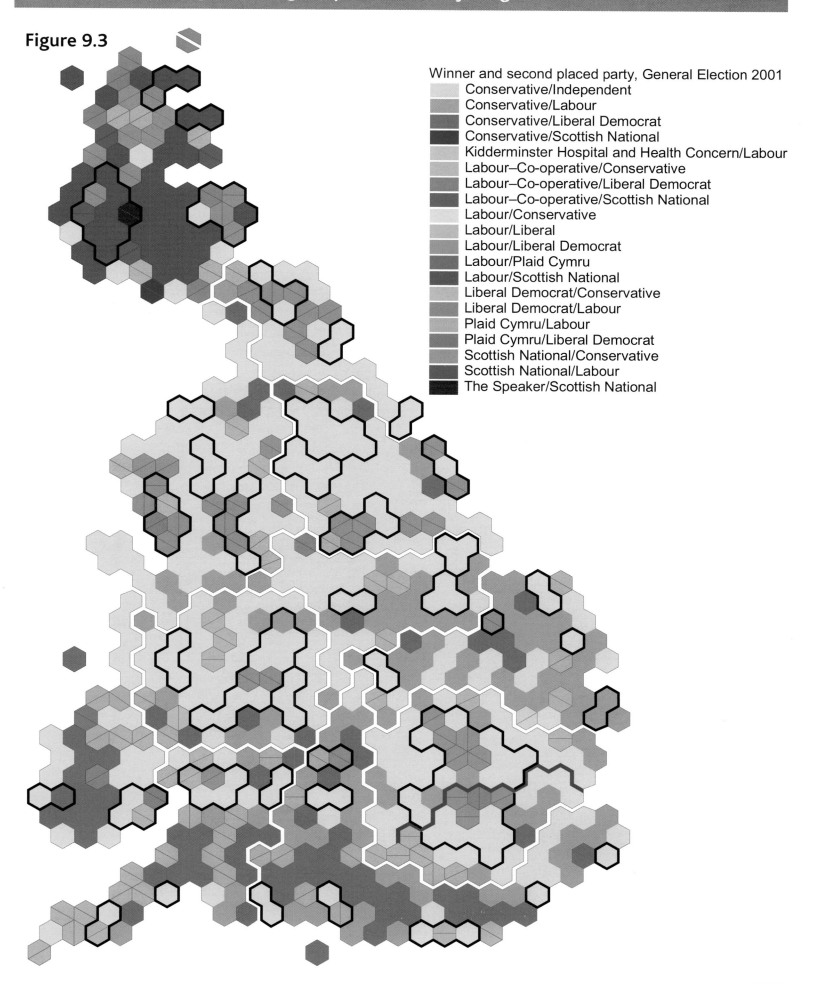

Winner and second placed party, General Election 2001
Conservative/Independent
Conservative/Labour
Conservative/Liberal Democrat
Conservative/Scottish National
Kidderminster Hospital and Health Concern/Labour
Labour–Co-operative/Conservative
Labour–Co-operative/Liberal Democrat
Labour–Co-operative/Scottish National
Labour/Conservative
Labour/Liberal
Labour/Liberal Democrat
Labour/Plaid Cymru
Labour/Scottish National
Liberal Democrat/Conservative
Liberal Democrat/Labour
Plaid Cymru/Labour
Plaid Cymru/Liberal Democrat
Scottish National/Conservative
Scottish National/Labour
The Speaker/Scottish National

9.4 Rich, poor, exclusive wealth, extreme poverty, and the rest in Britain at all ages

The *greatest of evils and the worst of crimes is poverty.* (George Bernard Shaw, 1907, Major Barbara, in G. Shaw, 1971, *The Bodley Head, Bernard Shaw: Collected plays with their prefaces, vol III*, London: The Bodley Head)

There are other forms of identity that we have not included here, not just because they cannot be easily subdivided by age, but because they most meaningfully refer to households or families rather than to individuals. The most important example of this in the context of identity in Britain is whether your household is living in poverty or has access to riches beyond the scope required to live a normal life.

Resources tend to be shared, albeit far from equally, within families and households, and poverty is most acutely felt when no one in the household has resources to share (especially when there is no one but you in that household).

With many colleagues (see Acknowledgements) we have recently worked to estimate the numbers of households living in each area that could be best categorised into five groups according to their material circumstances between 1968 and around the

time of the last census. The most recent patterning to poverty and wealth in Britain is shown opposite in Figure 9.4. In only two neighbourhoods is it normal to be in the most exclusively wealthy group (Amersham and Walton in Buckinghamshire and Surrey respectively). Nowhere in Britain are even a majority of the minority of households in the most excluded poor group. Below left and right we show also the geographies of those extremes.

Our five categories by proportions of household in them are defined as follows:

- 11% *core poor* (people who are income poor, materially deprived and subjectively poor)
- 16% *breadline poor* but not core poor (people in households living below a relative poverty line, and as such are excluded from participating in the norms of society, but above the core poor threshold)
- 50% *non-poor, non-wealthy*
- 17% *asset wealthy* (people with assets estimated to exceed the contemporary inheritance tax threshold, but excluding those with so many assets that they fall into the next group)
- 6% *exclusive wealthy* (people with sufficient wealth to exclude themselves from the norms of society).

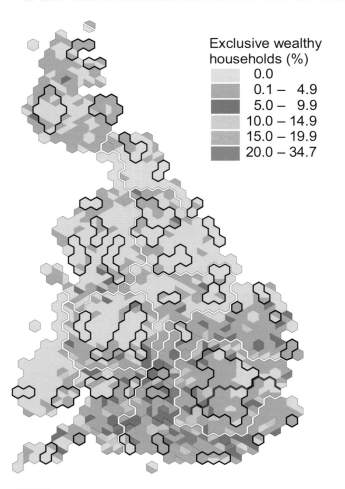

Exclusive wealthy households (%)
	0.0
	0.1 – 4.9
	5.0 – 9.9
	10.0 – 14.9
	15.0 – 19.9
	20.0 – 34.7

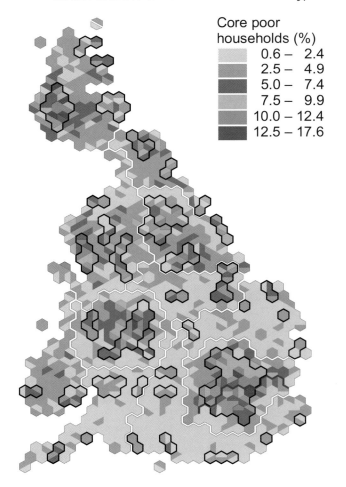

Core poor households (%)
	0.6 – 2.4
	2.5 – 4.9
	5.0 – 7.4
	7.5 – 9.9
	10.0 – 12.4
	12.5 – 17.6

9.4 Rich, poor, exclusive wealth, extreme poverty, and the rest in Britain at all ages

Figure 9.4

Households in poverty & wealth
- Exclusive wealthy/Asset wealthy
- Asset wealthy/Exclusive wealthy
- Asset wealthy/Non-poor, non-wealthy
- Asset wealthy/Breadline poor
- Non-poor, non-wealthy/Asset wealthy
- Non-poor, non-wealthy/Breadline poor
- Breadline poor/Non-poor, non-wealthy

9.5   From the fertile crescent to the peaks of despair: what is normal in Britain across all ages

Although people have a myriad of identities and not all are reducible, it would be very wrong to conclude from that reality that the overall map of human identity in Britain is incredibly complex. It is wrong to believe that it is a fractal entity that you can never quite get to grips with that always shows a little more nuance the further in you look. It is fractal, but more in the sense that the further you look, the more you begin to see the same old patterns repeated, both within areas and across issues of identity.

To help illustrate this, our last mosaic is a composite, a collage, created by combining parts of seven of the maps already shown. One issue of identity is taken from each life stage, chosen so that it fairly unequivocally differentiates advantage from disadvantage, but also so that there is a possible middle category. These three states of normality are then simply given a score of +1 for advantage being the norm in an area at the stage of life, –1 for disadvantage being the norm there, and 0 for neither. These scores can then be summed.

The table below shows the seven issues of identity we have chosen and what constitutes a neighbourhood being labelled as 'disadvantaged', 'average' (or 'normal') or 'advantaged' on each issue at each age if most people of those ages fit the label.

Thus in the most advantaged of areas most infants live in households that have access to at least two cars; most children, if housing wealth there were shared among them, would have access to £54,000 or more; young adults have at least a 41% chance of going to university; most in their midlife who live there are in social grade A or B occupations; in maturity (excluding those buying their home) the modal group are made up of people who own outright; most people living there in old age have good health; and the modal age at which people die when they are truly elderly is 83+. There are 47 neighbourhoods in Britain where all such is true and hence each of those are given a 'normalcy score' of +7 and shaded accordingly on Figure 9.5.

If you wanted a definition of what we mean by 'fertile crescent' in the pages above, these areas and their not-that-different neighbours define it. It is that part of Britain where it is normal to be advantaged no matter who are you or how hard you try (or don't try). That part of Britain where you are unlikely to appreciate you are advantaged because, after all, doesn't almost *everyone* have cars, money, go to college, get a good job, get to own their home, enjoy a healthy retirement, and die old? If you lived in any of these neighbourhoods, or any of the third of areas of Britain that only at most slip three points by this score card methodology, you would find it quite difficult to appreciate just how advantaged you mostly are, because you don't differ that much from your neighbours.

A summary score card for how being normal varies across Britain by life stage

Ages	Title	Issue	Disadvantage (−1)	Normalcy (0)	Advantage (+1)
0-4	Infancy	Number of cars household can access	None	1 car	2 or more
5-15	Childhood	Average housing wealth to inherit	Less than £20,000	£20,000-£54,000	Over £54,000
16-24	Young adulthood	Chance of having gone to university	Less than 20%	20%-40%	More than 40%
25-39	Midlife	Modal social grade of occupation	D or E	C1 or C2	A or B
40-59	Maturity	Modal tenure of those not buying	Social renting	Other renting	Owning
60-74	Old age	Modal health status	Poor	Fair	Good
75+	Truly elderly	Modal age of death	Less than 80	80, 81 or 82	83+

9.5 From the fertile crescent to the peaks of despair: what is normal in Britain across all ages

Figure 9.5

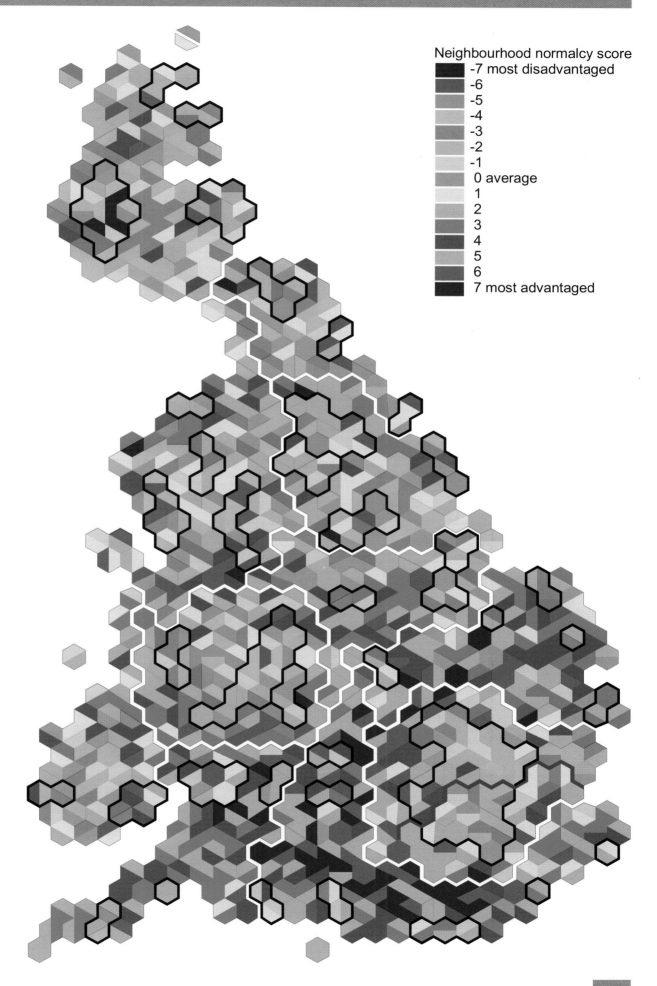

Neighbourhood normalcy score
- -7 most disadvantaged
- -6
- -5
- -4
- -3
- -2
- -1
- 0 average
- 1
- 2
- 3
- 4
- 5
- 6
- 7 most advantaged

9.5   From the fertile crescent to the peaks of despair: what is normal in Britain across all ages

At the other extreme of normalcy are what we have labelled the 'peaks of despair' in Britain. We have done this because, as can be seen from the score map just shown, they do not, at the extreme, tend to form a contiguous block in contrast to areas of most identity advantage. These are the areas where most infants are brought up in homes where no one has access to a car; where if all the housing wealth of the neighbourhood were shared out among all the children each would receive much less than £20,000; where far fewer than a fifth of children go to university; where most people in midlife are in social grade D or E jobs; where most who are not mortgaged in maturity are renting from the social sector; where most in old age live in poor health; and where the modal age of death for those who do reach their truly elderly years is less than 80.

Note that in areas that combine most of these characteristics the averages will usually be far worse than the upper limits just listed. Most children here will have recourse to *no* wealth; almost no young adults will go to university; many will not work and almost all who do work are in the worst paid jobs; average age of death will be much lower than 80; and so on – *and all of this in these neighbourhoods is normal.* However, unlike for the fertile crescent, people living in the peaks of despair do not need to look that far to realise that outside of their neighbourhood their situation is not normal. That not very far away from each of our poorest places are areas where most infants can be driven to a playgroup; where children's families are not usually near destitute and they can expect a chance of going to college; where it is normal to have an average job and fair health in old age, and not to have to rely on hand-outs throughout life.

It is because such normalcy is so easily locally visible that we have labelled these 'peaks of despair' in our categorisation of the neighbourhood geography of Britain. We use such a strong term also because there is good reason to be despairing if you find yourself so far down the geographical hierarchy of the country. That is because that hierarchy is quite skewed and appears to be becoming more so. A great many jumps are required to get far off these peaks.

The graph below shows how many neighbourhoods are of each score from −7 (the worst off) to +7 (where all life stages are advantaged), and illustrates how the distribution of normalcy is far from normal.

Distribution of neighbourhoods by normalcy score in Britain for all ages

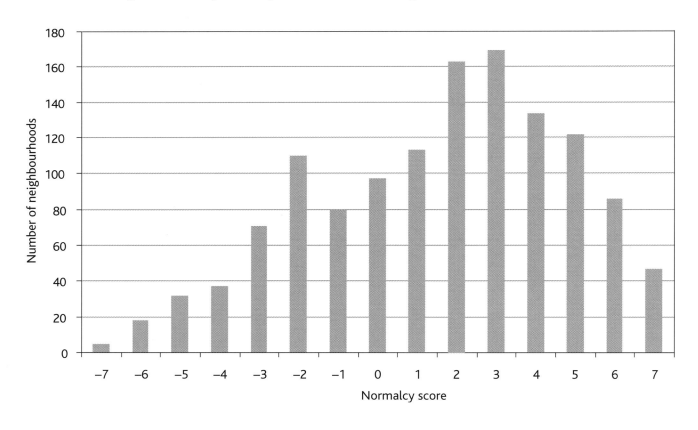

9.5 From the fertile crescent to the peaks of despair: what is normal in Britain across all ages

There are only five neighbourhoods which score −7 in the mosaic on page 293. In fact less than a third of neighbourhoods score under average. It is far from normal to be living in a deprived neighbourhood.

In the median neighbourhood, people are on average (net) advantaged in at least two stages of life. In the modal neighbourhood that is three; and there are more neighbourhoods where at least two (net) disadvantages are felt rather than just one, or none. The distribution shown in the preceding figure is bimodal with peaks at −2 and +3.

Bipolar distributions of geographical advantage and disadvantage were last common in Britain in the 1930s and seen then most clearly when looking at inequalities in health as measured between areas. After then a more bell-shaped geographical distribution formed whereby there were rich and poor places, but always more in between and both rich and poor were part of that normal-at-least-looking continuum.

When inequalities in post-war years fell the bell was squeezed to become thinner and when they rose it widened, but its shape remained much the same over time. However, what the preceding suggests is that there are now two distributions emerging. These are beginning to form out of what had been one. This is illustrated by the graph below which shows one possible way in which the overall distribution of identity advantage and disadvantage could be made up by one set of neighbourhoods where on average people are disadvantaged, but there is variation around that norm, and another set, where on average, people of most ages are advantaged.

Because the metamorphosis of the neighbourhood geography of identity advantage and disadvantage to a bipolar shape is quite a recent and still a tentative possibility, it will not become clear for some time whether it is truly happening, and here we are beginning to delve into an issue that this atlas has so far studiously avoided, the geography to neighbourhood change. But given all that we understand from looking at Britain now, and what we know of the recent and more distant past, the possibility that we are seeing the beginning of a new, more bifurcated world, within this richest of world islands, needs to be made clear now.

Bipolar distribution of neighbourhoods by normalcy score in Britain for all ages

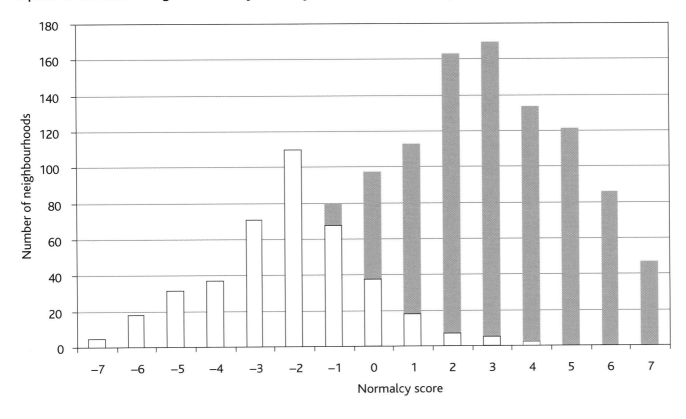

9.6   Concluding the conclusion: social topography of the stage

There are many analogies that can be made to the stages of life and the stage they are played out on. Here, maintaining cliché, we end with just one that is commonly used, of a playing field, to consider the neighbourhood geographies of identity and the opportunities and disadvantages associated with living in particular places.

These descriptions of the social stage may have it just termed 'playing field', 'level playing field', 'unfair playing field', 'tilted', 'sloped', 'steep', or 'rocky', but perhaps more accurately it should be described as a playing field so perilously pitted with sink holes, rucked and ruinous, that it bears no resemblance to anything that you would ever think of trying to roll a ball up or down, let alone set lives running across. Such identities and all that is associated with them, are not something we should be willing to impose on future generations. Moreover, identities are not simply imposed and unquestioningly adopted and are usually so multifaceted that you can choose what matters most and often change what you least like to be encumbered with.

That identity has many facets and is not simply given is not rocket science. As Amartya Sen reiterates for the unthinking:

> **In** *fact, of course, people of the world can be classified according to many other systems of partitioning, each of which has some – often far-reaching – relevance in our lives: such as nationalities, locations, classes, occupations, social status, languages, politics, and many others.* (Amartya Sen, 2006, *Identity and violence*, London: Penguin, p 10)

This argument can then be delivered to warn against the inevitability of the imposition of identity, as Sen does when discussing a man's fictitious identity crisis of exactly 150 years ago. That man then chooses to decide, whatever his various identities:

> *… to see himself as a human being who is at home …, not delineated by religion or caste or class or complexion.* (Amartya Sen, 2006, *Identity and violence*, London: Penguin, p 39)

Knowing your identities and those that are put on you, assumed of you from where you live, and held by your neighbours, constitutes a set of crucial discoveries but does not predetermine your future even if it does provide a good guide to the likely lives of the group of people most like you. As the passage just quoted above ends:

> **Important** *choices have to be made even when crucial [identity] discoveries occur. Life is not mere destiny.*

At the start of this atlas we described our aim as an attempt to produce a model of a Gilroy-scope (see page 4), a social scope, inspired by the arguments of Paul Gilroy for considering what it is that constitutes a human identity. We have sliced society up in numerous ways, taking common themes of work, class, health, home, caring, 'race' and religion throughout most of our seven ages, and interspersing these with issues of particular relevance to particular people, or more commonly things our scope could only see brief aspects of, as the data for more are simply not there.

Most people think they are average when asked. In most things most are not. Most say they are normal, but what is normal changes rapidly as you travel across the social topography of human identity in Britain, from the fertile crescent of advantage, where to succeed is to do nothing out of the ordinary, to the peaks of despair, where to just get by is extraordinary.

However, this map of identity is rapidly changing, and although we may currently be going through times where the topography is becoming more unfair and uneven, and the differences between certain identities are becoming more sharply contrasted, there is a great deal of hope among many of those who study society that the pendulum will soon begin to swing back to a more humane view of people than we often currently manage now to achieve.

This will occur not least when we begin to accept that it is the stage we are willing to live on that most determines the fate of the players on it and there is no preordained set of stage directions. Both historical and international studies are revealing more and more clearly how the stage we have inherited is not well set. As we discover this we can become better at learning not to blame individuals for where they find themselves on that stage, nor to be unduly impressed by the shallow achievements

9.6   Concluding the conclusion: social topography of the stage

of those who were best placed to end up where they now are. And we begin to ask more and more clearly how the stage can better be re-set. Look where the bar is set and why, and then break it:

> **Some** *societies seem to demand more resilience than others. But where the bar is set – whether a society has two or twenty percent unemployed, or five or twenty-five percent of children growing up in poverty – it is always the most vulnerable who suffer the consequences.* (Richard Wilkinson, 2006, in Mel Bartley, ed, *Capability and resilience*, p 2, www.ucl.ac.uk/capabilityandresilience)

People and places

A 2001 Census atlas of the UK

Daniel Dorling and Bethan Thomas

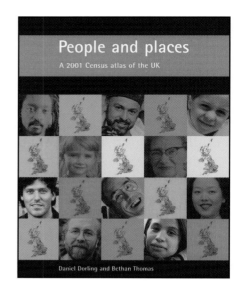

"... a compendium of facts that will have anyone interested in policy flipping through, manically, as well as wagging their fingers at their friends demanding 'did you know...?' From the precipitate rise of single living in London, Nottingham and Glasgow to the nation's unshakeable addiction to commuting by car – it is all here." **Audacity**

This extraordinary book provides an at-a-glance guide to social change in the UK at the start of the new millennium. It is the first comprehensive analysis of the 2001 Census and offers unique comparisons with the findings of the previous census a decade ago. Over 500 full-colour maps covering 125 topics clearly illustrate the state of UK society today and how it is changing, with trends explained and elaborated on in the accompanying text.

PB £29.99 US$55.00 ISBN 978 1 86134 555 4
HB £59.99 US$90.00 ISBN 978 1 86134 586 8
240 x 303mm 224 pages June 2004

Poverty, wealth and place in Britain, 1968 to 2005

Daniel Dorling, Jan Rigby, Ben Wheeler, Dimitris Ballas, Bethan Thomas, Eldin Fahmy, David Gordon and Ruth Lupton

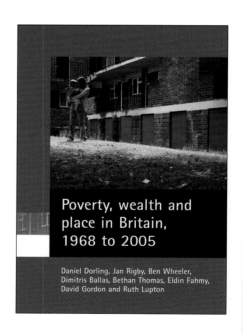

This is the first detailed study of the recent geographical distribution of poverty and wealth in Britain presenting the most comprehensive estimates of the changing levels of poverty and wealth from the late 1960s.

Statistics are mapped in detail to explore geographical patterns over the last four decades, and analysed to determine whether poverty and wealth have become more or less polarised.

PB £15.95 US$29.95 ISBN 978 1 86134 995 8
297 x 210mm 112 pages July 2007
Published in association with the Joseph Rowntree Foundation
Free pdf version available online at www.jrf.org.uk

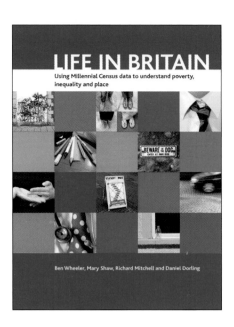